Object-Oriented Development with C++

A SOFTWARE ENGINEERING APPROACH

Kjell Nielsen

Science Applications International Corporation

International Thomson Computer Press

I(T)P® An International Thomson Publishing Company

Boston • London • Bonn •Johannesburg • Madrid • Melbourne • Mexico City • New York • Paris
Singapore • Tokyo • Toronto • Albany, NY • Belmont, CA • Cincinnati, OH • Detroit, MI

For more information, contact:

International Thomson Computer Press
20 Park Plaza, 13th Floor
Boston, MA 02116 USA

International Thomson Publishing Europe
Berkshire House
168-173 High Holborn
London WC1V 7AA England

Nelson International Thomson Publishing Australia
102 Dodds Street
South Melbourne, NSW
Victoria 3205 Australia

Nelson Canada
1120 Birchmount Road
Scarborough, Ontario
Canada M1K 5G4

International Thomson Publishing Southern Africa
Building 18, Constantia Park
240 Old Pretoria Road
P.O. Box 2459
Halfway House 1685 South Africa

International Thomson Publishing GmbH
Königswinterer Straße 418
53227 Bonn, Germany

International Thomson Publishing Asia
60 Albert Street #15-01
Albert Complex
Singapore 189969

International Thomson Publishing Japan
Hirakawa–cho Kyowa Building, 3F
2-2-1 Hirakawa–cho
Chiyoda–ku, Tokyo 102 Japan

International Thomson Editores
Seneca, 53
Colonia Polanco
11560 Mexico D. F. Mexico

International Thomson Publishing France
Tour Maine–Montparnasse
33 avenue du Maine
75755 Paris Cedex 15
France

A catalog record for this book is available from the Library of Congress.

ISBN 1-85032-905-2

Publisher/Vice President: Jim DeWolf, ITCP/Boston
Project Director: Vivienne Toye, ITCP/Boston
Marketing Manager: Christine Nagle, ITCP/Boston

Manufacturing Manager: Sandra Sabathy, ITCP/Boston
Editor: Theron Shreve, ITCP/Boston

Production: Multiscience Press, Inc., New York

To Vicki,
who survived the creation of another book!

Table of Contents

Preface

This book is about the development of applications using C++. This is not intended as an introductory treatment of C++; it is assumed that the reader already has a working knowledge of C++ syntax and semantics. A summary of the most important C++ object-oriented programming concepts is provided in Part 2 as a refresher.

This book places a significant amount of emphasis on the design aspects of C++ development. We are providing guidelines for creating C++ applications and omitting the gory details. This still requires a reading knowledge of C++, however, since all the coding examples are written using compilable C++ syntax and semantics. C++ code readability is also required for the understanding of templates and exception handling.

Successful C++ programmers cannot simply rely on syntax and semantics for creating large applications. A major trend in recent development strategies is the reuse of existing C++ libraries, interfacing with various forms of databases, CASE tools that include C++ code generation, and the use of GUI C++ development systems. Today's C++ programmers must become proficient not only with C++ design and implementation techniques, but also with using and interfacing to the new (and old!) development technologies.

The primary goal of this book is to provide practical guidelines and heuristics for designing and implementing C++ applications:

- Provide a background for object-oriented development using Domain Analysis, OOA, OOD, and OOP
- Provide design guidelines for implementing object-oriented concepts in C++
- Incorporate the use of C++ templates into the design
- Design and implement fault tolerant applications using C++ exception handling
- Use the standard C++ template library, STL
- Handle persistent data with RDBMS and ODBC
- Understand and use C++ frameworks
- Describe the mechanisms used in Microsoft Foundation Class (MFC) framework

This book is divided into five major parts. Part 1 lays the foundation for object-oriented development with C++ and describes the major software development phases:

Domain Analysis, OOA, OOD, and OOP. Even though this book is primarily about C++, most of this part is language independent.

Part 2 provides a summary of C++ class construction principles. The emphasis here is on how object-oriented concepts are implemented with C++ classes and other constructs. This also includes a description of well-defined classes, and answers the question of whether there is a given number of member functions that should always be part of a C++ class.

Part 3 includes a number of advanced C++ topics, such as the use of templates, and the incorporation of an exception handling strategy to support a fault-tolerant design. Special treatment is given to the use of the Standard Template Library (STL). Numerous examples are included to show how the various STL container classes can be used. Chapter 15 includes guidelines for creating robust code using the various forms of the C++ `const construct`.

Part 4 describes the handling of persistent data. This includes the use of C++ static data. A discussion is included about the main structure and features of an RDBMS. An illustration of the Open Database Connectivity (ODBC) mechanism provides an example of how we can interface C++ code to an existing RDBMS.

Part 5 is devoted to C++ frameworks. After a general discussion of the primary elements of a C++ framework, we provide numerous examples of the design and mechanisms included in the Microsoft MFC framework. This includes the structure of the C++ library, the two complementing mechanisms of virtual member functions and message mapping, the document/view paradigm, and the use of ODBC.

Appendix A contains a summary of the C++ design guidelines mentioned throughout the book. It also references the various design patterns that are included in some of the C++ examples.

A comprehensive list of OT, design, and C++ programming texts is included in the References section (as appropriate).

This book is intended for C++ developers who need to go beyond the mere syntax and semantics of the programming language. The emphasis of this book is on the practical aspects of creating large C++ applications. The intended audience includes C++ programmers, application designers, and software managers responsible for the entire development cycle.

Three major movements associated with C++ programming have evolved over the last few years: (1) an increasing reliance on GUI designs for a multitude of applications, (2) the use of visual software development environments and C++ frameworks, and (3) the development of applications for multiple platforms and databases. It is now essential for successful C++ programmers to be proficient in all of these areas, and the appropriate topics are emphasized throughout this book.

It is recommended that all readers become familiar with the material in both Parts 1 and 2. This will provide an overview of the development process and a summary of C++ class design and implementation concepts.

The chapters in Part 3 can be read in any order that matches the reader's interest. Chapter 13 is highly recommended to anyone interested in fault tolerant systems, and how to build an exception handling strategy into the overall design. Chapter 14 provides a comprehensive overview of the various container classes that are now part of the C++ standard, and how to use these containers. Chapter 15 describes how to create robust applications.

Part 4 includes the important interaction between C++ code and databases, and is recommended for anyone responsible for creating applications with persistent data.

Part 5 is highly recommended to anyone using or designing a framework that includes a visual development environment. Even though most of the examples are taken from Microsoft's MFC, any one of the modern development environments use similar techniques and mechanisms. The choice of using the MFC to demonstrate a C++ framework structure and the associated mechanisms is not accidental. Several independent C++ development system vendors are now licensing the use of MFC with their own systems. C++ developers can now use the MFC on a multitude of platforms and development systems. This is not intended as an endorsement of a Microsoft product; it is simply acknowledging a prevalent use of a C++ development environment.

This book can also be used in an upper-class or graduate curriculum of a Software Engineering program, where the emphasis is on the development of object-oriented applications in general, and the design and implementation of C++ applications in particular.

All the C++ examples have been compiled, linked. and executed using the Microsoft Visual C++ Version 5.0 development system, running under Windows NT 4.0, and Version 4.2 running under Windows NT 3.51. The source code for the C++ examples are included on the enclosed floppy disk. This floppy also includes the Rational Rose files used to create the design diagrams in the book. For further information refer to "About The Floppy Disk ..." located at the end of the book, after the index.

PART 1

Object-Oriented Software Development

In Part 1 we first present an overview of the various steps involved in an object-oriented software development process. It is important to realize the significance of having a software engineering approach to software development, and that we should never jump directly into the programming phase, even for small and medium-sized systems. The modern, visually oriented development systems with code-generating "wizards" may offer a temptation to jump directly on a computer to start creating a new system. We need to resist that temptation, take a step back, and proceed with an orderly process of analysis, design, and, finally, implementation.

The initial step in the development process is the domain analysis. There are three primary tasks to accomplish during this step:

- Analyze and understand the system requirements
- Assess the potential for large-scale reuse
- Determine a "build" structure to support an incremental development strategy

The Object-Oriented Analysis (OOA) step is used to create a system model of the requirements that reflects the real-world entities of the application.

The Object-Oriented Design (OOD) step is used to create an overall architecture which serves as the foundation for the implementation.

The Object-Oriented Programming (OOP) provides for the implementation of the architecture created during the design phase. For an application implemented with C++, this means creating a number of classes and their proper relationships that will support the user requirements.

Even though this book is primarily about C++ programming (i.e., OOP), we will introduce the concepts of OOA and OOD here. It is highly recommended that C++ developers precede their programming efforts with proper analysis and design steps. These steps will provide the basis for a stable design and more robust code.

1

Introduction

This chapter presents an overview of the steps utilized in the object-oriented software development process and the purpose of each step. The primary intent of this chapter is to introduce the concepts and methods of object-oriented development. Details of the development steps will follow in Chapters 2–5.

A number of object-oriented analysis and design methods have emerged over the last few years. The merits of two of the most popular methods are discussed with regard to notation and utility for the various development phases.

This book is exclusively devoted to object-oriented techniques and does not discuss the relative merits of structured versus object-oriented methods. (Such a discussion can be found in [1].)

1.1 The Overall Software Development Process

A sequence of development steps should precede the implementation task for any significant application. The development of non-trivial software products is a complex task. The complexity manifests itself in the understanding of detailed customer requirements, as well as specific analysis, design, and implementation techniques that are necessary to produce a high-quality software product.

A software product is viewed differently by its ultimate users and the software developers. The users are interested in desired features and how easy the product will be to use. The developers look at a software product with regard to design and programming techniques, and how efficient the product will be in terms of execution time and the amount of storage required.

Because of the limited capabilities of humans (even the most gifted!) to comprehend a large number of new and complex concepts, an immediate problem arises at the communication level between users and developers. Neither of these two groups fully understands the domain of the other, and some means of communication has to be created to bridge the gap of understanding.

Every software product is created to satisfy the needs of actual or perceived customers. These needs are specified in a system requirements document if a real customer is contracting to have the work done. This document represents the requirements for the new product. If a new software product line is being planned, there are a number of perceived customers who are the potential buyers of the product. In this case the requirements may be less formally stated, but they exist nevertheless, and should be documented in a system requirements specification just as for a real customer.

Software products can be created by programming directly from loosely formulated requirements specifications. This is usually referred to as "hacking" (coding without any design documentation) and rarely results in high-quality software that can form the basis for a product line with reusable components. An extensive analysis of the system requirements and a subsequent design effort should be performed prior to the start of the actual programming effort. The analysis effort will ensure that the product we are about to create will satisfy our customers' needs. The design effort will help in the construction of reusable software entities.

The discussion above implies that any software development effort should consist of at least three steps: analysis, design, and implementation. These three steps represent a development process. This does not imply that the steps are necessarily performed in a strict sequential order. For a large system, there are usually parallel activities happening simultaneously for several smaller portions of the system. The different development teams are dependent on the work produced by the other teams from other phases of the development.

The three suggested steps of analysis, design, and implementation are not sufficient, and we are adding a domain analysis (see Chapter 2) to precede the analysis phase.

To summarize the discussion above, we need a development process to manage the inherent complexity of producing software. This process is repeatable (i.e., reusable!) and scales up to large projects.

The primary phases of a software development process are shown in Figure 1.1. Even though the phases are drawn from left to right, this does not mean that each phase is completed in a strict, sequential order. We could have connected the boxes with backward arrows to signify the real, iterative process. This would make the diagram too unwieldy, however, and the iteration between phases is implied.

Figure 1.1 The Overall Development Process

A brief description of each major development phase is given below. Subsequent chapters will provide detailed accounts of these steps.

Domain Analysis

The domain analysis represents the first primary phase of the software development cycle. The major parts of this phase include the following:

- Determine a set of requirements in terms of functions or features. The purpose of this step is to gain a thorough understanding of user requirements. This involves significant input from users to determine their view of the application.
- Analyze the potential for reuse with a buy-or-develop decision. Based on the requirements determined in the previous substep, we investigate the commercial availability of an application that can satisfy all or most of the user requirements. If such a product already exists, and its cost is considered reasonable, we will buy that product. Otherwise, we will continue the process and develop the application in-house.
- Determine a "build" structure, which supports early prototyping of GUI interfaces and an incremental development strategy. Assuming that we have made the decision to develop the application in-house, we now determine a set of builds (increments), which will support an incremental development approach. Each build contains a portion of the user requirements.

Object-Oriented Analysis (OOA)

In the OOA phase, we transition the user requirements into a set of abstractions which can be represented as a set of classes (a class is a collection of objects with common characteristics) with known relationships. The major parts of this phase include the following:

- Determine the key abstractions. The purpose of this substep is to take the user requirements and identify the real-world entities that can be used as building blocks for an architecture of the application. Each key abstraction encapsulates a portion of the user requirements, e.g., a Customer, Invoice, or Product.
- Apply classification. This substep involves the transitioning of the key abstractions into a set of classes. These classes are used to create the initial system architecture and will eventually (after the design phase) be implemented as C++ classes.
- Determine class relationships. Classes cannot exist in isolation; there is always

some type of relationship between them. For example, we may send a message to an object created from a class and expect a reply. There are a number of different relationships that can be established between classes. For example, an Invoice is created for exactly one Customer. These relationships are determined and documented in the OOA model during this substep.

At the completion of the OOA phase, we have the initial system structure modeled as a set of classes with known relationships. This is usually referred to as the static class model (also called the static object model). This model provides the primary input to the OOD phase where we create the overall design for the application. The OOA model is free of implementation artifacts, i.e., we continue with the design (in the OOD phase) for a specific implementation.

Object-Oriented Design (OOD)

In the OOD phase, we refine the initial class structure and add implementation specific design elements. The major parts of this phase include the following:

- Transitioning from OOA to OOD. The static model created during the OOA phase becomes the starting point for the design. The classes and their relationships are now analyzed with a specific implementation in mind, e.g., a GUI design for X/Motif or Windows 95.

- Refining the class relationships. The initial class structure is analyzed to determine if a finer grain of relationships can be determined, e.g., additional inheritance structures.

- Adding architecture classes. The class model created from the key abstractions will usually not provide a complete implementation model. We need to add a set of architecture classes, such as lists, stacks, queues, interprocess communication (IPC) mechanisms, and message handling facilities.

- Refining the classes. Each class must be designed for a certain encapsulation in terms of attributes and operations, i.e., the data elements associated with an instance of a class and the expected behavior of that instance. One of the most important design criteria supported by OOD is *information hiding*. The level of information hiding is implemented in C++ via the access constructs of `private`, `protected`, and `public`. The last part of the OOD phase is spent on determining the proper level of information hiding for all the classes in the architecture. Some of these issues are quite complex and may not be settled until the OOP phase.

At the end of the OOD phase we have a design architecture. This architecture is intended for a specific implementation, e.g., a Windows NT platform or a Unix platform. The class/object models resulting from the OOD analysis can now be transitioned into a set of C++ constructs during the OOP phase.

Object-Oriented Programming (OOP)

In the OOP phase, we transition the design architecture (from the OOD phase) into the corresponding C++ constructs. Programming constructs are added to create software modules, which can be compiled and linked into an executable image, i.e., the application. The major parts of this phase include the following:

- Transitioning from OOD to OOP. The OOD models are transformed into C++ constructs to represent all the classes and their relationships. For example, a design class becomes a C++ class, an attribute is a C++ data member, and an operation is a C++ member function.
- Implementing OOD relationships in C++. Many OOD structures have direct C++ equivalents. C++ has syntactic constructs for inheritance, for example, but other relationships (e.g., aggregation or composition) have to be implemented via programming guidelines, e.g., using collection classes or "containers."

At the end of the OOP phase we have a C++ implementation for a specific platform. This will usually include a set of software modules organized into header files, source files, and resource files (for GUI interfaces) that can be compiled and linked into an executable image. The application must then be thoroughly tested before it is released as a product.

Testing

This phase involves finding errors ("bugs") in the software, as well as making sure the user requirements have been met. Steps used in testing include the following:

- Debugging. Software developers (sometimes an independent test team) execute a series of test cases (usually created from test scenarios) in an effort to uncover as many bugs as possible.
- Break testing. Designated testers (sometimes referred to as "gorilla testers") are attempting to "break" the system by applying random keyboard sequences and menu selections. This is usually done to provide a measure of the robustness of the application.
- Performance testing. Software developers (or an independent test team) measure how well the application will perform under certain conditions. Performance information may include response time from keyboard or menu selections, and

multitasking performance when several programs are competing for the use of the same resources.

- Acceptance testing. Users, under the guidance of the software developers, perform a thorough test of the entire system. The acceptance of a system usually signifies a formal event, sometimes a legally binding event.

At the end of the test phase, we have a product that can be released as an application. Note that we perform a test phase for each of the incremental builds with bug fixes applied to subsequent builds. If discrepancies are found between the implemented features and the user requirements, we may have to iterate between any of the primary development phases to correct the missing or erroneous requirements.

Each phase of the process shown in Figure 1.1 includes a number of intermediate analysis and design products, which ease the communication barrier between users and developers, and between various development teams working on different portions of a large system. An example of an intermediate product is a set of screen templates used to illustrate the layout of menus, buttons, toolbars, and dialog boxes in a GUI design.

An important aspect of the development steps shown in Figure 1.1 is that they are normally used in tracking the progress and achievement of intermediate goals for large projects.

1.2 Object-Oriented Methods

The traditional structured analysis and design techniques are being replaced by a number of OOA and OOD methods. This trend has been ongoing since approximately 1990, and is expected to continue. Many of the OOA/OOD methods utilize similar models to express various views of the system requirements and the architecture to be implemented. The primary differences between the methods are the graphical notations of the models and the transitioning from the analysis phase to the design phase.

Each object-oriented method has its origin with one or more authors who have published textbooks describing the models and features of their respective method. Some of these methods include Booch [2], Object Modeling Technique (OMT) [3], and Object-Oriented Software Engineering (OOSE) [4]. Some of the models used by these methods include

- Use-Case Analysis—describing interfaces between persons or systems (actors) and the system to be developed. Some people may refer to this as the use of Scenarios, but they are not the same. A use-case is a generic description of an entire transaction involving several objects. A scenario is a specific instance of a use-case.
- Static Class Model—describing real-world entities (classes and objects) and their associations in a static view (see Figure 1.2).

- Dynamic Model—describing the dynamic behavior of individual objects during the execution of an application, including potential concurrent relations. One form of this model is the State Transition Diagram (STD) (see Figure 1.3).

- Process or Functional Model—depicting a process- or procedure-oriented view of complex operations. An older version of this model used data flow diagrams (DFDs). Current versions use an "object view" with a sequencing of operations and their associated objects (see Figure 1.5).

As object-oriented methods are maturing, the models and features used by some of the original authors are starting to merge. An example of this is the cooperation between Grady Booch, James Rumbaugh, and Ivar Jacobson who are all working at Rational Software to create a unified OOA&D method and a CASE tool (Rational Rose) to support the new notation.

The use of a CASE tool for OOA and OOD is not strictly necessary—adequate models can be constructed using ordinary drawing tools. The significant potential for the use of CASE tools is the automated maintenance of analysis and design documentation, and the generation of C++ code from the OOD models. One important feature of a good CASE tool is the support for notations of different methods. We may want to use the OMT notation for the static model, for example, but the Booch notation for the dynamic model.

The remainder of this chapter contains descriptions of two of the most popular OOA&D methods and their associated models. The methods chosen for this discussion (OMT and Booch) represent the predominant use of the OT models currently in use. The details of the notations used in the various models will be described in later chapters when we use the concepts in OOA and OOD.

Object-Modeling Technique (OMT)

The primary references for OMT are Rumbaugh's book [3] and a number of articles in the *Journal of Object-Oriented Programming (JOOP)*, a SIGS publication, which he has written to explain extensions and modifications to the original OMT models [5]. The extended method is sometimes referred to as OMT-2, and will be absorbed in the Unified Booch/OMT Method. We will only be describing the original OMT here.

OMT covers both the analysis and design phases, and is based on the following three models.

The Static Model

This is used to describe the primary classes and objects that represent the requirements of the system, and their static relationships. Different views are used to describe generalized classes and associated specialized classes for inheritance hierarchies, weaker associations between classes, and embedded objects of other classes as attributes - sometimes referred to as aggregation. Class diagram notations include cardinality (the number of objects related within each relationship), class attributes, and class operations.

The result of the static modeling activity is a view of the key real-world abstractions and their relationships. These abstractions are represented as classes and are obtained from the application requirements.

Rumbaugh et al. refer to the "Object Model" as the static model in their book [3]. This is unfortunate and is easily confused with Booch's dynamic "Object Model." We will avoid this confusion and simply refer to the "static model" and "Class Diagram" to describe the elements of the static model for both OMT and Booch.

An example of an OMT static model is shown in Figure 1.2. This is a small snapshot of a class diagram for an automated inventory tracking system which we will use to describe the OOA, OOD, and OOP phases in Chapters 3–5. This particular snapshot illustrates the classes and relationships involved in the creation of an invoice.

The rectangles are representations of real-world entities (classes), and the lines connecting them depict various class relationships. The diamond between the class Invoice and Entry signifies that an Entry is a part of (an aggregate of) an Invoice. The other connecting lines demonstrate a weaker relationship between classes and their associated cardinalities. For example, at least one Entry is required for the creation of an Invoice. The two compartments below the class name are used for adding attributes (empty here) and operations. This will be explained in detail in Chapters 3–5.

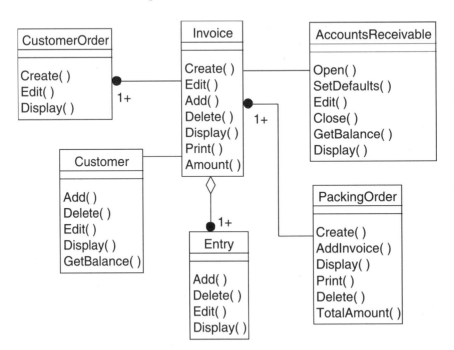

Figure 1.2 OMT Static Model

The static model provides the initial structure between the classes that represent the real-world abstractions of the system requirements. This model will later be refined and transitioned into a design architecture. This may look similar to an Entity Relationship (ER) model. The primary difference is that the ER model is primarily concerned with data elements and their attributes. We are adding operations (behavior) as another important modeling ingredient.

The Dynamic Model

This model is based on state transition diagrams (STDs) at the object level to describe how certain events affect state changes in individual objects. A second part of this model uses Event Trace Diagrams to show time-ordered interactions between objects. The third part of this model uses Event Flow Diagrams to depict dynamic interactions between objects without regard for any time sequencing. The latter diagrams represent the dynamic equivalent of the corresponding static object diagrams.

The result of the dynamic modeling activity is a consolidated view of time-ordered events, event flows between the key abstractions, and state changes (if any) that take place within each object.

We will only illustrate the first part of the dynamic model here; for the other two parts, see [3]. An example of an STD for the creation of an invoice is shown in Figure 1.3. Each rounded rectangle represents a state of an instance (object) of an Invoice class. The annotated connecting lines illustrate how the Invoice object changes its state during execution of the application. The annotations also show which objects are involved in a particular transition from one state to another. The dotted lines indicate messages that will trigger other operations. The solid black circle illustrates a start state, and the circle with the inner black target indicates a stop state. The semi-circle on top of the AddingEntries state indicates a looping action, i.e., we may have several entries for a single invoice.

This model is used to illustrate the operations and objects involved in the complex run-time behavior of a particular object that depends on several states. Other potential complex operations that would require STDs for an Invoice object are Edit(), Add(), Delete(), and Display(). The simpler operations such as Print() and Amount() do not require the effort involved in creating STDs.

The Functional Model

This model is used to describe interactions between objects, especially where we have to deal with complex functional operations. The original notation for this model was a traditional hierarchy of data flow diagrams (DFDs) where the data flows correspond to objects and attributes in the object diagram.

This OMT model has been the subject of severe criticism (i.e., it does not support an object-oriented view) and has subsequently been replaced by the Object-Interaction Diagram [3]. This is essentially the same as the Booch Object Diagram shown in Figure 1.5.

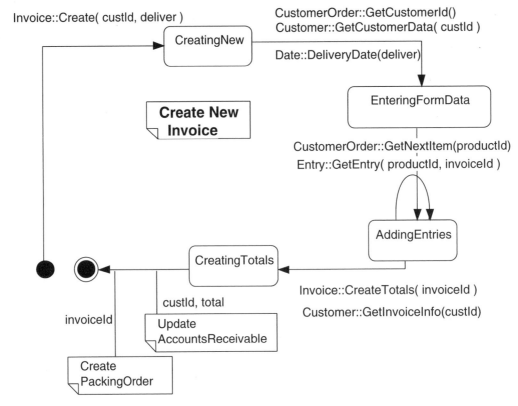

Figure 1.3 OMT Dynamic Model (STD)

The functional model is used to document the behavior of a complex algorithm or function. This view may be especially useful where the execution of a function involves a calling tree that reaches across several objects.

Booch

The Booch method also supports an OOA/OOD approach. The primary reference is [2]. This method also includes the three models described above for OMT, as well as some additional models. We will focus our attention on the same three models here and describe some of the differences in the graphical notation of the diagrams.

The Class Model

This is the static model referred to as the Object Model in OMT, and depicts classes and their relationships. An example of the Booch notation is shown in Figure 1.4 for the invoice application. Compare this to the OMT notation shown in Figure 1.2.

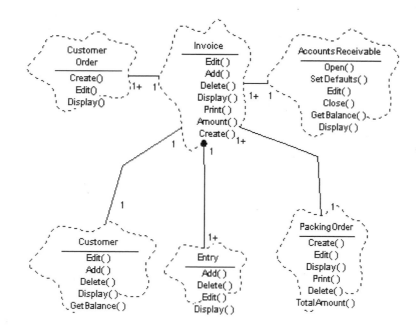

Figure 1.4 Booch Class Diagram

One major difference from OMT is the use of clouds for the classes in the Booch method. Another major difference is the notation used to depict class relationships. The latter can be a source of significant confusion: An open, small circle in Booch denotes a weak association ("using") between two classes. In OMT, this symbol refers to a cardinality of 0 or 1. A solid, small circle in Booch depicts an aggregation relationship between two classes, e.g., between Invoice and Entry. In OMT, this symbol refers to a cardinality of 0 or more. The cardinalities in Booch are written as annotations next to their class relationship line.

Since the Booch/OMT unified notation [6] for the static model will be based on the OMT rectangles, we will use the OMT notation for class diagrams in this book.

The Dynamic Model

This is the same as the dynamic model used in OMT and shown with the same STD notation (see Figure 1.3).

The Object Model

This is equivalent to the OMT functional model and is used to depict interactions between objects for complex operations. Note that the Booch "Object Model" is describing complex operations, whereas the OMT "Object Model" is depicting a static class model.

The Booch notation for the Object Model is illustrated with the object message diagram shown in Figure 1.5. This example is taken from the Rational Rose CASE tool [7]. The clouds with the solid lines represent objects, and the annotated connecting lines show the functions involved in a complex operation. The figure shows the operations involved with the calculation of the net cost for a particular crop C (netCost(C)). The number in front of each function shows the order in which the various functions are called to complete the operation, i.e., the netCost(C) calculation is only completed when operations 1–5 are completed. The PlanMetrics is a globally visible utility class which can be used by any client.

The Booch object model can be used effectively whenever a sequence of operations is required to complete a single, complex operation. This is similar to the use of DFDs in structured analysis and design. But we are not passing data elements between processes. We are trying to understand the sequencing of behaviors and their associated objects.

This has only been a cursory look at the OMT and Booch models. We will use and explain some of these models later in the various OOA and OOD activities.

If you find the two notations confusing, here is a recommendation and summary:

- Use the OMT notation for class diagrams in the static model (Figure 1.2).

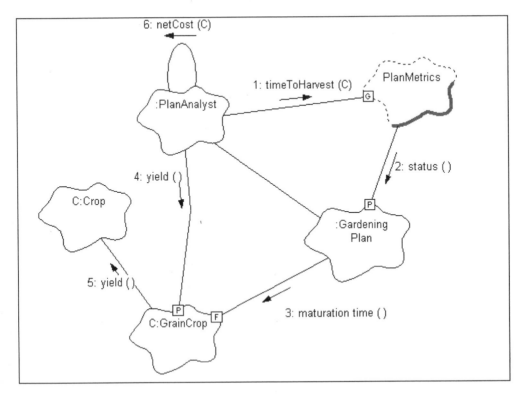

Figure 1.5 Booch Object Message Diagram

- The STD notation of the dynamic model is the same for both OMT and Booch (Figure 1.3).
- Use the Booch Object Diagrams for object interactions (Figure 1.5).

This combination of models and notation takes advantage of the best features of the two methods. It will also provide an easy transition to the unified notation when neither Booch nor OMT will be supported in their present forms. An additional reference for using OMT can be found in [8].

The Unification of OMT and Booch

OMT and Booch are the two most popular OOA/OOD methods in use today. Rumbaugh and Booch have been cooperating for some time to unify their respective methods into a single, comprehensive OOA/OOD method.

One of the early criticisms leveled at the Booch method was that the cloud notation was not intuitive, and that rectangles are easier to draw and manipulate. The unified notation will be based on the OMT rectangles, not the Booch clouds.

The CASE tool Rational Rose version 3.0 or later can handle both the OMT as well as Booch notation. This tool has been used to create all the object-oriented modeling diagrams in this book. The OMT notation is used for all the static models, since this is the closest to the unified notation.

Various articles describing the elements of the unified notation have been published by Rumbaugh in the *Journal of Object-Oriented Programming*, a SIGS publication. The latest information can be obtained from the Rational Web site at http://www.rational.com. This site includes a summary of the Unified Modeling Language (UML) [6] as well as the entire text of UML notation and semantics.

1.3 Object-Oriented Software Development: Hype or Reality?

The use of the expression "object-oriented" has permeated the software development industry over the last few years. There is no question about the existence of the hype associated with object technology (OT). But is the use of OT worth the cost of tools and training necessary to implement an object-oriented approach?

One of the primary benefits of an object-oriented approach is the invariant nature of the models as we move from OOA to OOD to OOP. The classes established during the analysis phase are transitioned to the OOD phase. Additional classes are added during the design phase to provide an architecture. The complete set of classes is then transitioned directly into C++ classes. The primary activities of the programming phase are to implement the class associations, level of access (public, protected, private, etc.), and the implementation of the class members.

The transitioning of models between development steps supports directly an incremental approach, where the higher levels of abstraction of a previous development step are replaced by detailed mechanisms to implement those abstractions. This approach can provide a better design and more robust code, which is not possible with structured techniques.

Another positive element of the OT strategy is that the terminology and diagrams we are using seem to be well accepted and understood by the customers. The class abstractions have names that are readily recognized as real-world elements of the application to be developed. That has not been the case with the documentation of structured analysis and design.

References

1. Nielsen, K.W., *Software Development with C++: Maximizing Reuse with Object Technology*, Academic Press, Cambridge, MA 1995.

2. Booch, G., *Object-Oriented Analysis and Design with Applications*, Second Edition, Benjamin/Cummings, Redwood City, CA 1994.

3. Rumbaugh, J., et al., *Object-Oriented Modeling and Design*, Prentice Hall, Englewood Cliffs, NJ, 1991.

4. Jacobson, Ivar., et al., *Object-Oriented Software Engineering: A Use Case Driven Approach*, Addison-Wesley, Reading, MA 1992.

5. Rumbaugh, J., OMT: The Functional Model, *JOOP*, March-April, 1993.

6. Unified Modeling Language (UML) Summary, version 1.0, 13 January 1997, Rational Software Corporation, Santa Clara, CA.

7. Rational Rose User's Guide, Version 3.0, Rational Software Corporation, Santa Clara, CA 1995.

8. Derr, K.W., *Applying OMT, A Practical Step-by-Step Guide to Using the Object Modeling Technique*, SIGS Books, New York, NY 1995.

2

Domain Analysis

The domain analysis represents the first primary step of the software development cycle. During this step, we first determine a set of user requirements, i.e., what the application must accomplish in terms of features and capabilities.

Once the user requirements have been established, we can investigate the potential for reuse for the new application. The remaining effort of the domain analysis is the determination of a series of "builds" for an incremental development strategy.

The domain analysis concepts will be illustrated with the development of an automated product distribution application for the Horizon Distributing Company ("Horizon"), a distributor of yogurt, ice cream, and other related products. We will use the requirements for this application to illustrate a number of design and implementation topics throughout the book.

2.1 Requirements Analysis

Regardless of the software development approach we are employing, the initial development step should always be to understand and document the user requirements. Without this step, an application may never comply with the expectations of users and future customers. It is essential that we spend a sufficient amount of time working with the users before any design and subsequent coding is attempted.

Requirements analysis has traditionally been based on a functional approach where we document the features (functions) required for an application. The documentation may consist of textual descriptions of primary functions and associated subfunctions. A context diagram is usually used to illustrate neighboring systems that our application will be interfacing with (see Figure 2.1).

A more recent approach to requirements analysis utilizes a use-case approach [1, 2]. A use-case represents an encapsulation of one or more requirements. The difference from the traditional functional approach is that a use-case presents requirements from a user's point of view, rather than simply a description of a feature.

Functional Approach

We will illustrate the functional analysis approach by specifying a set of requirements for the Horizon application. This application will automate the many business activities involved in the daily operations of such a company. Specific business activities will include, at least, the following:

- Order Entry—Orders must be created for customers who call in and request specific products to be delivered on a certain day
- Purchasing—Products must be ordered from suppliers to satisfy customer orders
- Receiving and Storage—All perishable products kept as inventory must be stored in a freezer and/or cooler for future deliveries
- Shipping—Packing orders must be assembled from available stock and delivered to the customers
- Inventory Tracking—The various products must be tracked as stock items from the time they are ordered from a supplier until they are delivered to a customer.
- Accounting—Various accounting functions that are required to operate a business successfully.

A high-level context diagram for the Horizon application is shown in Figure 2.1. The circle depicts the application we will develop. The rectangles represent existing systems our new application will interface with.

The Word Processor will be used to create business correspondence, including sending faxes to suppliers for ordering products.

The File Handler will be used for storage and retrieval of the miscellaneous files and reports that have been created.

The Network System will provide client/server access for remote platforms that have the necessary communications equipment.

This application is intended for Microsoft Windows 95 and NT platforms, and will use the Microsoft Win32 operating system (OS) interface for the necessary memory and resource management.

Use-Case Approach

We can also specify requirements with a use-case approach. Each use-case has a name (preferably in the form of an affirmation, starting with a verb) and represents

one or more requirements. Use-cases differ from the traditional functional requirements by specifying requirements from a user's point of view. This approach is especially useful for GUI developments, but not for typical number crunching applications.
Some of the use-cases we can list for the Horizon distributing application include:

- Take Customer Order
- Place Product Order with Supplier
- Assign Product to Freezer/Cooler
- Create Invoice
- Assemble Packing Order for Delivery (pick list from invoices)
- Track Inventory (adjustments, back orders, ...)
- Deliver Order (route, map, invoices)
- Track Accounts Receivable
- Track Accounts Payable
- Prepare Accounting Reports

This set of use-cases encapsulates the same set of functional requirements specified earlier. One important benefit of employing the use-case approach is that a number
of scenarios can be specified for each use-case with a corresponding set of test cases
that will track directly to a requirement. Each scenario (and associated test case)
represents a thread through the system and can be followed from an external stimu-
lus through the internal system responses.

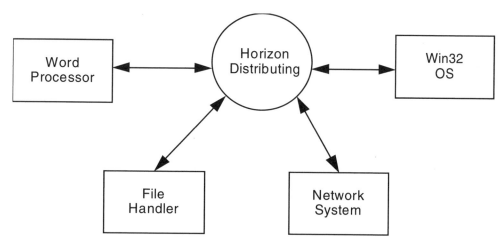

Figure 2.1 System Context Diagram for Horizon Distributing

Now that we have specified a set of requirements for the Horizon application, we can analyze the potential for reusable entities for this application. This is one of the primary activities of the domain analysis effort.

2.2 Planning for Large-Scale Reusability

The most important result of this step will be a buy-or-develop decision. If an existing application satisfies most of the features required, we should probably buy that application, providing, of course, that the licensing fees are reasonable. If very few of the requirements are available as a product, or if existing products include numerous features that will never be used, we should continue with the process and develop the application in-house.

In our case, we are looking for existing applications that can automate some or all of the functions of Horizon Distributing. One possibility is Peachtree Accounting for Windows (PAW). This application satisfies the requirements for the accounting functions, but is weak in tracking of inventory. The primary drawback here is that we would need separate applications to satisfy all of the requirements.

Another possibility is Quicken and the associated QuickBooks for Windows. This has similar capabilities to PAW and the same shortcomings. We are also discarding this as a solution for the Horizon application. (Note that this is not intended as negative criticisms of these Windows products; we are simply illustrating the type of analysis we use to come up with a buy-or-develop decision.)

Based on the (admittedly short!) reuse analysis presented above, we decide to continue the development process and create the application in-house. If, on the other hand, we had decided that an application such as PAW had all the desired features (including price!), we would end the development process here after a formal documentation stating the rationale for the decision. One approach could be to obtain a single-user version of PAW and employ it until we finish the new application.

This short exercise illustrates why the domain analysis is such an important initial step and should never be skipped. The reuse issue should always be explored before we embark on a lengthy and costly software development effort.

2.3 Planning for Incremental Development

The third major part of the domain analysis phase is to determine a "build" plan for an incremental development approach. It is not sufficient just to determine which requirements and use-cases should be included in a particular build; we must also determine the proper order for the development. There is usually a definite dependency of the components needed for the application, and this dependency determines the development order.

The structuring of the various builds should be made to include some of the required features in the initial build, and with a significant portion of the GUI interfaces. This will serve as an early prototype and will demonstrate the proposed interfaces to the users. Later builds will include requirements for additional features that will provide a similar user interface to what was illustrated in the initial build.

Here is a proposed build structure for the Horizon application in terms of use-cases, features, and requirements:

Build 0

- Take Customer Order
- Create Invoice

The focus of the initial build is to provide an order entry capability, and to create invoices. This will represent the early prototype, and should be presented to the users for their approval. The GUI design accepted by the users for this build should provide the template for all later builds. This will support a uniform "look and feel" for all of the application features. Since this application will execute on Windows platforms, the user interfaces should conform to the interface guidelines for Windows 95 and NT [3].

Only a small subset of the total requirements is included in this build. These requirements include a rudimentary set of business operations for taking customer orders and generating invoices. The subset is chosen such that as much of the GUI design as possible is demonstrated to the users. User feedback is extremely important at this stage, and relevant comments regarding suggested changes will be incorporated in the next and later builds.

The initial build includes a small, but well-defined set of requirements. Another important part of this build is to validate the development process. At the completion of this build, we have exercised all of the steps in the process, i.e., domain analysis, OOA, OOD, and OOP. Any adjustments to the steps in the process can be made at this point, before we embark on the subsequent, larger builds. It is possible that we may have overlooked some important features of the development approach that does not scale up. Now is the time to fix the problems.

Build 1

- Track Inventory
- Place Product Order with Supplier
- Assign Product to Freezer/Cooler
- Assemble Packing Order for Delivery
- Deliver Order
- Implement Help Functions (not a use-case)

The second build adds features that require a significant design and implementation effort. Similarly, the context-sensitive help facility also requires a significant development effort. Note that the latter is not part of the initial system requirements. Some developers may argue that this is strictly a software issue that should be delayed until the design phase. We are introducing it here as a feature that should be included into the development schedule.

The user interfaces for the new features should be similar to what we demonstrated in the initial build, and they should not come as a surprise to the users.

Build 2

- Track Accounts Receivable
- Track Accounts Payable
- Prepare Accounting Reports
- Implement the client/server architecture (not a use-case)

The final build contains the remaining set of requirements. We have included the internal systems requirements for the client/server architecture. The accounting reports will probably be subject to significant user feedback regarding formats and contents. Since these reports are independent of the daily business operations we are trying to automate, we saved them for the last build, even though they may elicit significant user comments.

2.4 Reuse Repository

A reuse repository for C++ components should be established as early as possible. The first set of components required for every C++ application is a set of container classes (see Chapters 7 and 14). This can be as simple as an ordinary C/C++ array, but will also require queues, stacks, lists, and maps (association between a key and an object).

The key to a successful repository is how well the components can be found and retrieved. At a minimum, the documentation of the components should include a list of available components. For each component, the following information should be provided.

- Type of component
- Purpose and functionality
- Restrictions and limitations
- Description
- Examples of how to use the component in an application
- Header and source files required
- File locations

We have so far only mentioned C++ components as candidates for the repository. Another category includes design patterns with actual C++ implementations. This is emerging as a major trend throughout the software development community [4], and can save significant development time when a suitable design pattern is recognized for a particular application. We will be referring to some of the well-known design patterns in later chapters.

2.5 Summary

The domain analysis represents the first primary step of the software development cycle. The major parts of this phase include

- Determine a set of requirements in terms of functions (features) and/or use-cases.
- Analyze the potential for reuse with a buy-or-develop decision.
- Determine a build structure that supports early prototyping of GUI interfaces and an incremental development strategy.
- Create a reuse repository of C++ components.

References

1. Jacobson, Ivar., et al., *Object-Oriented Software Engineering: A Use Case Driven Approach*, Addison-Wesley, Reading, MA 1992.

2. Wyder, T., Capturing Requirements with Use Cases, *Software Development*, February 1996, p.36.

3. *The Windows Interface Guidelines for Software Design*, Microsoft Press, Redmond, WA 1995.

4. Gamma, E. et al., *Design Patterns*, Addison Wesley, Reading, MA 1995.

3

Object-Oriented Analysis

The Object-Oriented Analysis (OOA) step is used to create a system model of the requirements that reflects the real-world entities of the application. These entities are used to create the initial set of classes that we need as elements from which we will create a design architecture.

The emphasis of this chapter is on how we discover real-world entities and how we transform them into an initial set of high-level classes that are used to create the OOA class model.

3.1 Real-World Entities

Real-world entities are system requirements formulated in terms that the users can recognize. Examples of entities for the Horizon application include orders, invoices, inventory, customers, suppliers, and accounting reports. These entities will emerge from written requirements documents or from discussing the system to be automated with the users.

It is important to recognize the real-world entities of a system, because they form the initial set of building blocks for an object-oriented development approach. Here is a list of real-world entities for the Horizon Distribution application:

- Orders—Orders created for customers who call in and request specific products to be delivered on a certain day

- Purchasing—Ordering of products from suppliers to satisfy customer orders

- Receiving and Storage—Reception, logging, and assignment of stock items to be stored in the warehouse for future deliveries

- Invoice—List of product items from which a packing order will be created.
- Shipping—Packing orders assembled from available stock and delivered to the customers.
- Inventory—The various products tracked as stock items from the time they are ordered from a supplier until they are delivered to a customer.
- Accounts Receivable—Outstanding accounts to be paid by our customers.
- Accounts Payable—Outstanding accounts that we must pay to our suppliers for products delivered.
- Chart of Accounts—Collections of accounts required for all of the various business operations.

These entities represent high-level requirements of the problem domain. They don't quite have the flavor of something we can build a design architecture from yet. We will illustrate the transformation from real-world entities to abstractions and classes in the next sections.

3.2 Abstractions

Real-world entities are sometimes referred to as the "key abstractions" of the system, but there is a distinction between these two concepts. Each key abstraction encapsulates a specific requirement that will eventually become a part of the system design. A real-world entity is simply a high-level representation of a system requirement.

A justifiable question then becomes, "If the two concepts are different, how do we get from one to the other?". Initially, we list every conceivable real-world entity that seems important in the problem domain. An intermediate step is to eliminate irrelevant or duplicate entities that will not be needed for the design. The resulting set of key abstractions is kept for further analysis and will be transformed into the classes that form the basis for the object-oriented model.

The answer to the hypothetical question posed above is that the key abstractions reflect entities that we will follow through the analysis, design, and implementation phases of the development. Each key abstraction will be classified as a high-level "class" which will later be implemented as one or more C++ classes. Here is a list of key abstractions for the Horizon application:

- Account—an accounting entity used to track the flow of payments, e.g., Accounts Receivable and Accounts Payable.
- Accounting report—a report providing detail about some aspect of the business operation.
- Customer—a client who orders products from us.
- Customer order—a customer's request for certain items to be delivered at a

certain time.

- Entry—a line item on an invoice specifying the product, quantity, and price.
- Inventory—a list of stock items by quantity and location.
- Invoice—a report specifying items, quantities, and prices for a customer's order.
- Packing order—a list of products generated from one or more invoices.
- Stock item—an item received from suppliers and assigned to the warehouse or kept on the truck.
- Stock order—our request to a specific supplier for certain stock items
- Supplier—a vendor who supplies us with products.

These key abstractions encapsulate the basic requirements for the Horizon application and will be transformed into a set of elements ("classes") via the process of classification.

3.3 Classification and Objects

The key abstractions of the problem domain are transformed into a set of classes via a process called classification. This process can be as simple as taking each key abstraction and giving it a name, using a special naming convention. This is referred to as an "ad hoc" classification scheme. Our naming convention will be to have class names as singular nouns starting with an uppercase letter.

We will be using the concept of a class at two different levels. In the present context, a class can be loosely defined as a set of high-level entities ("objects") that share a common structure. Later on, in an implementation context, we will see C++ classes as user-defined types. The latter classes will be created using C++ syntax and semantic rules.

Here are the high-level classes we get from the key abstractions of the Horizon Distribution application using ad hoc classification:

- Account
- AccountingReport
- Customer
- CustomerOrder
- Entry
- Inventory
- Invoice
- PackingOrder
- StockItem

- StockOrder
- Supplier

In this case, we used an ad hoc classification scheme and transformed the key abstractions directly into a set of classes. The significance of this set is that it forms the basis for our object-oriented analysis and provides the building blocks for the class model. These classes will not exist as isolated entities; we will later assign associations between them similar to what has traditionally been done for entity relationships in data modeling schemes.

The set of classes encapsulates the requirements of the problem domain for the Horizon Distribution application, and will be used in tracking the progress through our development cycle.

One of the problems we are faced with in our development effort is the "overloading" of the word "object." What we are calling real-world entities are sometimes referred to as high-level objects, i.e., "things" that represent requirements in the problem domain. As we get further into our development cycle, we will be using "object" to denote an instance of a class, i.e., one of many objects belonging to the same class. As an example, we can have an invoice number 10043 for customer X and invoice number 20167 for customer Y. The two different invoices represent two instances (objects) of the Invoice class.

Just as we noted for the class concept above, we will be encountering objects at two different levels. There are high-level objects ("things") as instances of high-level classes, and C++ objects as instances of C++ classes (types).

A common characteristic of both high-level and C++ objects is that they are associated with attributes and behavior. An Invoice, for example, has attributes such as Invoice Number, Date, and Total Amount. Behaviors ("functions") include Create an invoice for customer X, Display an invoice, Print an invoice, and Edit an invoice.

The determination of attributes and behaviors associated with high-level objects can help us refine the identification of the initial set of classes. We loosely defined a class above as a set of high-level entities that share a common structure. A tighter definition is that a class is a collection of objects that have common attributes and behaviors. This definition covers both high-level classes and objects and C++ specific classes and objects. We will expand on the significance of objects as instances of classes in later sections and chapters.

3.4 Identifying Real-World Entities and Classes

The first step of our OOA effort is to identify a proper set of key abstractions and to classify them. Here are some hints for finding real-world entities and to create the initial set of classes:

1. The first place to look for real-world entities is in a requirements document. Noun

phrases representing key domain abstractions will suggest the initial set of high-level objects. Simply collecting nouns will not work for a large system. Too many irrelevant "objects" will then be collected, and will have to be disposed of later. If a requirements document does not exist, discussing the problem domain with users and domain experts will usually yield a set of key abstractions. General categories for finding the high-level objects include:

• Tangible things	stock items, cars, sensors, satellite links, devices
• Roles	customer, air traffic controller, teacher, politician
• Events	shipping, landing, interrupt, request
• Concepts	account, company, employee
• Mechanisms	network communications protocol

2. The set of key abstractions must be transitioned into classes. The class names should clearly reflect the corresponding domain entities. We can use an ad hoc classification scheme to transition the key abstractions into abstract classes. We can also use a more formal method by attempting to identify the high-level entities within a set of predefined class categories that may fit a particular problem domain [1]:

- Device Interface Classes
- External System Classes
- User Interface Classes
- Computational Classes
- Role Classes
- Data Abstraction Classes
- Entity Object Classes
- Interface Object Classes
- Control Object Classes

The last three categories support the use-case analysis approach developed by Jacobson [2]. Objects belonging to an Entity Object Class are the real-world entities mentioned above. Objects to be classified as instances of an Interface Object Class can be determined by examining the boundary between the users and the system we are developing. Examples of an interface object include a Window and a Menu. Any object that cannot be classified as either an Entity or an Interface object is classified as a Control Object in the Jacobson approach.

3. After discovering the initial set of candidate classes, we usually have a very large number of classes, many of which are not unique. We can use the following list of criteria to eliminate unwanted classes [3]:

   - Redundant classes
   - Irrelevant classes
   - Vague classes
   - Attributes (assign to another class)
   - Operations (assign to another class)
   - Potential Collections (e.g., list, queue, stack)
   - Implementation Constructs (e.g., database, IPC mechanism)
   - External Objects (draw system context diagram to determine these)
   - Roles reflecting a relationship between two classes

   Sometimes we discover classes that are really potential collections or implementation constructs. We don't throw those classes away; we save them as Architecture Classes for the design phase.

4. Names must be chosen carefully:

   - A name should show the problem domain nature of a class, attribute, or operation
   - Use singular nouns for classes, starting with an uppercase letter to distinguish a class name from a key abstraction (Account, Radar, SatelliteLink)
   - Use noun phrases for attributes (name, address, speed, heading, account status)
   - Use verb phrases for operations; use predicates for boolean functions (receive message, send reply, is message queue full)
   - The type of data dictionary used will determine how soon we have to use computereeze names (SatelliteLink, accountStatus, receiveMessage(), sendReply(), isMsgQFull(), etc.)

The first step of OOA is to determine a set of high-level classes from the key abstractions of the problem domain. These classes do not exist in isolation; most of them are related in some ways. An Invoice, for example, is created for a specific Customer. There is thus a relationship between an Invoice class and a Customer class.

The second step of the OOA effort is to determine and document the proper relationships between the set of high-level classes that encapsulate the user requirements for a specific application.

3.5 Class Relationships

To complete the class model, we must show how the various classes are related. This can be done with textual descriptions, but a better way is to use certain graphical icons that have special meanings when displayed on class model diagrams.

Unfortunately, there are a number of different graphical representations developed by a variety of authors. Some of these representations use the exact same icons to display entirely different class relationships.

Two of the prevalent notations that have been used extensively by OOA/OOD modelers are representations of the OMT [3] and Booch [4] methods. These two methods are currently being merged into a Unified Notation, which is closer to OMT than Booch. We will primarily use OMT notation throughout this book. Occasionally, we may switch to the Booch notation to demonstrate concepts that are not present in the OMT method. Relationships between classes can be placed in the four categories that follow.

Aggregation

Aggregation is represented by the Has-A relationship. This is also referred to as Whole-Part, Composition, and Embedding. An example of an aggregation relationship is an Invoice composed of a number of Entries, as shown in Figure 3.1.

The diamond icon represents the Has-A relation, which depicts that an Invoice is composed of Entries. Why plural? The solid circle augmented with "+1" depicts the cardinality of one-or-more ("many").

The cardinality of a relation represents the number of instances that will be related in the implementation of the class model. An Invoice must thus have at least one Entry, and we have an aggregation with a one-to-many cardinality.

The correct cardinality is determined from business rules. In this case, one of these rules dictates that for an Invoice to exist, it must have at least one entry.

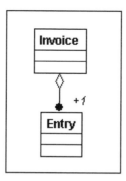

Figure 3.1 Aggregation Relationship

Inheritance

Inheritance represents the relationship that one class is derived from a base class. This is also referred to as the Is-A relation: a derived class Is-A representation of its base class. In the Horizon application, an AccountsReceivable and AccountsPayable class can both be derived from an Account base class, as shown in Figure 3.2.

The apex of the triangle icon points to the base class. This notation can be extended to include entire hierarchies of new classes deriving from a derived class functioning as a lower-level base class.

The use of the inheritance relation is primarily a design notation. The key abstractions may reveal possibilities for inheritance, but do not directly represent real-world entities as requirements.

Note that there is no cardinality associated with the inheritance relation, since an instance of a derived class is not necessarily associated with an instance of a base class. We can have abstract base classes for which there are no instances. Also, there are no business rules that apply to inheritance relations, since these relations are primarily design artifacts.

The primary use of the inheritance relation is to describe a general base class from which we can derive similar, specialized classes that have some of their attributes and operations in common with the base class. This relation is also referred to as generalization/specialization.

Association

The association relation is used when objects of two classes need to communicate, or there is a dependency that doesn't fit the category of aggregation or inheritance. As an example from the Horizon application, an Invoice is created from a CustomerOrder and on behalf of a Customer, as shown in Figure 3.3.

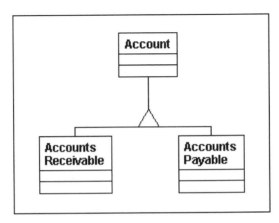

Figure 3.2 Inheritance Relationship

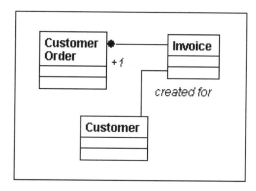

Figure 3.3 Association Relationship

The line segment between the class icons depicts the association (weak dependency) between instances of the classes. The annotation describes the particular association.

Business rules are also used to determine the appropriate cardinalities for associations. In our example, one Invoice is created on behalf of exactly one Customer, i.e., a cardinality of one-to-one. Also, one Invoice is created from at least one CustomerOrder, i.e., a cardinality of one-to-many. This business rule implies that several customer orders can be associated with one invoice.

The distinction between aggregation and association is sometimes blurred, and some developers even consider aggregation to be a special case of association. One way to distinguish these two relationships, however, is to consider a car and a driver. A car is composed of (i.e., aggregation) one chassis, one body, four wheels, one engine, etc. A driver is not a component of the car; the car exists without a driver. When a car is driven, it is associated with a particular driver. The reverse association is that a driver can only drive a particular car at a time, and a driver exists (as a person) without driving a car. There is thus a binary association between a car and a driver, but definitely not a Has-A relationship.

Using

There is a fourth relationship, commonly referred to as a "using" relationship. This doesn't usually show up when we determine the key abstractions and use the business rules to establish the proper relationships.

The using relation is primarily used during OOD, when we add architecture classes. An example of a using relationship is the reference to a display class used to draw a graphical object. This class is referenced by including a graphics library and calling a member function in the display class. There is neither an aggregation, inheritance, nor association relationship between the client class and the supplier class that is referenced. We will return to this relationship in later chapters.

3.6 Completing the Class Model

With an understanding of classes, relationships, and cardinalities, we can create a class model by connecting the high-level classes created from the key abstractions. This model will serve as the primary product of the OOA phase and is the basis for creating an architecture during the OOD phase.

Note that the initial set of classes determined during the OOA phase is not sufficient for creating an architecture that can be implemented as an application. Additional classes will be defined during the OOD phase and added to the OOA class model.

One of the primary differences between OOA and OOD is that OOA is a *discovery* phase: We determine and discover classes and their relationships from the key abstractions of the problem domain. We *define* additional classes during OOD and add them to the OOA classes. The Horizon application, for example, will need a database, but there is nothing in the key abstractions that reflects such a structure. This will be defined during OOD.

We will now illustrate the elements of the class model by creating a class model diagram for the Horizon application using OMT notation. First, we describe class relations and the associated business rules:

An Invoice is composed of one or more Entries

An Invoice is created for exactly one Customer

An Invoice is created from one or more CustomerOrders

An Invoice is used to update the AccountsReceivable account

An Inventory is composed of zero or more StockItems

A PackingOrder is initiated from one or more Invoices

A PackingOrder is created from Inventory items

A PackingOrder is used to update the Inventory

A StockOrder is received from a Supplier

A StockOrder is used to update the Inventory

A StockOrder is used to update the AccountsPayable account

The class relations and associated business rules are stated for each pair of classes expected to have instances that need to communicate. The Horizon class model diagram is shown in Figure 3.4.

The associations between two classes are considered binary, i.e., there is a direction associated with an association. A PackingOrder, for example, is created from Inventory. The reverse association is that a PackingOrder updates Inventory. Many of the reverse associations are not interesting and are not annotated. We see from the diagram that an Invoice is made up of at least one CustomerOrder. The reverse association, that a collection of CustomerOrders is related to a specific Invoice, is of no consequence for this model.

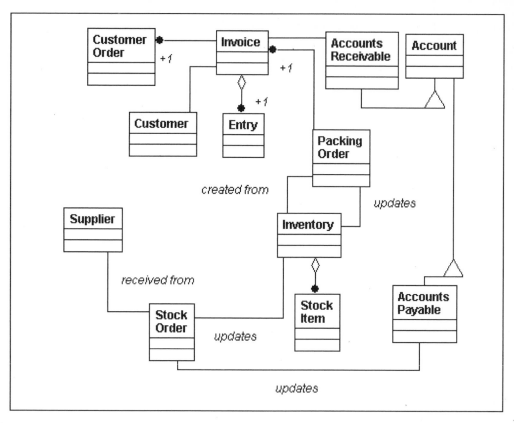

Figure 3.4 Horizon Static Class Model

The static class model for the Horizon application is the primary product of the OOA phase. This model will be refined during the OOD phase by adding attributes and behaviors for each class. Additional classes required for a design architecture will also be added.

3.7 Summary

The first step of the OOA effort is the determination of the key abstractions of the problem domain. These abstractions are transformed into high-level classes via an informal ad hoc classification or by using a set of predefined class categories.

The classes we discover do not exist in isolation, they have certain relations. There are three primary relationships between classes determined during the OOA phase:

- Aggregation, described as a Has-A relation (also referred to as Composition or Embedded relations).

- Inheritance, described as an Is-A relation (also referred to as Generalization/Specialization).
- Association, a weaker relation that doesn't belong in either of the previous categories.

The fourth relationship of "using" (i.e., a weak reference to another class) is usually determined during the OOD phase.

The Aggregation and Association class connections are also related by cardinalities (multiplicities). This describes how many instances in a class pair are related. The proper cardinalities are determined by examining the business rules associated with the key abstractions. Cardinalities are not applied to the inheritance relationship. There are four cardinalities to consider:

- One-to-one—One object of a class has a relationship with exactly one object in the other class of the class pair.
- One-to-many (many-to-one)—One object of a class has a relationship with many (zero or more) objects in the other class of the class pair.
- Many-to-many—Many objects of a class have a relationship with many objects in the other class of the class pair.
- Optional—There can be zero or exactly one object involved on either side of a relation.

The class model diagram is the primary documentation of the OOA phase. This model is obtained by connecting the high-level classes with their appropriate relationships and associated cardinalities. This model is referred to as the "Object Model" in the OMT reference literature [3]. A better name would have been a "Class Model," as used in the Booch method. The Rational Rose tool supports both the OMT and Booch notations and uses the Class Model for both methods.

References

1. Nielsen, K.W., *Software Development with C++: Maximizing Reuse with Object Technology*, Academic Press, Cambridge, MA 1995.

2. Jacobson, Ivar., et al., *Object-Oriented Software Engineering: A Use Case Driven Approach*, Addison-Wesley, Reading, MA 1992.

3. Rumbaugh, J., et al., *Object-Oriented Modeling and Design*, Prentice Hall, Englewood Cliffs, NJ, 1991.

4. Booch, G., *Object-Oriented Analysis and Design with Applications*, Second Edition, Benjamin/Cummings, Redwood City, CA 1994.

4

Object-Oriented Design

Object-Oriented Design (OOD) is the next major phase in the object-oriented lifecycle development process. The major product of the OOA phase is the class model developed from the key abstractions of the problem domain. This model will be transitioned into an architecture during the OOD phase. The architecture is the primary result of the OOD phase and provides a design structure from which we can create a C++ application during the OOP phase.

The OOA model focused exclusively on representing high-level abstractions in terms that would be familiar to the users of the proposed application. One major shift that takes place during the OOD phase is that we now introduce design mechanisms and technology into our model. An example of a design mechanism is the type of exception handling we decide to use. The introduction of technology could also include the use of relational or object database approaches.

Even though we are describing the OOA, OOD, and OOP phases in sequential chapters, this does not mean that we are completely finished with the OOA phase during OOD, or with the OOD phase during OOP. As we stated in Chapter 1, the development is iterative and incremental and does not follow the waterfall model. If a new and important requirement is discovered during OOD, we may have to go back to the OOA model to make the necessary adjustments. Similarly, if we discover design flaws during the OOP phase, we may have to return to the OOD model and make additions or corrections.

The emphasis of this chapter is to describe how we transition the OOA class model into the foundation for an architecture, and what type of design elements we must add to the class model to create a design structure.

4.1 Transitioning from OOA to OOD

During the last step of the OOA phase, we created an abstract class model from the key abstractions of the problem domain. The classes were modeled as nodes with certain relations connecting them. Annotations for cardinalities (derived from business rules) were added to the class model diagram to describe the expected number of objects that will interact in an application.

The starting point for the OOD model is to take the final OOA class model and simply transition it "as-is" into an OOD model, as shown in Figure 4.1. This may, at first, elicit a "so what?" reaction. One thing to realize about the object-oriented approach is that the exact same diagram and notations are used for OOA and OOD. This is a drastic improvement, for example, over structured analysis and design (SASD) where we used data flow diagrams for the analysis part, and structure charts for the design phase. It was very difficult to provide a smooth transition between analysis and design using the SASD approach.

The class icons depicted in Figure 4.1 only have the class names included. The empty compartments are used for attributes and operations. These will be added during the OOD phase.

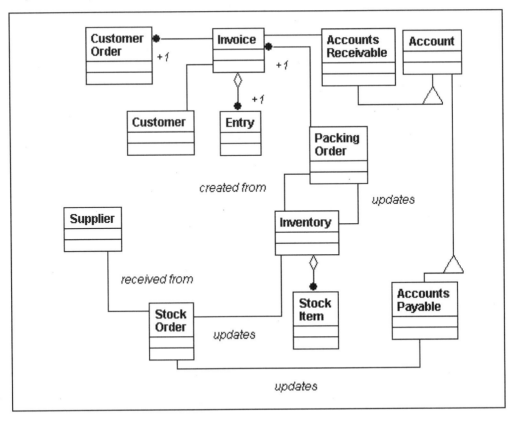

Figure 4.1 Horizon Static Class Model

Detractors of the object-oriented approach have pointed out that the smooth transitioning from OOA to OOD has a bad side effect of not being able to establish a clear dividing line between analysis and design. This does not really affect the over-all quality of the design, but may have an impact on how progress is reported. This issue is now primarily of academic interest and will not be pursued further here.

4.2 Refining the Class Model

After the transitioning of the class model, we must determine the appropriate set of attributes and operations for each class. Note that "operations," "behaviors," and "functions" are used interchangeably. In C++ terms, class attributes will become C++ class data members, and operations will become member functions.

There is some controversy over exactly what should be included in the class model during OOA. Some developers insist on determining attributes and operations during OOA, and adding their types and initial values during OOD. We have chosen to do all of this during the OOD phase. The recommendation here is to keep the OOA model as simple as possible, and to avoid terminology such as "attributes" and "behaviors." Users and domain experts are our primary interfaces during OOA and may be confused by terminology belonging to the design phase. They are primarily interested in making sure that their requirements will be met.

4.3 Adding Attributes and Operations

There is no simple way to determine the proper set of attributes and operations for a class. Some of the attributes may appear as noun phrases or adjectives in a requirements document. Similarly, operations may appear as verb phrases in the same type of document. In most cases, however, we have to simply consider each class and determine which attributes we need and which operations are required for affecting the behavior of a particular class. As an aid in determining the initial set of operations, we can use a taxonomy for classifying the required operations [1, p. 62 and 2, p.223].

Taxonomy of Class Operations:

The taxonomy of class operations includes the following:

1. Implementers—Primary client interface reflected in the requirements.
2. Access—Will return values of (hidden) attributes.
3. Managers—Object (instance) creation, initialization, destruction, memory management, etc.
4. Helpers—Internal operations used by the operations in categories 1–3.

The determination of a set of attributes and operations for the classes in the class model should be made in cooperation with the domain experts. They do not have to be designers or fluent in OOA/OOD concepts. Here is the initial list for some of the classes in the Horizon application:

Class: Account

Attributes	Operations
Number	Open
Description	Set Defaults
Status	Edit
Balance	Close
	Set Initial Balance
	Display

Class: Customer

Attributes	Operations
Name	Edit
Description	Add
Shipping Address	Delete
Mailing Address	Display
Phone	Show Balance
Contact	
Account Number	
Discount	
Payment Terms	

Class: CustomerOrder

Attributes	Operations
Customer Name	Record
Order Date	Edit
Delivery Date	Display
Item List (embedded objects)	Print

Class: Entry

Attributes	Operations
Product Number	Add
Description	Delete
Quantity	Edit
Unit Sales Price	
Amount	
Tax Code	

Class: Inventory

Attributes	Operations
Product Location	Check on Item
Description	Display
Phone	Edit
Contact	Update
Item List (embedded objects)	Print

Class: Supplier

Attributes	Operations
Name	Add
Description	Edit
Address	Delete
Phone	Display
Contact	Show Balance
Account Number	
Discount	
Payment Terms	

Class: Invoice

Attributes	Operations
Number	Create
Date	Edit
Status	Add
Customer Reference	Delete
Payment Terms	Display
Entries (embedded objects)	Print
Total Amount	Amount
Discount	
Sales Tax	
Amount to be Paid	
Account Number	

Class: StockItem

Attributes	Operations
Name	Update Quantity
Description	Edit
Quantity	
Storage Location	

Some of the elements listed as attributes of a class do not really belong to that particular class. An Invoice, for example, has a list of Entries. This collection is considered a set of embedded Entry objects and will be implemented with the aggregation (whole-part) relation. The Invoice is the "whole" and the Entries the "parts."

4.4 Adding Types and Initial Values to Attributes

The attributes determined for each class will eventually be implemented in C++ as data members. This requires a type specification for each attribute. Many of these types will be selected from the predefined types delivered with a particular C++ development system. Some of the types will be taken from the standard C++ library or from C++ libraries supplied by independent software vendors.

Here are the types and initial values (if any) for the attributes associated with the classes in the Horizon application:

Class: Account

Attribute	Type
Number	String
Description	String
Status	Enumeration = Active
Balance	Double = 0.0

Class: CustomerOrder

Attribute	Type
Customer Name	String
Order Date	Date
Delivery Date	Date
Item List (embedded objects)	Entry*

Class: Inventory

Attribute	Type
Product Location	String
Description	String
Phone	String
Contact	String
Item List (embedded objects)	StockItem*

Class: StockItem

Attribute	Type
Name	String
Description	String
Quantity	Integer
Storage Location	String

Class: Supplier

Attribute	Type
Name	String
Description	String
Address	String
Phone	String
Contact	String
Account Number	String
Discount	Double 0.0
Payment Terms	Enumeration = Net 30 days

Class: Customer

Attribute	Type
Name	String
Description	String
Shipping Address	String
Mailing Address	String
Phone	String
Contact	String
Account Number	String
Discount	Double = 0.0
Payment Terms	Enumeration = Net 30 days

Class: Entry

Attribute	Type
Product Number	String
Description	String
Quantity	Integer
Unit Sales Price	Double = 0.0
Amount	Double = 0.0
Tax Code	Integer

Class: Invoice

Attribute	Type
Number	String
Date	Date
Status	Enumeration
Customer Reference	Customer
Payment Terms	Enumeration = Net 30 days
Entries (embedded objects)	Entry*
Total Amount	Double = 0.0
Discount	Double = 0.0
Sales Tax	Double = 0.0
Amount to be Paid	Double = 0.0
Account Number	String

Some of the types listed for the attributes are now available in the Standard C++ library. Examples of these include String and Date. The types listed for embedded objects, e.g., Customer Reference in the Invoice class, may end up as pointers or references to the respective class types. Other embedded objects, e.g., the Item List in the Inventory class, may become collection classes. These are implementation issue that will be resolved during the OOP phase.

The use of an asterisk (e.g., StockItem* in the Inventory class) implies a variable number of elements in an array type.

The primary purpose of assigning types to the attributes is to prepare the classes for transitioning to C++ constructs, and to uncover any additional classes or types that may be required. Two additional classes were uncovered above: String and Date.

Both of these types are available, and we only have to find the correct include statements to use them.

4.5 Refining Operations

The next step in the OOD phase is to refine the class operations by adding parameter names and types, and return types. The operations are written as prototypes in C++ syntax. Here are sample prototypes for some of the Horizon classes:

Class: Invoice
```
    void Create (CString custId, Date deliver);
    void Edit (CString invoiceId, Date deliver, Entry&
                                              entry);
    void Add (CString invoiceId, Entry& entry);
    void Delete (CString invoiceId, int entryLine);
    void Display (CString invoiceId);
    void Print (CString invoiceId);
    double Amount (CString invoiceId);
```

Class: Customer
```
    void    Add ();
    void    Delete (CString custId);
    void    Edit (CString custId);
    void    Display (CString custId);
    double GetBalance (CString custId);
    Customer& GetCustomerData (CString custId);
    InvoiceInfo& GetInvoiceInfo (CString custId);
```

Where did the *CString* type come from? Let's assume that we have decided to use the Microsoft Visual C++ development system, and *CString* is available in the MFC C++ class library.

The determination of the return types for the operations is dependent on the type of error reporting we choose. The return types for the prototypes shown as void anticipate the use of the C++ exception handling mechanism instead of returning C-style error conditions. Requesting the deletion of a Customer object that doesn't exist, for instance, would return a properly named exception. If we should decide to use a mechanism that returns an error condition, all of the void return types should be replaced by integer types instead. The recommendation throughout this book is to use the C++ exception handling mechanism to implement fault tolerance.

4.6 Determine Exception Handling Strategy

The older C/C++ programming style made use of special error handling by having a number of error codes or character strings as error messages. This was usually not implemented uniformly across all modules in a large programming project and depended on preferences of individual programmers. In many cases, error handling was added to a project as an afterthought and was not very well integrated with the overall design.

Modern C++ style programming has the opportunity to use the built-in exception handling mechanism to implement an overall fault tolerance strategy. This is more than simply anticipating error handling. A strategy can be designed into the application for detecting, reporting, and, correcting, at least some, predefined exceptional conditions.

Here are the choices we are faced with in determining an overall exception handling strategy:

- C++ constructs—Built-in syntax and semantics now available with most modern C++ development systems (see Chapter 13 for details).

- Using the assert() function—Can be sprinkled throughout the application for checking pre- and post-conditions within a function.

- Error messages—Creating error numbers and/or character strings for reporting error conditions.

- Structured Exception Handling (SEH)—Unique Microsoft exception handling mechanism using macros to simulate the real C++ mechanism. Included in the Microsoft Foundation Class (MFC) framework prior to Visual C++ version 4.0.

- setjmp/longjmp—Special low-level functions (setjmp is usually implemented as a macro) that can be used to vector certain error conditions when they are detected. The setjmp macro is used to set up information about the current calling context similar to a callback mechanism. The longjmp function is used to affect a non-local jump to the area set by the corresponding setjmp macro.

- Combinations of the above—We can mix any of the strategies listed above in a single application. The Microsoft SEH can, of course, only be used if our development platform is Visual C++.

It is highly recommended that the C++ exception handling mechanism be used as the single, or at least primary, strategy for a fault tolerance scheme. This mechanism is now implemented on all major C++ development systems, and the run-time overhead is extremely low. One disadvantage is the increased amount of design activity required for a successful implementation. This extra effort is by far outweighed by increased robustness of execution and ease of extensibility when (not if!) requirements change.

Let's assume that we decide on using the C++ exception handling mechanism for the Horizon application. The return types of the sample function prototypes will be void:

Class: Invoice
```
void Create (CString custId, Date deliver);
void Edit (CString invoiceId, Date deliver, Entry&
          entry);
```

```
void Add (CString invoiceId, Entry& entry);
void Delete (CString invoiceId, int entryLine);
void Display (CString invoiceId);
void Print (CString invoiceId);
```

If an invalid invoiceId is detected, an exception will be raised within the function and must be handled by the caller. (See Chapter 13 for raising and handling C++ exceptions.)

Class: Customer
```
void    Add ();
void    Delete (CString custId);
void    Edit (CString custId);
void    Display (CString custId);
```

If we are not successful in adding a new customer to our database, an exception will be raised. Similarly, if we are calling any of the functions that manipulate existing customer data with an invalid custId, an appropriate exception will be raised.

Note that this discussion of return types only applies to implementer operations. The access operations will have return types different from *void*:

```
Customer& getCustomer(CString custId);
```

The return type is now a reference to a Customer class and not void. An exception will be raised if an invalid customer id is passed to this function.

We will now return to the class model diagram and focus on the class relationships. In particular, the inheritance relations need additional scrutiny.

4.7 Refining Class Relationships

An inheritance relation is shown in Figure 4.2 with the Account class as a base class and AccountsReceivable and AccountsPayable as derived classes. It is important to decide on the common attributes and operations that belong to the general class, and to determine which ones are unique for the specialized classes. The suggested split of attributes and operations for these three classes is illustrated in Figure 4.2.

The unique attributes for the two derived classes are determined to be customerId for the AccountsReceivable class and supplierId for the AccountsPayable class. All the other attributes are common and are kept in the abstract base class.

The only unique operation listed for the two derived classes is Open(). This will be a virtual member function which we have to override in each of the two derived classes to make sure we get the desired class type.

In looking for additional inheritance relations, we should expect to have a GeneralLedger class, also derived from the Account base class. This does not directly affect the structure of our class model and does not have to be added at this time.

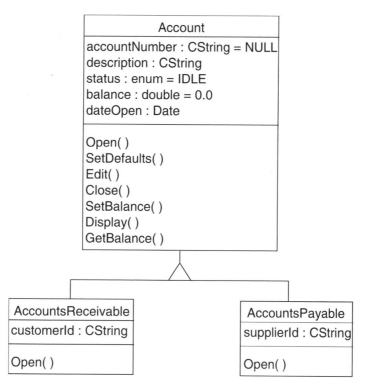

Figure 4.2 Attributes and Operations

When we filled in the attributes for the CustomerOrder, we included Item List as an embedded object and assigned it the type Entry. We also have Entry as a type for Entries as an embedded object of the Invoice class. It appears that we have two similar but slightly different "Entry" types that we need to account for. This may, at first, suggest an Entry base class with OrderEntry and InvoiceEntry as derived classes. On closer scrutiny, however, the "entry" for a CustomerOrder can be derived from a product identifier. This does not warrant a new inheritance hierarchy with the associated run-time overhead. We will keep the original Entry class and use it with the Invoice class relation.

The analysis made in this section is intended to illustrate the kinds of considerations we perform in refining the OOA class model. This is by no means a complete analysis, but by expanding the points made here, this limited analysis will scale up to a large application.

A major effort in the OOD phase is the determination of the additional classes required for the creation of a structure that can be implemented with an object-oriented programming language, i.e., C++ in our case. Most of what we have discussed so far will apply to implementations in Smalltalk and Eiffel as well as C++.

The additional classes we need are referred to as "architecture" classes and will almost never be found in requirements documents or from discussions with users.

These classes are strictly design artifacts that are necessary for a successful implementation. Some authors refer to these classes as "technology" classes, since we are leaving the high-level abstractions of the problem domain and diving into the technology required to implement the application.

4.8 Adding Architecture Classes

The necessity for adding architecture classes arise from a number of different design considerations:

- An exception handling strategy
- Use of GUI for communicating with users
- Type of I/O
- Database requirements for persistent data
- Client/server architecture
- Help features

Assuming we are implementing our application using the recommended C++ exception handling strategy, we will need a set of exception classes for exception objects that can be raised and propagated during execution. We can build our own classes, e.g., for the taxonomy of exceptions suggested in Chapter 13. We can also use predefined classes that are part of a library. The MFC, for example, includes the hierarchy of exception classes shown in Figure 4.3 [3].

This set of classes may not be sufficient for our application and we then have the choice of making new, independent exceptions (see Chapter 13) or derive additional classes from the MFC classes.

The use of GUI for communicating with users implies that we will be using a C++ library or a windows-oriented development framework such as X Window or Motif or Microsoft Windows 95 or NT. We will integrate our application with the existing GUI classes to form the architecture of the solution.

The type of I/O we decide to use will determine which architecture classes we will be interfacing with. Simple I/O to a monitor, for example, can be handled with the existing C++ extraction and insertion operators available in the iostream library. This library also contains classes and operations for file I/O. If we are interfacing with a GUI, even simple text I/O will have to be handled via the GUI functions, usually with device independent context layers or wrapper functions.

One of the major design decisions for a large project is what type of database system we should use. All large applications have requirements for persistent data, but C++ does not have any database features built into the language. We could, of course, save data to a flat file using the iostream library, but this is not what we have in mind for a "database."

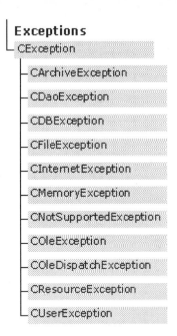

Figure 4.3 The MFC Exception Classes

There are a number of object-oriented databases (ODBMSs) available from independent vendors, e.g., POET and O2. There are also a number of relational databases (RDBMSs) that can be accessed from a C++ application via the Object Database Connectivity (ODBC) drivers [4]. Suffice it to say here that the design decisions made regarding the architecture classes and databases to be used in the application will have a profound effect on the utility and efficiency of the application. These topics are described further in later chapters.

The requirement for a client/server architecture will add another set of classes to implement the necessary communication schemes. This may be as simple as using an existing C++ TCP/IP library, or it may involve the design of a multi-threaded application that includes e-mail features and asynchronous message passing.

The addition of help features will require yet another set of architecture classes for "canned" help messages as well as context sensitive help via "hot areas" and mouse clicks. We may also decide to include a tutorial with a number of sample cases to illustrate the primary features of the application.

List of Architecture Classes

Here is a partial list of the Architecture classes we will need for the Horizon application:

Class	Library/Header File
Address	Horizon (TBI)
CString	MFC
COblist or List	MFC or STL
CObArray or Vector	MFC or STL
Date, CTime	MFC
CException	MFC
InvoiceInfo	Horizon (TBI)

Most of the architecture classes listed here are available in the MFC library. The Address class is something we have to implement (TBI = to be implemented). Additional architecture classes required for the implementation are likely to be discovered during the OOP phase.

4.9 Decomposing Complex Operations

We will take a small snapshot of the Horizon application to illustrate how we can use the dynamic model to determine the operations and associated objects involved in a complex function. The static model for the classes involved with the creation and maintenance of invoices is shown in the class diagram in Figure 4.4.

The Create() function of the Invoice class is a complex operation of an object (instance of the Invoice class) that has a number of different run-time states. Here is a list of possible states:

- Start—"idle" state waiting for the command to create a new invoice
- CreatingNew—The creation of a new invoice for a particular customer
- EnteringFormData—Entering data common to all invoices
- AddingEntries—Adding entries for the products ordered by the customer
- CreatingTotals—Using entry amounts, possible discounts, and tax data to create the total invoice amount
- Stop—Update AccountsReceivable with the total amount for the customer, and send trigger for creating a PackingOrder

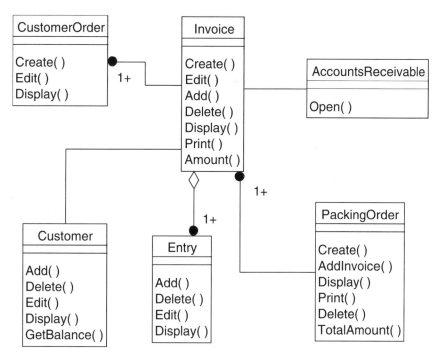

Figure 4.4 Class Diagram for the Invoicing Sub-Function

The STD for the creation of a new invoice is shown in Figure 4.5. The rounded rectangles correspond to the states listed above. The annotations illustrate the operations and their associated objects (listed with class names and the C++ scope operator: `CustomerOrder::GetCustomerId()`) that are involved with each transition from one state to another. An object-level STD can be constructed for each complex function that is an operation of a class.

When the STD shown in Figure 4.5 was created, additional operations were discovered. This is a byproduct of trying to understand complex operations. The initial set of operations we determine for each class is usually not sufficient. The further we get into the design activity, the more we understand about the required operations, and, sometimes, the attributes. The new operations, e.g., CustomerOrder::GetCustomerId() have been added to the operations list in the Data Dictionary, discussed in the next section.

4.10 Updating the Data Dictionary

As we refine the OOD class model, the design decisions we make must be recorded. The best place for such recordation is in a CASE tool that supports our OOA/OOD method and notation. Several of these tools exist today. The main problem in using them is that the notation changes and new versions are released periodically by the tool vendors.

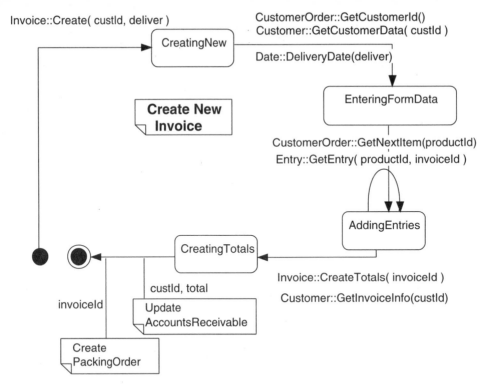

Figure 4.5 STD for Create New Invoice

The OOA/OOD class model and the STD shown for the Horizon application were created with Rational Rose. This tool records all the information we enter for the various diagrams and stores it in its internal data dictionary. Here is a summary of the data associated with attributes and operations for some of the invoice classes:

Class: **AccountsReceivable**
Class Persistence: Persistent

Operations:
```
 void Open (CString custId);
```

Attributes:
```
 CString customerId
```

Class: **Invoice**
Class Persistence: Persistent

Operations:
```
 void Create (CString custId, Date deliver);
```

```
void Edit (CString invoiceId, Date deliver, Entry&
          entry);
void Add (CString invoiceId, Entry& entry);
void Delete (CString invoiceId, int entryLine);
void Display (CString invoiceId);
void Print (CString invoiceId);
double Amount (CString invoiceId);
void CreateTotals (CString invoiceId);
```

Attributes:
```
CString number
Date deliveryDate
enum status = NOTPAID
CString customerId
enum paymentTerms = COD
Entry* entry
double totalAmount = 0.0
double discount = 0.0
double salesTax = 0.0
double amountToBePaid = 0.0
CString accountNumber
```

Class: **Customer**
Class Persistence: Persistent

Operations:
```
void    Add ();
void    Delete (CString custId);
void    Edit (CString custId);
void    Display (CString custId);
double GetBalance (CString custId);
Customer& GetCustomerData (CString custId);
InvoiceInfo& GetInvoiceInfo (CString custId);
```

Attributes:
```
CString customerId
CString description
Address shippingAddress
Address mailingAddress
CString phone
CString contact
CString accountNumber
double discount = 0.0
enum paymentTerms = COD
enum taxCode = NOTAX;
```

Class: **CustomerOrder**
Class Persistence: Transitory

Operations:

```
void Create (CString custId);
void Edit (CString orderId);
void Display (CString orderId);
void Print (CString orderId);
int& GetNextItem(CString& productId);
CString& GetCustomerId ();
```

Attributes:
```
CString orderId
CString customerId
Date orderDate
Date deliveryDate
CObList itemList
```

Class: **Entry**
Class Persistence: Transitory

Operations:
```
void Add (CString invoiceId);
void Delete (CString invoiceId, int entryIndex);
void Edit (CString invoiceId);
void Display (CString invoiceId, int entryIndex);
Entry& GetEntry (CString productId, CString invoiceId);
```

Attributes:
```
CString productId
CString description
int quantity = 0
double unitPrice = 0.0
double amount = 0.0
enum taxCode = NOTAX
```

Class: **PackingOrder**
Class Persistence: Persistent

Operations:
```
void Create (CString invoiceId);
void AddInvoice (CString packOrder, CString invoiceId);
void Display (CString packOrder);
void Print (CString packOrder);
void Delete (CString packOrder, CString invoiceId);
double TotalAmount (CString packOrder);
```

Attributes:
```
CString orderId
CString customerId
Address shippingAddress
Date deliveryDate
CObList listofInvoices
```

Additional data dictionary items, such as levels of data access, concurrency, cardinalities, etc., are stored in the Rational Rose CASE tool.

Note that there is usually a considerable amount of iteration and refinement between the design decisions made during OOD and the implementation phase of OOP. This is normal, since it is almost impossible to anticipate all the architectural details necessary to implement a complex application during the OOD phase.

This chapter has provided an outline of some of the design decisions we need to make during OOD. Many of these decisions involve complex C++ issues, which are discussed in later chapters. In the next chapter, we look at how the refined class model is transitioned to the OOP phase and how we implement the classes and their relations in C++.

4.11 Summary

It should be quite clear from the above discussion that there is a significantly different focus in the OOD phase than in the OOA phase. The latter is occupied with understanding the requirements and creating an initial class model based on the key abstractions of the problem domain. The OOD phase is concerned with refining the OOA class model and determining the architectural elements that must be added.

The structural elements of the design consist of the refined class model, function prototypes of the operations belonging to each class, and the class attributes with associated types and initial values. A list of architecture classes to be added, and the C++ libraries where they can be found, completes the products of the OOD phase. We are assuming that these additional classes are available via reuse and that we (hopefully!) do not have to develop them.

References

1. Nielsen, K.W., *Software Development with C++: Maximizing Reuse with Object Technology*, Academic Press, Cambridge, MA 1995.

2. Lippman, S., *C++ Primer*, Second Edition, Addison-Wesley, Reading, MA 1991.

3. Visual C++ 4.0, Programming with MFC, Volume 2, p. 402, Microsoft Press, Redmond, WA 1995.

4. Microsoft ODBC 3.0 Programmer's Reference and SDK Guide, Microsoft Press, Redmond, WA 1997.

5

Object-Oriented Programming

Object-Oriented Programming (OOP) is the process of transforming a design into an application by using the available constructs of a particular programming language, i.e., C++. The architecture created during the OOD phase anticipated the use of C++ by including C++ "technology" as design elements. Existing C++ libraries, for example, were introduced as architectural elements for our application.

We went to great lengths during the OOA and OOD phases to create a class model that takes advantage of object-oriented concepts such as inheritance and encapsulation. We are now ready to implement these concepts in C++.

Some of the implementation schemes are quite complex and will be revisited in later chapters after we have reviewed the basics of C++ class construction. The emphasis of this chapter is to describe the transitioning process from the OOD model to the OOP model with C++ as the implementation language.

5.1 Transitioning from OOD to OOP

The starting point for our implementation is the refined class model developed during the OOD phase. The new version of the class model for the invoicing sub-function of the Horizon application is shown in Figure 5.1.

This is the same class model as we had before, now also showing the attributes and operations for each class. The attributes include types and default values (if any). The operations only include the name. The parameters and return types are kept in the data dictionary.

Additional design elements include the architecture classes Address, CString, Date, CObList, and InvoiceInfo. The class relationships and cardinalities are the same as we saw earlier for the less detailed class diagrams. The problem facing us now is how we can implement the architecture in Figure 5.1 using C++ constructs.

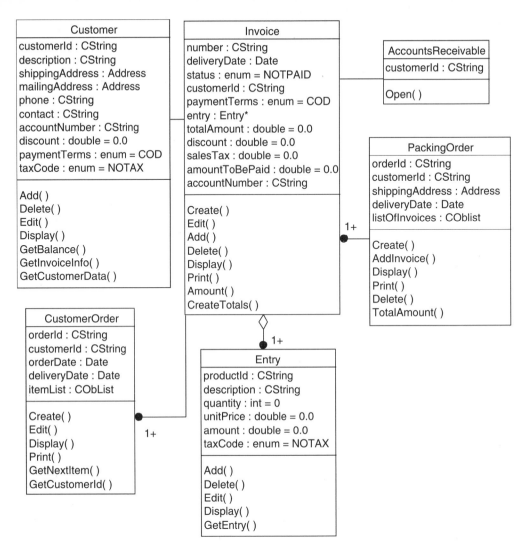

Figure 5.1 Horizon Invoicing Refined Class Model

5.2 Implementing OOD Structures in C++

Some of the architectural elements in the refined class model can be implemented directly with C++ constructs; others have to be created with certain programming idioms (generally accepted programming practices for a particular programming language). Here is a list of how we intend to accomplish the C++ implementation:

- classes   =>   C++ classes
- abstract classes   =>   abstract C++ classes via pure virtual member functions
- class operations   =>   member functions
- class attributes   =>   data members
- information hiding   =>   private or protected access
- encapsulation   =>   a C++ class containing all of its attributes and operations
- direct data access   =>   friend privilege
    - class
    - member function
    - non-member function
- inheritance   =>   C++ constructs with public (in most cases), protected, or private inheritance
- polymorphism   =>   declare base member functions as virtual
- exception handling   =>   C++ constructs with throw, try, and catch

All the design elements listed above can be implemented directly with C++ constructs. We will illustrate these transitions with actual C++ code in later chapters.

We will now address some of the more complex transitions, which do not have corresponding C++ constructs. These design elements are implemented using C++ constructs and a set of programming idioms:

- aggregation   =>   data members as objects of other classes
- association   =>   passing objects of other classes as arguments via reference or pointer
- information hiding   =>   separate header (.h) and source (.cpp) files
- STD   =>   finite state machine
    - traditional, using switch statements
    - object-oriented, using C++ classes

Aggregation (whole-part) is implemented with the "whole" class having "parts" as data members of other classes. Here is an example for the Invoice/Entry relation:

```
class Invoice {
public:
  // ...
private:
  // ...
  Entry* entry;
};
```

Our business rules stated that an Invoice is composed of one or more Entries. We have shown the data member `entry` as a pointer to an Entry object. This can also be interpreted as an array of Entry elements. The design decision for this type of relation usually leaves us with a choice of two basic implementations: an array or a collection class. This can be a tricky C++ implementation issue of an object-oriented design and will be explored further in Chapters 7 and 14.

The simple Using relationship is used where an object of one class makes references to an object of a different class. Here is an example for the creation of an invoice for a particular customer:

```
class Invoice {
public:
   // ...
   void Create (CString& custId, Date& deliver);
private:
   // ...
   Entry* entry;
};
```

The customer id makes a reference to a particular customer object about which we need data to create a portion of the invoice.

The primary difference between aggregation and association can be stated as ownership and persistence issues:

- An object in an association relationship does not own the object it references. The referenced object may exist before or after the referencing object is created and destroyed.

- An object that contains an embedded object of another class (aggregation relationship) has ownership of the embedded object or collection of objects. The embedded object is created and destroyed with its owner.

Again, we are touching on very detailed C++ issues that are not easily understood. We will continue to explore these issues in the chapters that follow.

5.3 Designing Proper Visibility

One of the primary features of an object-oriented architecture is the use of encapsulation and information hiding. The information hiding part is the packaging mechanism used to prevent casual users from gaining direct access to attributes and internal operations. This is implemented in C++ by creating code sections prefaced by the `protected` and `private` keywords. Here are some design guidelines for accomplishing the information hiding goal:

- Initially, make all attributes private
- If a class is designed as a base class, make those attributes that are allowed to be manipulated by a derived class protected
- If instances of a base class should only be created by a derived class, make the base class constructor(s) protected
- Make Implementer and Access operations (see Section 4.3) public
- Make Manager operations public, with a possible exception of memory management operations
- Make Helper operations private
- Don't grant friend privilege unless absolutely necessary and harmless, e.g., for output functions that do not modify the data they display or print

This set of guidelines will help us determine the initial visibility for attributes and operations of each class. There will usually be iterations between the OOD and OOP phases before this issue is completely resolved.

Another element of the information hiding issue is how we package our classes in header and source files:

- Put all class declarations in header files (.h)
- Put all class definitions in separate source files (.cpp)
- Defer #include statements to the module where they are needed, e.g., put them in the .cpp file where needed, rather than nested within another header file

These design guidelines provide for a low level of coupling between compilation units and hide implementation details. The class declarations should serve as mere interfaces for user programs and derived classes. If we should decide to change the implementations of the class operations, we can change the C++ code in the .cpp files without affecting the users of the changed classes. This is assuming, of course, that we are not changing the class declarations, i.e., the class interfaces.

5.4 Summary

The OOD class model is transitioned into an OOP class model, which includes the class relationships and cardinalities.

Many of the OOD design elements can be implemented directly with C++ constructs. The remaining elements are implemented using a number of different programming idioms, where an idiom is a generally accepted programming practice for a particular programming language.

Visibility is controlled by declaring the desired level of access using the keywords public, protected, and private.

PART 2

C++ Class Design and Implementation

In this part we present a synopsis of how we implement many of the object-oriented concepts with C++ class constructs. This digest provides a review of the most important elements of C++. The emphasis is placed on the following elements:

- The general use of classes and objects to implement a design
- The use and design of collection classes
- Elements of class construction and well-designed classes
- Use of overloading to create complete sets of class interfaces
- The mechanism of inheritance and polymorphism
- Implementation of proper class relationships
- Implementation of object-oriented finite state machines
- Using the Factory Method design pattern to implement virtual constructors
- Use of structs as data structures vs. classes
- Converting binary objects to byte streams

The original specification of the C++ programming language (the ARM) has been the subject of numerous changes as the standards committees have continued their work towards a C++ ISO/ANSI standard. This has presented a significant problem for both C++ programmers and tool vendors. The programmers need to understand the proper syntax and semantics to create their applications. The vendors need to implement the language requirements, and they need to have a reasonable chance to anticipate forthcoming changes.

The basic reference text serving as the original ARM has been [1]. Other important references are [2, 3]. The document that will eventually replace [1] as the official C++

ARM is a draft of the ANSI standards committee working paper [4]. Copies of the latest changes to the C++ standard can be obtained via Internet access at `http://www.cygnus.com/misc/wp/dec96pub/`. (The references listed here are found at the end of Chapter 6.)

6

Classes and Objects in C++

We have seen the progression through the development cycle and the refinement of the class model as we move from OOA to OOD to OOP. A general strategy for implementing OOD structures with C++ constructs and programming idioms was outlined in Chapter 5. An idiom is a generally accepted programming practice for a particular programming language.

The objective of this chapter is to continue the discussion of how we can implement an OOD design using C++ classes and objects.

6.1 Implementing Design Entities

The refined class model that is the product of the OOD phase represents the architecture for our application. This can be likened to a set of architectural drawings used to construct a building. The carpenters don't start framing until the foundation has been laid, and electricians don't start laying cables and putting in switch boxes until the frame is up, but before the walls are completed. The blueprints and constant verbal communication between the various work crews ensure that the construction of the building progresses steadily.

The static OOD class model must contain sufficient architectural detail that the real-world abstractions can be implemented with the intended technology. An example of what we mean by "technology" is a particular C++ development environment that we will use to develop an executable application. This could include the Microsoft Visual C++, Borland C++, or HP SoftBench.

Once we choose one of these environments, we will have to make our application classes fit with the rest of the classes and framework of the development platform. One such architecture is the Microsoft Foundation Classes (MFC) and the associated framework that are part of the Microsoft Visual C++. A great deal of code reuse can be realized by taking advantage of the built-in Visual C++ tools ("wizards"). By using these tools, however, we are accepting the architecture and structure of that particular framework, since a significant amount of C++ code is generated.

If we decide to use the wizards available in Microsoft Visual C++, we are automatically buying into the predefined document/view architecture. This architecture is implemented with a "document" object holding and owning all the data for the application, and this data can be displayed to a user in a number of different "views." This means that we must make design decisions for how to fit our application classes that represent the real-world abstractions into an existing document/view design paradigm. We could also choose to implement our application by using some of the framework classes independent of the document/view, but this would require a significantly larger programming effort and less opportunity for reuse on future, similar projects.

By accepting an existing design structure, such as the document/view architecture, how are we assured that this is an acceptable solution for our application? There is no simple answer to this question. But a compelling number of Windows applications have been developed with it. If we are developing an application with a significant amount of GUI requirements, the document/view paradigm is an ideal candidate for such an application. This concept was not developed by Microsoft, by the way, it originates from the Smalltalk development environment [5] as the Pane-ViewManager concept, and has been accepted as the design pattern Mediator [6]. There is thus ample precedence for the use of this particular implementation strategy.

In the remaining sections of this chapter, we will enlarge the discussion of the type of design decisions we need to make to successfully implement an architecture.

6.2 C++ Classes as User-Defined Types

The classes we transition from the OOD class model to the C++ OOP model will be implemented as user-defined types. A Customer class in the Horizon application, for example, can be implemented as follows:

```
class Customer {
public:
  Customer ();
  Customer (const Customer&);
  Customer& operator= (const Customer&);
  ~Customer ();
  // exceptions
  ...
  void Add (CString custId);
  void Delete (CString custId);
  void Edit (CString custId);
  void Display (CString custId);
  double GetBalance (CString custId);
  Customer& GetCustomerData (CString custId);
  InvoiceInfo& GetInvoiceInfo (CString custId);
  void Print (String custId = NULL);
```

```
private:
  CString   customerId;
  CString   description;
  Address shippingAddress;
  Address mailingAddress;
  CString   phone;
  CString   fax;
  CString   contact;
  double    discount;
  Terms paymentTerms;
  Taxes taxCode;
};
```

We have created a new type Customer which we can add to our application modules. By including this as a header file into any of our classes, we can then use this class as any other predefined type that comes with the C++ environment.

Notice the two major code sections prefaced by "public:" and "private:," respectively. All the operations (the C++ term is "member functions") have been placed in the public section. This means that a program wanting to use this class can merely include it to gain access to all the member functions. The attributes (the C++ term is "data members") have all been placed in the private section. This prohibits direct access to the data members by programs using this class. Only the member functions of Customer have access to the data members of this class.

The issue of controlling visibility with the correct level of data access is much more complex than simply choosing between public and private. We will pursue this further in Chapter 8, when we add considerations for the use of "protected" in connection with base and derived classes, and the optional "friend" keyword for granting unlimited access.

There is a major design decision implicitly included in the prototypes for the Customer class member functions. Add(), Delete(), Edit(), etc., all have a return type of void. What if we are passing an invalid customer id to any of these functions—shouldn't we then return some type of error flag or message? The implicit design decision here is that we will be using the C++ exception handling mechanism rather than sending error flags or messages. This design decision was made during the OOD phase and will be implemented during the OOP phase.

Here is another class we will need for our Horizon application:

```
class Invoice {
public:
  Invoice ();
  Invoice (const Invoice&);
  Invoice& operator= (const Invoice&);
  ~Invoice ();
  // exceptions
  ...
  void Create (CString custId, Date deliver);
  void Edit (CString invoiceId, Date deliver, Entry&
            entry);
  void Add (CString invoiceId, Entry& entry);
```

```
        void Delete (CString invoiceId, int entryLine);
        void Display (CString invoiceId);
        void Print (CString customerId = NULL);
        double Amount (CString invoiceId);
        void CreateTotals (CString invoiceId);
    private:
        CString number;
        Date deliveryDate;
        CustomerStatus status;
        CString customerId;
        Terms paymentTerms;
        Entry* entries; // collection of entries
        double totalAmount;
        double discount;
        double salesTax;
        double amountToBePaid;
        CString accountNumber;
    };
```

One of the data members of the class Invoice is the embedded collection of "entries." The collection has been indicated with an array notation here (Entry*), but this is not the only way this can be implemented. This is an example of the whole-part paradigm with a cardinality of one Invoice to many Entries. The design decisions we make for a "collection" class is described in detail in Chapter 7.

6.3 Encapsulation

One of the key features of an object-oriented design and implementation is the use of encapsulation. The class Customer includes all attributes and operations required for the creation, destruction, and manipulation of Customer objects. In other words, this class encapsulates everything associated with Customer objects required for the Horizon application. The same is true for the Invoice class.

The C++ code we have shown for the Customer and Invoice classes are class declarations contained in separate header files and represent the respective interfaces for these two classes. A by-product of this type of encapsulation is that the implementation is completely hidden from the users of these two classes, i.e., we have separated the implementation from the interface. This supports a level of information hiding that is different from and in addition to the use of the special keywords (e.g., public or private) to control the class access.

The class encapsulation supports the localization concept, i.e., when changes have to be made to an operation or attribute of a class, we have only one place to look to make those changes.

The accomplishment of the information hiding concept, by separating the implementation from the interface, adds significantly to the goal of having loose coupling between program modules. When the implementation of an operation needs to be changed, the program modules that use that particular class does not have to be changed. They don't even have to be recompiled, as long as the class interface doesn't change! These conditions are now detected by development systems using incremental compilation schemes, and save significant development time.

6.4 Classes as Collections of Objects

Each class we design represents a template or blueprint for one or more objects that will be instantiated during the execution of an application. We have described a class as a collection of objects with a set of common attributes and operations. Every instance of a class has a set of unique attributes and a set of operations for creating, destroying, and manipulating the instances. In C++, storage is allocated for the attributes of each instance of a class. The operations, however, are shared among all the objects of a particular class. This saves considerable amounts of storage when several objects of a given class are present during the execution of an application.

There must thus be a mechanism to distinguish between different objects of the same class calling the same operation. The following mechanism is used in C++:

- Each object must be declared with a unique name:

```
Customer aCustomer, bCustomer;
```

- "Dot" notation is used to call an operation via an object:

```
aCustomer.Display (id1);
bCustomer.Edit (id5);
```

- Pointer notation is used to call an operation via a pointer to an object:

```
Customer* ptrCustomer;
// ...
ptrCustomer->Edit (id5);
```

- An internal "this" pointer is used as an invisible parameter in the parameter list and points to the object on whose behalf an operation is invoked

This mechanism is pervasive in C++ and is implemented with a minimum of run-time overhead.

We have seen the use of a class as a collection of objects in an entirely different context than the general definition of a class just described. The other context is where one class contains an embedded object of a different class as an attribute. This was expressed with the aggregation relationship (whole-part) and is difficult to implement in C++, since there is no direct construct to support this concept. This is an extremely important topic, because every application involving database issues must implement this relationship. This is a complex issue, and we have devoted the entire next chapter to describe various design strategies and solutions.

6.5 Summary

Every C++ application is based on the implementation of classes modeled as an OOD design architecture. C++ has constructs for the creation of classes as user-defined types. It also supports the class relationships of inheritance and association. Aggregation is not supported and must be implemented with certain C++ programming idioms.

Visibility to operations and attributes is controlled by creating code sections prefaced by a keyword denoting the particular access level.

Each C++ class declaration encapsulates everything required for the creation, destruction, and manipulation of objects of that class. The class declaration represents the class interface. A level of information hiding is provided by placing the class implementation in a separate source file.

When multiple instances of the same class are created, each instance has its own set of attributes. One set of operations is shared by all the instances of the same class. A run-time mechanism utilizing the "this" pointer is used to designate the particular object on whose behalf an operation is invoked.

References

1. Ellis, M.A., and Stroustrup, B., *The Annotated C++ Reference Manual*, Addison-Wesley, Reading, MA, 1990.

2. Stroustrup, B., *The C++ Programming Language*, Second Edition, Addison-Wesley, Reading, MA, 1991.

3. Stroustrup, B., *The Design and Evolution of C++*, Addison-Wesley, Reading, MA, 1994.

4. Working Paper for Draft Proposed International Standard for Information Systems - Programming Language C++, Doc No: X3J16/96-0225, WG21/N1043, 2 December 1996.

5. LaLonde, W., *Discovering Smalltalk*, Benjamin/Cummings, Redwood City, CA, 1994.

6. Gamma, E. et al., *Design Patterns*, Addison Wesley, Reading, MA 1995.

7

Collection Classes

We have seen the need for collection classes whenever a class has an embedded object as an attribute. This is expressed as the aggregation (or whole-part) relationship, where the "part" is the embedded object of the "whole." Synonyms for aggregation are embedding (data members are embedded as attributes of other classes), composition (the current class is composed of attributes of other classes), and layering (the current class is layered on top of other classes as attributes).

The focus of this chapter is on how we can implement collection classes using C++ constructs and programming idioms. After a general description of the different types of collection classes, we provide guidelines for the selection of a particular collection class that best fits our application.

Collection classes are now available both as part of the STL (see Chapter 14), as well as with the major C++ development systems (see chapter 21 for a discussion of the MFC collection classes). We will discuss trade-offs between these two sources for selecting collection classes.

Some of the material in this chapter is based on the assumption that the reader has a basic understanding of C++ template syntax and semantics. If you don't feel comfortable with C++ templates, see Chapter 12 for a review before tackling this chapter.

7.1 Types of Collection Classes

A C++ collection is a container which holds a set of user-defined class objects or a set of built-in objects. The simplest form of a collection is an array of integers. In our case, we need more complex collections which can hold sets of embedded objects. For example, we may need a collection containing a set of Invoice Entries.

A collection object will appear in the application as a single object. A set of member functions will be associated with the collection object and can operate on all the elements in the collection. Two basic sets of collections can exist in an application: *homogeneous* collections, where all the objects are of the same type, and *heterogeneous* collections, where objects of different types make up each collection.

Collection Categories

Collections can be classified into three different categories according to their "shape":

- List—An ordered collection that is not indexed. The order refers to the insertion and deletion of objects, and does not necessarily imply that they are sorted in that order.
- Array—An ordered collection that is indexed. The elements can be retrieved via an integer index.
- Map—An indexed collection that may be ordered. Fast access methods are available for inserting an element and for searching for a specific element. Each element is associated with a key.

Reviewing the various shapes of collection classes can help us choose a particular class that fits our application. Table 7.1 presents an example of features for the shapes available in the MFC [1]:

Table 7.1 Shapes Available in the MFC

Shape	Ordered	Indexed	Insert	Search	Duplicates
List	Yes	No	Fast	Slow	Yes
Array	Yes	By int	Slow	Slow	Yes
Map	No	By key	Fast	Fast	No (key) Yes (value)

This table can be used to compare the available classes in a C++ library and make the necessary trade-offs to determine the best fit for our application.

The way collection classes are implemented can be described by two basic types:

- Template-Based Collections—These use the C++ template constructs.
- Non-Template Collections—These are implemented as arrays, lists, etc., and do not use the C++ templates.

Template-Based Collections

One advantage of using a template-based collection is that it usually provides better type-safety than a non-template collection. Here is an outline of a template-based collection class:

```
// File: collection.h

template<class Type>
class Collection {
public:
// Constructors/destructor

// Overloaded operators

// Implementer Functions
  virtual void Add(const Type&);
  virtual void Delete(const Type&);
  // ...

  // Access Functions
  virtual int NumberOfItems() const;
  virtual Type& First() const;
  virtual Type& Last() const;
  virtual void Iterator();
  // ...

protected:
  // Helper Functions
  virtual void Lock();
  virtual void Unlock();
  Type* elements;
  // ...
};

// File: msghandler.cpp

#include "collection.h"
# include "message.h"
// ...
Collection<Message> msgContainer;
Message msg("Hi Priority Alert");
msgContainer.Add(msg);
```

This is an example of a generalized collection class, i.e., we can derive other collection classes from this base type. We have included an iterator (gets us to the next element in the collection) member function here; later we will discuss iterator classes as well. The instantiation with the Message type creates the `msgContainer` object, and we are invoking the Add() function to insert the new message.

Non-Template Collections

If we are working with a C++ compiler that does not support the template features, we don't have much choice: non-template collections is the only solution. One advantage of non-template collections is that they are simpler to implement and easier to understand. The biggest disadvantage is that separate classes will have to be created even if the only difference is the type of objects to be contained.

We can illustrate the creation of non-template collections with a generalized stack class:

```
// File: stack.h

typedef Message Type;
const int BOS = -1; // bottom of stack
const int stackSize = 24;

class Stack {
public:
  Stack (int sz = stackSize); // default ctor
  ~Stack ( ); // dtor
  int isEmpty( ) {return top == BOS;}
  int isFull( )  {return top == size-1;}
  virtual void push(Type value);
  virtual Type pop( );
protected:
  int top;
  int size;
  Type* array;
};
```

The data member `array` points to a collection of objects, which, in this case, has been `typedef`ed to a `Message`. This may, at first, appear to be a fairly general class, which can be used for any type, including built-ins. It can also serve as a base class for special, derived stack classes.

The primary disadvantage with this approach is that we will have to modify the `typedef` declaration for each new stack type. This will require a recompilation of all client software that references this stack class. This can prove to be a significant additional effort and use of resources for a large project. A much more preferable approach is the use of templates, which will only require an instantiation of a particular type in the client source code, as shown above for the generic Collection class.

7.2 Choosing a Collection Class

The terms Collection classes and Container classes are used interchangeably as synonyms. When a collection class is instantiated, it will contain a number of objects, which are "owned" by the object in whose class they are declared. The objects in a collection will persist as long as the owner-object persists.

When we need collection classes, we have to decide on one of four basic choices for creating the collections:

- Designing our own "home-grown" collections
- Using the collections available in the C++ Standard Template Library (STL)
- Using the collections included in our development environment
- Buying an add-on C++ library from an independent vendor

Home-Grown Collections

This should be our last resort. Creating an efficient and complete set of collection classes is a significant development effort. Not only do we need the classes themselves, we also have to develop a set of iterators and algorithms for accessing the elements in the collections. This is not a simple task and should be avoided unless some very peculiar requirements prevent us from using either the STL or the development environment classes.

Using Collection Classes in the STL

The latest version of the STL includes a complete set of collection classes, including iterators and algorithms. This would be a good choice if we anticipate moving between different development platforms, where each platform has its own C++ library and framework mechanism. One problem with this choice is that we have to integrate the STL classes with the framework classes. The latest C++ features include the use of Namespace, which can prevent name ambiguities of classes and functions with the same names.

Using Collection Classes in the Development Environment

If we expect to use a single development platform for our applications, we are better off using the collections included in that framework. The collection classes will be integrated with the rest of the classes in the framework, and we can usually capitalize on a maximum of code reuse.

One of the reasons why the Microsoft MFC has reached its current popularity is the fact that several C++ vendors are now licensing the MFC to be included as an option with their development environment. If the Microsoft Visual C++ is our development platform, the MFC should be our first choice for attempting to locate the collection classes we need.

Buying an Add-On C++ Library

Several independent vendors are now selling C++ libraries, which can be integrated with a development environment. As an example, Rogue Wave has a number of different C++ libraries (including a version of the STL), which can be added to the existing library of our development environment.

A particular add-on library may have exactly the features we desire from the shape determination, and could be a good candidate for our collection classes.

One major disadvantage with this approach is that the library structure may not be easily integrated with the existing library. Another potential disadvantage is the possibility of having two separate structural and implementation approaches, e.g., with regard to the exception handling mechanism.

7.3 Example of a Collection Class

To illustrate the level of effort required to create even a simple template-based collection class, here is an example:

```
template<class Type>
class CollectionIterator;

template<class Type>
class Collection {
public:
  // Constructors/destructor
  Collection(); // default ctor
  Collection(const Collection<Type>&); // copy ctor
  virtual ~Collection(); // virtual dtor

  // Overloaded operators
  virtual Collection<Type>& operator=
                    (const Collection<Type>&);
  virtual bool operator==(const Collection<Type>&) const;
  virtual bool operator!=(const Collection<Type>&) const;

  // Implementer Functions
  virtual void Add(const Type&);
  virtual void Delete(const Type&);
  virtual void ReplaceAt(int, const Type&);
  virtual void DeleteAll();

  // Access Functions
  virtual int NumberOfItems() const;
  virtual Type& First() const;
  virtual Type& Last() const;
  virtual bool IsEmpty() const;
  virtual Type& ItemAt(int) const;
  virtual int Position(const Type&) const;
```

```
  virtual int Duplicate(const Type&) const;

protected:
  // Helper Functions
  virtual void Lock();
  virtual void Unlock();

// Friends
  friend class CollectionIterator;
};
```

This "simple" container is implemented as a template-based base class.

The forward declaration of the iterator implies that this will be implemented as an independent class. The same iterator can then be used for a number of different collection classes. A less general approach would be to include a unique iterator as an access member function of the Collection class.

This class provides a common interface for any collection class we wish to derive from this base class. If we need a queue, for example, we can derive a Queue class as follows:

```
class Queue : public Collection<Type> {
public:
  // Ctors & Dtor
  // ...
  // Overridables
  void Add(const Type&);
  void Delete(const Type&);
  void ReplaceAt(int, const Type&);
  void DeleteAll();
  // ...

private:
  // ...
};
```

A complete implementation of the collection class will require a significant development effort. And this is only one of many collection classes required for most applications.

This simple example demonstrates why we try to reuse existing collection classes for our applications, unless, of course, we are in the business of creating frameworks for use by other developers.

7.4 Summary

Collection classes can be broadly categorized as homogeneous (all the objects contained are of the same type) and heterogeneous (objects contained can be of mixed types). C++ collections are created as template-based or non-template classes.

The concept of "shape" can be used to determine what kind of collection class to choose for a particular application:

- List—An ordered collection that is not indexed. The order refers to the insertion and deletion of objects, and does not necessarily imply that they are sorted in that order.
- Array—An ordered collection that is indexed. The elements can be retrieved via an integer index.
- Map—An indexed collection that may be ordered. Fast access methods are available for inserting an element and for searching for a specific element. Each element is associated with a key.

The creation of a set of collection classes requires a significant software development effort. The initial approach for acquiring a set of collection classes should be to first investigate their availability within the C++ library delivered with the development environment. If not available, the STL should be checked next. Developing a set of collection classes in-house should be the last resort.

The use of STL containers will be described in Chapter 14. The MFC containers are discussed in Chapter 21.

References

1. Microsoft Visual C++ Version 4.0, Programming with MFC, Volume 2, p. 186, Microsoft Press, Redmond, WA 1995.

8

Class Construction

The most important part of the OOP phase is the creation of C++ classes. Each class presents an interface to the users of that class. This interface consists of the member functions necessary to create and manipulate instances of that class in an application.

The focus of this chapter is on how to design proper class interfaces for user access, implementing the creation of objects, and initializing data members.

8.1 Class Interfaces

Throughout this chapter we are acting as "class providers" rather than "class users." Every class intended for reuse in various applications must be designed with the users in mind. This implies that we provide a class interface consisting of four categories of member functions:

- Managers—Object creation, initialization, destruction, memory management, etc.
- Implementers—Primary client interface reflected in the requirements
- Access—Will return values of (hidden) attributes
- Helpers—Internal operations used by the operations in categories 1–3

We will refer to these categories as we describe the C++ constructs available for creating proper class interfaces, and the various design decisions we have to make. The String class shown in Figure 8.1 will be used to illustrate the various member functions that make up a typical class interface.

```
// File: stringx.h
#ifndef STRINGX_H
#define STRINGX_H

class Exception { // general exception
public:
  Exception(const char* ptr) {}
};
class MemAlloc { // memory allocation exception
public:
  MemAlloc(const char* ptr) { }
};

class String {
public:
  String(); // default ctor, null string
  String(const String& rhs); // copy ctor
  String (const char* aPtr); // initialization ctor
  String (int len); // initialization ctor
  virtual ~String(); //dtor
  String& operator=(const String& rhs);
  String& operator[](int index); // index (lhs)
  String operator[](int index) const; // index (rhs)
  char operator()();  // iterator
  ...
protected:
  int    length;
  char* theString;
  int index;
};
```

Figure 8.1 String Class Declaration

8.2 Constructors

The creation of objects in an application is done with constructors. These are special member functions with any number of parameters but no return type. There can be any number of constructors for each class. There are three basic categories of constructors:

- Default Constructor—No parameters, or all parameters have default values. There can only be one default constructor for each class.
- Copy Constructor—A new object of the class is created and initialized with the data members of an existing object of the same class. The existing object is passed as a parameter. There can only be one copy constructor for each class.
- Initialization Constructor—A new object of the class is created and initialized with

the data from objects passed as parameters. There can be any number of initialization constructors for each class.

Default Constructors

The default constructor is used to create an object that does not have any special initialization requirements, or where all the initializations can be set by default values in the parameter list. The default constructor for the String class shown in Figure 8.1 is of the first type.

```
String() : Length(0), theString(0) {  }  // default ctor
```

When an object of type String is created, the data members len and pStr are both set to 0.

A default constructor with no arguments will be created by the compiler for each class that does not have any constructors declared. If we declare a constructor of any type, the compiler does not create a default constructor.

The default constructor created by the compiler will create the necessary constructor calls for the creation of embedded objects as data members. The default constructor causes storage to be allocated for data members, but data members of built-in types are not initialized.

We can thus create a class without any constructors and still declare instances of that class. Only embedded data members can be initialized by their respective constructors. The declaration and implementation of default constructors should be considered a necessary part of the class interface design. Default constructors should only be omitted in rare cases. The task of initializing data members is extremely important and should not be left to the compiler.

Here is an illustration of how we could create an object without having any constructors specified:

```cpp
// File: emptyobj.cpp
// Illustrating the creation of an empty object

#include <iostream.h>

class X {
public:
  void set(int a, char* str) {
    i = a;
    ptr = str;
  }

  int  get_a() {return i;}
  char* get_ptr() {return ptr;}

private:
```

```
    int i;
    char* ptr;
    };

int main() {
  X myX;
  myX.set(10, "Hello");
  cout << " myX.get_a() = " << myX.get_a() << endl;
  cout << " myX.get_ptr() = " << myX.get_ptr() << endl;
  return 0;
}
```

Output:

```
myX.get_a() = 10
myX.get_ptr() = Hello
```

This is not a very useful class, since we must concoct an initialization scheme via a set() function outside the regular constructor mechanism. It does illustrate, however, that an object gets created without having specified any constructors in the class interface.

Copy Constructors

The copy constructor shown in Figure 8.1 for the String class has a constant reference to another String object as its only parameter:

```
String(const String&); // copy ctor
```

When a new String object is created, all of its data members will be initialized to the values of the data members of the existing object passed in as a parameter.

If we do not provide a copy constructor, the compiler creates one for us. This is not an acceptable solution if we have data members that are pointers to other objects. The default copy constructor created by the compiler will only perform a memberwise copy (also referred to as *shallow* copy). A pointer to a character string, for example, would be copied as an address without actually copying the string itself. This means that we could end up with aliases and dangling references if the string referenced by the original object is destroyed.

A typical implementation of a copy constructor will include explicit copying of data elements pointed to by one or more of the data members. Here is an example for the String class:

```
String::String(const String& rhs) {
  length = rhs.length;
  theString = new char[length + 1];
  if (theString == NULL)
```

```
        throw (MemAlloc("String::String(const String& rhs"));
    strcpy (theString, rhs.theString); // deep copy
}
```

A new instance of String is created dynamically and initialized with the data elements of the rhs instance using deep copy. An exception, including the name of the copy constructor, is thrown if `new()` was not successful in allocating memory for the new instance.

Initialization Constructor

Two different initialization constructors are shown in Figure 8.1. The first has an int object as its parameter:

```
String(int len); // initialization ctor
```

When a new String object is created, its string length will be set to this value, and the string pointer will be set to the first element of the (empty) character array:

```
String::String(int len) {
    length = len;
    theString = new char[length + 1];
    if (theString == NULL)
        throw (MemAlloc("String::String()"));
}
```

Another Initialization Constructor

The other initialization constructor takes a character string as a formal parameter and creates a String object with the same length and character elements as the actual parameter passed in.

One use for this type of constructor is where we want to allocate a fixed-, or maximum-sized storage area from static memory and reuse the same area as new String objects of different sizes are created dynamically. The overloaded new() with placement syntax can be used for the dynamic creation:

```
// File: stringx.h

#ifndef STRINGX_H
#define STRINGX_H

class Exception { // general exception
public:
    Exception(const char* ptr) {}
};
class MemAlloc { // memory allocation exception
```

```
public:
  MemAlloc(const char* ptr) { }
};

class String {
public:
  String(); // default ctor, null string
  String(const String& aStr); // throw(Exception, MemAlloc);
  String (char* aPtr);        // throw(Exception, MemAlloc);
  String (int len);           // throw(MemAlloc);
  virtual ~String(); //dtor
  String& operator=(const String& rhs);
  String& operator[](int index); // index (lhs)
  String operator[](int index) const; // index (rhs)
  char operator()();  // iterator
  char* getString() {return theString;}
protected:
  int   length;
  char* theString;
};

#endif


// File: stringx.cpp

#include <string.h>
#include "stringx.h"

String::String(char* aPtr) {
  if ((theString = aPtr) == 0) // invalid string
    throw Exception("Invalid input string in
                    String::String(const char* aPtr)");
  length = strlen(aPtr);
  theString = new char[strlen(aPtr) + 1];
  if (theString == NULL)
    throw MemAlloc("String::String(const char* aPtr");
  strcpy(theString, aPtr); // init with input string
}


String::String(int len) {
  length = len;
  theString = new char[length + 1];
  if (theString == NULL)
      throw MemAlloc("String::String()");
}

String::~String() {
  delete [] theString;
}

// File: dynstrng.cpp
```

```
// Illustrate use of placement syntax

#include <iostream.h>
#include <stddef.h>
#include "stringx.h"

void* operator new(size_t size, void* address) {return address;}

int main() {
  char buffer[512];

  String* pString1 = new(buffer) String("Short string");
  cout << " pString1 = " << pString1->getString() << endl;

  String* pString2 = new(buffer) String("A somewhat longer
string");
  cout << " pString2 = " << pString2->getString() << endl <<
endl;
  return 0;
}
```

Output:

```
pString1 = Short string
pString2 = A somewhat longer string
```

We have used the so-called "placement syntax" to place the two strings at the location of `buffer`, which has storage allocated statically.

Note that we can't tell from the class interface how the different constructors create objects and initialize data members. This can only be seen when we look at the implementation in the source file, and is an example of how we implement the concept of information hiding.

8.3 Assignment Operators

Here is an example from the String class that can serve as a general "template" for creating assignment operators:

```
String& String::operator=(const String& rhs) {
  if (this != &rhs) {// assignment to 'this'?
    delete [] theString;
    length = rhs.length;
    if (theString = rhs.theString) == 0)
      return *this;
    theString = new char[length + 1];
    if (theString == NULL)
      throw (MemAlloc("String::operator="));
    strcpy (theString, rhs.theString); // deep copy
```

```
    }
    return *this;
}
```

The strategy for an assignment operator is to delete the elements of the 'this' object before the elements are assigned. This type of assignment operator allows slicing, since the new length is set to the length of the rhs object. Deep copy is necessary here to make sure the elements get copied, not just the pointer address.

8.4 Destructors

The prototype form of a destructor is just like a default constructor, but prefaced with a tilde:

```
String::~String() { delete [] theString; }
```

A destructor, like constructors, has no return type. Destructors are automatically called when any object created on the stack, or globally, exits its scope. There can only be a single destructor declared in the class interface. If a destructor is not declared, the compiler creates a default destructor.

Whenever we are creating an interface for a class that may serve as a base class, the destructor should always be made virtual. The compiler will create code for the destructor to call other destructors in the inheritance hierarchy. This will provide for adequate destruction of derived and embedded objects. This is explained in more detail in Chapter 10.

8.5 Class Architecture

The architecture of a class consists of a declaration, which specifies its interface, and the implementation, which is hidden from the users of the class. The declaration is made up of the user interface, which consists of the public member functions, and the data members, which are usually in a private section. Users gain access to a class by "including" the declaration as a header file.

Most classes designed for reuse have a number of overloaded operators (see Chapter 9). This provides a set of common operations that programmers can use just like the ones they are familiar with for built-in types. There is thus a specific part of the class architecture that must support a sufficient and complete set of operators.

Access to Class Members

The most important part of the class architecture is how users are allowed access to the member functions, and how the data members are protected from potential misuse. The String class shown in Figure 8.1 includes a public section for the constructors, destructor, implementer functions, and access functions. The two data members are contained within the protected section.

A complete guideline for class access is complicated by the additional design decisions that have to be made for base classes and derived classes. Here is a preliminary guideline for class access aside from inheritance considerations:

- Managers (object creation, initialization, destruction, memory management, etc.) should be public
- Implementers (primary client interface reflected in the requirements) should be public
- Access functions (return values of hidden attributes) should be public
- Helper functions (internal operations used by the operations in the other categories) should be private or protected
- Data members should be private or protected

We will augment these guidelines later when we discuss the ramifications of inheritance on the relations between base classes and derived classes.

Information Hiding

A form of information hiding is gained with the programming convention of placing the class declaration in a separate header file. The implementations of the member functions are placed in a corresponding source file. The header file for the String class is sketched out in Figure 8.1. A portion of the corresponding implementation file is shown in Figure 8.2.

```
// File: stringx.cpp

#include <string.h>    // needed for strcpy()
#include "stringx.h"

String::String(char* aPtr) {
if ((theString = aPtr) == 0) // invalid string
  throw Exception("Invalid input string in
              String::String(const char* aPtr)");
length = strlen(aPtr);
theString = new char[strlen(aPtr) + 1];
if (theString == NULL)
  throw MemAlloc("String::String(const char* aPtr");
strcpy(theString, aPtr); // init with input string
}
```

```
String::String(int len) {
  length = len;
  theString = new char[length + 1];
  if (theString == NULL)
      throw MemAlloc("String::String()");
}

String::~String() {
  delete [] theString;
}
// ...
```

Figure 8.2 String Class Implementation

This source file will contain all the implementations of the member functions. By separating the implementation from the declaration, this file is hidden from the users of the String class.

We thus provide a measure of information hiding via the programming convention of placing the class declaration and implementation in two separate files. Note that there is nothing inherent in C++ syntax or semantics to preclude us from creating a monolithic file that contains both the declaration and the implementation. Each development project must establish and follow the suggested programming convention.

Return Types

Class member functions (in fact, any C++ function) can return objects and values, references, and pointers. Reference types should be used to minimize the amount of copying required for large objects. Pointers and references are essentially equivalent even to the point of using casts. So when should we use pointers over references? The only time to choose a pointer over a reference is if a NULL value is allowed. A pointer type always requires that we return the address of an object. If the calling program is expecting a possible NULL value returned, it can only test for it if the return type is a pointer.

Irrespective of the choice between a pointer and a reference type, remember never to return an address to an object that exits the function scope when the function completes! This can create the infamous dangling references when the local pointer goes out of scope.

The return type of most implementer and access functions must be determined in connection with the overall fault tolerance strategy. Consider these two prototypes:

```
int Open(File&);   // error flag may be returned
void Open(File&);  // exception may be raised
```

For the first function, if the file cannot be opened, an error flag is returned to the caller, e.g., a value of -1. If the same condition is detected in the second function, an exception is raised. This exception must be handled with a special handler, and the program logic is completely different from simply returning an error flag.

This simple illustration indicates that a major design decision regarding a fault tolerance strategy must be made for the entire development project before the class architecture can be constructed. Since C++ supports an exception handling approach with special keywords and a run-time mechanism (see Chapter 13), this is a likely candidate for a C++ application.

We will revisit the topic of return types when we discuss overloading of operators in the next chapter. In the context of operators, we must make design decisions that pertain to whether a returned object will appear to the left or the right of an operator symbol, i.e., the concept of l-values and r-values. This is also discussed further in the next chapter.

Static Data Member Shortcut

The separation of a class declaration and its corresponding implementation creates a problem if we need a simple, shared constant. All class data members are considered *instance* variables unless they are declared with the *static* keyword. This implies that every object has its own set of data members with unique values. These data members cannot be shared among instances of the same type.

C++ does allow for shared *class* variables when a data member is declared static:

```
// File: newclass.h

class NewClass {
public:
  //...
private:
  //...
  static const int MaxBuff = 1024; // error!
  char str[MaxBuff];
};
```

The static data member cannot be initialized within the class declaration, and the value of MaxBuff will have to be set in the source file:

```
// File: newclass.cpp

#include "newclass.h"

const int NewClass::MaxBuff = 1024;

// implementation of member functions
...
```

The data member MaxBuff is now considered a shared class variable that can be used by any object of NewClass. It doesn't solve the related problem of allocating storage for a data member, however. This is still an error:

```
// File: newclass.h

class NewClass {
public:
    //...
private:
    //...
    static const int MaxBuff;
    char str[MaxBuff]; // error!
};
```

This seems like a cumbersome method for creating a simple, shared constant, especially since it does not even solve the storage allocation problem. Here is a short-cut for a shared data member that can be created as an enumerated type within the architecture of the class declaration:

```
class NewClass {
public:
    //...
private:
    //...
    enum {MaxBuff = 1024}; // ok
    char str[MaxBuff]; // ok
};
```

MaxBuff is now just like the static class variable that can be shared among all objects declared of the NewClass type. Note that this is a shortcut, since MaxBuff does not have to be initialized outside the class declaration. This is sometimes considered a work-around for a feature that should perhaps have been included in the C++ specification. Some developers refer to this as a "grotesque hack" and a misuse of the language.

If a constant such as NewClass::MaxBuff is to be used outside the class scope, it will have to be placed in the public section.

8.6 Order of Constructor Invocation

Embedded objects are used to implement the aggregation relationship between two classes. This has an impact on the order in which objects and sub-objects get created. The compiler uses certain rules for how constructors are called for complex objects:

- Constructors for sub-objects are called before the constructor for the containing object

- If there are multiple sub-objects, their constructors get called in the order they are declared as data members
- Constructor invocation for sub-objects is recursive

The Customer class from the Horizon application has a number of sub-objects:

```
class Customer {
public:
  Customer();
  Customer(const Customer&);
  Customer& operator=(const Customer&);
  ~Customer();
  // exceptions
  ...
  void Add (CString custId);
  void Delete (CString custId);
  void Edit (CString custId);
  void Display (CString custId);
  double GetBalance (CString custId);
  Customer& GetCustomerData (CString custId);
  InvoiceInfo& GetInvoiceInfo (CString custId);
  void Print (String custId = NULL);
private:
  CString  customerId;
  CString  description;
  Address shippingAddress;
  Address mailingAddress;
  CString  phone;
  CString  fax;
  CString  contact;
  double  discount;
  Terms paymentTerms;
  Taxes taxCode;
};
```

All of the data members of the class Customer are embedded objects as instances of other classes, except for `discount`. These embedded objects get created in the order of their declaration, and before an instance of Customer is created.

When an object containing other objects goes out of scope, the destructors are called in the reverse order of their creation.

Whenever objects are created dynamically using `new`, a multi-step operation takes place. For example, for the declaration of a Screen object:

```
Screen* pScreen = new Screen;
if(pScreen == NULL)
  throw MemAlloc("Unsuccessful attempt to create Screen object");
// ...
```

The following steps are involved:

- `new` attempts to allocate dynamic storage for a Screen object
- If successful,
  - the constructor for Screen is invoked. This may involve other constructor invocations if Screen has sub-objects
  - `new` assigns the address of the Screen object to pScreen
- Otherwise,
  - `new` assigns the NULL address to `pScreen` (future compiler versions will raise the exception `bad_alloc`)

It is a good design practice to always check the value of the pointer containing the address of the new object.

8.7 Initializing Data Members

All data members should be initialized in a constructor. There are two different ways to accomplish this:

- Use executable statements in the body of the constructor
- Use the special member initialization syntax.

Initialization in the Constructor Body

Here is an example from the String class, where all the initialization takes place within the body of the constructor:

```
String::String(char* aPtr) {
if ((theString = aPtr) == 0) // invalid string
   throw Exception("Invalid input string in
                   String::String(const char* aPtr)");
length = strlen(aPtr);
theString = new char[strlen(aPtr) + 1];
if (theString == NULL)
   throw MemAlloc("String::String(const char* aPtr");
strcpy(theString, aPtr); // init with input string
}
```

Values for both the two data members (`length` and `theString`) are set with ordinary executable statements. If we have a simple constructor, the special member initialization syntax can be used instead of (some or all) executable statements. Here is the other initialization constructor with executable statements:

```
String::String(int len) {
   length = len;
   theString = new char[length + 1];
   if (theString == NULL)
      throw MemAlloc("String::String()");
}
```

Member Initialization Syntax

C++ includes a special syntax for initializing data members outside a constructor body. Here is the use of the member initialization syntax for the same constructor that was shown in the previous example:

```
String::String(int len)
         : length(len), theString(new char[length + 1]) {}
```

The initialization list follows the ":" and individual data members are separated by commas. This is a short hand notation for initializing data members without any executable statements.

It used to be that this form of a constructor was more efficient than the equivalent set of executable statements. Modern compilers, however, are likely to optimize the executable code of an ordinary constructor into the equivalent set of member initialization statements.

The primary difference between the two forms shown for the last constructor is that the member initialization syntax doesn't allow for checking if new was able to allocate the required storage. We could combine the two forms to include the checking and throwing the exception:

```
String::String(int len)
         : length(len), theString(new char[length + 1]) {
   if(theString == NULL)
      throw MemAlloc("String::String()");
}
```

Some compilers may complain if the declaration order of the data members were reversed for length and theString:

```
class String {
public:
   // ...
protected:
   char* theString;
   int   length;
};
```

We are now asking new to allocate storage before the length data member has been initialized, since the order is determined by the declaration order and not the order in the member initialization list.

Mandatory Use of Member Initialization Syntax

The two examples for the String constructor showed that we could choose between the two forms for initialization of data members. There are two cases where we have to use the member initialization syntax:

- `const` non-static data members
- reference type data members

```
// File: newclass.h

class NewClass {
public:
  NewClass(int size, int buf) : x(size), MaxBuff(buf), ref(x) {}
  NewClass();
  //...
private:
  int x;
  const int MaxBuff;
  int& ref;
};
```

Since a non-static constant data member (or any other C++ constant identifier) cannot appear as a left operand in an assignment statement after its declaration, it must be set with the member initialization syntax.

The reference variable *ref* is an alias for an int and must have an lvalue when it is created. This cannot be done with an assignment statement in the class declaration. The only way to accomplish the aliasing is with the special member initialization syntax.

Initializing Static Data Members

C++ offers two different types of data members associated with a class: (1) Non-static data members created as part of each instance of a class; and (2) Static data members that are class variables shared among all instances of a class.

We have illustrated how non-static data members are always initialized by the constructors. Static class variables are not associated with any instance and must be initialized after the class declaration, typically in the associated class source file or an application source file. Here is an example including both static and non-static data members:

```
// File: newclass.h

class NewClass {
public:
```

```
    NewClass(int size);
    NewClass();
    ~NewClass();
    //...
  private:
    int x; // instance variable
    enum {MaxBuff = 1024};
    char str[MaxBuff]; // instance variable
  static unsigned int numObjects; // class variable
  };

  // File: newclass.cpp

  #include "newclass.h"

  unsigned int NewClass::numObjects = 0; // class variable

  NewClass::NewClass(int size) : x(size) {
    numObjects++;
  }

  NewClass::NewClass() : x(512) {
    numObjects++;
  }

  NewClass::~NewClass() {
    numObjects-;
  }
```

The initialization of a static class member must be done after the class declaration. This could be done at the end of the header file. However, modern compilers provide incremental compilation and linking via precompiled header (pch) files. Some compilers simply refuse to create a pch (with an appropriate warning) if they detect initialization statements of static members in the header file.

Static members retain their access and visibility role, even though they appear to be initialized as global variables. The private, static numObjects is set within the class scope, but can only be accessed by the NewClass member functions.

Initializing Base Constructors

When a derived object is being created, the C++ constructor mechanism will automatically call a base constructor before the constructor of the derived object is called. If we do not specify how this should be done, the compiler will use the default constructor of the base class, if one exists.

In most cases, we do not want to leave this mechanism to the compiler, and will specify our own explicit calls to the base constructors via the special member initialization syntax.

We will use a base class and a derived class to illustrate two different uses of the member initialization syntax. Here is an example of how we can use the member initialization list for the data members in the base class:

```
// File: student.h

// ...
enum Year {fresh, soph, junior, senior, grad};

class Student { // base class
public:
  Student (String nme, Address adr, long id, Year y,
           double grade=0.0)
      : name(nme), studentId(id), addr(adr), year(y), gpa(grade)
{}
  virtual void display();
  virtual void update(String name, Address adr,
                      Year year,   double gpa);
  virtual long getId(String name);
  virtual double getGpa(String name);
protected:
  String  name;
  Address addr;
  long    studentId;
  Year    year;
  double  gpa;
};
```

The constructor passes the data values received as actual parameters to the data members with the member initialization list.

We'll now look at a derived class and how we can use the initialization syntax in two different contexts:

```
// File: gradstnt.h

#include "student.h"

enum support {NSFGrant, teach, resAssist, fellowship};

class GradStudent : public Student { // derived class
public:
  GradStudent(String name, Address addr, long id,
              double grade, Year year, String suprt,
              String dpt, String  thsis)
      : Student(name, addr, id, year, grade),
        support(suprt), dept(dpt), thesis(thsis) {}
  void display();

private:
  String support;
  String dept;
  String thesis;
};
```

The constructor first makes an explicit call (via the initialization syntax mechanism) to the base constructor and passes up five of the values received as actual parameters. This is the only way we can properly set up the inherited data members. The constructor next passes the remaining three parameters to the data members of the derived class.

We have illustrated here how we can use the special initialization syntax mechanism in two different contexts: (1) to initialize data members without executable statements in the constructor body, and (2) to pass data values up to a base constructor for initialization of inherited data members.

Declaring and Initializing Arrays

C++ presents somewhat of a puzzle regarding the declaration and initialization of arrays as data members. Consider the following code:

```
// File: newclass.h

class NewClass {
public:
  NewClass(int size) : MaxBuff(size) {}
  NewClass();
  //...
private:
  const int MaxBuff;
  char str[MaxBuff]; // illegal!
};
```

This appears to be a perfectly legal way to declare the array `str`, where the array size is a constant `int` and is set via the member initialization syntax. Here is the error message created by the Microsoft C++ compiler (version 4.2):

```
c:\msdev\projects\include\newclass.h(13) : error C2327:
'NewClass::MaxBuff' : member from enclosing class is not a type
name, static, or enumerator
```

The Borland C++ compiler (version 5.01) has the following error message and associated help text:

```
newclass.h(13,20): Constant expression required // compiler mes-
sage

Help Text:
Arrays must be declared with constant size.
This error is commonly caused by misspelling a #define constant.
```

These messages add to the confusion, since `MaxBuff` is certainly a constant. Here are different ways of solving this problem:

```
(1)
// File: newclass.h

const int MaxBuff = 1024;

class NewClass {
public:
  NewClass(int size) {}
  NewClass();
  //...
private:
  char str[MaxBuff]; // now legal
};
```

```
(2)
// File: newclass.h

class NewClass {
public:
  NewClass(int size) {}
  NewClass();
  //...
private:
  enum{ MaxBuff = 1024};
  char str[MaxBuff]; // now legal
};
```

```
(3)
// File: newclass.h

class NewClass {
public:
  NewClass(int size) {}
  NewClass();
  //...
private:
  char str[1024]; // legal but ugly!
};
```

```
(4)
// File: newclass.h

class NewClass {
public:
  NewClass(int size) {}
  NewClass();
  //...
private:
char str[]; // legal according to Borland but not Microsoft
};
```

Solutions (1) and (2) use either a global constant value or a type enum, respectively. Which one of these to pick depends on whether we need the constant at class scope (solution (1)) or not. Solution (3) will always work, but goes against all recommendations of never to include literals in the code.

Solution (4) is accepted without error or warning by the Borland compiler, but elicits both an error and a warning by the Microsoft compiler. The issue here is an illegal use of a zero-sized array extension. This seems to imply that the Microsoft compiler will accept this in a future version. (Version 5.0 only issues a warning.)

8.8 Using Preprocessor Statements

The use of preprocessor statements should be minimized, and we avoid the use of define declarations as much as possible:

```
#define maxBuff  1024 // avoid
const int maxBuff = 1024; // preferred
```

The define statement will result in text substitution everywhere maxBuff is referenced throughout the code. The compiler does not check the types of literals, and we have thus lost an important aspect of strong typing.

We do want to use preprocessor statements as brackets in header files to prevent multiple inclusions of the same classes:

```
// File: stringx.h

#ifndef STRINGX_H
#define STRINGX_H

class String {
public:
  String();
  // ...
protected:
  // ...
};

#endif
```

This should be implemented as a project-wide guideline to prevent linker problems when multiple modules (.cpp files) are combined into an application.

Some linkers may complain about duplicate declarations. The potential problem is that a declaration is associated with a memory location at link time. If you run into this problem, use enums instead of the constant type declarations.

8.9 Summary

Instances are created with the use of three different categories of constructors:

- Default Constructor—No parameters, or all parameters have default values. There can only be one default constructor for each class.
- Copy Constructor—A new object of the class is created and initialized with the data members of an existing object of the same class. The existing object is passed as a parameter. There can only be one copy constructor for each class.
- Initialization Constructor—A new object of the class is created and initialized with the data from objects passed as parameters. There can be any number of initialization constructors for each class.

Access to class members is carefully controlled via encapsulation and selected information hiding:

- Managers (object creation, initialization, destruction, memory management, etc.) should be public.
- Implementers (primary client interface reflected in the requirements) should be public.
- Access Functions (return values of hidden attributes) should be public.
- Helper Functions (internal operations used by the operations in the other categories) should be private or protected.
- Data members should be private or protected.

The compiler uses certain rules for how constructors are called for complex objects:

- Constructors for sub-objects are called before the constructor for the containing object.
- If there are multiple sub-objects, their constructors get called in the order they are declared as data members.
- Constructor invocation for sub-objects is recursive.

Data members are initialized in constructors using either executable statements in the body of the constructors or the special member initialization syntax. The member initialization syntax must be used in the following cases:

- `const` non-static data members
- reference type data members

- passing initialization data to base constructors

Static class instances must be initialized after they are declared in a header file, and preferably in a source file to allow the compiler to create precompiled header (pch) files.

Class declarations should only occur in header files, and preprocessor statements should bracket all class declarations to prevent multiple inclusions of the same classes in large applications consisting of multiple source files.

9

Well-Designed Classes

We have already established (see Chapter 8) that the creation of a proper class interface requires that we provide member functions in the following categories:

- Managers—functions for the creation, management, and destruction of instances, including constructors and destructors
- Implementers—functions that alter the values of the data members (sometimes referred to as mutators)
- Access—functions that return the values of private and protected data members
- Helpers—functions that are used by the functions in the other categories, but are not available to clients of the class

Another set of functions we must usually provide for a proper class interface is a set of overloaded operators. These are not invoked directly by the clients, but are usually invoked by the compiler when it parses an expression.

Some of the issues discussed in Chapter 8 included a description of the different categories of constructors, and the order of constructor invocation for embedded objects and derived objects. The focus of this chapter is on the set of constructors, destructor, and overloaded operators that we must provide as an interface for a well-behaved class, i.e., a class designed for reuse but without any superfluous constructors or overloaded operators. We also attempt to answer the question of whether or not there is a minimal set of operations we must provide for every class.

9.1 Creating the Class Interface

As class providers, it is our responsibility to create a class interface that will make it easy for the users to understand and use the class. In other words, we are attempting to create classes with reusability as a primary motive.

There is no cook-book formula that applies to creating an interface for every conceivable class. We will use the following String class to illustrate many of the concepts and design decisions pertaining to class interfaces:

```
// File: stringx.h

#ifndef STRINGX_H
#define STRINGX_H

class Exception { // general exception
public:
  Exception(const char* ptr) {}
};
class MemAlloc { // memory allocation exception
public:
  MemAlloc(const char* ptr) { }
};


class String {
public:
  String(); // default ctor, null string
  String(const String& aStr); // copy ctor
  String (const char* aPtr); // initialization ctor
  String (int len); // initialization ctor
  virtual ~String(); //dtor
  String& operator=(const String& rhs);
  String& operator[]() ; // index (lhs)
  String operator[]() const; // index (rhs)
  char operator()(); // iterator
  ...
protected:
  int    length;
  char* theString;
  int    index;
};
```

9.2 Constructors

We have three categories of constructors that we must consider for each class:

- Default constructor—a constructor with no parameters or with all parameters set to default values. There is only one of these.

- Initialization constructor—a constructor that initializes data members based on a set of parameters. We can have any number of these.

- Copy constructor—a constructor that creates a new instance of the class and initializes this instance with the data members of an existing instance which is passed as a parameter. There is only one of these.

Default Constructor

The compiler will create a default constructor if no other constructors have been declared. A reasonable semantic interpretation of a default constructor for a String object could be a null string. There is no way that a compiler could make that kind of interpretation, and we should always furnish a default constructor for this type of class. Here is one way to accomplish the expected semantics for the String class:

```
String::String() {
  length = 0;
  theString = new char[1];
  if (theString == NULL)
      throw (MemAlloc("String::String()"));
  theString[0] = '\0'; // null string
}
```

This default constructor creates a null string. If memory is not available, the exception for unsuccessful memory allocation is raised.

When should we create a default constructor? The default constructor created by the compiler will not initialize data members of built-in types—they will be undefined. This is certainly one condition we should avoid by providing our own default constructor. Anytime an instance has data members that should have initial values, we should create a default constructor. It makes no sense to concoct special "set()" functions to initialize data members after the instance has been created.

Initialization Constructor

An initialization constructor is a special constructor that initializes data members based on a set of values passed as parameters. There can be any number of these constructors; each has a unique set of parameters. Here is an example for the String class:

```
String::String(const char* aPtr) {
if ((theString = aPtr) == 0) // invalid string
    throw Exception("Invalid input string in
                    String::String(const char* aPtr"));
  length = strlen(aPtr);
  theString = new char[length + 1];
```

```
    if (theString == NULL)
        throw MemAlloc("String::String(const char* aPtr"));
    strcpy(theString, aPtr.theString); // init with input string
}
```

This initialization constructor uses the input string as the source for the new string instance. Exceptions are thrown if the input string does not exist and if `new()` is not able to allocate sufficient storage for the new instance.

The decision to provide constructors in this category always requires some thought. We have to anticipate all the different conditions for which the users may want to pass parameters to initialize the data members.

Copy Constructor

The purpose of a copy constructor is to create a new object of the same class as an existing object and to initialize the new object with the values of the data members of the existing object.

We should always include a copy constructor if any of the data members are based on pointer types. The compiler will create a copy constructor if we don't include one, but it will only perform memberwise copy, e.g., it will copy member addresses but not the data elements pointed to.

A typical implementation of a copy constructor will include explicit copying of data elements pointed to by one or more of the data members. Here is an example for the String class:

```
String::String(const String& rhs) {
    length = rhs.length;
    theString = new char[length + 1];
    if (theString == NULL)
        throw (MemAlloc("String::String(const String& rhs"));
    strcpy (theString, rhs.theString); // deep copy
}
```

A new instance is created dynamically and initialized with the data elements of the rhs instance using deep copy. An exception, including the name of the copy constructor, is thrown if `new()` was not successful in allocating memory for the new instance.

The only time we have to provide a copy constructor is when deep copy is required, or we have complex, embedded objects as data members. The compiler will always create an acceptable copy constructor for memberwise or shallow copy.

We do not need to provide a copy constructor if an application will always only have one instance of a given class. Examples of one-of-a-kind objects include a track manager, syntax parser, and alerts manager.

If we have a derived class, and we let the compiler create a copy constructor, that constructor will automatically call the base class copy constructor. When we create our own copy constructor, however, we decide which one of the base class constructors to call, and it doesn't necessarily have to be the copy constructor.

9.3 Destructor

A destructor is automatically invoked when an instance goes out of scope. Each class has exactly one destructor. If we don't provide one, the compiler creates one for us. For the String class, for example, we must make sure that all the characters in the string get deleted:

```
String::~String() {
  delete [] theString;
}
```

Remember that the pointer theString is allocated statically and it is what it is pointing to that gets reclaimed by delete, not the pointer itself. The pointer is automatically reclaimed when it goes out of scope, just like any other static variable.

There may be cases when a destructor should not be invoked. An interesting example is shown in [1] for a special memory allocation scheme and an automatic garbage collection that is different and separate from the normal C++ new/delete mechanism. If we want to prevent instances from being allocated on the stack, we can declare a private destructor:

```
// File: privdtor.cpp

#include <iostream.h>

class X {
public:
  // ...
private:
  // ...
  ~X(); // private dtor
};


int main() {
  cout << " attempting to allocate a static X instance" << endl;
  X myX;
  return 0;
}
```

Static instances of X cannot be created, since they cannot be destroyed. Here is the error message created by the Microsoft Visual C++ 4.2 compiler:

```
'X::~X' : cannot access private member declared in class 'X'
```

Note that the compiler catches this and not the run-time mechanism upon exiting from main().

Having the private destructor does not prevent us from creating an instance of X off the heap:

```
// File: privdtor.cpp

#include <iostream.h>

class X {
public:
  X() {
     cout << " X object created" << endl;
  }
  // ...
private:
  // ...
  ~X(); // private dtor
};


int main() {
  cout << " Attempting to allocate a dynamic instance of X" <<
endl;
  X* ptrX = new X;
  return 0;
}
```

            Output:

```
Attempting to allocate a dynamic instance of X
X object created
```

We cannot use `delete` on `ptrX` to reclaim X, however, since the destructor is private.

9.4 Overloaded Operators

There is no minimal set of overloaded operators that we have to provide for each class. The only default operator generated by the compiler is the assignment operator.

One of the major design decisions we have to make for operators is what the return type should be. A major source of confusion for the novice C++ programmer is the sight of the reference symbol (&) in a return type, and the rationale for its use is certainly less than obvious. Here are the primary reasons for the use of a reference type as a return type for operators:

- It is more efficient to return a large object as an alias rather than having to make a copy

- We are required to return an object as a reference type whenever an *lvalue* is expected:
  - in a statement with multiple operators, e.g.: `x = y = z;`
  - returning an object as a left-hand operand, e.g.: `x[i] = y[j];`
- We are required to return an object as an *lvalue* in a compound statement including multiple member function invocations separated by periods:

```
#include "screen.h"
// ...
Screen scr1(0, 0);
//...
scr1.clear().move(100, 100); // left associativity
```

The last case accommodates the legal, but dubious, use of placing multiple operations on behalf of the same instance in one statement. After the `scr1.clear()` operation is completed, we must return the "this" object as an *lvalue* to permit the second operation `scr1.move(100, 100)` to be executed.

Assignment Operator

The purpose of an assignment operator is to assign the values of the data members of an existing object to the data members of another existing object of the same class. This is similar to a copy constructor, but this operator does not create a new object.

The compiler will generate an assignment operator for us if we don't declare one, and it will generate calls to it. But do we always need this operator? The answer is "no." The reasoning for this answer parallels the discussion of the copy constructor, since the two member functions are closely related. Any time we have an application using a class for which there will always only be a single object, we do not need an assignment operator or a copy constructor. Examples of one-of-a-kind objects include a print manager, memory manager, and alerts handler.

Using The Singleton Design Pattern

If we want to limit the creation of instances to a single object, the Singleton design pattern can be used, as suggested in [2, pp.127-136]. The purpose of this design pattern is to ensure that a class has only one instance and to provide a global entry point for this instance.

The suggested Singleton class declaration and implementation for a Print Manager class is as follows:

```
// File: printmgr.h
```

```cpp
class Time{};
class String{};

class PrintManager {
public:
    static PrintManager* Instance();
    void SpoolJob(char* name);
    void Print(int seq);
    void DeleteJob(char* name);
protected:
    PrintManager();
private:
    static PrintManager* instance;
    String printerName;
    int     seqNumber;
    String status;
    String docName;
    String owner;
    Time    printedAt;
    int     numPages;
    long    memorySize;
    int     priority;
};


// File: printmgr.cpp

PrintManager* PrintManager::instance = 0;

PrintManager* PrintManager::Instance() {
    if(instance == 0) {
        instance = new PrintManager;
    }
    return instance;
}
```

Clients of the class PrintManager can only create a single object via the public member Instance(). The constructor PrintManager() has been placed in the protected section and will create a compiler error if an application attempts to declare an instance of PrintManager.

The control variable for the creation of a single object is initialized to 0 in the source file and is checked inside the Instance() member function. An object is only created if the value of the control variable is 0. The address of the new object is returned by Instance() when an object is created.

Here is an example of how we can create an application using the Singleton design pattern for the PrintManager class:

```cpp
// File: printmain.cpp

#include "printmgr.h"
```

```
int main() {
  PrintManager* pPrintManager;
  pPrintManager = pPrintManager->Instance();

  // Can now use the PrintManager instance via pPrintManager:
  pPrintManager->SpoolJob("job1");
  pPrintManager->Print(2);
  pPrintManager->DeleteJob("job1");

  return 0;
}
```

The Singleton design pattern can also be used to control any number of objects, besides just one. A separate control variable can be used as a counter to control a specific number of instances of a class.

Restricting Access

For some applications we may want to specifically prohibit the use of a copy constructor and an assignment operator, e.g., for a class used to create login passwords:

```
// File: password.h

class Password {
public:
  Password(const char* userName) :
  user(userName), aPassword("Huldra") {};
  void change(const char* userName, Password& pass);
  void remove(Password& pass);
private:
  Password(const Password& pass);
  const Password& operator=(const Password& pass);
  const char* user;
  char* aPassword;
};


// File: pswdmain.cpp

#include "password.h"

int main() {
  Password passw1("Peer Gynt");
  Password passw2("Henrik Ibsen");

  Password passw3 = passw2; // illegal

  passw2 = passw1; // illegal

  // ...
```

```
    return 0;
  }
```

If we do not provide the dummy copy constructor and assignment operator in the private part, the compiler will create them for us as public members and allow the two operations we are trying to prohibit.

Iterators

Generally speaking, an iterator is an operator that provides us with the "next" element in a data structure, or a suitable end indicator if it has reached past the last element. C++ provides a special operator that can be given iterator semantics for the String class:

```
class String {
public:
  // ...
  char operator()();  // iterator
  // ...
protected:
  char* theString;
  int   length;
  int   index;
};
```

This is usually referred to as the "call" operator, and can be implemented as follows:

```
char String::operator()() {
  char temp = theString[index]; // current char
  if(index < length)
    index++; // increment to next element
  else
    index = 0; // reset to start
  return temp;
}
```

Here is how we can invoke this operator in an application:

```
// File: strnmain.cpp

#include <iostream.h>
#include "stringx.h"

int main() {
  char ch;
  String str1("String1");

  while(ch = str1())
```

```
        cout << ch;

    return 0;
  }
```

This illustration shows how we could implement an iterator for this class using the C++ call operator. There is a major problem associated with this approach, however. There can only be one call operator active on each object during the execution of the application. The call operator cannot be overloaded in the class interface. If we needed additional iterators for each object, we would have to implement them in terms of other classes, or as data members with unique names.

While we have shown how we can use C++ to create home-grown iterators, this should not be the chosen approach for a large C++ project. The recommended approach is to use the iterator mechanism built into the Standard Template Library (STL) implementation. This implementation contains five different categories of iterators. We should only spend the effort to create our own iterators if none of the iterators in the STL (or comparable library) will satisfy a specific requirement. The STL iterators are described in Chapter 14.

9.5 Inheritance

Base classes are provided for ease of extending a class hierarchy via inheritance. The compiler uses certain rules regarding which constructors and operators are inherited. The thing to remember is that a derived object may be drastically different (almost always larger) from a base object in terms of the data members that make up the structure of a derived object.

There is no way the compiler can guess what kind of classes will derive from a base class. Base class constructors are thus not inherited and will have to be provided for each derived class.

Similarly, the assignment operator is never inherited from a base class for the same reason that the constructors are not inherited. Suitable constructors, including the copy constructor, and the assignment operator should be provided in derived classes. This rule holds for any class that will serve as a concrete data type for multiple instances within the same application. The copy constructor and assignment operator should not be included for a class that will only contain a one-of-a-kind instance.

Destructors are also not inherited and should be included for derived classes.

There is a special case to consider for classes with virtual member functions. The polymorphism mechanism allows a pointer declared for a derived object to also point to a base object. If this pointer is pointing to a base object when we do a `delete` on the pointer, how do the derived objects (which have additional data members) get reclaimed?

Whenever we have virtual functions declared in a base class, we should also declare a virtual destructor. The destructor mechanism will then automatically call the destructors for all derived objects in the reverse order of how they were created. This will prevent the kind of memory leaks that could occur if only a base object was reclaimed.

Table 9.1 provides a summary of the inheritance rules that apply to constructors, destructors, and overloaded operators [3, p. 306].

This table provides a handy reference for the various characteristics of several operators and member functions regarding the rules of inheritance, who can be virtual functions; requirements for a return type; who can be member versus friend; and whether constructors, destructors, and operators are generated by the compiler by default.

Table 9.1 Characteristics of Various Operations

Operation	Inherited	Can Be Virtual	Can Have Return Type	Member or Friend	Generated by Default
constructor	no	no	no	member	yes
destructor	no	yes	no	member	yes
conversion	yes	yes	no	member	no
=	no	yes	yes	member	yes
()	yes	yes	yes	member	no
[]	yes	yes	yes	member	no
->	yes	yes	yes	member	no
op=	yes	yes	yes	either	no
new	yes	no	void*	static member	no
delete	yes	no	void	static member	no
other operator	yes	yes	yes	either	no
other member	yes	yes	yes	member	no
friend	no	no	yes	friend	no

9.6 Well-Designed Classes

The premise of this chapter was how we can construct a class interface for a maximal reuse potential by the users. We have already answered the frequently asked question of "is there a standard, minimal set of operations to specify for every class?" with a "no." We can suggest, however, a recommended set of operations for well-behaved classes (also called "nice" classes [1]) as a starting point:

- Default constructor
- Copy constructor
- Destructor
- Assignment operator
- Equality operator
- Inequality operator (can be based on the equality operator)

Using this set as a basis, we can determine if some of these don't make any sense for a particular class or if additional operators must be specified.

For any one-of-a-kind object, we can eliminate the copy constructor, assignment operator and the two equality operators. Examples of such an object include a print manager, memory manager, and a parser.

9.7 Summary

There is no minimal set of operations we must provide for every class. Each class must be evaluated carefully to determine the proper interface.

Letting the compiler create a default constructor with shallow copy may be appropriate for some classes, but not for others. A deep copy constructor should be provided whenever we have data members as pointers to embedded objects.

There is a close coupling between a copy constructor and an assignment operator. In general, if we define a copy constructor, we also need an assignment operator

A virtual destructor should be provided any time we have virtual functions declared in a base class.

References

1. Carroll, M., and Ellis, M., What functions should all classes provide?, *C++ Report*, November-December 1994, p. 26.
2. Gamma, E. et al., *Design Patterns*, Addison-Wesley, Reading, MA 1995.
3. Ellis, M.A., and Stroustrup, B., *The Annotated C++ Reference Manual*, Addison-Wesley, Reading, MA, 1990.

10

Inheritance and Polymorphism

Inheritance and polymorphism are closely linked concepts. Inheritance is the design concept that allows us to reuse a base class and derive a specialized class where we add members that are unique to the derived class. Polymorphism is an implementation mechanism that associates a member function with an object in the inheritance hierarchy at run-time. The mechanism of polymorphism is sometimes referred to as dynamic binding.

The focus of this chapter is to review the general mechanism of inheritance and polymorphism, and to explain how to prepare classes in an inheritance hierarchy with regard to visibility and being able to take advantage of polymorphism.

The use of abstract classes is explained in terms of design guidelines for when these classes would be most beneficial or crucial.

Multiple inheritance is a C++ language feature that is sometimes receiving bad press and recommended not to be used by novices. Examples are included for when this feature can be used safely. This chapter concludes with an explanation of how the polymorphism mechanism is implemented via the primary data structure: the virtual table.

10.1 Preparing a Base Class for Derivation

As an example of preparing a base class for derivation, we will use the MFC CObject class to illustrate some of the design issues we are faced with.

The purpose of the CObject base class is to present a common interface for all of the subsequent derived classes. Here is a snapshot of the class declaration in the `<afx.h>` header file:

```
// class CObject is the root of all MFC compliant objects

class CObject {
public:
    // Diagnostic Support
    virtual void Dump(CDumpContext& dc) const;
    virtual void AssertValid() const;

    // RTTI support
    virtual CRuntimeClass* GetRuntimeClass() const;
    BOOL IsKindOf(const CRuntimeClass* pClass) const;

    // Serialization
    virtual void Serialize(CArchive& ar);
    BOOL IsSerializable() const;

    virtual ~CObject();

protected:
    CObject();

private:
    CObject(const CObject& objectSrc); // no implementation
    void operator=(const CObject& objectSrc); // no implementation
    ...
};
```

The generalized functions available to any derived class of CObject include support for run-time diagnostics with the Dump() function, RTTI support, and the ability to store and retrieve persistent data with the Serialize() and IsSerializable() functions.

The default constructor is protected to allow the construction of objects in the derived classes. No parameters are required, since there are no data members that need to be initialized. Note the private copy constructor and assignment operator. This prevents copying of CObject instances that may not be related, since they could be base objects for entirely different derived objects.

The virtual destructor was added to ensure that all the sub-objects get reclaimed when a *delete* operation is performed on a pointer pointing to a base object when it goes out of scope The virtual destructor mechanism will call the destructors of all existing derived objects to prevent memory leaks. This issue was mentioned in Chapter 9 and is discussed further in Section 10.6.

10.2 Abstract Classes

Abstract classes are created when no instances of that class will ever be constructed. The primary purpose of an abstract class is to provide a common interface for a class hierarchy derived from the abstract base class.

A C++ abstract class is created by declaring one or more member functions as pure virtual:

```
class NewClass {
public:
  //...
  virtual void Display() const = 0; // pure virtual
  //...
};
```

A pure virtual function has the effect of making the compiler force every derived class that overrides this function to include an implementation for the function.

Even though instances of the abstract class will never be created, we can still include an implementation of a pure virtual function. This implementation will represent a default functionality that is common to all of the derived classes.

An example of an inheritance hierarchy involving an abstract class is a Shape class. A shape by itself is an abstraction, and we could never describe a real object of such a class. Objects of type Shape could include a circle, rectangle, polygon, etc.:

```
// File: shape.h

class Angle;
class Coordinate;
class Color;

class Shape {
public:
  Shape();
  virtual ~Shape();
  virtual void rotate(Angle& a);
  virtual void move(Coordinate& xy);
  virtual void draw() = 0; // pure virtual
  virtual void erase();
  virtual void redraw();
protected:
  Coordinate center;
  Color      color;
};
```

The class Shape has been prepared as an abstract base class for any number of derived classes from which concrete shapes can be instantiated. The member function draw() has been declared pure virtual, and will have to be overridden in the derived classes.

We can also include an implementation of a general draw() class for the Shape class. The overridden classes will then call the base draw() first, e.g., to create a general window frame with associated menu bar, tool bar, etc. This general window frame is not a Shape object and will be the same for all of the derived shape objects. The overridden `draw()` functions will implement the unique features of their particular concrete shape. Here is one example of a derived class for rectangles:

```
// File: rectangl.h

#include "shape.h"

class Rectangle : public Shape {
public:
   Rectangle(Coordinate& center, long x, long y);
   ~Rectangle();
   void rotate(Angle& a);
   void draw();
   void move(Coordinate& coord);
   Coordinate origin() const;

protected:
   long sideX, sideY;
};


// File: rectangl.cpp

#include rectangl.h

void Rectangle::draw() {
   Shape::draw(); // create window frame
   // now draw the rectangle within the window frame
   // ...
}
```

The design decision to use abstract classes applies to a wide range of applications. Any time a class occurs as a key abstraction, but for which we cannot think of a concrete instance without further specification, it becomes a candidate for an abstract class. The abstract class mechanism provides an excellent design vehicle for a common interface that can be used by several derived classes as an extension of the base class.

The creation of an abstract class is not limited to just the root class of a hierarchy. Successive classes in a hierarchy can be used as abstract base classes for the derivation of concrete classes. In particular, an abstract root class can be followed by abstract base classes for two separate branches of the hierarchy as shown in Figure 10.1.

The `Message` class provides a common interface for all alerts and communications messages. The `Alert` class is an abstract class for the concrete `LANAlert` and `HWAlert` classes. Similarly, the `CommMessage` abstract class is a base class for the concrete `Stream` and `Packet` classes.

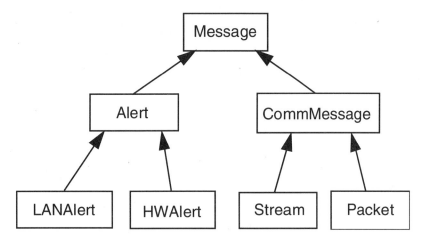

Figure 10.1 Multiple Abstract Classes

10.3 Multiple Inheritance

The use of multiple inheritance may at first seem like a panacea for reuse. C++ supports this paradigm (unlike Smalltalk) and we should be able to make substantial use of this feature. Heavy use of multiple inheritance can be very counterproductive, however, and this paradigm must be approached with caution.

If we are using a C++ library that consists of several branches which are all anchored by the same base class, two major problems occur:

- Ambiguous calls to virtual functions
- Inclusion of multiple objects of repeated base classes

The Problem with Ambiguous Virtual Functions

We have seen how we prepare a class with virtual member functions to take advantage of the built-in C++ polymorphism mechanism. This may not work as expected if we are using multiple inheritance and deriving from two or more classes that have been derived from the same base class.

An example of a hierarchy for using multiple inheritance is shown in Figure 10.2. The corresponding C++ code is listed in Figure 10.3.

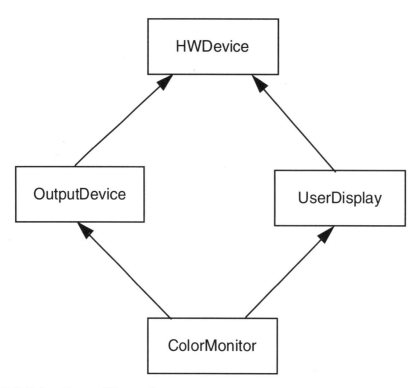

Figure 10.2 Inheritance Hierarchy

```
// File: nvertinh.h
// Illustrating non-virtual multiple inheritance

class HWDevice {
public:
  HWDevice();
  virtual ~HWDevice();
  virtual void print(); // problem for non-virtual multiple in-
heritance
};
class OutputDevice : public HWDevice {
public:
  OutputDevice();
};

class UserDisplay : public HWDevice {
public:
  UserDisplay();
};

class ColorMonitor : public OutputDevice,
                     public UserDisplay {
public:
```

```
     ColorMonitor();
};


// File: nvertinh.cpp

#include <iostream.h>
#include "nvertinh.h"

HWDevice::HWDevice() {
   cout << " Constructor for hardware device " << endl;
}

HWDevice::~HWDevice() {
   cout << " Virtual destructor for hardware device  "
             << endl << endl;
}

void HWDevice::print() {
   cout << " Virtual print() in the base class " << endl;
}

OutputDevice::OutputDevice() {
   cout << " Constructor for output device " << endl;
}

UserDisplay::UserDisplay() {
   cout << " Constructor for user display " << endl;
}

ColorMonitor::ColorMonitor() {
   cout << " Constructor for color monitor " << endl;
}


int main() {
   ColorMonitor cMonitor;
   cMonitor.print(); // which print() ?
   return 0;
}
```

Figure 10.3 Using Non-Virtual Inheritance

The declaration for the multiple inheritance includes both the OutputDevice and UserDisplay classes, each of which derives from the HWDevice class. When we attempt to use the virtual print() function, the compiler creates the following message:

```
C:\MSDEV\projects\book\nvertinh.cpp(30) : error C2385:
'ColorMonitor::print' is ambiguous
C:\MSDEV\projects\book\nvertinh.cpp(30) : warning C4385: could be
```

```
the 'print' in base 'HWDevice' of base 'OutputDevice' of class
'ColorMonitor'
C:\MSDEV\projects\book\nvertinh.cpp(30) : warning C4385: or the
'print' in base 'HWDevice' of base 'UserDisplay' of class
'ColorMonitor'
```

This compile-time error message clearly shows the problem of attempting to use a virtual function of a base class. Since both the OutputDevice and UserDisplay classes inherit from the same HWDevice class, the compiler cannot determine which of the two HWDevice objects to use in the polymorphic call.

This is not a problem for a virtual destructor. The destructor is simply called once for each of the two HWDevice objects, as shown in Figure 10.4 (with the offending cMonitor.print() statement commented out).

The problem with ambiguous virtual functions can be solved by declaring the derived class with virtual inheritance, as illustrated in the next section.

Using Virtual Inheritance

We have already seen how the virtual keyword is used in preparing an inheritance hierarchy to participate in the polymorphism mechanism. This keyword is overloaded in C++ and can take on a significantly different semantics when it is used to declare the particular kind of inheritance desired:

```
class Base {
// ...
};

class Derived : public virtual Base {
// ...
};
```

This type of inheritance avoids the problem of ambiguous calls to member functions in a base class used by two different derived classes. The modified C++ code from Figure 10.3 is listed in Figure 10.5, now using multiple, virtual inheritance.

```
Constructor for hardware device
Constructor for output device
Constructor for hardware device
Constructor for user display
Constructor for color monitor

Virtual destructor for hardware device

Virtual destructor for hardware device
```

Figure 10.4 Using a Virtual Destructor in Multiple, Non-Virtual Inheritance

```
// File: vertinh.h
// Illustrating virtual inheritance

class HWDevice {
public:
  HWDevice();
};

class OutputDevice: public virtual HWDevice { // virtual
public:
  OutputDevice();
};

class UserDisplay : public virtual HWDevice { // virtual
public:
  UserDisplay();
};

class ColorMonitor: public OutputDevice,
                    public UserDisplay {
public:
  ColorMonitor();
};


// File: vertinh.cpp

#include <iostream.h>
#include "vertinh.h" // virtual inheritance

// rest of the implementation is exactly as in Figure 10-3
// ...

int main() {
  ColorMonitor cMonitor;
  cMonitor.print(); // which print() ?
  return 0;
}
```

```
        Output:

                Constructor for hardware device
                Constructor for output device
                Constructor for user display
                Constructor for color monitor
                Virtual print() in the base class
```

Figure 10.5 Using Virtual Inheritance

The earlier problem with the ambiguous call to `print()` has disappeared. There is now only a single print() function to be referenced. Virtual inheritance should be used whenever a hierarchy includes two or more branches, and the use of multiple inheritance from these branches is anticipated.

The Problem with Multiple Base Objects

If we reexamine the output shown in Figure 10.4, we notice two constructor invocations for the hardware device, and one each for the output device, user display, and color monitor. This illustrates the fact that we are inheriting two identical base objects when we inherit from two or more classes that derive from the same base class, using non-virtual inheritance.

The multiple object structure that results for our application when we use non-virtual inheritance is shown in Figure 10.6. The recursive order of constructor invocations starts with the `HWDevice` and `OutputDevice` objects of the left branch. It then continues with the `HWDevice` and `UserDisplay` object of the right branch, and, finally, the `ColorMonitor` object.

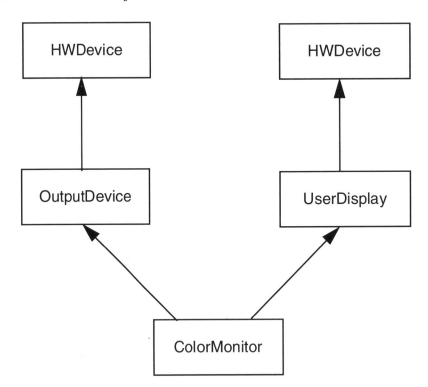

Figure 10.6 Object Structure Using Non-Virtual Inheritance

The use of virtual inheritance eliminates the multiple object problem, as we notice from the output section in Figure 10.5. The constructor for the base class is now only called once, and the object structure shown in Figure 10.7 matches the inheritance hierarchy in Figure 10.2.

We were able to avoid both the problem with ambiguous calls to member functions and the problem with multiple objects in this case because we had complete control over the source code. We simply made the required modification from non-virtual to virtual inheritance.

If we are using a purchased C++ library such as the MFC, we don't have the opportunity to modify the source code, and we are stuck with whatever mechanism is built into the underlying framework. In the case of the MFC, multiple inheritance is simply prohibited, thus making the library less flexible but avoiding the problems associated with non-virtual inheritance. Resorting to cloning and using mixins is the only solution in this case if we want to use multiple classes that are deriving from the same base classes.

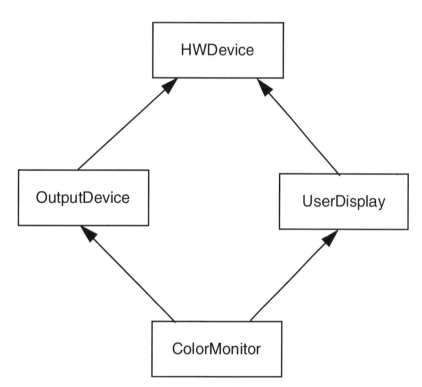

Figure 10-7 Object Structure Using Virtual Inheritance

Creating Mixin Classes

If we discover two or more classes we would like to use in a multiple inheritance relationship, we can clone all but one of the classes from the inheritance hierarchy as stand-alone, independent classes with different class names. Multiple inheritance will now only involve a single branch down the inheritance hierarchy, and the problems with ambiguous calls and multiple base objects are avoided.

By "cloning" we simply mean to copy as much of the existing classes as we need and to give the corresponding mixins similar, but different, names (or use the Namespace feature and keep the same names).

Cloning all but one of the classes in the inheritance hierarchy assumes that we have access to the source code of the library classes we are cloning as mixins. If we do not have access to the source code, we can still use the class interfaces. The member functions will then have to be coded as new and different implementations. This could even be beneficial in some cases, since we could tailor the implementation exactly to our application needs and omit unnecessary services.

10.4 Polymorphism

Polymorphism is the implementation mechanism that associates a member function with an object in the inheritance hierarchy at run-time (dynamic binding). We will illustrate this mechanism via a hierarchy using the three classes GParent (grandparent), Parent, and Child, and their associated member functions (we are ignoring the data members for now):

```
class GParent {
public:
    void F1();
    void F2();
    virtual void V1();
    virtual void V2();
};

class Parent : public GParent {
public:
    void F1(); // Hides GParent::F1() (not overloaded)
    void V1(); // Polymorphic with GParent::V1()
            // (the 'virtual' keyword is not required)
};

class Child : public Parent {
public:
    void F1(); // Hides Parent::F1()
    void V1(); // Polymorphic with Parent::V1() and
            //    GParent::V1()
    virtual void V3();  // new virtual fn
};
```

The class Parent has been derived publicly from the GParent base class, and the further derived class Child from its base class Parent. The name of the member function F1() in Parent hides the F1() function in GParent. This type of hiding is different from the overloading mechanism we can have within a single class, and only depends on the name, not the return type and/or parameters. Here are different ways to access F1() (static binding):

```
. . .
Parent p;
Child c;

p.F1(); // F1() in Parent
p.GParent::F1(); // F1() in GParent
((GParent)p).F1(); // F1() in GParent
static_cast<GParent>(p).F1();// F1() in GParent
```

The use of the `static_cast< >` is a new C++ language feature that may not yet be implemented by some current compilers. This feature is intended to provide a standard way of performing a cast from one object type to another. A companion feature is the `dynamic_cast< >` for dynamic downcasts associated with polymorphism.

There is a language restriction regarding the way we must implement our C++ code to take advantage of polymorphism: We can only access member functions polymorphically via pointers or references to objects. For the class hierarchy listed in this section, here is some sample code to illustrate this:

```
c.F1(); // F1() in Child (static)
((GParent)c).V1(); // V1() in GParent
c.GParent::V1(); // V1() in GParent
((GParent*)&c)->V1(); // V1() in Child

void Draw(GParent& obj) {
    obj.V1(); //  GParent::V1(), Parent::V1(), or Child::V1()
    ...
}
```

The run-time binding will associate the member function V1() with any of the objects in the hierarchy, i.e., a GParent, Parent, or Child object. This association will only take place if we are passing the object via a reference or a pointer. Passing an object by value results in the creation of an internal, local copy based on the type of the formal parameter.

10.5 The Virtual Table

The primary data structure used to implement polymorphism is the virtual table (usually referred to as the `vtable` or `vtbl`). Each class in the hierarchy has its own vtbl, which consists of pointers for each virtual function to its corresponding code segment.

The code segment pointed to depends on whether or not a member function in a derived class overrides a function in a parent class. If it is not overridden, the pointer is to a code segment in a parent class. Overridden functions have pointers to code segments of their own class. These relationships are illustrated in Figure 10.8.

The pointers are listed in the order in which the virtual member functions are declared within each class. The class name is listed with each class vtable. This provides access to the class name for each (unknown) object that is simply pointed to, e.g., via a call to `typid()->name()`.

The vtable for the next level of derivation is shown in Figure 10.9. Only the pointers from the Child::vtable have been included in the figure. The pointers from GParent and Parent are still there.

The Object Pointer

When an object is built by the compiler, the object's data structure includes pointers to the virtual tables of base classes in the hierarchy from which this class was derived. There is thus an efficient link between a virtual function call and the object on whose behalf the function was called, as shown in Figure 10.10.

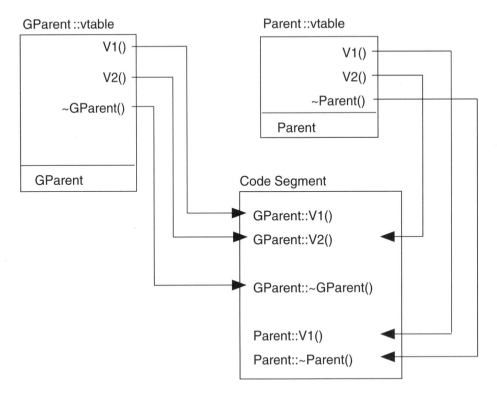

Figure 10-8 vtable for First-Level Derivation

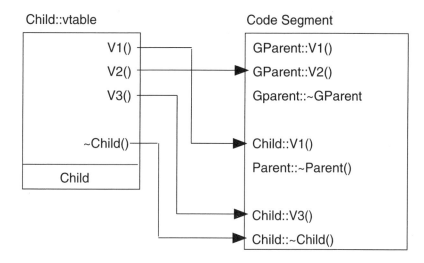

Figure 10.9 vtable for Second-Level Derivation

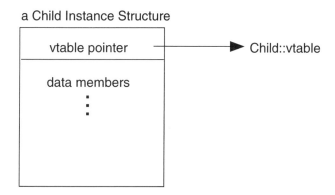

Figure 10.10 Instance Structure in a Virtual Hierarchy

Each object of a virtual derived class has a pointer added to the regular storage of its data members. Other overhead for virtual classes includes one virtual table for each class. There is also some run-time overhead associated with the run-time binding of virtual member function invocation. These spatial and run-time overheads are minimal for most applications, and are far outweighed by the advantages of code re-use and extensibility associated with polymorphism.

If the overhead of using polymorphism is worrisome, e.g., for a real-time system, a profiler can be used to isolate potential trouble spots. The well-known "90-10 Rule" applies to most applications: ten percent of the code represents ninety percent of the execution time. If the profiler can identify the ten percent of code, this can be re-written and optimized for our application.

10.6 Virtual Destructors

We have seen how we prepare a base class for inheritance by declaring virtual member functions that can be overridden in the derived classes. Constructors are never inherited and cannot be virtual, and the data members in a derived class can only be initialized by their corresponding, derived constructor. Destructors are also never inherited, but there is a special mechanism associated with virtual destructors.

Whenever we invoke the run-time binding of member functions via polymorphism, we use pointers or references to a mixture of base objects and derived objects. A special design consideration arises when we have declared a pointer to a base class and that pointer is pointing to a base object when a `delete` is invoked for the pointer. The relevant question is whether or not all of the associated sub-objects get deleted properly. This issue is illustrated with the code and corresponding output shown in Figure 10.11.

```cpp
// File:  vehicle.h

#ifndef VEHICLE_H
#define VEHICLE_H

class Vehicle {
public:
  Vehicle();
  /*virtual*/ ~Vehicle(); // non-virtual destructor
};

class Truck : public Vehicle {
public:
  Truck();
  ~Truck();
};

class Pickup: public Truck {
public:
  Pickup();
  ~Pickup();
};
#endif


// File: vehicle.cpp

#include <iostream.h>
#include "vehicle.h"

Vehicle::Vehicle() {
  cout << " Vehicle() ctor" << endl;
}

Vehicle::~Vehicle() {
```

```
    cout << " ~Vehicle() dtor" << endl;
}

Truck::Truck() {
    cout << " Truck() ctor" << endl;
}

Truck::~Truck() {
    cout << " ~Truck() dtor" << endl;
}

Pickup::Pickup() {
    cout << " Pickup() ctor" << endl;
}

Pickup::~Pickup() {
    cout << " ~Pickup() dtor" << endl;
}


// File: vclmain.cpp

#include <iostream.h>
#include "vehicle.h"

int main() {
    Vehicle* ptrV = new Pickup;
    delete ptrV; // which object is deleted?
    cout << " ptrV deleted in main()" << endl;
    return 0;
}
```

                    Output

                Vehicle() ctor
                Truck() ctor
                Pickup() ctor
                ~Vehicle() dtor
                ptrV deleted in main()

Figure 10.11 Using Non-Virtual Destructor

In this case, since the base destructor is not virtual, only the base object gets deleted, and we have a memory leak.

By making the Vehicle destructor virtual, both the Truck and Pickup destructors also become virtual. The output produced with this modification is shown in Figure 10.12.

```
Vehicle() ctor
Truck() ctor
Pickup() ctor
~Pickup() dtor
~Truck() dtor
~Vehicle() dtor
ptrV deleted in main()
```

Figure 10.12 Using Virtual Destructors

All of the sub-objects are now properly destroyed and thus prevents the potential memory leak we saw for the non-virtual destructor case. Also note that the order of destructor calls is performed in the reverse order of the constructor calls.

This simple illustration suggests that we should always include a virtual destructor for a base class that is being prepared for an inheritance hierarchy.

10.7 Summary

A base class that is prepared for an inheritance hierarchy should include a virtual destructor to avoid potential memory leaks of sub-objects. Member functions expected to be overridden should be made virtual in the base class. The keyword `virtual` does not have to be repeated in the declarations of the derived classes.

The data members that are expected to be manipulated by member functions in the derived classes should be in a protected section. Other data members should be private.

Abstract classes are used to create a common interface for a number of derived classes. An abstract C++ class has one or more member functions that are pure virtual.

The use of multiple inheritance has the potential problem of ambiguous function calls and multiple base objects. These problems can be avoided with virtual derivation.

Mixin classes can be used to prevent the problems associated with multiple inheritance via base classes that derive from a common root class. A mixin class is an independent class that can be used with another class derived from an inheritance hierarchy.

Polymorphism is implemented using a virtual table structure for each class that has virtual functions. A pointer in the virtual table connects the member function of a derived class to the corresponding code section of an overridden function or a function of a base class. An object pointer is created for each instance of a class and points to the corresponding virtual table for that class.

Overhead associated with the use of virtual functions and polymorphism includes one virtual table for each class and a pointer added to the regular storage of the data members for each class instance. There is also some run-time overhead associated with the run-time binding of virtual member function invocations. This overhead is negligible for most applications.

11

Implementing Object-Oriented Concepts in C++

The primary reason for choosing C++ as a programming language is the close mapping of OOA/OOD concepts and their corresponding implementations in C++. Many of the OOA/OOD concepts can be implemented *directly* using C++ constructs. Other concepts have to be implemented by *modeling* them using various C++ constructs.

The focus of this chapter is to describe how the various OOA/OOD concepts can be implemented for a C++ application. An emerging trend for implementing OOD paradigms is the use of Design Patterns [1]. We will illustrate the implementation of some C++ applications in terms of the State and Factory Method patterns.

11.1 Transitioning from OOD to OOP with C++

In earlier chapters, we illustrated how we first created a set of domain classes based on the key abstractions. This was the primary OOA activity. During the OOD phase, we refined the domain classes and added architecture classes.

In this chapter, we demonstrate how we accomplish the transitioning phase from an OOD architecture to an application implemented in C++. Here is a summary of the OOD design entities and concepts and the corresponding transitioning strategy:

- classes   =>   C++ classes
- abstract classes   =>   abstract C++ classes via pure virtual member functions
- class operations   =>   member functions

- class attributes   => data members
- information hiding   => private or protected access
- encapsulation   => a C++ class containing all of its attributes and operations
- data access   => member access functions or friend privilege for
  - class
  - member function
  - nonmember function
- inheritance   => C++ constructs with public or private (rare) inheritance
- polymorphism   => declare one or more member function as virtual in the base class
- exception handling   => C++ constructs (try, throw, catch)
- association   => data members as pointers or references to objects of other classes
- aggregation   => data members as objects of other classes
- "using"   => #include, or forward class reference
- extensibility   => derive C++ classes from base classes
- reusability   => generic functions and classes using templates
- STD   => finite state machine using C++ classes
- dynamic inheritance   => "virtual" constructors with the Factory Method
- data structures   => structs and classes

Every C++ application will have to be implemented in terms of these design concepts. All these features may not be utilized for small, simple applications, but medium to large applications will certainly require most of them.

We will use the Horizon application to demonstrate the implementation concepts that apply to this architecture. Other applications will be used to illustrate the remaining implementations. Figure 11.1 shows the class diagram we developed in Chapter 5 as the static architecture for the Horizon application.

11.2 Implementing Domain and Architecture Classes

Many of the current OOA/OOD CASE tools will generate C++ code from the static class model. All the diagrams for this book were created with Rational Rose/C++ version 3.0. How well the class design is generated by the tool, is entirely dependent on how much detail is entered by the developer creating the static model, and how much code is generated as boilerplate by the tool.

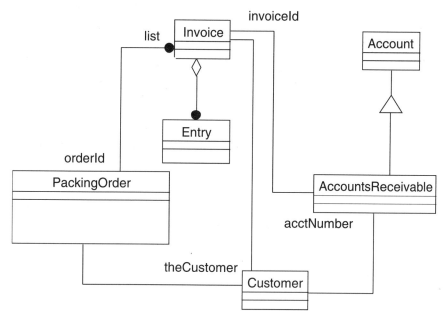

Figure 11.1 Horizon Class Diagram

Rose takes it upon itself to create a number of set()/get() member functions for all the attributes declared in the model. It also creates a set of overloaded operators that may or may not be useful. A careful pruning of the generated code is required to create the desired class interface for each class.

The Class Interface

The design decisions involved in a well-designed class interface were discussed in Chapter 9. We will use the PackingOrder class to discuss the various design decisions that deal with the class interface. A packing order in the Horizon application is a list of items that have to be delivered to a specific customer at a given address on a specific date. The items are associated with a particular invoice. Here is a version of the class PackingOrder:

```
// File: packordr.h

#ifndef Packordr_h
#define Packordr_h

#include "invoice.h"
#include "customer.h"
#include "string.h"
#include "map.h"
```

```
#include "date.h"

// Persistence: Persistent

class PackingOrder {
public:
    // Managers
    PackingOrder(const Customer& cust, Invoice& inv, Date& deliv);
    PackingOrder(const PackingOrder& pkOrder);
    ~PackingOrder();

    // Implementers
    void AddInvoice(Invoice& inv);
    void Replace(Invoice& inv);
    void DeleteItem(String invoiceId, int first=-1, int last=-1);
    // Access Functions
    void Display() const;
    void Print() const;
    String GetCustomerId() const;
    String GetOrderId() const;
private:
    //Helpers
    String createOrderId();
    // Data Members
    String orderId;
    const Customer& theCustomer;
    Address shippingAddress;
    Date deliveryDate;
    map<String, Invoice&, less<String> > invoiceMap;
};

#endif
```

Member Functions

Member functions have been provided for the four different categories. The copy constructor has the usual semantics. The first constructor creates a new packing order instance based on the customer id, initial invoice, and delivery date. Note that we are passing in entire object references for Customer and Invoice. This is based on a design decision that considers how much of the object passed as the actual parameter is required for creating the new object. We could, for instance, have passed in the customer id, address, phone number, etc., as separate parameters, rather than passing the entire object. There is no hard and fast rule to guide us here; each case must be evaluated on its own merit regarding the ease or difficulty in creating the new instance.

The implementer functions provide services for adding the items of an invoice, replacing the items of an existing invoice, and deleting the items of an invoice. Here, again, we have to decide how much of an object should be passed as a parameter. Deleting items only requires an invoice id and the first and last item number to be deleted. Defaults of negative one are provided if all of the items of an invoice should be deleted.

The access functions include services to display a packing order on the screen, to print it, to return the customer id, and to return the order id.

Only one helper function is provided: the creation of a new order id.

Data Members

Data members include the order id, customer id, delivery address, and date of delivery. The major data structure for an instance of this class is the map of invoice ids and the associated invoices with the items to be delivered. We are anticipating using the Standard Template Library (STL) for this data structure, with a map as an associative container (this is covered in detail in Chapter 14). Each invoice in the list is associated with one or more items to be delivered to the customer.

There is no need to store entire objects for the customer and the various invoices. The customer id is stored to associate the packing order with a specific customer. The invoice id is used as a reference into the item list of an invoice.

11.3 Providing Encapsulation and Information Hiding

All the services to be provided by the PackingOrder class have been placed in the public section. The one helper function is in the private section, along with the data members. Access functions have been provided for returning the values of certain data members. No protected members are provided here, since there is no expectation of inheritance for this class.

A secondary level of information hiding (aside from placing helper functions and the data members in the private section) is accomplished with a "clean" header file. All the code resides in a separate .cpp file. This effectively hides the implementation and minimizes the amount of recompilation required when the implementation is modified, i.e., recompilation is limited to the implementation module. If the implementation is part of the header file, the entire application must be recompiled when changes are made. Many modern C++ compilers create precompiled header modules only if the header files are clean. These modules can contribute significantly to reducing the amount of recompilation required for large systems.

11.4 Association

Two classes have a binary association relationship when there is a semantic connection between these classes that requires a two-way navigation between instances of these classes. This is probably the most complex relationship to understand and implement in C++; there is no direct language construct to employ, and the binary relationship adds a level of complexity to the run-time maintenance of the related instances.

One way to think of this relationship is that neither class instance contains or owns the other instance. Each of the two instances exists as part of the application as independent entities. Cardinalities between the two class objects can be one-to-one or one-to-many.

An example of an association between two classes is shown in Figure 11.1 for the relationship between Invoice and AccountsReceivable. The particulars of an invoice, such as the invoice id, total dollar amount, discount rate, and date are associated with a specific account number for tracking accounts receivable with a one-to-one cardinality. The items of each invoice are associated with exactly one account number. Conversely, each account is tracked against one or more invoices with a one-to-many cardinality. If an item in an invoice is returned or rejected by a customer, the outstanding balance for the corresponding account will have to be modified. Thus we see the added complexity resulting from having to update a second object each time certain values change in the first object.

Associations are, typically, implemented in C++ using buried pointers [2, p. 312]. For an association with a one-to-one cardinality, each of the two associated classes contains a pointer that references the other class. For a one-to-many cardinality, referencing in the "many" direction can be implemented as an array of pointers.

We will now illustrate these concepts using the relationship between Invoice and AccountsReceivable. Here is the header file for the Invoice class:

```
class Invoice {
public:
   friend class AccountsReceivable;
   Invoice ();
   Invoice (const Invoice&);
   Invoice(const Customer cust, const Date& deliver);
   ~Invoice ();
   Invoice& operator= (const Invoice&);
   // exceptions
   ...
   void Edit (String invoiceId, Date deliver, Entry&
                                          entry);
   void Add (const String& invoiceId, const Entry& entry);
   void Delete (const String& invoiceId, int entryLine);
   void Display (const String& invoiceId);
   void Print (const String& customerId = NULL);
   double Amount (const String& invoiceId);
   void CreateTotals (const String& invoiceId);
private:
   String invoiceNumber;
   Date deliveryDate;
   CustomerStatus status;
   String customerId;
   Terms paymentTerms;
   Entry* entries; // collection of entries
   double totalAmount;
```

```
    double discount;
    double salesTax;
    double amountToBePaid;
    AccountsReceivable* acctRec; // association
};
```

The data member `acctRec` is used as a reference to the account object that is tracking the receivables associated with this invoice. An array is not necessary, since each invoice is associated with exactly one account.

Each time a new invoice is created for a customer, a reference to the associated account number is created as a data member of the invoice object. If there is an update to an invoice that affects the accounts receivable, the account reference is used to update the receivables amounts. Here is the header file for the AccountsReceivable class:

```
class AccountsReceivable : public Account {
  AccountsReceivable(const Customer& cust);
  void addInvoice(const Invoice& inv);
  void updateReceivable(const String& invoiceId, double amount);
  double totalOwed() const;
  double amountOwed(const String& invoiceId) const;
  // ...
private:
  String acctNumber;
  String custNumber;
  Invoice** invoiceRef; // association
  // ...
  double totalOwed;
};
```

The second part of the binary navigation must be implemented for the one-to-many cardinality: Each account is tracking zero or more unpaid invoices. This is implemented here with invoiceRef as an array of pointers to the invoice instances. The actual invoice instances exist somewhere in the application, but are not part of the account object. In an actual implementation, we would normally create a collection of pointers using a templatized container, e.g., List<Invoice*>, as described in Chapter 14.

An account object must extract the information required to accurately track unpaid invoices. The Invoice class issued a friend privilege to the data members of the AccountsReceivable class to allow this extraction without having to create access functions for every detail required.

We have discussed the implementation of the most complex relationship, i.e., the binary association, first, to set the stage for the other three relationships, which are considerably simpler to implement. Some of these can even be considered a special case of association.

11.5 Aggregation

The class relationship of aggregation is implemented in C++ by the "whole" containing a "part" as a data member of the class in the relationship. There are three variations of aggregation:

- By Value—The embedded object is owned by the containing object and has a lifetime that matches the lifetime of the object. The regular C++ constructor mechanism is invoked to initialize the embedded object, i.e., the constructor for the embedded object is invoked before the constructor for the containing object.

- By Reference—This does not imply ownership, and the lifetime of the referenced, contained object is independent of the object. An implied restriction has the semantics that the contained object must exist as long as the containing object exists. The contained object must be initialized by the constructor(s) of the containing object using member initialization syntax. The contained reference must reference an object that exists when the constructor is invoked.

- By Pointer—Same as By Reference, except that the pointer can be null. This can be used when the embedded objects are transient in nature and are created dynamically as the application is running. This form of aggregation is sometimes considered a special, one-way case of association. It is a one-way relationship, because the contained object pointed to does not have any knowledge of the containing object.

We will now use the PackingOrder class to illustrate how we can implement these three variations of aggregation in C++:

```
class PackingOrder {
public:
  // ...
private:
  // ...
  // Data Members
  String orderId;
  const Customer& theCustomer;
  Address shippingAddress;
  Date deliveryDate;
  map<String, Invoice&, less<String> > invoiceMap;
  Invoice** invoiceList;
};
```

By Value

This is the most straightforward type of aggregation and is shown as the relationship between PackingOrder and Address. Each packing order created must have a shipping address. The address is a distinct part of the packing order which owns it. The address object has the same lifetime as the packing order object (aside from the exact timing and order of destructor invocations). Other examples of aggregation by value for this class include the data members orderId, deliveryDate, and invoiceMap.

By Reference

A PackingOrder object will always be created for a specific customer. A Customer object is not owned by the PackingOrder; the latter simply needs to access some information within the Customer object which can exist beyond the life of the PackingOrder. We have used this relationship here to reference a specific Customer object, which exists independent of any PackingOrder object.

By Pointer

Aggregation via a pointer is used whenever the containment is transient, and includes the case where the pointer can be null. To demonstrate this type of aggregation, we have included an alternate data structure for the invoice list as an array of invoice pointers. This list is transient, depending on how many invoices are represented in a particular PackingOrder object. If a blank packing order is allowed, the list will be empty, otherwise there will be at least one invoice pointer in the list. The order may be modified by adding other invoices, thus adding invoice pointers to the list.

By comparing the implementation of this relationship to the way we implemented the relationship between the Invoice and AccountsReceivable, we can now see how this is sometimes considered a special case of association. Syntactically, there is no difference between these two statements:

```
Invoice** invoiceRef;  // binary association
Invoice** invoiceList; // one-way aggregation
```

Semantically, however, the first structure reflects a binary relationship between the Invoice and AccountsReceivable classes, whereas the second is used in a one-way relationship of the PackingOrder class knowing about Invoices. Invoices are only created from customer orders and are not associated with packing orders.

11.6 Using

The "Using" relationship implies the weakest coupling between class instances. The most common form of this relationship is where an object is passed as an actual parameter to a function. This is illustrated with the constructor for the AccountsReceivable class:

```
AccountsReceivable(const Customer& cust);
```

A Customer object is passed in as a parameter and parts of this object are used to create an AccountsReceivable object. The entire object is not contained within the object using it. The using object simply needs a reference to a particular object.

This relationship doesn't always show up in the class interfaces. The implementations of the member functions may sometimes require "using" relationships within their code, e.g., for the use of I/O libraries:

```
// File: acctmgr.h
#include "acctrecv.h" // "using" as parameter type

class AcctsMgr{
public:
  // ctors and dtor
  void appAcctRecv(const AccountsReceivable& acctRecv);
  // other member functions
private:
  // data members
};


// File: acctmgr.cpp
#include "acctmgr.h"
#include "acctrecv.h" // "using" as parameter type
#include <iostream.h> // "using" in implementation
#include <fstream.h> // "using" in implementation

void AcctsMgr::appAcctRecv(const AccountsReceivable& acctRecv) {
  char* acctRecvFile = "receivables.csv";
  fstream recvFile;
  recvFile.open(acctRecvFile, ios::app); // open for 'append'
  if(!recvFile)
    throw FailedOpenFile(acctRecvFile);
  recvFile << acctRecv;
  recvFile.close();
}
```

The member function appAcctRecv() makes references to the fstream and ios classes in its implementation. These references are examples of "using" relationships in the function implementation. They do not show up in the class interface, since the #include directives are placed in the source file (.cpp).

The "using" relationship is used: (1) when a member function has the referenced class as a type of a formal parameter, or (2) a member function has to create a local, temporary object of the referenced class. Both of these two cases are illustrated in the previous example. Case (1) shows up as a type in the member function parameter list in the header file:

```
appAcctRecv(const AccountsReceivable& acctRecv);
```

Case (2) shows up inside the body of the member function where the local object is created, and where an enumerated value is used:

```
fstream recvFile; // local object
recvFile.open(acctRecvFile, ios::app); // enumerated value
ios::app
```

This relationship represents the weakest coupling between two classes, and is the easiest to implement. We only have to place a #include directive in the header and/or source file making a reference to the used class.

11.7 Inheritance

Inheritance should be used whenever we discover an "Is-A" relationship in the form of a parent/child class hierarchy. C++ has direct language support for this relationship with base/derived class syntax and semantics. We will use the class diagram shown in Figure 11.2 to illustrate the features and merits of inheritance for the Horizon application.

The generalized Account class serves as a common interface for any of the special account classes. We will focus on the AccountsReceivable and AccountsPayable classes here. The common interface includes the member functions payInvoice() as an implementer, and balance(), yearEnd(), and totalPaid() as access functions. The manager function is close(). These functions are all pure virtual, and will have to be overridden in the derived classes.

The common data members in the base class are all protected, whereas the unique data member in each of the derived classes are private.

The same set of member functions is shown in all the classes, because all the member functions in the base class are declared pure virtual, and there are no other unique member functions in the derived classes.

Abstract Classes

An "account" is simply an abstraction, comparable to a "shape" abstraction. The only instances of accounts that will occur in the Horizon application will be accounts for tracking of receivable amounts from customers, payable amounts to suppliers, payroll account, etc. This is similar to actual shape instances of triangle, polygon, square, etc.

We will design the Account class as an abstract base class that simply provides a common interface. Actual instances will only be created from the derived classes. C++ provides syntax and semantics for an abstract base class via pure virtual member functions (see Chapter 10):

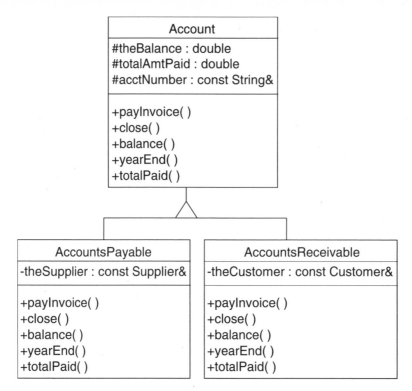

Figure 11.2 Inheritance of Account Classes

```
// File: account.h
// Common interface for account classes

class Summary;
class String;
class Date;

class Account {
public:
  Account(double bal, double amtPaid, String& acctNum);
  virtual ~Account();
  virtual void payInvoice(const String& invoiceId,
                          double amt,
                          const Date& date,
                          const String& pmtMethod) = 0;
  virtual void close(const String& acctNum) = 0;
  virtual double balance(const String& acctNum) = 0;
  virtual Summary& yearEnd(const String& acctNum) = 0;
  virtual double totalPaid(const Date& start, const Date& end) =
0;
protected:
  virtual String& getNewAcctNumber() = 0;
```

```
    double theBalance;
    double totalAmtPaid;
    String& acctNumber;
};
```

The use of the pure virtual functions will require us to override these member functions in the derived classes. This does not preclude the inclusion of a definition of any of these functions in the .cpp file for the abstract class.

Note the use of the forward declarations for the class Summary, String, and Date classes used to provide visibility to these types. This will not work for any data member that is an embedded object "by value." We have to suffer a level of indirection via a pointer or reference to use this type of forward declaration. Here is the compiler error created by the Microsoft Visual C++ compiler if acctNumber is an embedded object by value:

```
C:\MSDEV\projects\abstract\account.h(24) : error C2079:
'acctNumber' uses undefined class 'String'
```

The source file for the abstract Account class can be implemented as follows:

```
// File: account.cpp

#include "account.h"

Account::Account(double bal, double amtPaid, String& acctNum)
  :theBalance(bal), totalAmtPaid(amtPaid), acctNumber(acctNum) {
}
```

The only source code required is the member initialization of the common data members. The constructors in the derived classes will have to pass the three parameters to the base constructor before the other data members of the derived object are initialized. Remember, we cannot create any instances of the type Account. The base constructor is only preparing the inherited part of a derived object.

Derived Classes

The two classes deriving from the abstract Account class shown in Figure 11.2 are AccountsReceivable and AccountsPayable. The Horizon application will have other derived classes as well, but we are ignoring them here since the two chosen classes are sufficient to demonstrate the design principles. Here is a partial header file for the derived classes:

```
// File: deraccts.h
// Interface for derived accounts classes

#include "account.h"
```

```
class Customer;
class Supplier;

class AccountsReceivable : public Account {
  AccountsReceivable(const Customer& cust, double bal,
                     double amtPaid, String& acctNum);
  void payInvoice(const String& invoiceId,
                     double amt,
                     const Date& date,
                     const String& pmtMethod);
  void close(const String& acctNum);
  double balance(const String& acctNum);
  Summary& yearEnd(const String& acctNum);
  double totalPaid(const Date& start, const Date& end);
private:
  String& getNewAcctNumber();
  const Customer& theCustomer;
};

class AccountsPayable : public Account {
  AccountsPayable(const Supplier& suppl, double bal,
                     double amtPaid, String& acctNum);
  void payInvoice(const String& invoiceId,
                     double amt,
                     const Date& date,
                     const String& pmtMethod);
  void close(const String& acctNum);
  double balance(const String& acctNum);
  Summary& yearEnd(const String& acctNum);
  double totalPaid(const Date& start, const Date& end);
private:
  String& getNewAcctNumber();
  const Supplier& theSupplier;
};
```

Each of the two derived classes has a unique data member: an embedded Customer object for the AccountsReceivable class, and an embedded Supplier object for the AccountsPayable class.

The constructor for each of the derived classes must pass the values of the common data members up to the base constructor before the unique data members can be initialized:

```
// File: deraccts.cpp

#include "deraccts.h"

AccountsReceivable::AccountsReceivable(const Customer& cust,
                                       double bal,
                                       double amtPaid,
                                       String& acctNum)
  : Account(bal, amtPaid, acctNum), theCustomer(cust) { };
```

```
AccountsPayable::AccountsPayable(const Supplier& suppl,
                                 double bal,
                                 double amtPaid,
                                 String& acctNum)
   : Account(bal, amtPaid, acctNum), theSupplier(suppl) { };
```

Each of the pure virtual functions must include an implementation in the source file of the respective derived class. We are not showing that here, since we are only demonstrating the general implementation techniques of transitioning from OOD to C++.

11.8 Finite State Machines

State transition diagrams (STDs) are used to depict the various run-time states of an object and the events and actions that cause transitions from one state to another. The implementation of the STD structure is usually referred to as a finite state machine (FSM).

FSMs have traditionally been implemented in C using lookup tables for the various events and state transitions, and pointers to functions for the corresponding actions. These table-driven FSMs are usually quite efficient, but the code is difficult to read and hard to understand.

The State Design Pattern

We will illustrate an alternative, object-oriented FSM approach based on the State design pattern [1, p. 305]. This model is also suggested in [3]. The State pattern is based on a hierarchy of state classes, and allows an object to alter its behavior and class when its internal state changes. The general class diagram for this pattern, using a TCP application as an example, is shown in Figure 11.3.

A TCPConnection object is composed of an abstract TCPState object that can have three different states. The state object provides the common interface to the various subclasses that represent the finite states of the FSM. The behaviors of the different states are accomplished via the overridden member functions of each subclass.

We will now illustrate this mechanism for a serial printer connection, whose class diagram is shown in Figure 11.4.

The serial printer exists in one of three states: Idle, Suspended, or Txing (transmitting). The UserInterface object can be implemented as a main() program with a pointer to a SerialPrnState object that is created with new() and initially set to an Idle object (we'll show the actual C++ code later in this section).

The events that cause state transitions are represented as public member functions of the current state object, and the corresponding actions are modeled as private (internal) member functions that are executed before the state transition is completed.

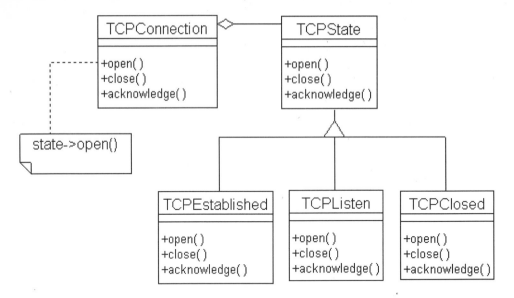

Figure 11.3 State Design Pattern

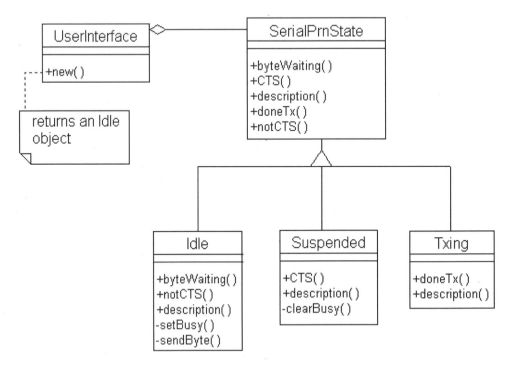

Figure 11.4 Serial Printer Class Diagram

Serial Printer State Transition Diagram

The STD for the serial printer is shown in Figure 11.5.

The initial printer state is Idle. For the event that the printer is not clear to send (notCTS()), the action setBusy() is executed, and the object is transitioned to the Suspended state. The CTS()/clearBusy() event/action combination transitions the state object back to the Idle state. The byteWaiting()/sendByte() event/action pair results in the Idle object transitioning to the Txing state. The event doneTx() transitions the object back to the Idle state.

The events shown in the STD in Figure 11.5 correspond to the public member functions shown in the class diagram in Figure 11.4. Similarly, the actions in the STD correspond to the private member functions for their respective classes in the class diagram.

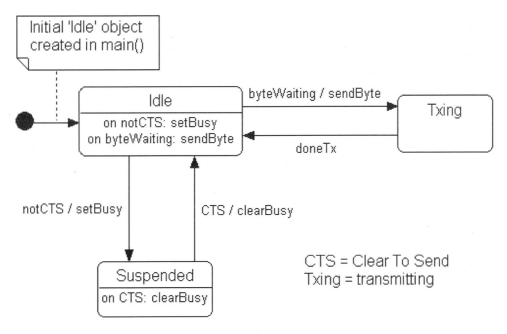

Figure 11.5 Serial Printer STD

Implementing the Serial Printer State Transitions

We will now show one implementation of the serial printer, based on the class diagram in Figure 11.4 and the STD in Figure 11.5. Here is the C++ code for the state class hierarchy:

```
// File: ooFSM.h

class SerialPrnState {
public:
  virtual ~SerialPrnState() {}

  virtual SerialPrnState* notCTS() {return this;}
  virtual SerialPrnState* byteWaiting() {return this;}
  virtual SerialPrnState* CTS() {return this;}
  virtual SerialPrnState* doneTx() {return this;}
  virtual char* description() {return "Invalid State";}
};


class Idle : public SerialPrnState {
public:
  virtual ~Idle() {}
  SerialPrnState* notCTS(); // to Suspended
  SerialPrnState* byteWaiting(); // to Txing
  char* description() {return "Idle";}
private:
  void setBusy();
  void sendByte();
};

class Txing : public SerialPrnState {
public:
  virtual ~Txing() {}
  SerialPrnState* doneTx(); // to Idle
  char* description() {return "Txing";}
};

class Suspended : public SerialPrnState {
public:
  virtual ~Suspended () {}
  SerialPrnState* CTS(); // to Idle
  char* description() {return "Suspended";}
private:
  void clearBusy();
};


// File: ooFSM.cpp

#include <iostream.h>
#include "oofsm.h"
```

```
SerialPrnState* Idle::notCTS() {
  setBusy();
  delete this;
  return new Suspended;
}

SerialPrnState* Idle::byteWaiting() {
  sendByte();
  delete this;
  return new Txing;
};

SerialPrnState* Suspended::CTS() {
  clearBusy();
  delete this;
  return new Idle;
}

SerialPrnState* Txing::doneTx() {
  delete this;
  return new Idle;
};

void Idle::setBusy() {
  cout << endl << " setBusy executed" << endl;
}

void Suspended::clearBusy() {
  cout << endl << " clearBusy executed" << endl;
}

void Idle::sendByte() {
  cout << endl << " sendByte executed" << endl;
}
```

Each event is declared as a public member function and is implemented by first calling any actions expected for that state object. When the action is completed, the event function deletes the current object (this), and creates a new object for the next state. For example, when the notCTS() event is invoked on behalf of the Idle object, it first calls the setBusy() action. When this action is completed, the event deletes its own object and returns a Suspended object via new() as the next state object.

This model removes any knowledge about the various states from the high-level FSM and simplifies the transition logic by localizing this information to the individual objects.

The actions in the serial printer example have simply been modeled with "cout" statements. In a real application, the action functions would execute the various printer functions.

Implementing an FSM Application

A user interface was created to demonstrate how the FSM works. This interface is based on the scheme reported in [3]. Here are the interface functions and the main program:

```cpp
// File: oofsmain.cpp

#include <iostream.h>
#include "oofsm.h"

void PromptForNextEvent(SerialPrnState& state, int& event) {
  cout << endl << " Current state = " << state.description();
  cout << endl;
  cout << " Event types:" << endl
       << " 1 - notCTS" << endl
       << " 2 - byteWaiting" << endl
       << " 3 - CTS" << endl
       << " 4 - doneTx" << endl << endl;
   cout << " Event selected = ";
  cin >> event;
}

SerialPrnState* ProcessNextEvent
      (SerialPrnState& state, int& event) {
  const int
    notCTS      = 1,
    byteWaiting = 2,
    CTS         = 3,
    doneTx      = 4;

  // Identify the event, and invoke the associated
  // member function
  switch (event) {
    case notCTS:
      return state.notCTS();
    case byteWaiting:
      return state.byteWaiting();
    case CTS:
      return state.CTS();
    case doneTx:
      return state.doneTx();
    default:
      return 0;
  }
}


void main() {
  // set the initial state
  SerialPrnState* currentState = new Idle;
                 // initial state object
  int event;
```

```
do {
  PromptForNextEvent(*currentState, event);
  currentState = ProcessNextEvent (*currentState, event);
} while (currentState);
delete  currentState;
}
```

An Idle object is first created dynamically in main(). The user is then prompted for a series of events that will cause state transitions. Here is a sample output for a particular scenario of selected events:

```
Current state = Idle
Event types:
1 - notCTS
2 - byteWaiting
3 - CTS
4 - doneTx

Event selected = 1

setBusy executed


Current state = Suspended
Event types:
1 - notCTS
2 - byteWaiting
3 - CTS
4 - doneTx

Event selected = 3

clearBusy executed


Current state = Idle
Event types:
1 - notCTS
2 - byteWaiting
3 - CTS
4 - doneTx

Event selected = 2

sendByte executed


Current state = Txing
Event types:
1 - notCTS
2 - byteWaiting
```

```
3 - CTS
4 - doneTx

Event selected = 4

Current state = Idle
Event types:
1 - notCTS
2 - byteWaiting
3 - CTS
4 doneTx
```

This application demonstrates the feasibility of this approach and clearly shows the various transitions resulting from the selected events. The handling of the state information has been decoupled from the system determining the various event scenarios, as shown in Figure 11.6.

Summary of the Object-Oriented FSM Approach

Here is a summary of the features, merits, and liabilities of the object-oriented FSM approach:

- The STD model is represented directly by a class diagram
- A base class serves as an abstract root class
- Each state is modeled as a derived class

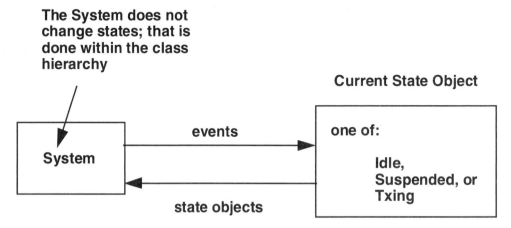

Figure 11.6 Handling of Events and State Transitions

- The public virtual member functions represent events and are overridden in the derived classes
- State transitions are represented by class instances, inside the class hierarchy
- State objects are created and destroyed with each state transition
- Events that don't cause state transitions are ignored at the base class level
- The hierarchical structure makes it very easy to add states
- The coding convention of placing all events in a public section, and the corresponding actions in a private section, makes it easy to verify that the entire STD has been implemented
- There are no look-up tables for finding handler functions based on the system state
- Once an event is classified in the function ProcessNextEvent(), a single polymorphic function call is bound at run-time to the object representing the current state
- An unknown issue is the run-time efficiency of the create/destroy mechanism for each state transition

11.9 Virtual Constructors

The C++ syntax and semantics does not support virtual constructors similar to the way that virtual member functions can be invoked polymorphically at run-time. We have seen how we can create objects dynamically using new() via a pointer to a class in an inheritance hierarchy:

```
class Base { ... };
class Derived : public Base { ... };

int main() {
  Base* ptrBase = new Base;
  // ...
  ptrBase = new Derived;
  // ...
}
```

This will work whenever we know a priori exactly how many different types of objects to create, and where in the application this code should reside. In other words, we still have to hard-code the pointers even though we are able to use new() to create objects dynamically and reference their member functions polymorphically via the pointers. What if we want to create objects at run-time from a selection of known classes? This is a common problem, for example, where users can open one or more documents using menu items and dialog boxes.

The design pattern Factory Method [1, p. 107] was created to solve this problem. This pattern is also known as the Virtual Constructor paradigm [4, p. 140].

This pattern can be used when a class cannot anticipate the class of objects it is required to create, or when a base class wants its derived classes to specify the objects to be created.

Window Factory Class Diagram

We will illustrate the use of this design pattern with a Window base class and FrameWnd and View subclasses. The class diagram is shown in Figure 11.7.

The Window class provides the common interface for the creation of subclass objects. The Factory Method is the virtual `create()` function. The static pointer `head` points to the start of a singly-linked list of objects of type FrameWnd and/or View, which have been added via the templatized RegisterClass<T>.

RegisterClass<T> is used to create objects and register classes from which additional clone objects can be created during run-time by specifying the class name. Each time RegisterClass<T> is instantiated with a class, that class name is added to the list (Window::addClass()) pointed to by `head`.

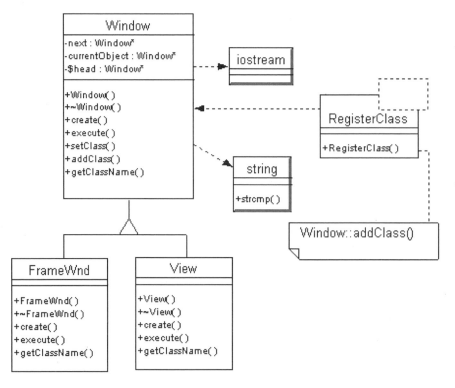

Figure 11.7 Window Factory Class Diagram

The directed graphs with the dotted lines are a new representation in OMT diagrams that is supported by Rational Rose. This notation depicts the "using" relationship (making a reference to) described in earlier chapters. A Window instance, for example, is making use of the functions in the `iostream` library.

We will now show how this pattern can be used in an application by designing a user interface which allows requests for cloned objects to be entered on the command line.

Window Factory Application

A Window factory application is shown in Figure 11.8. The Application class will be implemented as a main() program that contains a Window object and *N* RegisterClass<T> objects for *N* instantiations. In our case there are two instantiations: one each for the FrameWnd and View classes.

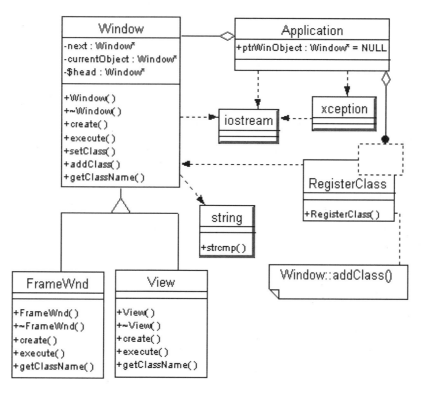

Figure 11.8 Window Factory Application

Implementation of Window Factory Application

The implementation of the class model shown in Figure 11.8 is focused on the cloning of FrameWnd and View instances. One instance of each of these two classes is first created and registered with a RegisterClass template object. Any number of instances from these types can then be created dynamically. Here is the class specification for the inheritance hierarchy:

```cpp
// File: factory.h

#ifndef FACTORY_H
#define FACTORY_H 1

class Window {
public:
  Window();
  virtual ~Window();
  virtual Window* create() const;
  virtual int execute();
  int setClass(const char* className);
  static void addClass(Window* bcp);
  virtual const char* getClassName() const;
private:
  Window* next;
  Window* currentObject;
  static Window* head;
};


template<class T>
class RegisterClass {
public:
  RegisterClass() {Window::addClass(new T);}
};


class FrameWnd : public Window {
public:
  FrameWnd();
  ~FrameWnd();
  virtual Window* create() const;
  virtual int execute();
  virtual const char* getClassName() const;
private:
  // ...
};


class View : public Window {
public:
  View();
  ~View();
```

```
    virtual Window* create() const;
    virtual int execute();
    virtual const char* getClassName() const;
private:
    // ...
};

#endif
```

The virtual `create()` function is the Factory Method used to clone instances of FrameWnd or View types. The `execute()` function is called after an instance is created to perform the necessary processing for that object.

Factory Method Source Code

Here is the source file for implementation of the Factory Method member functions:

```cpp
// File: factory.cpp

#include "factory.h"
#include <iostream.h>
#include <string.h>

Window* Window::head = NULL;

Window::Window() {
  cout << " Window::Window() called" << endl;
  currentObject = NULL;
}

Window::~Window() {
  cout << " Window::~Window() called" << endl << endl;
}

Window* Window::create() const {
  return currentObject ? currentObject : (Window*)0;
}


int Window::execute() {
  return currentObject ? currentObject->execute() : 0;
}

int Window::setClass(const char* className) {
  cout << className << endl;
  currentObject = (Window*)head;

  while(strcmp(currentObject->getClassName(), className) &&
    currentObject != (Window*)NULL) {
      currentObject = currentObject->next;
```

```
    }
    return currentObject ? 1 : 0;
}

void Window::addClass(Window* bcp) {
  if(!head) {
    head = bcp;
    head->next = NULL;
  }
  else {
    bcp->next = head;
    head = bcp;
  }
}

const char* Window::getClassName() const {
  return "Window";
}

template<class T>
RegisterClass<T>::RegisterClass() {
  Window::addClass(new T);
}

FrameWnd::FrameWnd() {
  cout << " FrameWnd::FrameWnd() called" << endl;
}

FrameWnd::~FrameWnd() {
  cout << " FrameWnd::~FrameWnd() called" << endl;
}

Window* FrameWnd::create() const {
  return new FrameWnd;
}

int FrameWnd::execute() {
  cout << " FrameWnd::execute()" << endl;
  return 1;
}

const char* FrameWnd::getClassName() const {
  return "FrameWnd";
}

View::View() {
  cout << " View::View() called" << endl;
}
View::~View() {
  cout << " View::~View() called" << endl;
}

Window* View::create() const {
```

```
    return new View;
}

int View::execute() {
  cout << " View::execute()" << endl;
  return 1;
}

const char* View::getClassName() const {
  return "View";
}
```

Window Factory Application Source Code

We will now illustrate how we can use this design pattern with an application that registers one instance each of a FrameWnd and View type. The insertion and extraction operators are then used to interface with the user to determine which objects should be created dynamically:

```
// File: factmain.cpp
//
// This is the main program to exercise the
//   Factory Method pattern.
//
// The base class is Window, with derived classes FrameWnd and
//   View, as shown in the OMT class diagram

// The two derived classes are first registered. These classes
//   are displayed to the user (via 'cout') with a corresponding
//   index number.
//   The user is then asked to enter the index number for the
//   class he/she wants to clone. If an invalid index is
//   entered, the exception InvalidIndex is thrown, and the
//   user is asked to enter a legal index, or quit (index = 99)

#include "factory.h"
#include <iostream.h>
#include "xception.cpp"

int main() {
  string theIndex("Invalid Index"); // exception tag
  string quitString("time to quit");

  int classIndex; // input from user

  Window* ptrWinObject;
  cout << " Constructor calls to show the instances created:"
       << endl;
  Window winApp;
  RegisterClass<FrameWnd> frameReg;
```

```cpp
RegisterClass<View> viewReg;

cout << endl;
cout << " Summary of Registered Classes " << endl;
cout << " Class Index" << "    Class-Name" << endl;
cout << "\t" << 1 << "\t" << "FrameWnd" << endl;
cout << "\t" << 2 << "\t" << "View" << endl << endl;

try { // outer try block
  for(;;) { // user interface loop
    try { // inner try block
      cout << endl;
      cout << " Pick a class by entering the class index"
           << "\n (enter 99 to quit): ";
      cin >> classIndex;
      switch(classIndex) {
        case 1:
          if (winApp.setClass("FrameWnd"))
            ptrWinObject = winApp.create();
          else
            cout << " No FrameWnd class found" << endl;

          ptrWinObject->create(); // FrameWnd instance
          ptrWinObject->execute(); // executing the instance

          cout << " ptrWinObject->getClassName() "
               << ptrWinObject->getClassName() << endl;
          break;

        case 2:
          if (winApp.setClass("View"))
            ptrWinObject = winApp.create();
          else
            cout << " No View class found" << endl;

          ptrWinObject->create(); // View instance
          ptrWinObject->execute(); // executing the instance

          cout << " ptrWinObject->getClassName() "
               << ptrWinObject->getClassName() << endl;
          break;

        case 99:
          cout << " Time to quit in main()" << endl;
          throw Quitting(quitString);
          break;

        default:
          cout << " Invalid index in main()" << endl;
          throw InvalidIndex(theIndex);
          break;
      } // end of switch
    } // end of inner try block
```

```
            catch (InvalidIndex& except) {
              cout << " 'InvalidIndex' exception caught in switch-loop"
                    << endl;
            }
            continue;
        } // end of for(;;)
    } // end of outer try block

    catch (Quitting& except) {
        cout << " 'Quitting' exception caught at end of main()"
              << endl;
    }

    catch (...) {
        cout << " Unknown exception at end of main()" << endl;
    }
    cout << " end of main()" << endl << endl;

    delete ptrWinObject;
    return 0;

} // end of main()
```

We note the general strategy of first registering the two instances with RegisterClass of types FrameWnd and View, respectively. The remaining processing involves the interface with the user to determine which clones should be created dynamically. Note how we have implemented exception handling as part of the design for dealing with illegal user choices, and for terminating the session. The output from one user session is illustrated in the next section.

Output from Window Factory Application

Here is the output from one session using the application from the previous section:

```
Constructor calls to show the instances created:
Window::wIndow() called
Window::wIndow() called
FrameWnd::FrameWnd() called
Window::Window() called
View::View() called

Summary of Registered Classes
Class Index      Class-Name
      1              FrameWnd
      2              View

Pick a class by entering the class index
```

```
(enter 99 to quit): 1
FrameWnd
Window::Window() called
FrameWnd::FrameWnd() called
FrameWnd::execute()
ptrWinObject->getClassName() FrameWnd

Pick a class by entering the class index
(enter 99 to quit): 2
View
Window::Window() called
View::View() called
View::execute()
ptrWinObject->getClassName() View

Pick a class by entering the class index
(enter 99 to quit): 6
Invalid index in main()
msg.data()=Invalid Index
'InvalidIndex' exception caught in switch-loop

Pick a class by entering the class index
(enter 99 to quit): 99
Time to quit in main()
msg.data()=time to quit
'Quitting' exception caught at end of main()
end of main()

View::~View() called
WIndow::~Window() called

WIndow::~Window() called
```

The progression of the creation and destruction of instances can be seen via the calls to "cout" that are included in the constructors and destructors. The user selected one FrameWnd and one View object for this session. An attempt to specify an illegal instance type was detected and handled with an exception. The session ended with the user specifying a class index of 99.

The implementation of the Factory Method is a reasonable design choice for the dynamic creation of instances of known types, where the subclasses decide which classes should be instantiated. This design pattern can be expanded to the Abstract Factory [1, p. 87], if we need to create families of related or dependent objects without specifying their concrete classes.

11.10 Creating Data Structures

Every C++ application needs data structures to implement the dynamic state values of the objects that model the solution. In this section, we will illustrate the use of *structs* versus classes by modeling a simple message passing scheme.

A common requirement in a message passing system is the ability to have clean interfaces for send and receive functions, with the details of how the messages are actually handled being hidden from the users.

An example of such a system is an interprocess(or) communication (IPC) mechanism. Messages are passed between applications residing in the different processes via the operating system facilities, e.g., the socket mechanism in Unix or Windows NT. When a source is ready to pass a message to a destination, it should be able to simply pass that message as a parameter without any knowledge of the intervening communication mechanism.

We will now illustrate a simple IPC mechanism, with an emphasis on the data structures required and how we can provide a clean user interface which only consists of a send() and a receive() function. In a real client/server system, there is usually also a registration mechanism to facilitate the management of multiple clients, which we are ignoring here.

Designing the Data Structures

The general scheme is for a client that acts as a *source* to create a message of a certain type and pass it to a communication facility via a send() function. The send() function transforms the message into a byte stream and passes it to the communication facility at the destination. Here is a header file, and the corresponding source file, that contains the data structure for the message and the encapsulated IPC facility:

```
// File: ipcmsg.h

#ifndef IPCMSG_H
#define IPCMSG_H

struct IPCMsg {
  IPCMsg(); // create a blank msg
  IPCMsg(int a, int b);
  int x;
  int y;
};

class IPC {
public:
  void send(IPCMsg& msg, const char* source,
            const char* dest);
  void receive(IPCMsg& msg, size_t length);
private:
```

```
    static char buf[]; // msg buffer (byte stream)
};

#endif

// File: ipcmsg.cpp

#include "ipcmsg.h"
#include<string.h>
#include <iostream.h>
char IPC::buf[]="            ";

void IPC::send(IPCMsg& msg, const char* source,
               const char* dest) {
  memcpy(buf, (void*)&msg, sizeof(msg));
// notify dest that it has a pending msg
}

void IPC::receive(IPCMsg& msg, size_t length) {
  memcpy((void*)&msg, buf, length);
  cout << " Copied msg in IPC::receive() x, y = "
       << msg.x << ", " << msg.y << endl;
}

IPCMsg::IPCMsg(int a, int b) : x(a), y(b) {}
IPCMsg::IPCMsg() : x(0), y(0) {}
```

We have used the struct IPCMsg to represent the data structure for the message. In this case, we are modeling a message with just two int components. In a real system, this could be a nested struct including a header, the length of the message, etc. The main point here, is that we chose a struct rather than a class because we are only dealing with data; there are no behaviors to encapsulate with a message object.

The message structure includes two constructors: the default constructor creates a blank message with x and y initialized to zero, and the second constructor initializes x and y with the values of the actual parameters passed. The default visibility for x and y is public. There is no compelling reason for making them private, since only the source and destination processes know anything about these messages, and each message will be passed as a byte stream.

The IPC utility is modeled with a class rather than a struct, since it encapsulates the message buffer and the behavior for sending and receiving messages.

The transformation of the message is performed within the send() function using memcpy(). Note how we have to cast the message type to (void*) to get around the C++ strong typing rules.

After a destination has received a notification that a message is pending (not shown here), that destination calls the IPC receive() function to get the waiting message. The receive() function copies the message from the stream buffer to the blank message object referenced as the actual parameter. The intermediary operations of creating the byte stream and the transmission of the message across the network are thus transparent to both the source and the destination.

Implementing an IPC Application

Here is an example of how we can model this message passing scheme in a C++ application:

```
// File: ipcmain.cpp
// Converting from a struct to a char string and back again

#include <iostream.h>
#include "ipcmsg.h"

IPC ipcClient1;
IPC ipcClient2;

int main() {

  IPCMsg aMsg(50, 23);
  IPCMsg bMsg; // blank msg

  cout << " Size of aMsg = " << (sizeof (aMsg)) << endl;

  cout << " Initialized aMsg in main() = " << aMsg.x << ", "
       << aMsg.y << endl;
  cout << " Blank bMsg in main() = " << bMsg.x << ", "
       << bMsg.y << endl;

  ipcClient1.send(aMsg, "TaskIdFrom", "TaskIdTo");
  ipcClient2.receive(bMsg, sizeof (bMsg));
  cout << " Received bMsg in main() x,y = " << bMsg.x
       << ", " << bMsg.y << endl;
  return 0;
}
```

Output from ipcmain():

```
Size of aMsg = 8
Initialized aMsg in main() = 50, 23
Blank bMsg in main() = 0, 0
Copied msg in IPC::receive() x, y = 50, 23
Received bMsg in main() x,y = 50, 23
```

The two clients have been modeled as two global IPC objects, that perform a send() and receive(), respectively. In a multiprocess environment, there would be an IPC client attached to each process as a shell between the process and the OS calls.

The primary purpose here is not to provide a complete IPC mechanism, but merely to show when we can effectively use a struct instead of a class.

Another benefit of this illustration is the transparent message transformation combining the C memcpy() and C++ cast to (void*). This scheme can be used anytime we can justify the necessity for casting to avoid the C++ strong typing rules. This should not be used as a general implementation to avoid the desired OOD encapsulation mechanism.

Using fstream Objects

The conversion mechanism shown in the previous section can also be used to write an object to a file as a byte stream. After the conversion from the object to the stream, the stream is written to a file as an ofstream object. The same stream can then be read back into memory as an ifstream object and converted back to the original object:

```cpp
// File: fipcmsg.cpp

#include "ipcmsg.h"
#include <string.h>
#include <iostream.h>
#include <fstream.h>

void IPC::send(IPCMsg& msg, const char* source, const char* dest)
{
   ofstream outfile("myFile.dat", ios::out);
   memcpy(buf, (void*)&msg, sizeof(msg));
   outfile.write(buf, sizeof(msg));

}

void IPC::receive(IPCMsg& msg, size_t length) {
   char buf1[256];
   ifstream infile("myFile.dat", ios::in);
   infile.read(buf1, length);
   memcpy((void*)&msg, buf1, length);
   cout << " Copied msg in IPC::receive() x, y = "
        << msg.x << ", " << msg.y << endl;
}

IPCMsg::IPCMsg(int a, int b) : x(a), y(b) {}
IPCMsg::IPCMsg() : x(0), y(0) {}
```

The send() function converts the binary object into a character array, and writes this byte stream to an output file. The receive() function reads the file into a local character array and converts the byte stream back into the original object.

11.11 Summary

In this rather lengthy chapter, we have demonstrated how we can implement many of the OOD design paradigms we are likely to encounter.

The four class relationships are implemented with a mixture of C++ constructs and programming idioms:

- Inheritance—directly using C++ constructs
- Aggregation—include embedded objects as data members of other classes
- Association—include a data member as a pointer to an object of the associated class for cardinality one; as a pointer to a set of pointers that matches the cardinality N.
- Using—include a header file, or make a forward class declaration.

Finite state machine can be implemented using the State design pattern. Each state is modeled as a derived class of an abstract "state" class.

Virtual constructors can be implemented using the Factory Method design pattern. Instances are created dynamically from known subclasses.

Data structures that include a collection of related data elements can be created using structs rather than classes if encapsulation and information hiding is not important or desired.

Binary objects can be converted to byte streams using memcpy() and void*. This type of conversion can be used for I/O operations with fstream file objects.

References

1. Gamma, E. et al., *Design Patterns*, Addison Wesley, Reading, MA 1995.

2. Rumbaugh, J., et al., *Object-Oriented Modeling and Design*, Prentice Hall, Englewood Cliffs, NJ, 1991.

3. Faison, T., Object-Oriented State Machines, *Software Development*, September 1993, p. 37.

4. Copelien, J., *Advanced C++:Programming Styles and Idioms*, Addison-Wesley, Reading, MA 1992.

PART 3

Advanced C++ Topics

In this part we present a number of advanced C++ topics. Long before the C++ ANSI/ISO standardization effort started, the C++ ARM [1] included the specification of template functions and classes, and the use of exception handling. These two features were both labeled as "experimental," but their use and implementations are now widespread. Most modern C++ compilation systems can handle the special syntax and run-time mechanisms necessary to support these important language features.

The importance of the use of templates is evidenced by the acceptance of the Standard Template Library (STL) as a part of the new C++ standard.

The use of exception handling is rapidly becoming a design solution for an integrated fault tolerance strategy.

The emphasis in this part is placed on:

- The creation and use of template functions and classes
- The syntax and semantics of exception handling, and how we can implement an overall fault tolerance strategy
- The structure and use of the STL
- The creation of robust code using the various features of `const`

12

Generic Programming with Templates

One of the most important code reuse features of C++ is the support for generic programming with templates. This allows us to declare a general function or class that can handle objects of any type. To use a templatized function, we simply instantiate it with a specific type. For a templatized class, we first need to instantiate the class with a particular type, and then to declare instances of the class.

A template can be described as a declaration of a class or a function that has one or more C++ types (including built-in types) as parameters. This is provided for in C++ with a special syntax [1, 2].

The focus of this chapter is first on how we create templatized classes and functions, and then we discuss the competition for reuse between the use of templates and inheritance

12.1 Function Templates

The concept of abstracting algorithms with procedures and functions dates back to the programming languages Basic, Fortran, C, and Cobol. Procedure and function prototypes are declared with a set of formal parameters. These abstractions are called by passing actual parameters to them at run-time. Each algorithm can be used as many times as required by each program.

The primary drawback to the use of the old-style procedures and functions is that they cannot be made generic for a set of different types. If we look at a function to determine the smallest element of an array, for example:

```
int minInt(const int* array, int size) {
  int minimum = array[0];
  for (int i = 1; i < size; ++i) {
    if (array[i] < minimum)
      minimum = array[i];
  }
  return minimum;
```

This function is restricted to finding the smallest element of an integer array. If we needed a min() function for doubles, we would have to create a second function:

```
double minDouble(const double* array, int size) {
  double minimum = array[0];
  for (int i = 1; i < size; ++i) {
    if (array[i] < minimum)
      minimum = array[i];
  }
  return minimum;
```

We now have two separate functions that perform the exact same algorithm. And if we need a min() function for a third type, we have to add a third function, etc.

The template feature raises the level of abstraction for algorithms to a higher level. The C++ template feature provides an excellent reuse facility for general functions that operate on different types of objects using the same algorithm. Here is a new version of our min() function:

```
template <class Type>
Type min(const Type* array, int size) {
  Type minimum = array[0];
  for (int i = 1; i < size; ++i) {
    if (array[i] < minimum)
      minimum = array[i];
  }
  return minimum;
}
```

This is a generic function that can be used to find the smallest element in any type of array, provided the assignment and less-than operators exist for the given type. The exact same algorithm is used to find the smallest element of an array of any type. The overloaded operators must be written with this algorithm in mind.

The new keyword *template* is reserved for the declaration of generic functions. The keyword `class` is overloaded here to specify that the formal parameter `Type` is a C++ type, including built-in types.

Instantiating Template Functions

The instantiation of template functions is accomplished by simply invoking the function with the appropriate set of parameters. The compiler determines the types associated with the names of the actual parameters and checks for appropriate matches with the corresponding types of the formal parameters. Code for the instantiated function is then created using the types of the actual parameters.

Here is an example of how we can apply the generic min() function to an array of integers and an array of doubles in the same program:

```
// File: mintempl.cpp

#include <iostream.h>

// Global arrays
int intA[] = {49, 35, 4, 2, 27}; // array of ints
double dblA[] = {4.3, 7.9, 2.7, 6.5, 1.9};
                                // array of doubles

// Application
int main() {
   int size = sizeof (intA) / sizeof (int); // # of elements
   int smInt = min(intA, size); // instantiate for ints

   cout << " Smallest integer = " << smInt << endl;

   size = sizeof (dblA) / sizeof (double); // # of elements
   double smDbl = min(dblA, size);
                        // instantiate for doubles

   cout << " Smallest double = " << smDbl << endl;
   return 0;
}
```

In this mini-application, we are instantiating the templatized min() function first for an array of integers and then for an array of doubles. This is a clear example of how easy it is to reuse existing template functions.

Here is another template function that can perform a swap operation:

```
template <class Type>
void swap (Type& a, Type& b) {
   Type temp (a);
   a = b; // need an assignment operator for Type
   b = temp;
}
```

Any two Type objects can be swapped by this function. If it is a complex type, e.g., including pointers to other embedded objects, the assignment operator must be designed to perform a deep copy rather than simply a copy of the pointer addresses.

Here is a brief summary of C++ generic functions and why they are so important for creating reusable algorithms:

• Generic functions represent a higher level of abstraction than old-style procedures and functions

- Functions that employ the same algorithm on data structures that only differ by type are ideal candidates for generic functions

- Template functions are instantiated with actual parameters at compile time. Storage is not allocated to a function template, only to a function that is instantiated with actual parameters

- The instantiation is automatic, i.e., the compiler creates the functions without the use of any special syntax (see min() for ints and doubles in the mini-application above)

The creation and use of template functions only represents one half of the C++ features regarding generic programming. Of equal, if not larger, importance is the facility for class templates, which is covered in the next section.

12.2 Class Templates

The derivation of new classes from base classes was discussed in Chapter 10, and demonstrated the great potential for reuse via inheritance and polymorphism. There are problems with the use of inheritance, however, such as run-time overhead of virtual functions and the potential lack of type safety.

The use of C++ templates also offers a great potential for reuse with the creation of classes. This becomes quite evident when we look at the STL (Chapter 14). A container class, for example, is an excellent candidate for parameterization. Each container holds a collection of similar objects. The algorithms used to access and manipulate different collections are identical, since each collection only differs from another by a C++ type.

One form of a generic class can be created with the use of only typedefs, and without any templates. Here is an example of a Stack class:

```
// File: stack.h

typedef int Type;
const int BOS = -1; // bottom of stack
const int stackSize = 24;

class Stack {
public:
    Stack (int sz = stackSize); // default ctor
    ~Stack (); // destructor
    bool isEmpty () {return top == BOS;}
    bool isFull ()  {return top == size-1;}
    void push (Type value);
    Type pop ();
private:
```

```
    int top;
    int size;
    Type* array; // int array
};
```

In this case, we have created a pseudo-generic class via the `typedef` declaration in the header file. If we need a Stack class for doubles, we can simply change the typedef declaration. But what are some of the problems with this approach?

The main problem with the typedef approach is that we have to modify the header file each time we need a new Stack class. This means that the class interface has changed. Whenever changes are made to a class header file, the associated source file and the application that depends on this header file must be recompiled. In other words, this is not a very elegant solution.

Another problem with typedefs is that the compiler performs a text substitution without any associated type checking.

Both of these problems associated with the use of typedefs can be overcome with the use of class templates. Here is the same Stack class in a generic form:

```
// File: stack.h
const int BOS = -1; // bottom of stack
const int stackSize = 24;

template<class Type>
class Stack {
public:
  Stack (int sz = stackSize); // default ctor
  ~Stack (); // destructor
  bool isEmpty () {return top == BOS;}
  bool isFull ()  {return top == size-1;}
  void push (Type value);
  Type pop ();
private:
  int top;
  int size;
  Type* array; // generic array
};
```

This is now a general, generic class that can be used to create a stack for any type of elements.

Implementing the Member Functions

As we recommended for the implementation of non-template member functions, the definitions are placed in one or more separate source files. The syntax for implementing class member functions is slightly more complex than for non-template classes:

```
// File: stack.cpp
```

```
#include <assert.h>
#include <stdlib.h>
#include <iostream.h>
#include "stack.h"

template<class Type>
Stack<Type>::Stack(int sz) {
  array = new Type[sz];
  assert(array != 0);
  top  = BOS;
  size = sz;
}

template<class Type>
Stack<Type>::~Stack() {
  delete [] array;
}

template<class Type>
void Stack<Type>::push( Type value ) {
  if (isFull()) {
    cerr << "Attempted push on full stack" << endl;
    exit(-1);
  }
  array[++top] = value;
}

template<class Type>
Type Stack<Type>::pop() {
  if (isEmpty()) {
    cerr << "Attempted pop on empty stack" << endl;
    exit( -1 );
  }
  return array[top-];
}
```

Note that the `template<class Type>` specifier precedes the member function return type, and that the class specifier includes the formal parameter.

Instantiating Template Classes

Instantiating template classes is more complex than we illustrated above for template functions. We first have to create a proper class by supplying the type of the actual parameters for the corresponding formal parameters. For the function templates, we only had to supply the names of the actual parameters; the compiler determined the associated types. Here is how we can use this class in an application:

```
// File: stakmain.cpp
```

```
#include <iostream.h>
#include "stack.h"

int main() {
   cout << "Stack<char>:" << sizeof(Stack<char>) << endl;
   cout << "Stack<int>:" << sizeof(Stack<int>) << endl;
   cout << "Stack<double>:" << sizeof(Stack<double>);
return 0;
}
```

Unlike the function template, the instantiation of a class template is not automatic. We must use the special syntax of the angle brackets to specify the particular C++ type for the instantiation.

The templatized Stack class has only a single formal parameter. We'll now show a graduated example, where we start with a single type parameter and add a non-type parameter as a second formal parameter. Here is an example of a templatized array class, where the fixed array size is declared as a global constant and the type of element is a formal parameter:

```
// File: fxdarray.h

const int ArraySize = 1024;

template <class Type> // formal parameter
class FixedArray {
public:
   FixedArray() // default ctor
      : size(ArraySize), array(new Type[ArraySize]) {}
   FixedArray(const FixedArray<Type>&); // copy ctor

   virtual ~FixedArray() {delete [] array;}

   int getSize() {return size;}
   virtual Type&
   operator[](int index) {return array[index];}
protected:
   int    size;
   Type* array;
};

// Instantiating FixedArray objects:
FixedArray<int> intA;
FixedArray<double> dblA;
FixedArray<String> strA;
```

This is a general class that can be used as-is for any type of array. This can also function as a generalized base class for specialized array classes. Note the virtual destructor and index operator, and the protected section for the attributes. The only problem with this class declaration is the fixed array size.

A more general solution can be obtained by declaring the array size as a second formal parameter:

```
template <class Type, unsigned aSize> // formal param's
class Array {
public:
  Array() : size(aSize) {} // default ctor
  Array(const Array<Type, aSize>&); // copy ctor

  virtual ~Array() {delete [] array;}

  unsigned getSize() {return size;}
  virtual Type&
  operator[](int index) {return array[index];}
protected:
  unsigned size;
  Type     array[aSize];
};

// Instantiating Array objects:
Array<int, 56> intA;
Array<double, 512> dblA;
Array<String, 1024> strA;
```

This is a more general solution, where both the class type and the array size are passed as actual parameters. This can be considered a more efficient version, since we are not invoking the operator new to allocate storage: each array is created on the stack.

A third version of the array class can be created with the array size passed to the default constructor:

```
template <class Type > // formal parameter
class Array {
public:
  Array(unsigned aSize = 1024) // default ctor
         : size(aSize) {array = new Type[size];}
  Array(const Array<Type>&); // copy ctor

  virtual ~Array() {delete [] array;}

  unsigned getSize() {return size;}
  virtual Type&
  operator[](int index) {return array[index];}
protected:
  unsigned size;
  Type*     array;
};

// Instantiating Array objects:
Array<int> intA(56);
Array<double> dblA(512);
Array<String> strA(1024);
```

Summary of Instantiating Template Classes

The instantiation of class templates is a little more complex than for function templates. The use of the angle-brackets is required, and the actual parameters must match the formal parameters by type and number of parameters. Here is a summary of the instantiations made in the examples given above:

```
cout << "Stack<char>:" << sizeof(Stack<char>) << endl;
cout << "Stack<int>:" << sizeof(Stack<int>) << endl;
cout << "Stack<double>:" << sizeof(Stack<double>);

FixedArray<int> intA;
FixedArray<double> dblA;
FixedArray<String> strA;

Array<int, 56> intA;
Array<double, 512> dblA;
Array<String, 1024> strA;

Array<int> intA(56);
Array<double> dblA(512);
Array<String> strA(1024);
```

The Stack and FixedArray classes have only a single formal parameter, whereas the Array class has two.

The type checking between formal and actual parameters is performed at compile time and does not create any additional run-time overhead.

12.3 Nested Template Classes

There is no limitation to the type of actual parameters we can specify in a template declaration, e.g., we can have a container of other containers as nested template classes:

```
Stack<Vector<char*> > strVecStack;
```

In this case, we have a stack of vectors, where each vector is represented with character strings. Note the syntax used for nested classes with a space between the closing angle brackets.

Here is another example, where we have combined the use of a generic array and a generic stack:

```
template<class T, int sz>
class Array {
public:
  Array();
  // ...
```

```
protected:
  int size;
  T    arr[sz];
};


template<class Type>
class Stack {
public:
  Stack();
  // ...
private:
  int    index;
  Type* item;
  int    top;
};


Array<Stack<char*>, 4> strStackArray;
```

We opened this section with the claim that there is no limitation to the kind of C++ types that can be specified as an actual parameter to instantiate a template declaration. This was illustrated with the use of nested template declarations. The use of nested template classes should not be carried to the extreme, however, as the complexity increases drastically and readability becomes a formidable challenge.

A reasonable guideline for a first C++ project is to limit the nesting to the level shown in the two examples above. These examples are typical of the way the STL containers are accessed (see Chapter 14). Any further nesting is almost guaranteed to create readability problems.

12.4 Parameterization versus Inheritance

We have now described two entirely different C++ mechanisms for achieving the desired result of a high degree of code reuse. Deriving new classes from base classes and taking advantage of the automatic mechanism of virtual functions and polymorphism was described in Chapter 10. In this chapter we have introduced the use of templatized functions and classes as another great potential for code reuse. We also mentioned the use of typedefs to create pseudo-generic classes. What are the advantages and disadvantages of each approach, and when do we use one over the other?

Here is a summary of the advantages of using C++ templates:

- Complete type safety. Type checking is performed at compile time to assure proper matching of formal and actual parameters.
- We don't have to derive new classes from base classes. This saves on development time, since there is no need for testing of new classes and associated member functions.

- Several C++ template libraries are now available, including the STL, which is part of the C++ standard.

With all these advantages for templates, where does this leave inheritance? Inheritance still has an important place in large C++ developments. Templates are ideal when we have algorithms operating on data structures that only differ by C++ types. We must also be able to specify a reasonable number of formal parameters for each template specification. For this type of classes and functions, the choice should be for templates. There are numerous instances, however, where a natural hierarchy of base classes and derived classes will occur. In this case, the choice is for inheritance.

One way to summarize the difference between the reuse aspects of inheritance and templatized functions and classes is to consider inheritance the extensibility and reuse of types (classes), and the use of templates as reuse of source code.

12.5 Summary

The use of C++ templates has a great potential for code reuse. Templates are used with functions and classes. Instantiations of function templates is automatic. Class templates must be instantiated using the special angle-bracket syntax. Special syntax is also required for the implementation of member functions.

The compiler performs type checking by matching formal and actual parameters by C++ type and by the number of parameters. Formal parameters can include a mixture of user-defined and built-in types. They can also include a mixture of C++ types and values.

The use of templates has a number of advantages over the derivation of new classes from base classes and using inheritance. They support type safety, and do not suffer any run-time overhead compared to the use of virtual functions.

Template classes are ideal candidates for collection classes, and are used extensively to support the C++ STL.

References

1. Ellis, M.A., and Stroustrup, B., *The Annotated C++ Reference Manual,* Addison-Wesley, Reading, MA, 1990.

2. Working Paper for Draft Proposed International Standard for Information Systems - Programming Language C++, Doc No: X3J16/96-0225, WG21/N1043, 2 December 1996.

13

Exception Handling

Most programmers have used some type of error handling mechanism to help them detect and report run-time errors. C programmers typically use some combination of run-time library functions and macros like `raise()`/`signal()`, `assert()`, and `setjmp()`/`longjmp()`. In many cases, these features are used as an individual programmer sees fit, without an overall design guideline for an entire project.

C++ has introduced exception handling as a potential mechanism for implementing a design strategy to support a measure of fault tolerance. There is language support for declaring, raising, and handling exceptions. What is missing is a design strategy to take full advantage of this language feature.

This chapter presents a detailed exposition of the exception handling features available in C++, and includes a suggested general design approach that makes efficient use of these features. Chapter 20 will describe how exception handling has been implemented in the Microsoft Foundation Class (MFC) library. Here we will explain in detail how to:

- Declare exceptions
- Raise exceptions
- Handle exceptions
- Propagate exceptions
- Position a try block

First, let's discuss the run-time situations when we should be concerned with exception handling, and how we can create a taxonomy of exceptions that can handle all of these situations.

13.1 A Taxonomy of Exceptions

Our goal is to create applications that are robust. This means that they should in-clude some means of fault tolerance for, at least, detecting and reporting run-time anomalies. It would also be great if we could include a *correction* mechanism to allow an application to continue executing, either automatically or after a user has taken corrective actions.

Another notion associated with the concept of robustness is that when a run-time problem occurs, it does not hang the entire computer, leaving the user with the only recourse of rebooting.

A properly designed exception handling mechanism can support the overall goal of robustness. It should be clear by now that we are not simply talking about error han-dling, i.e., the detection and reporting of run-time bugs, but an entire range of run-time problems. Here is a suggested taxonomy of exceptions that will support fault tolerance:

- Anticipated exceptional conditions

- Protection of server software

- Detection and reporting of hardware failures

- Detection and reporting of unanticipated errors (bugs)

Anticipated exceptional conditions refer to anomalies that are expected to occur during the normal execution of an application, especially if the application executes for long time periods. One example of an exception in this category is an end of file (EOF) condition; another is reaching the end of "handles" to graphics resources. Nei-ther of these two conditions should cause an application to hang, and we should be able to continue execution after handling such an exception.

Protection of server software is necessary to make sure the clients use that soft-ware properly. This applies, for example, to parameters that clients are passing when calling functions in a library. Examples of exceptional conditions in this category in-clude trying to get an element from an empty queue, or passing an integer value in-stead of a string to an ASCII-to-integer conversion function.

The ability to detect and report hardware failures can add a significant measure of fault tolerance. When such a condition is detected and reported, we have a chance to save valuable data, and we will know which particular hardware element failed.

Detecting and reporting unanticipated errors (bugs) is what we normally associate with error handling. Note that this is just one of several types of exceptions we would like to handle, i.e., our exception handling strategy encompasses much more than simply detecting and reporting bugs. A significant feature for this category is that we cannot give these exceptions a name, since they are unknown. All of the exceptions in the previous categories will be given specific names and we will create handlers for each named exception. Bugs can only be handled with unnamed exception handlers.

C++ examples for exceptions in each category will be given in a later section in this chapter.

13.2 Declaring Exceptions

C++ exceptions are treated as types and can be declared in several different ways:

- Nested classes
- Independent classes
- Enumeration types
- Inheritance hierarchy
- Throw list

Nested Classes

Here is a class library that is used by clients who need to manipulate mathematical entities:

```
class MathLib {
public:
   double mathFunc1(int n, int k, double x);
   double mathFunc2(...);
   ...
   Boolean mathFuncN(...);
// Exceptions:
   class OutOfRange { }; // empty class
   class Overflow { };   // empty class
   class InvalidData {
   public:
     int    index; // data elements associated
     double value; // with InvalidData
   };
private:
   // data members
};
```

The exception declarations shown here are nested within the `MathLib` class and are thus tightly coupled to this class, just as ordinary class members are tightly coupled to their encapsulating class.

A deliberate design decision has been made in declaring the exceptions as nested classes: They will only be associated with the `MathLib` class and are not needed for any other classes.

An exception class can be empty, as shown for `OutOfRange` and `Overflow`, or it can include data members as shown for `InvalidData`. The data members are used to provide details about a particular exception. These data members should be made public to simplify access. It does not make sense to have to provide special access member functions to gain access to data members associated with an exception.

Clients of the class `MathLib` must be prepared to handle the exceptions within the code that calls the `MathLib` functions. Exceptions declared in the `MathLib` class interface will not be handled within the member function implementations, they will be propagated out of the class and back to the clients that call a particular function that may raise an exception.

Independent Classes

Exceptions can be declared as individual, independent classes, i.e., not nested as was shown in the previous section. Independent exception classes can be reused anywhere within an application; they can also serve as base classes for derived exceptions. Here is an example of an independent exception class for a parameterized Array class:

```
// File: array.h
...
const int ArraySize = 256;

class ArrayError { // independent exception class
public:
  ArrayError (int size, void* vptr)
             : aErrSize(size), memPtr(vptr) {}
  int    aErrSize;
  void* memPtr;
};

template <class Type>
class Array {
public:
  Array(int siz = ArraySize) {
    if (siz < 1) // legal size array?
      throw ArrayError(siz, 0);
    size  = siz;
    array = new Type[size];

    if (array == 0) // memory allocated?
      throw ArrayError (siz, array);
  }

  virtual ~Array() {delete [] array;}
  int getSize() {return size;}
  virtual Type&
  operator[](int index) {return array[index];}

protected:
  int    size;
  Type* array;
};
```

The exception class `ArrayError` is not nested within the `Array` class, and can be used by any other class or function that needs this type of exception. If we had only wanted the `ArrayError` exception to be associated with the `Array` class, it should be nested within the `Array` class.

Note that the two data members of the `ArrayError` exception class have been placed in the public section. We don't want to create additional access functions for these data members.

Enumeration Types

Since an exception is a type, it does not have to be specified as a class. We can, for example, declare exceptions as a set of data values in an enumerated type [1, p. 302]:

```cpp
// File: excpenum.cpp

#include <iostream.h>

enum MathException {OutOfRange, Overflow, Underflow,
                    ZeroDivide, NotDefined};

void mathFunc(int index);

int main() {
  try {
   //mathFunc(-5); //  OutOfRange thrown here
    mathFunc(66000); // Overflow thrown here
  }

  catch (MathException& mathExcept) {
    switch (mathExcept) {
      case OutOfRange:
        cout << " OutOfRange exception in main()" << endl;
        break;
      case Overflow:
        cout << " Overflow exception in main()" << endl << endl;
        break;
      case Underflow:
        // ...
        break;
      case ZeroDivide:
        // ...
        break;
      case NotDefined:
        // ...
        break;
      default:
        cout << " default in main()" << endl;
    }
  }
  return 0;
}
```

```
void mathFunc(int index) {
  const int MaxSize = 65536; // overflow limit

  if (index < 0)
    throw OutOfRange;
  else if (index > 65536)
    throw Overflow;
  // ...
}
```
                         Output:

Overflow exception in main()

In this case, the handler in main() is prepared to catch any of the enumerated exceptions that can be thrown by `mathFunc()`. The exception is raised in the server software (e.g., a library function) and the handler is placed in the client software unit. We'll say more about the handling of exceptions in later sections.

Inheritance Hierarchy

Exceptions can be declared with an inheritance hierarchy to take advantage of polymorphism and run-time type information. The exceptions declared earlier for the `MathClass` could be derived as follows:

```
class MathException { };
class OutOfRange : public MathException { };
class Overflow :   public MathException { };
class Underflow :  public MathException { };
class ZeroDivide : public MathException { };
```

The inheritance rules that apply to instances of ordinary base and derived classes also apply to exceptions. Here is an inheritance hierarchy of exception classes from the STL that we will revisit in Chapter 14:

```
class exception { };
class bad_alloc : public exception { };
class logic_error : public exception { };
class invalid_argument : public logic_error { };
class length_error : public logic_error { };
class out_of_range : public logic_error { };
```

Another example of an exception hierarchy is the one used in the Microsoft Foundation Class (MFC) library [2]:

```
class CException { };
class CArchiveException : public CException { };
class CDaoException : public CException { };
class CDBException : public CException { };
class CFileException : public CException { };
```

```
class CMemoryException : public CException { };
class CNotSupportedException : public CException { };
class COleException : public CException { };
class COleDispatchException : public CException { };
class CResourceException : public CException { };
class CUserException : public CException { };
```

We will show how some of these exceptions are used in the MFC framework in Chapter 20.

Throw List

A function prototype can be augmented with a `throw` list as a suffix:

```
// Exceptions of type String and char* are expected
//    to be raised:
  void fException () throw (String&, char*);

// No exceptions will be raised:
  void fNoException () throw ();
```

The throw list includes a set of exceptions which are declared by type, and which can be raised when the function is called. No exceptions are expected to be thrown by a function whose throw list is empty. This may sound a bit vague as a specification, but there is only a limited amount of type checking performed for a throw list, and its use is primarily for documentation purposes. Throw lists will probably not be widely used until type checking is added.

13.3 Raising Exceptions

C++ exceptions can be raised with a `throw` expression wherever an executable statement is allowed, including within constructors and destructors. The keyword `raise` is already used by a function in the C run-time library, and throw is used instead. These two words (raise and throw) are normally used interchangeably when we describe verbally that an exception is "raised."

In the `Message` class that follows, the exception `NoConnection` is declared in the public section of the class interface. This exception is raised in the member function `SendMessage()`:

```
// File Message.h
//...
class Message {
public:
  Message ();
  ~Message ();
```

```
    void SendMessage (const char*);
    void RetrieveMessage (...);
    void DeleteMessage (...);
  // Exceptions:
    class NoConnection { }; // exception raised in
                            //   SendMessage
  private:
    date* timeTag;
    char* sender;
    char* receiver;
    char* text;
  };

  void Message::SendMessage (const char* msg) {
    // ...
    if (getConnection ())
      Send (msg);
    else
      throw NoConnection(); // raise exception
    // will not return here if exception is thrown
    ...
  }
```

When an exception is raised, the run-time system starts looking for an exception handler that corresponds to the thrown exception. The client program using the class `Message` should be prepared to provide the handler for the exception.

The C++ exception handling mechanism is considered non-resumptive, and the program control will not return to the statement immediately following the throw statement. The program will continue to execute after the code associated with an exception handler, or block of handlers (see below).

We have already seen how we can declare exception classes that include data members. These data members can be returned as parameters when an exception is raised (i.e., we are passing values to the exception constructor). Here is a different version of the `NoConnection` exception declaration in the `Message` class:

```
  class Message {
  public:
    // ...
    void SendMessage (const char*);
    class NoConnection { // exception class
    public:
      NoConnection (const char*); // constructor
      char* msg;   // data member
    };
  private:
    // ...
  };

  void Message::SendMessage (const char* msg) {
    // ...
    if (getConnection ())
```

```
        Send (msg);
    else
        throw NoConnection (msg); // raise exception and
                                  // pass the data to the
                                  // handler
}
```

The message we wanted to send (if we had received a proper connection) is now included as a parameter when the NoConnection exception is raised. We had to add a constructor to the exception declaration to allow for the passing of the message as a parameter.

Here is another example using the MathLib class shown earlier:

```
class MathLib {
public:
    double mathFunc1(int n, int k, double x);
    double mathFunc2(...);
    ...
    Boolean mathFuncN(...);
// Exceptions:
    class OutOfRange { };
    class Overflow { };
    class InvalidData {
    public:
        InvalidData (int i, double x)
                        : index(i), value(x){}

        int    index; // data elements associated
        double value; // with InvalidData
    };
private
    // ...
};

    double MathLib::mathFunc1(int n, int k, double x) {
    // ...
    trow InvalidData (n, x);
    ...
}
```

In this example, we are raising the exception InvalidData and pass parameters that correspond to the two data members index and value, respectively. The handler that catches this exception will interpret the values of the data members, and may, perhaps, be able to correct the erroneous values or print a report. In the next section, we will analyze how exceptions are handled.

13.4 Handling Exceptions

C++ exception handlers are encapsulated in catch statements. A handler is placed immediately after a `try` block, i.e., the set of statements where an exception can be raised:

```cpp
#include "Message.h"
// ...
int main () {

  Message localMsg;
  // ...
  try {
    // ...
    localMsg.SendMessage ("ack1");
    // ...
  }
  catch (Message::NoConnection) {
    cout << "NoConnection exception in SendMessage"
         << endl;
  }
  catch (...) { // unknown exception"
    cout << "Unknown exception captured in main()"
         << endl;
  }
  return 0;
}
```

The handler for the NoConnection exception is placed after the try block. This catch block will handle any exception raised as a result of executing `SendMessage()` or any lower functions in its calling hierarchy. In this case, we don't need to list a parameter name for the exception, since we are not referencing an actual exception object.

We can place any number of exception handlers at the end of a `try` block. The relative location of the handlers is extremely important, however, as the run-time system searches in lexical order for a match between an exception thrown and a suitable handler. The run-time system gives control to the handler of the first match (not the best match!). After that handler has completed its execution, control is transferred to the statement following the last catch block. Any handlers that may follow the one that is handling the current exception are skipped.

This example illustrates the importance of catch block positioning. We placed the handler to catch the unknown exceptions (`catch (...)`) *after* the exception handler for the named exception NoConnection. If we had placed the handler for the unknown exception first, this would "match" the named exception raised, and the named exception handler for NoConnection would not be executed.

Here we are catching an exception that is passed as an object:

```cpp
#include "Message.h"
// ...
int main () {

  Message localMsg;
  // ...
```

```
try {
  // ...
  localMsg.SendMessage ("ack1");
  // ...
}
catch (NoConnection& nConn) {
  cout << "NoConnection exception in SendMessage: "
       << nConn.msg << endl;
}
return 0;
}
```

The message we had attempted to send can be accessed as a data member of the exception object. This can provide additional information about why the exception was raised and support a level of fault tolerance.

Note how we are passing the exception object to the handler by reference, rather than by value. When an exception object is passed from within a `try` block, a copy of that object is made. The copy is passed to the handler; the original is destroyed when the stack is unwound. If we pass an exception object by value, a second copy is created for use within the handler. When we pass by reference, the copy made within the `try` block scope is used as the exception object within the handler, and we are saving the overhead of making a second copy.

13.5 Propagation of Exceptions

C++ exception handling is considered *non-resumptive*. Separate code sections are used to handle an exception that is raised anywhere within the scope of a handler. After the handler has completed its executable instructions, program control is not returned to the statement immediately following the point at which the exception was raised.

If a matching handler is not found after the `try` block where the exception was raised, a handler is sought in the next enclosing block of the calling chain. The stack is unwound and destructors are called as this process continues up the calling tree.

When a matching handler is found, control is transferred to that handler. After the handler has completed its executable instructions, control is transferred to a location following that handler (or set of handlers), regardless of how high up in the calling tree the match was found. Control will not be returned back down the calling tree to the point where the exception was raised. This mechanism is significantly different from calling ordinary functions.

If a matching handler is not found anywhere within the application, the run-time system transfers control to the function `terminate()`. This function will abort the program.

Special considerations should be given to exceptions that are raised and propagated from a constructor. This is illustrated with an example in Section 13.9.

13.6 Implementing the Exception Taxonomy

The design guidelines listed above suggest that we need to prepare handlers for four different categories of exceptions. Examples for these four categories are given below.

Anticipated Exceptional Conditions

An application that executes for a long period of time may experience certain run-time conditions that can be handled with exceptions. Let's assume that a system uses a global resource "handle" (nHandle) that has a fixed range of values. When the last value is reached, we can use an exception to reinitialize the handle:

```
long getHandle () {
  // ...
  try {
    nHandle++;
  }
  catch (...) {
    nHandle = 0; // reinitialize
  }
  return nHandle;
}
```

An alternative strategy could be to check the current value of nHandle with an if-statement before it is incremented. This would create a larger run-time overhead, since we would have to check every time the function is called. The overhead of raising and handling the exception will only be incurred each time we run out of values, which is rare, and may never happen. The overhead of maintaining the try block when an exception is not raised is minimal compared to the use of an if-statement.

Protection of Server Software

Software which is functioning in a "server" role, and is used by a number of clients, should be protected from erroneous or inconsistent input data furnished by these clients:

```
class MathLib {
public:
  class OutOfRange { };
  // ...
  int math1 (int);
  // ...
private:
  // ...
};
```

```
MathLib::math1 (int i) {
  if (i < 0) // check for erroneous input data
    throw OutOfRange (); // caller must handle exception
  // normal processing
  ...
}
```

Unreliable results and potentially corrupted data are prevented by checking the data values passed by the clients. Note that if an exception is raised, it is propagated back to the caller.

Detection and Reporting of Hardware Failures

Exceptions can be used to detect and report hardware devices that fail to respond to expected commands:

```
{
  // ...
  hwOutBuf = 0;
  hwInBuf  = input; // expect device to respond by putting
                    // data in hwOutBuf
  // ...
  for (int i = maxRetries; i > 0; i-) { // polling loop
    if (hwOutBuf)
      return hwOutBuf;
  }
  throw deviceXFault; // device X did not respond within
                      // maxRetries
}
```

The polling loop counts down for a maximum number of retries for the device to respond by placing a value in a register that we have mapped to a memory location (hwOutBuf). No catch block is included here to handle the exception when it is raised. The handling will be done at a higher level.

Detection and Reporting of Unanticipated Errors (Bugs)

Here we are using an exception to detect and report bugs:

```
void func (int x, double y) {
  try {
    // normal processing here
  }
  catch (...) { // unexpected exception (bug)
    cerr << "bug detected in func() " << x << y << endl;
    throw; // re-raise exception
  }
}
```

Note that this handler is unnamed, since we are catching an unexpected bug. We report the bug by printing out a message, and propagate the exception up the calling chain by re-raising the same (unnamed) exception.

Positioning of Exception Handlers

As we have illustrated with the four examples given above, the positioning of an exception handler depends on the exception category we are implementing. In the first case (anticipated exceptional conditions), the handler is placed immediately following the try block. Normal processing continues after the re-initialization of the handle (nHandle).

In the second case, the exception OutOfRange is declared in the class specification of MathLib. This tells a client of this class that the exception can be raised in one or more of the class member functions. The client software has to handle this exception; no handler is placed inside the function math1() which raises the exception.

In the third case, we are not including a handler, since this function can only detect the fault, and not correct it. The detection of a hardware fault is propagated out of the function via the deviceXFault exception. Any potential fault correction will have to be done at a higher level.

In the fourth, and last, category, we are detecting an unknown bug. The exception we are catching may have been raised by the run-time system or by one of our application functions raising an unknown exception. The handler for the unknown exception is placed at the end of the try block, and we can thus catch any unknown exception that is raised during the execution of func(). After the bug is reported, the exception is re-raised, and may be handled at a higher level. The most important point to note here is that we report the bug immediately, and then determine how the exception should be handled (or not handled at all). We could also choose to end the program right here by calling terminate() which, by default, calls abort().

A strategy for initial debugging of a large system is to encapsulate all functions by a try block with a handler for an unknown exception. This can provide early detection of bugs. The exception handling features can subsequently be removed prior to releasing a production version to avoid the run-time overhead that exception handling imposes.

13.7 Exception Handling in C++ Libraries

Exception handling of the second category should be included for all C++ libraries. This provides for a level of protection of the server software and a uniform exception handling mechanism that the client software can respond to.

All exceptions raised within class member functions and exported to the callers should be shown in the class specification. There should be no internal, hidden exceptions that could be propagated out from any of the library functions. Clients of the class libraries must include the necessary exception handlers, and expect to handle all the exceptional conditions.

A basic assumption for using the recommended strategy is that the C++ compiler and run-time platform we are using can support the mechanism. Most major C++ development platforms now support a full implementation. Some platforms have utilized an interim "structured exception handling" mechanism using macros for the corresponding throw, catch, and try constructs. This mixing of macros with pure C++ code is less than ideal; it is not portable between platforms and may become non-supportable at the vendor's whim.

A design issue to be aware of is the introduction of non-local program flow and the potential loss of resources [3]:

```
void f() {
  Widget* w = new Widget;
  g (); // exception could be raised from here
  delete w;
}
```

If an exception is raised in g() or in any function it may call, the destructor for the object w will not be called. Any widget resource that is normally freed when w exits the scope of f(), will now not be freed, and thus causing memory and resource leaks. A low level of remaining resources can sometimes be more serious than low memory for windows-oriented programs. One solution to this problem is to include a try block for the statements that may raise an exception, and an unnamed local handler:

```
void f() {
  Widget* w = new Widget;
  try {
    g (); // exception could be raised from here
  }
  catch (...) {
    delete w;
    throw WidgetException; // handle elsewhere
  }
  delete w; // normal case
}
```

If an exception is raised, cleanup of the resource created with the operator new is now performed within the exception handler. The exception WidgetException is raised in the handler and will be handled at a higher level. Precious resources are retained here and execution can continue from the next handler.

There is no problem with the cleanup of local objects that are allocated statically. If an exception is propagated out of a function scope, C++ guarantees that destructors for lo objects are invoked when the call stack is unwound. The problem associated with objects allocated using the operator new is thus avoided for objects allocated statically.

13.8 Sample Application Using Exception Handling

We will now create an application to illustrate the concepts described above. This application was picked to demonstrate the combined use of template classes, inheritance, and exception handling. It also provides a summary of the various exception handling design decisions we have to make.

The classes provided for the sample application include a parameterized array class and a derived class that provides for range checking of array indexes:

```
// File: array.h

#ifndef ARRAY_H
#define ARRAY_H

const int ArraySize = 12;

class InvalidArray { // exception for Array
public:
  InvalidArray (int sz, void* vptr)
                      : asize(sz), memptr(vptr) {}
  int   asize;
  void* memptr;
};


template <class Type>
class Array {
public:
  Array(int sz=ArraySize) {
  if (sz < 1)
    throw InvalidArray(sz, 0);

  size = sz;
  ia = new Type[ size ];

  if (ia == 0) // rather than assert()
    throw InvalidArray (sz, ia);
  }

  virtual ~Array() { delete [] ia; }
int getSize() { return size; }
virtual Type&
  operator[](int index) { return ia[index]; } // no checking

protected:
  int size;
  Type *ia;
};

#endif
```

```
// File: arrngchk.h

#ifndef ARRNGCHK_H
#define ARRNGCHK_H

#include "array.h"

class IndexError { // exception for RangeCheckArray
public:
   IndexError(int indx)
     : index(indx) {}
   int index;
};

template <class Type>
class RangeCheckArray : public Array<Type> {
public:
   RangeCheckArray(int sz = ArraySize) : Array<Type>( sz ){};
   Type& operator[](int index) {
     if (index < 0 || index >= size) // range checking
       throw IndexError(index);
     return ia[index];
   }
};

#endif
```

Declaring Exceptions

We have seen that exceptions can be declared as classes or enumerated types. The exception classes can be represented as an inheritance hierarchy, as individual classes, or as nested classes. In this case, we decide to declare the exception associated with the Array class as an independent class:

```
class InvalidArray{
public:
   InvalidArray(int sz, void* vptr)
                          : asize(sz), memptr(vptr) {}
   int   asize;
   void* memptr;
};
```

This exception will be raised whenever an instantiation of Array<T> is attempted with an invalid array size, or if memory cannot be allocated by the new operator. The checking, and potential raising of an exception, is done in the constructor. We decided to make the two data members public here to avoid having to add two access functions to support the exception handlers.

To illustrate that template classes, inheritance, and exception handling can work in perfect harmony, we declare another exception for the derived class that includes range checking of indexes:

```
class IndexError {
public:
  IndexError(int indx)
    : index(indx) {}
  int index;
};
```

This exception will be raised in the index operator of the class `RangeCheckArray` if an illegal index size is detected. Again, the data member is public, since it doesn't make sense to provide an access function.

Raising Exceptions

An exception is raised whenever an exceptional condition occurs. This includes expected events for which we can write named handlers, and unexpected events that can only be handled with an unnamed handler.

The constructor for the Array class first checks if the current instantiation is invoked with a valid size. If not, the `InvalidArray` exception is raised with the invalid size and a constructor message.

```
Array::Array(int sz=ArraySize) {
  if (sz < 1)
    throw InvalidArray(sz, "Array::Array()");

  size = sz;
  ia = new Type[ size ];

  if (ia == 0)
    throw InvalidArray (sz, 0);
}
```

If the size is OK, but `new` fails to allocate sufficient dynamic storage, the `InvalidArray` exception is raised with the size and 0 as the parameters.

The exception for an invalid index is raised inside the `operator[]` of the `RangeCheckArray` class:

```
Type& RangeCheckArray::operator[](int index) {
  if (index < 0 || index >= size) // range checking
    throw IndexError(index);
  return ia[index];
}
```

This exception is thrown with the illegal index as a parameter.

Positioning of Exception Handlers

The positioning of exception handlers is determined by when the exception should be handled and by whom. In the current application, the handlers are placed at the end of the main program. This means that there will not be any handlers inside the `Array` constructor or the RangeCheckArray index operator. We thus have a design which represents the second category of Protection of Server Software.

Figure 13.1 shows the application using the `Array` and `RangeCheckArray` classes with the exception handlers:

```cpp
// File: arrmain.cpp

#include <iostream.h>
#include "array.h"
#include "arrngchk.h"

template <class Type>
void swap(Array<Type> &array, int i, int j) {
  int tmp = array[i]; // no checking of index range
  array[i] = array[j];
  array[j] = tmp;
}

template <class Type>
void swapRC(RangeCheckArray<Type> &array, int i, int j) {
  int tmp = array[i]; // index range checked
  array[i] = array[j];
  array[j] = tmp;
}


int main() { // application
  try {
    Array<int> intArr(-1); // illegal size (excception raised)
    RangeCheckArray<int> intRCArr;

    cout << " swap() with Array<int> intArr" << endl;
    int size = intArr.getSize();
    swap( intArr, 1, size ); // illegal swap (no exception)

    cout << " swap() with RangeCheckArray<int> intRCArr" << endl;
    size = intRCArr.getSize();
    swapRC( intRCArr, 1, size ); // illegal swap
                                 // (exception raised)
    cout << " end of try-block" << endl;
  } // end of try block

  catch (InvalidArray& iA) {
    cout << "\n InvalidArray exception in main().  size="
         << iA.asize;
    cout << "\t memptr=" << (char*)iA.memptr << endl;
```

```
    }

    catch (IndexError& iE) {
       cout << " IndexError exception in main().  index="
            << iE.index;
       cout << endl;
    }

    catch (...) {
       cout << " Unknown exception in main()" << endl << endl;
    }
    return 0;
}
```

Figure 13.1 Application Using the `Array` and `RangeCheckArray` Classes

The exception handlers have been placed in sequence at the end of the application. Note the last handler for an unknown exception. This type of handler must always be placed last in a sequence of handlers. If it is not, the named exceptions will not be caught, since an unnamed handler will catch any exception, named or unnamed.

Scope of The Try Block

The scope of a try block includes all the statements between the opening and closing brace following the *try* key word. This scope determines the range of executable statements for which an exception can be handled. Widely different run-time results can occur, depending upon how the try block is arranged and which exception handlers are available. We will discuss these concepts using a number of different scenarios.

Scenario 1

The scope shown in Figure 13.1 will catch any exception raised anywhere in the program, since it includes the declaration of the objects `intArr` and `intRCArr` and all of the executable statements within the program. The first of the objects is declared with an illegal size parameter to illustrate the exception being raised within the Array constructor with the following result:

```
InvalidArray exception in main().  size=-1
memptr=Array::Array()
```

The program terminates normally via the return statement after the execution of the exception handler. The exception raised in the Array constructor was propagated to the enclosing block, i.e., main(). Program control gets transferred directly to the named handler and terminates with the return statement.

Scenario 2

If we reduce the scope of the try block to exclude the object declarations, a different scenario takes place, as shown in Figure 13.2.

```
int main() {
  Array<int> intArr(-1); // illegal size (excception raised)
  RangeCheckArray<int> intRCArr;

  try {
    cout << " swap() with Array<int> intArr" << endl;
    int size = intArr.getSize();
    swap( intArr, 1, size ); // illegal swap (no exception)
    // same as in Figure 13.1
  } // end of try block

  catch (InvalidArray& iA) { // now outside the scope
    cout << "\n InvalidArray exception in main().  size="
         << iA.asize;
    cout << "\t memptr=" << (char*)iA.memptr << endl;
  }
  // same as in Figure 13.1
  return 0;
} // end of main()
```

   Output:

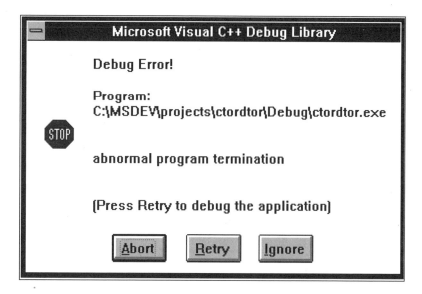

Figure 13.2 Reducing the Scope of the `try` Block

The exception `InvalidArray` is still raised within the Array constructor. In this case, however, the handler for this exception is outside the scope of the `try` block. The exception gets propagated from the `Array` constructor to `main()` as in scenario 1, but since the handler is outside the scope, the exception gets propagated further to the enclosing block of `main()`, which is at the system level. The result is the abnormal program termination via a call to `terminate()` and `abort()`.

Scenario 3

In the two previous scenarios, the program never executed beyond the attempt to declare the invalid instance of Array<int>. Figure 13.3 illustrates a third scenario, which makes valid declarations for the two instances, invokes an illegal swap for the Array<int> object intArr, and then attempts to make an illegal swap for the RangeCheckArray<int> object intRCArr:

```
int main() {
  try {
    Array<int> intArr; // legal size
    RangeCheckArray<int> intRCArr;

    cout << " swap() with Array<int> intArr" << endl;
    int size = intArr.getSize();
    swap(intArr, 1, size); // illegal swap (no exception)

    cout << " swap() with RangeCheckArray<int> intRCArr" << endl;
    size = intRCArr.getSize();
    swapRC(intRCArr, 1, size); // illegal swap (exception raised)
    cout << " end of try-block" << endl;
  }
  // same as in Figure 13.1
  // ...
  return 0;
}
```

```
        Output:

          swap() with Array(int) intArr
          swap() with RangeCheckArray(int) intRCArr
```

There is no exception raised for the illegal swap of the Array<int> object, since the `Array::operator[]()` does not do any index checking when the arrays in swap() are accessed with an illegal size. The system detects a program abnormality ("Damage: after Normal block (#30) at 0x00420A70") and gives us a chance to start the debugger.

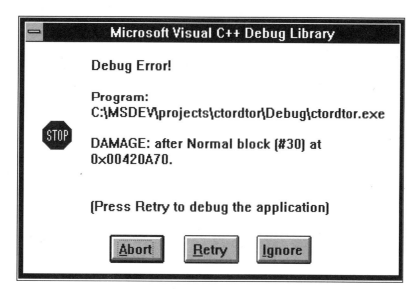

Figure 13.3 Attempting an Illegal Swap

Scenario 4

In the final scenario, the object constructions are legal, the swap for the Array object is legal, and the swap for the `RangeCheckArray` is illegal, as shown in Figure 13.4.

```
int main() {
  try {
    Array<int> intArr; // legal size
    RangeCheckArray<int> intRCArr;

    cout << " swap() with Array<int> intArr" << endl;
    int size = intArr.getSize();
    swap( intArr, 1, size-1 ); // legal swap

    cout << " swap() with RangeCheckArray<int> intRCArr" << endl;
    size = intRCArr.getSize();
    swapRC( intRCArr, 1, size ); // illegal swap
                                 // (exception raised)
    cout << " end of try-block" << endl;
  }
  // same as in Figure 13.1
  // ...
  return 0;
}
```

```
Output:
swap() with Array(int) intArr
swap() with RangeCheckArray(int) intRCArr
IndexError exception in main().  index= 12
```

Figure 13.4 Legal and Illegal Swaps

When swapRC() is accessed with an illegal index, the RangeCheckArray::operator[]()
detects this condition and raises the IndexError exception. This exception is propagated to main() with program control transferred to the second exception handler. A normal
program termination is then executed via the return statement.

It should be clear from these scenarios that the scope of a try block and the positioning of the exception handlers are the two most important design decisions
that must be made for any application that uses the suggested exception handling
strategy.

13.9 Exceptions and Interrupts

We have seen how C++ exceptions get propagated out of a local scope if there is no
handler in that scope. The run-time propagation mechanism automatically starts looking for a handler in the next enclosing scope.

We would like to take advantage of this same mechanism in the context of interrupt handlers. A common strategy for detecting when an interrupt handler has completed its processing, is for the function that issued the interrupt to sit in a polling
loop and check a flag, or check if something has been written to a certain memory
location. This mechanism can be greatly simplified if the interrupt handler can simply raise an exception when it is finished with its processing. For this to work as we
would like, the exception must be propagated out of the interrupt handler and back
to the function that affected the interrupt.

We will now test this mechanism by combining the signal() and raise() functions
from the C run-time library with the C++ exception strategy:

```
// File: exinterr.cpp
// Program to check how an exception gets propagated
//    from an interrupt handler

#include <iostream.h>
#include <signal.h>

void handleInterrupt(int x);

class CException {};

int main() {
```

```
    cout << " Setting up the interrupt handler in main()" << endl;
    signal(SIGINT, handleInterrupt); // register the interrupt
                                     // handler

    try {
      cout << " Raising the interrupt in main()" << endl;
      raise(SIGINT); // execute the interrupt
      cout << " Exception not propagated back to main() if here "
           << endl;
    }

    catch (CException& cexpt) {
      cout << " CException caught by handler in main()" << endl;
    }

    catch (...) {
      cout << " Unknown exception caught in main()" << endl;
    }
    return 0;
  }

void handleInterrupt(int x) {
  cout << " Throwing the CException in handleInterrupt()" <<
endl;
  throw CException();
}
```

```
    Output:

        Setting up the interrupt handler in main()
        Raising the interrupt in main()
        Throwing the CException in handleInterrupt()
        CException caught by handler in main()
```

After registering handleInterrupt() with the signal() function, control is transferred to that interrupt handler via the raise() function. The exception CException is thrown within the interrupt handler. Since there is no exception handler inside handleInterrupt(), the exception gets propagated out of this function. We can tell from the output that the exception gets handled by the first catch() statement in main(), which is exactly the expected effect.

We have thus demonstrated that we can effectively combine the signal()/raise() mechanism of the C run-time library with a C++ exception handling strategy. This mechanism will only work if we are within the context of one process. C++ exceptions will not get propagated across multiple processes.

13.10 The Cost of Using Exceptions

The cost of implementing an exception handling strategy can be attributed to the following factors:

- Additional system data structures
- Run-time execution overhead
- Extra coding
- Additional complexity

Additional system data structures are required to implement the exception handling mechanism. This may include such things as pointers to the start and end of `try` blocks and lists of exception handlers. This will not amount to any more storage overhead than what we would have to include for a traditional error handling strategy.

There is a definite amount of run-time overhead associated with the use of C++ exceptions. One part of this overhead comes from the maintenance of the `try` blocks. This represents a minimal amount of overhead, and will be less than the traditional use of `assert()` functions or macros. The major part of the run-time overhead is associated with executing a `throw` statement. This event will set off a chain of related events such as locating a handler, propagating an exception, unwinding of stacks, and invoking destructors. In the (hopefully) rare case when an exception is raised, this overhead should simply be regarded as a necessary cost for implementing more robust software.

There is an additional coding and testing effort required for implementing the recommended exception handling strategy. This effort includes declaration of exceptions, determination of `try` blocks, writing `throw` statements, and the implementation of the `catch` blocks. These extra coding costs are not any higher than the comparable costs of using assert(), raise()/signal(), or setjmp()/longjmp(). Another reason for not using these coding combinations is that they don't provide for C++ destructors. If we have stack-based objects in a function that calls `longjmp`, for example, the objects will go out of scope undestructed.

There is definitely an additional complexity and a learning cost associated with the implementation of exceptional handling. This complexity will only manifest itself on the first major C++ project within an organization using these new features. It is important to realize that all of the features regarding the declaration, raising, handling, and propagation of C++ exceptions are specified in the ARM.

The use of an exception handling taxonomy will greatly reduce the ad-hoc nature of the way we have handled exceptions (error handling) in the past. An exception handling taxonomy will support a uniform and reusable design strategy that can be utilized across applications and multiple development organizations.

13.11 Summary

The benefits of C++'s exception handling mechanism include:

- A syntax for declaring, raising, and handling exceptions is built into the language
- A run-time mechanism for propagating exceptions during execution is built in, and destructors are automatically invoked as the stack is unwound
- A uniform design guideline can be implemented to support fault tolerance
- A minimal run-time overhead is associated with the use of exceptions during normal program execution

C++ exceptions are treated as types and can be declared in several different ways:

- Nested classes
- Independent classes
- Enumeration types
- Inheritance hierarchy
- Throw List

A uniform exception handling strategy should be implemented for the following categories of exceptions:

- Anticipated exceptional conditions—handler is placed in the function or block where the exception is raised
- Protection of server software—handler is placed in the client software
- Detection and reporting of hardware failures—handler is placed in the function or block where the exception is raised
- Detection and reporting of unanticipated errors (bugs)—handler can be placed in every function during the debugging and test phase. The handlers can be disabled or removed in the release version

The exception handling mechanism implemented for C++ is non-resumptive: Separate code blocks are required for handling exceptions, and program control is not returned to the statement following the point at which an exception is raised.

C++ exceptions are types and can be declared as nested or independent classes. These classes can be empty, without any implementation, or they can include member functions and data members. Data members should be public to avoid having to provide access functions for displaying the members.

An exception is raised with a `throw` statement for named and unnamed exceptions.

The latter is used to re-raise an exception within a handler.

Exception handlers are created with the `catch()` statement for named and unnamed exceptions. The lexical order of multiple exception handlers determines the matching order of named exceptions. A handler for an unnamed exception must be the last of multiple handlers.

Exceptions are propagated up to the next enclosing block in the calling hierarchy. This unwinds the stack, and the appropriate destructors are called.

C++ libraries should include exceptions that are propagated to the client programs for fault tolerance. These exceptions are declared in the visible class interface.

We can effectively combine the signal()/raise() mechanism of the C run-time library with a C++ exception handling strategy.

References

1. Stroustrup, B., *The C++ Programming Language*, Second Edition, Addison-Wesley, Reading, MA, 1991.

2. Microsoft Visual C++ Version 4.0: MFC Library Reference, Volume 3, p. 647, Microsoft Corporation 1995.

3. Carroll, M., and Ellis, M., Error Handling in C++ Library Code, *C++ Report*, May 1994, p. 43.

14

The C++ Standard Template Library

The use of C++ templates, i.e., generic classes, was originally introduced as an "experimental" language feature. [1, p. 341]. This has become a permanent part of the language specification and is now implemented by most of the modern C++ compilation systems.

Most C++ applications need data structures such as strings, lists, queues, stacks, etc. Prior to the STL, the creation and manipulation of these data structures were implemented using hand-crafted algorithms that were unique for each application. The arrival of the STL solves two major problems:

- The availability of a standard interface for a number of common data structures
- The representation of efficient algorithms for the construction and manipulation of common data structures

A more subtle problem facing C++ developers has been the extensive use of inheritance and the penalty of storage required for the vtables and run-time overhead associated with polymorphism. The STL is composed of a set of generic classes using the C++ template features. Developers electing to use the STL classes should expect less run-time overhead where these classes replace a comparable inheritance hierarchy.

One of the C++ standards subcommittees has created a specification for a standard template library (STL) similar to the iostream library, which has been available since the early C++ versions.

The STL specification [2] is now a subset of the complete C++ Language Reference [3]. It includes the container, iterator, and algorithm part of the C++ standard library specification. Strings, I/O streams, etc., are not part of the STL.

The creation of the STL library is a major addition and improvement to the C++ language specification. Various C++ container libraries have been in existence for some time, but most of them had some common problems:

- Lack of portability—library interfaces were unique for each implementation.
- Limited functionality—only the functionality considered important by the particular vendor was implemented.
- Inefficient—most of the early C++ libraries were tailored after the Smalltalk model with heavy emphasis on inheritance and the use of virtual functions. This design suffers a significant run-time penalty.
- Embedded memory management—memory management was embedded deep into the container code. This makes it difficult to allocate memory for anything (e.g., shared memory) other than the local heap.

The original STL specification [4] was proposed as a solution to these problems, and represents a standard set of collection classes with a uniform interface. The current standard [3] has evolved from the original and is expected to undergo some further changes before it is finalized.

The focus of this chapter is on the elements and structure of the STL, how the template features are used to support this library, and how a C++ application can make use of the various STL container classes and the associated functions.

14.1 Overview

A major part of an object-oriented design effort is the determination of a set of architecture classes that we must add to the major abstractions in the problem domain. These architecture classes include basic data structures such as lists, queues, stacks, sets, binary trees, etc. The classes that implement these data structures are usually referred to as container classes or collection classes. Some authors prefer to make a distinction between these two types of classes: Containers hold whole objects, whereas collections hold pointers to other objects. We will not make this distinction here and for our purposes, the containers and collections are synonyms, unless otherwise specified.

Collection classes serve as the basic framework for organizing embedded objects, i.e., they support the implementation of the aggregation relationship between classes. Another view of collection classes is that they support the creation and retrieval of persistent data.

Collections that are common across a large number of different applications have been identified and implemented as C++ libraries of function and class templates. The functions include a set of algorithms used to visit individual elements of a collection.

These functions are referred to as *iterators* and make up a very important part of the library mechanism regarding how the elements are accessed and manipulated.

The use of templates is ideal for container classes because the logic to manage the collections is independent of the elements themselves. The same set of algorithms can be used to manipulate sets of objects that only differ by their C++ types.

One of the problems associated with using the STL is the fact that it is not very "standard." Compiler vendors are implementing their own versions of the STL that they integrate with their own C++ libraries. Independent software vendors are also creating different, commercial STL products. Examples of commercial products include *STL++*, from Modena Software [5]; *STL<toolkit>*, from ObjectSpace [6], and, *The Standard C++ Library*, from Rogue Wave Software [7].

The first version of the STL library was developed at HP [4] and has been incorporated into the C++ standard [3] as the Standard Template Library (STL). This is primarily the version we will consider here.

14.2 Basic STL Components

Quoting from the STL specification document ([2, p. 6]):

> "The Standard Template Library provides a set of well structured generic C++ components that work together in a seamless way. Special care has been taken to ensure that all the template algorithms work not only on the data structures in the library, but also on built-in C++ data structures. For example, all the algorithms work on regular pointers."

The basic components of the STL fall into the following five main categories:

- Container classes
- Iterators to provide traversal through containers
- Algorithms
- Function objects that encapsulate functions in objects for use by other components
- Adapters that adapt components to provide a different and suitable interface for other components

The components shown in Figure 14.1 interact with each other to provide the necessary mechanisms for creating and managing the data structures abstracted by the various STL template classes and functions.

14.3 Header Files

The interfaces to the STL components are contained in a set of header files. Each header file represents a set of classes that encapsulate certain data structures and the associated algorithms, iterators, etc. A list of all the header files (and some documentation files) that are shipped with the STL is shown in alphabetical order in Figure 14.2.

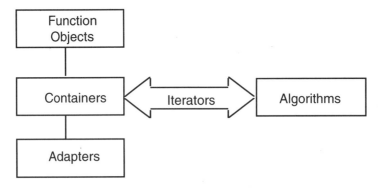

Figure 14.1 STL Components

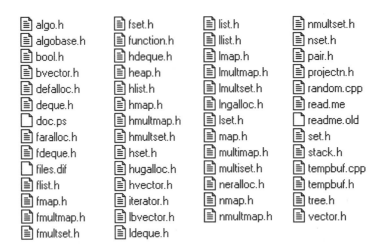

Figure 14.2 STL Header Files

The header files are given names that correspond to the functionality contained within the template classes and functions of that header file. A code snippet of the vector class declaration in the `vector.h` file is shown in Figure 14.3:

```
// File: vector.h

#include <function.h>
#include <algobase.h>
#include <bool.h>

template <class T>
class vector {
public:
    typedef Allocator<T> vector_allocator;
    typedef T value_type;
    typedef vector_allocator::pointer pointer;
    typedef vector_allocator::pointer iterator;
    typedef vector_allocator::const_pointer const_iterator;
    typedef vector_allocator::reference reference;
    typedef vector_allocator::const_reference const_reference;
    typedef vector_allocator::size_type size_type;
    typedef vector_allocator::difference_type difference_type;
    typedef reverse_iterator<const_iterator, value_type,
        const_reference, difference_type> const_reverse_iterator;
    typedef reverse_iterator<iterator, value_type, reference,
                             difference_type> reverse_iterator;
protected:
    static Allocator<T> static_allocator;
    iterator start;
    iterator finish;
    iterator end_of_storage;
    void insert_aux(iterator position, const T& x);

public:
    iterator begin() { return start; }
    const_iterator begin() const { return start; }
    iterator end() { return finish; }
    const_iterator end() const { return finish; }
    reverse_iterator rbegin() {
        return reverse_iterator(end());
    }
    const_reverse_iterator rbegin() const {
        return const_reverse_iterator(end());
    }
    reverse_iterator rend() {
        return reverse_iterator(begin());
    }
    const_reverse_iterator rend() const {
        return const_reverse_iterator(begin());
    }
    size_type size() const {
        return size_type(end() - begin());
```

```
      }
      size_type max_size() const {
            return static_allocator.max_size();
      }
      size_type capacity() const {
            return size_type(end_of_storage - begin());
      }
      bool empty() const { return begin() == end(); }
      reference operator[](size_type n) {
            return *(begin() + n);
      }
      const_reference operator[](size_type n) const {
            return *(begin() + n);
      }
      vector() : start(0), finish(0), end_of_storage(0) {}
      vector(size_type n, const T& value = T());
      vector(const vector<T>& x);
      vector(const_iterator first, const_iterator last);
      ~vector();
      vector<T>& operator=(const vector<T>& x);
      void reserve(size_type n);
      reference front() { return *begin(); }
      const_reference front() const { return *begin(); }
      reference back() { return *(end() - 1); }
      const_reference back() const { return *(end() - 1); }
      void push_back(const T& x);
      void swap(vector<T>& x);
      iterator insert(iterator position, const T& x);
      void insert (iterator position, const_iterator first,
                   const_iterator last);
      void insert (iterator position, size_type n, const T& x);
      void pop_back();
      void erase(iterator position);
      void erase(iterator first, iterator last);
};


template <class T>
inline bool operator==(const vector<T>& x, const vector<T>& y) {
    return x.size() == y.size() && equal(x.begin(), x.end(),
                                          y.begin());
}


template <class T>
inline bool operator<(const vector<T>& x, const vector<T>& y) {
    return lexicographical_compare(x.begin(), x.end(), y.begin(),
                                                       y.end());
}
```

Figure 14.3 Snapshot of Vector Class Declaration

The public interface includes a number of member functions that can be used to manipulate and manage vectors. In particular, we note the begin(), end(), push_back(), pop_back(), insert(), erase(), and swap() functions. Each header file also contains a number of typedefs and general non-member functions that support the algorithms in the class member functions. In this case, we note that the equality and less-than operators have been declared as non-member functions. Section 14.5 provides a synopsis of some of the most common STL functions.

14.4 Container Classes

A container class holds a collection of related objects. This supports the implementation of the notion of aggregation (or embedded objects) with cardinality of 1:*N*. A data member of the "whole" class is represented as a "part" with a container class as the type for the embedded data member:

```
class Whole {
public:
  Whole();
  //
private:
  Container aPart;
};

// Example:
  vector<char*> strVector; // an array of char strings
```

The STL provides services for ten basic categories of containers:

- vector<T>—sequential array
- deque<T>—sequential, double-entry queue, e.g., FIFO
- list<T>—doubly linked list
- set<key, compare>—set of items, elements are accessed with the key in an associative look-up
- multiset<key, compare>—same as set<T> with duplicate elements
- map<key, T, compare>—collection of 1:1 mappings between key and object
- multimap<key, T, compare>—collection of 1:*N* mappings
- stack<Container<T> >—adapter to use a container as a stack; LIFO only
- queue< Container<T> >—FIFO only
- priority_queue< Container<T>, compare>—sorted FIFO queue

This list of STL container classes can be placed in three primary groups:

1. Sequence containers maintain elements in a linear fashion, similar to an ordinary C/C++ array or linked list:
   - vector<T>
   - deque<T>
   - list<T>

2. Associative containers maintain elements in ordered structures that support fast, associative access, e.g.,:
   - set< key, compare>
   - multiset<key, compare >
   - map< key, T, compare >
   - multimap< key, T, compare >

   The associate containers are usually implemented as binary trees with fast traversal between nodes and leaves. An example of using an associative container includes locating a Person object associated with a Social Security Number as a key.

3. Adapter containers provide an "adapted" interface to an existing container, e.g., a prioritized queue:
   - stack<Container<T> >
   - queue< Container<T> >
   - priority_queue< Container<T>, compare>

14.5 Common Member Functions

The various container classes have several common member functions that can be used to create and manipulate different types of container objects. Here is a sample of these functions, using the vector class as an example:

```
iterator begin()     — return iterator positioned at first item
iterator end() — return iterator positioned after last item

T& front()     — return a reference to the first element
T& back()      — return a reference to the last element

bool empty() const — return true if no entries

void erase(iterator pos) — erase the element at pos
void erase(iterator first, iterator last) — erase elements in
range [first,last)
```

```
void insert(iterator pos, const T* first, const T* last) — insert
copies of the elements in range [first,last) starting at location
pos

void insert(iterator pos, size_type n, const T& value) — insert n
copies of values starting at location pos

iterator insert(iterator pos, const T& value) — insert value at
pos and return an iterator pointing to the next element

size_type max_size() const — return the maximum number of entries
that can be contained
size_type size() const — return the number of entries in the
container

void swap(deque<T>& deque) — swap contents of "this-deque" with
deque

void push_back(const T& value) — Add value to the end
void push_front(const T& value) — Add value in front of the first
element

void pop_back() — Erase the last element
void pop_front() — Erase the first element
```

Note that there are different functions for inserting and erasing elements. The insert() function takes an argument which indicates the object that will succeed the new object that is inserted. The three insert functions include a single object, a range of objects, and n number of the same object. The two erase() functions specify the position of the object to be removed, or a range of objects.

There are also a number of common constructors, destructor, and overloaded operator functions provided with each container class. Here is a set of these functions for the vector<T> container:

- vector()—default constructor that creates an empty vector
- vector(const vector<T>& X)—copy constructor
- ~vector()—non-virtual destructor with the usual C++ semantics
- vector<T>& operator=(const vector<T>& X)—assignment operator
- bool operator==(const vector<T>& X) const—equality operator returning *true* if the two vector objects contain the same items in the same order
- bool operator<(const vector<T>& X) const—comparison operator returning *true* if the "this" object is lexicographically less than the X object

The only comparison operators listed above are "==" and "<." The STL includes template functions for the other comparison operators in terms of these two operators. We simply need to provide the two operators for any of our user-defined types that we want to store as objects in any of the container classes.

Some of the usual overloaded operators don't make sense in certain cases. For example, the index operator operator[ ]() can be used with both vector<T> and deque<T>, but not with list<T>. A list must be traversed before a particular object can be identified.

14.6 Using vector<T>

The vector<T> container is a linear array with contiguous storage that can change its size transparently as we are adding elements. Block moves are required when objects are inserted or removed from within the array. Fast inserts are accommodated at the end only.

Sample vector<T> Application

Figure 14.4 illustrates how we can interface a simple application to the STL when we need an array of character strings:

```
// File: vecmain.cpp
#include <iostream.h>
#include <vector.h>

const int maxStrs = 3;

int main() {
  vector<char*> vec; // create an empty vector

  vec.insert(vec.end(), "San Diego");
  vec.insert(vec.end(), "San Francisco");
  vec.insert(vec.end(), "Los Gatos");

  for (int i = 0; i < maxStrs; ++i) {
    cout << " " << vec[i] << endl;
  }
  return 0;
}
```

                          Output:

                  ┌─────────────────────┐
                  │ San Diego   │
                  │ San Francisco   │
                  │ Los Gatos   │
                  └─────────────────────┘

Figure 14.4 Inserting Single Objects Into a Vector

In this example, we have instantiated vector<T> with the type of a character string, and have inserted three strings at the end of the array using the single-object insert iterator. Note how we use the index `operator[ ]()` to move through the array of strings.

Another vector<T> Application

In the previous example, we used the insert() function to add strings to the end of the vector container. Figure 14.5 is a different example that illustrates the use of the pushback() function to add elements.

```cpp
// File: vecmain1.cpp
#include <vector.h>
#include <iostream.h>

int main() {

   vector<int> vInt;
   vector<double> vDbl;
   vector<char*> vChar;

   cout << endl;
   cout << " Empty = " << vInt.empty() << endl;
   cout << " Size = " << vInt.size() << endl;
   cout << " Max Size = " << vInt.max_size() << endl << endl;
   vInt.push_back(42);
   vInt.push_back(84);
   cout << " vIntSize = " << vInt.size() << endl;
   cout << " vInt[0] = " << vInt[0] << endl;
   cout << " vInt[1] = " << vInt[1] << endl << endl;

   vDbl.push_back(10.5);
   vDbl.push_back(64.8);
   cout << " vDblSize= " << vDbl.size() << endl;
   cout << " vDbl[0] = " << vDbl[0] << endl;
   cout << " vDbl[1] = " << vDbl[1] << endl << endl;
   vChar.push_back("Harald");
   vChar.push_back("Haarfagre");
   cout << " vCharSize = " << vChar.size() << endl;
   cout << " vChar[0] = " << vChar[0] << endl;
   cout << " vChar[1] = " << vChar[1] << endl;
   return 0;
}
```

```
        Output:
            Empty = 1
            Size = 0
            Max Size = 1073741823
```

```
vIntSize = 2
vInt[0] = 42
vInt[1] = 84

vDblSize= 2
vDbl[0] = 10.5
vDbl[1] = 64.8

vCharSize = 2

vChar[0] = Harald
vChar[1] = Haarfagre
```

Figure 14.5 Adding Elements with pushback()

In this case, we use the functions empty() to see if the vector had any elements, max_size() to determine the maximum number of elements that can be stored, and size() to determine the current number of elements contained in the vector. The function push_back() is used to insert elements at the end of the vector.

These small examples illustrate how simple it is to interface to the STL, once we understand the capabilities that are encapsulated in the various header files, and how to use them.

Recommended Use of vector<T>

This container can be used when elements need to be inserted or erased at the front, end or middle. The most efficient use is for insertions and erasures at the end. Efficient random access (with access time O(k)) is available via the operator[ ](). This operator can be modified to perform bounds checking.

One major difference between an ordinary C/C++ array and the STL vector<T> is the feature allowing the size of the vector to be automatically increased as elements are added.

Another difference is an assignment operator that permits slicing, i.e., a subset of elements can be assigned from one vector to another.

Here is a summary of the implementer member functions:

```
void push_back(const T& x);
void pop_back();
void swap(vector<T>& x);
iterator insert(iterator position, const T& x);
void insert (iterator position, const_iterator first,
             const_iterator last);
void insert (iterator position, size_type n, const T& x);
void erase(iterator position);
void erase(iterator first, iterator last);
```

Note the absence of the otherwise-normal container functions of push_front() and pop_front().

The most efficient member functions for inserting and erasing are

- `push_back()`
- `pop_back()`

This container should not be used as a FIFO queue with insert() and erase() at the front and back, respectively. Additional storage can only be allocated from the back, and inserting from the front will result in frequent moves of the entire set of elements.

14.7 Using deque<T>

The container deque<T> is similar to a vector, except that it supports efficient algorithms for inserting and removing elements from either end of the queue. This can be useful as a FIFO data structure where we can insert at the head and remove from the tail. Here is an example of using this container:

```
// File: deqmain.cpp

#include <iostream.h>
#include <deque.h>

int main () {
  deque<int> deq;

  deq.push_back(4); // add after end.
  deq.push_back(9);
  deq.push_back(16);
  deq.push_front(1); // insert at beginning.
  for (int i = 0; i < deq.size(); i++)
    cout << " deq[" << i << "] = " << deq[i] << endl;

  cout << endl;
  deq.pop_front(); // Erase first element.
  deq[2] = 25; // Replace last element.
  for (i = 0; i < deq.size(); i++)
    cout << " deq[" << i << "] = " << deq[i] << endl;

  return 0;
}

                      Output:

                          deq[0] = 1
                          deq[1] = 4
                          deq[2] = 9
                          deq[3] = 16
```

```
deq[0] = 4
deq[1] = 9
deq[2] = 25
```

Recommended Use of deque<T>

This container is specialized for inserting and removing elements at the front and end, and is thus ideal for creating FIFO queues. Random access (with access time O(k)) is available via the operator[ ](); although it is not quite as efficient as for vector<T>. Here is a summary of the implementer member functions:

```
void push_front(const T& x);
void push_back(const T& x);
void pop_front();
void pop_back();
void swap(deque<T>& x);
iterator insert(iterator position, const T& x);
void insert(iterator position, size_type n, const T& x);
void insert(iterator position, const T* first, const T* last);
void erase(iterator position);
void erase(iterator first, iterator last);
```

The most efficient member functions for inserting and erasing are

- `push_back() / pop_back()`
- `push_front() / pop_front()`

14.8 Using list<T>

The list<T> structure is implemented as a doubly-linked list and provides an efficient data structure for insertion and removal from anywhere in the list. There are no "previous" and "next" pointers to access as part of the list structure. Navigating through a list is performed just like the vector and deque containers.

List structures created in C and C++ will, typically, have a NULL in the "next" pointer to signify the end of the list. The STL is implemented as a circular list, where the last list element will point to the first, rather than containing a NULL value. Similarly, the "previous" pointer in the root element points to the last element in the list.

Sample list<T> Application

In this application, we have two arrays of doubles that we include as two list objects dList1 and dList2, respectively. The merge() function is used to merge the dList2 elements with the dList1 elements. The merged elements in dList1 are then sorted:

```cpp
// File: list.cpp

#pragma warning (disable : 4290) // new, exception

#include <iostream.h>
#include <list.h>

class ListException {};

template<class T>
void dumpList(T& t);

double darray1[] = {6.4, 3.14, -2.9, 0.0};
double darray2[] = {3.88, 7.1, 24.0, 2.3};

int main () {
  list<double> dList1(darray1, darray1 + 4);
  list<double> dList2(darray2, darray2 + 4);

  dList1.merge(dList2);
  cout << " Merged lists dList1 & dList2:" << endl;
  dumpList(dList1);
  cout << endl << endl;

  dList1.sort();
  cout << " Sorted dList1:" << endl;
  dumpList(dList1);
  cout << endl << endl;

  cout << " Checking dList2:" << endl;
  dumpList(dList2);
  return 0;
}

template<class T>
void dumpList(T& t) {
  T::iterator iter;

  try {
    if ((iter = t.begin()) == t.end())
      throw ListException();

    for (iter = t.begin(); iter != t.end(); iter++)
      cout << " " << (*iter) << " ";
  }

  catch (ListException) {
    cout << " Empty list found in dumpList()" << endl;
  }
}
```

```
        Merged lists dList1 & dList2:
        3.88  6.4  3.14  -2.9  0  7.1  24  2.3
```

```
Sorted dList1:
-2.9  0  2.3  3.14  3.88  6.4  7.1  24

Checking dList2:
Empty list found in dumpList()
```

The behavior of the merge() function is a bit unexpected. The elements from dList2 that are less than the first element of dList1 (only 3.88 in this case) are moved to the front of dList1. The remaining elements are moved to the end of dList1. The sort() function orders the elements in ascending order, as expected.

We can deduce from the printout that the merge() function freed the storage for the source list dList2.

Note how we implemented a general, templatized display function to dump the elements of the list. This exact form can be used for any of the sequence containers: list, vector, and deque.

A simple exception handling mechanism is included in the display function. In this case, we decided to place the handler inside the display function and simply report the discovery that a list is empty. The main program can thus continue to execute without interruption. This falls in the category of Anticipated Exceptional Conditions (see Chapter 13 for the additional categories).

Recommended Use of list<T>

This container is specialized for doubly-linked list structures. The ideal use is for lists of large objects. A linked list of several small objects incurs a significant overhead since each element is stored in objects that have two links (pointers), i.e., previous and next.

Random access via the operator[ ]() is not available, since the access time is O(n). Here is a summary of the implementer member functions:

```
void push_front(const T& x);
void push_back(const T& x);
void pop_front();
void pop_back();
void swap(list<T>& x);
iterator insert(iterator position, const T& x);
void insert(iterator position, const T* first, const T* last);
void insert(iterator position, const_iterator first,
            const_iterator last);
void insert(iterator position, size_type n, const T& x);
void erase(iterator position);
void erase(iterator first, iterator last);
```

All of the various member functions for inserting and erasing are equally efficient:

- push_back() / pop_back()
- push_front() / pop_front()
- insert() / erase()

14.9 Using set< > and multiset< >

The main characteristic of associative containers is their capability to store objects based on a key value, and the efficient retrieval of objects via the keys. The STL specification includes four associative containers:

- set<key, compare>—ordered collection of keys. This does not allow duplicate keys and is an ideal candidate for a group of unique, sorted records
- map<key, T, compare>—collection of objects that can be referenced by a key value. This is an ideal candidate for a lookup of non-sequential elements
- multiset<key, compare>—same as set<key, compare>, but allows duplicate keys
- multimap<key, T, compare>—same as map<key, T, compare>, but allows duplicate values

The difference between a set and a map is that a set is an ordered collection of keys, whereas a map is a collection of objects that can be referenced by their associated keys. A map stores the associated object with the key value. A set only stores the key.

The difference between the single-version of a set and map and their corresponding multi-versions is that the latter two allow duplicate values.

These containers are implemented as sorted, balanced trees, and support rapid data retrieval based on a key value. Whereas the sequence containers have retrieval times proportional to the number of elements in the container or have constant times (O(N) or O(k), respectively), associative containers perform similar operations in significantly less time (O(log(N))).

One major difference between sequence containers and associative containers is that the latter supports an index that does not have to be an integer or simple scalar value, e.g. a key can be a string.

Sample set<key, compare> Application

Here is an example of how we can create and manipulate a set<T> container:

```
// File: set1.cpp

#pragma warning (disable : 4290) // exception, new

#include <iostream.h>
#include <set.h>

int main () {
  set<int, less<int> > intSet;

  cout << " count(-10) = " << intSet.count(-10) << endl;
```

```
intSet.insert(-10);
cout << " count(-10) = " << intSet.count(-10) << endl;
cout << " count(1024) = " << intSet.count(1024) << endl;
intSet.insert(1024);
cout << " count(1024) = " << intSet.count(1024) << endl;
int numElements = intSet.erase(1024);
cout << " " << numElements << " element(s) erased" << endl;
numElements = intSet.erase(-10);
cout << " " << numElements << " element(s) erased" << endl;

    return 0;
}
```

```
        Output

                count(-10) = 0
                count(-10) = 1
                count(1024) = 0
                count(1024) = 1

                1 element(s) erased
                1 element(s) erased
```

The insert() and erase() functions are used for adding and removing elements to and from the set. The count() function, with the key as the parameter, is used to read if there are any elements with that value in the set.

Sample multiset<key, compare> Application

The functions for the multiset container are exactly the same as for the set:

```
// File: multset1.cpp

#pragma warning (disable : 4290) // exception, new

#include <iostream.h>
#include <multiset.h>

int main () {
  multiset<int, less<int> > mSet;

  cout << " Number of keys with value 1024: " << mSet.count(1024)
       << endl;
  mSet.insert(1024);
  cout << " Number of keys with value 1024: " << mSet.count(1024)
       << endl;
```

```
   mSet.insert(1024);
   cout << " Number of keys with value 1024: " << mSet.count(1024)
        << endl;

   multiset<int, less<int> >::iterator mIt = mSet.find(512);
   if (mIt == mSet.end())
     cout << " Did not find key with value 512 " << endl;
   else
     cout << " Found " << *mIt << endl;

   mIt = mSet.find(1024);
   if (mIt == mSet.end())
     cout << " Key not found" << endl;
   else
     cout << " Key " << *mIt << " Found "<< endl;
   int numElements = mSet.erase(1024);
   cout << " Erased " << numElements << " elements with key 1024"
        << endl;
   return 0;
}
        Output
```

```
            Number of keys with value 1024: 0
            Number of keys with value 1024: 1
            Number of keys with value 1024: 2
            Did not find key with value 512
            Key 1024 Found
            Erased 2 elements with key 1024
```

We have used the functions insert(), erase(), find(), and count(), just as we did for the set container.

Sets and multisets are fairly primitive containers that have limited use in an object-oriented implementation. The maps and multimaps are much more important, since they support the implementation of the aggregation relationship with complex objects. This is illustrated in the sections that follow.

14.10 Using Maps

Maps are associative containers that maintain pairwise relationships between a key and its corresponding object. There are two types of maps supported in the STL:

- map<key, T, compare>—a collection of objects that can be referenced by a key value. This is an ideal candidate for a lookup of non-sequential elements.

- multimap<key, T, compare>—same as map<key, T, compare>, but allows duplicate values associated with the same key.

We will illustrate the features of map containers by creating a list of customers and their associated invoice numbers. The customer names are implemented as *string* types, and the corresponding invoice numbers as *unsigned long*. The pragmas have been included to avoid annoying warning messages from the C++ compiler Microsoft Visual C++ version 4.2; they are not needed in version 5.0:

```cpp
// File: mapmain.cpp

#pragma warning (disable : 4270)
#pragma warning (disable : 4761)
#pragma warning (disable : 4786)
#pragma warning (disable : 4290)

#include <iostream.h>
#include <bstring.h>
#include <map.h>

typedef unsigned long ULONG;

int main() {
  map<string, ULONG, less<string> > myMap;

  myMap["Caterina's"]  = 101331;
  myMap["Big Olaf"]    = 101456;
  myMap["Yogurt Mill"] = 101348;
  myMap["Cafe Blend"]  = 101232;
  cout << " Invoice for Big Olaf = "
       << myMap["Big Olaf"] << endl;
  cout << " Invoice for Cafe Blend = "
       << myMap["Cafe Blend"] << endl;
  cout << " Invoice for Caterina's = "
       << myMap["Caterina's"] << endl;
  cout << " Invoice for Yogurt Mill = "
       << myMap["Yogurt Mill"] << endl;

  return 0;
}
          Output:

          Invoice for Big Olaf = 101456
          Invoice for Cafe Blend = 101232
          Invoice for Caterina's = 101331
          Invoice for Yogurt Mill = 101348
```

This illustrates how we can access map objects using operator[ ]() with the key as the index. Hard-coding this output is rather clumsy, however, and we could be using the available iterators instead:

```cpp
int main() {
// same as above
```

```
// ...
  cout << " Customer Name " << "\tInvoice Number" << endl;
  cout << "  _____  " << "\t_____" << endl;

  map<string, ULONG, less<string> >::iterator mapIt;
    for (mapIt = myMap.begin(); mapIt != myMap.end(); mapIt++) {
      cout << " " << (*mapIt).first;
      cout << "\t";
      cout << " " << (*mapIt).second << endl;
    }
  return 0;
}
```

```
        Output:

            Customer Name     Invoice Number
            -------------     --------------
            Big Olaf          101456
            Cafe Blend        101232
            Caterina's        101331
            Yogurt Mill       101348
```

In this case, we created the iterator mapIt and used the begin() and end() iterators as the for-loop parameters. The dereferencing expression (*mapIt).first returns the value of the key; (*mapIt).second returns the value of the associated object.

Using iterators to access map objects is certainly more elegant and requires less code. Note also that the output is automatically sorted on the key in ascending order, based on the comparison we specified, i.e., less<string>. If we had specified greater<string> instead, the output would be automatically sorted in descending order:

```
int main() {
  map<string, ULONG, greater<string> > myMap;

  myMap["Caterina's"]  = 101331;
  myMap["Big Olaf"]    = 101456;
  myMap["Yogurt Mill"] = 101348;
  myMap["Cafe Blend"]  = 101232;

// same as above
// ...

  map<string, ULONG, greater<string> >::iterator mapIt;
  for (mapIt = myMap.begin(); mapIt != myMap.end(); mapIt++) {
    cout << " " << (*mapIt).first;
    cout << "\t";
    cout << " " << (*mapIt).second << endl;
  }
  return 0;
}
```

```
Output:
```

```
Customer Name    Invoice Number
--------------   ---------------
Yogurt Mill       101348
Caterina's        101331
Cafe Blend        101232
Big Olaf          101456
```

The output is now automatically sorted in descending order, based on the `greater<string>` comparison.

Do not try to mix the comparison types of the map object and the corresponding iterator. They must both be `less`, `less_equal`, `greater`, `greater_equal`, or any other pertinent comparator specified in `function.h`.

All the STL containers include templatized iterators that can be used in a similar way to what we have demonstrated here.

14.11 Using Multimaps

We will now illustrate the use of a multimap by creating more than one invoice for the same customer. The primary difference between the use of map and multimap is that we cannot insert elements using the operator[ ](). Since the key is used as the index for this operator, and we can have multiple keys with the same value, a potential ambiguity may occur regarding which object should be referenced. The insert function with a pairwise parameter is used instead:

```cpp
// File: mmapmain.cpp

#pragma warning (disable : 4786)
#pragma warning (disable : 4290)

#include <iostream.h>
#include <bstring.h>
#include <multimap.h>

typedef unsigned long ULONG;

int main() {
  multimap<string, ULONG, less<string> > myMMap;

  myMMap.insert(pair<string, ULONG> ("Caterina's", 101331));
  myMMap.insert(pair<string, ULONG> ("Big Olaf", 101456));
  myMMap.insert(pair<string, ULONG> ("Caterina's", 101368));
  myMMap.insert(pair<string, ULONG> ("Big Olaf", 101470));
  myMMap.insert(pair<string, ULONG> ("Yogurt Mill", 101348));
  myMMap.insert(pair<string, ULONG> ("Cafe Blend", 101232));
  myMMap.insert(pair<string, ULONG> ("Big Olaf", 101420));
```

```
      cout << " Customer Name " << "\tInvoice Number" << endl;
      cout << " _____ " << "\t_____" << endl;

      multimap<string, ULONG, less<string> >::iterator mapIt;
      for (mapIt = myMMap.begin(); mapIt != myMMap.end(); mapIt++) {
        cout << " " << (*mapIt).first;
        cout << "\t";
        cout << " " << (*mapIt).second << endl;
      }
    return 0;
    }
```

        Output:

Customer Name	Invoice Number
Big Olaf	101456
Big Olaf	101470
Big Olaf	101420
Cafe Blend	101232
Caterina's	101331
Caterina's	101368
Yogurt Mill	101348

Two of the customers have multiple invoices associated with their respective keys. A new object is placed after the existing objects with the same key, according to their insertion order. There is no secondary sorting performed using the actual object.

The use of the iterators is exactly the same for maps and multimaps. Removing elements can be done with the erase() functions:

```
    int main() {
      // same as above
      // ...

      int numErased = myMMap.erase("Big Olaf");
      cout << " Number of Big Olaf invoices erased = "
           << numErased << endl;
      cout << " Remaining invoices: " << endl;

      for (mapIt = myMMap.begin(); mapIt != myMMap.end(); mapIt++) {
        cout << " " << (*mapIt).first;
        cout << "\t";
        cout << " " << (*mapIt).second << endl;
      }
    return 0;
    }
```

        Output

```
Customer Name     Invoice Number
-------------     --------------
Big Olaf          101456
Big Olaf          101470
Big Olaf          101420
Cafe Blend        101232
Caterina's        101331
Caterina's        101368
Yogurt Mill       101348

Number of Big Olaf invoices erased = 3
Remaining invoices:
Cafe Blend        101232
Caterina's        101331
Caterina's        101368
Yogurt Mill       101348
```

When the key is used as the parameter in the erase() function, all the objects associated with that key are removed.

14.12 Using stack<Container>

This container is an adapter that can make some of the other containers perform as a stack. The use of the stack container is restricted to deque, list, and vector objects.

The typical stack functions of pop(), push(), and top() can be used regardless of which one of the three container types is being adapted. We will now illustrate the use of this adapter for deque and list objects.

Sample stack<Container> for Deque Objects

In this application, we are adapting a deque<double> container to perform as a stack object. All of the normal stack operations can be applied to the deque<double> elements:

```cpp
// File: dqstack.cpp

#pragma warning (disable : 4290) // new
#pragma warning (disable : 4146) // deque
#pragma warning (disable : 4018) // deque

#include <iostream.h>
#include <stack.h>
#include <deque.h>
```

```
int main () {
  stack<deque<double> > dqStack;
  dqStack.push (68.43);
  dqStack.push (3.14159);
  dqStack.push (2345.45);
  cout << " Emptying the deque-stack: " << endl;

  while (!dqStack.empty()) {
    cout << " " << dqStack.top() << endl;
    dqStack.pop();
  }
  return 0;
}
```

        Output

            Emptying the deque-stack:

            2345.45
            3.14159
            68.43

The stack operations top(), push() and pop() are not available to ordinary deque<T> containers. We are able to use them here because the stack adapter makes the deque object perform as a stack object. The exact same operation can be used on vector and list objects. The next section includes an illustration of a stack adaptation of a list object.

Sample stack<Container> for List Objects

Here is a sample of the use of the stack operations for a list object:

```
// File: stacklst.cpp

#pragma warning (disable : 4290) // new

#include <iostream.h>
#include <stack.h>
#include <list.h>

int main () {
  stack<list<const char*> > listStack;

  listStack.push ("San Diego");
  listStack.push ("San Francisco");
  listStack.push ("Bozeman");

  cout << " Emptying the list-stack: " << endl;
```

```
      while (!listStack.empty()) {
        cout << " " << listStack.top() << endl;
        listStack.pop();
      }
   return 0;
   }
```

            Output:

                  Emptying the list-stack:

                  Bozeman
                  San Francisco
                  San Diego

Again, just as with the deque object, we are treating the list object as if it were a stack object. The stack adapter can be used any time we need a LIFO behavior for a deque, vector, or list container.

14.13 Using The Queue Adapter

Whereas the stack adapter handles elements strictly in a LIFO order, a queue adapter maintains elements in a FIFO order. The queue adapter can only be used with list and deque containers. Since vectors can only grow from the end, they are not good candidates for a FIFO mechanism.

Sample Queue Application

The push() function adds a new element to the end (tail) of the queue, while the pop() function removes an element from the front (head) of the queue. The first element inserted (the oldest) can be read by calling the front() function. The newest element can be read by calling the back() function. Some of these functions are used in the following application:

```
// File: quelist.cpp

#pragma warning (disable : 4290) // exception, new
#pragma warning (disable : 4237) // queue.h

#include <iostream.h>
#include <queue.h>
#include <list.h>

int main () {
queue<int, list<int> > qList;
   qList.push(321);
```

```
    qList.push(-50);
    qList.push(1024);
    while (!qList.empty()) {
      cout << qList.front() << endl;
      qList.pop();
    }
    return 0;
}
```

Output:

```
321
-50
1024
```

The `push()` function is used to add the three integer elements to the tail, and `front()` is used to read the elements at the head of the queue. The `pop()` function removes the oldest element from the head of the queue.

14.14 Using priority_queue< >

The third adapter is the prioritized queue which orders elements based on the comparison function that is specified. This adapter can only be used with a deque or vector container. New elements can be added, and the largest element can be retrieved or removed based on the specified comparison function.

Sample priority_queue< > Application

The `push()` function is used to add elements into the sorted queue, and `pop()` is used to remove the element with the highest priority. The function `size()` can be used to obtain the current number of elements remaining in the queue. Here is a sample application using some of these functions:

```
// File: queprty.cpp

#pragma warning (disable : 4290) // exception, new
#pragma warning (disable : 4237) // queue.h
#pragma warning (disable : 4146) // deque.h

#include <iostream.h>
#include <function.h>
#include <queue.h>

int main () {
    priority_queue<deque<int>, less<int> > dqQueue;
```

```
//dqQueue.push ((char*) "San Francisco");
//dqQueue.push ((char*) "San Diego");
//dqQueue.push ((char*) "Bozeman");
dqQueue.push (61);
dqQueue.push (-10);
dqQueue.push (48);

while (!dqQueue.empty()) {
  cout << dqQueue.top() << endl;
  dqQueue.pop();
}
return 0;
}

        Output:

              61
              48
              -10
```

We have now provided an overview of the use of all the ten different containers. The collection of these containers provides a significant arsenal of data structures that can be used for any large C++ application. The learning curve for understanding the differences between the containers and when and how to use them is well worthwhile.

The alternative to using the STL is to hand-craft a set of data structures at great development expense. These type of structures may or may not be usable across development projects, depending upon how well the developers have paid attention to the concepts of software reusability.

14.15 Iterators

Iterators are used as index markers to provide the location of an element in a data structure. An iterator can be compared to a pointer that represents a location in memory, but it is important to realize that it is not a C/C++ pointer. A simple iterator can be advanced or reversed with incrementing and decrementing operations. An iterator can be considered the "glue" that connects containers and the algorithms that operate on them.

STL uses different iterators to support the various data structures represented by the generic C++ classes. We used a number of these iterators in the sample container programs in the previous sections. Here are some general characteristics regarding iterators:

- Access to data structures is made via generic iterators rather than allowing direct manipulation via pure, C++ pointers.

- Each data structure uses the most efficient iterator available for the current

STL version.

- Iterators provide access to generic algorithms as well as generic data structures, i.e., iterators are not used exclusively with containers.

Based on these general characteristics, an optional view of iterators and the other STL components is shown in Figure 14.6. The components are all interacting with each other, and the use of iterators is not reserved exclusively as an interface between the containers and algorithms.

Access to iterator interfaces is available from the <iterator.h> header. Here is a list of some of the iterators contained in this header:

```
iterator
back_insert_iterator
front_insert_iterator
insert_iterator
iostream_iterator
istreambuf_iterator
ostream_iterator
ostreambuf_iterator
reverse_bidirectional_iterator
reverse_iterator
```

The explicit use of these iterators is usually hidden from us, but they operate behind the scene when we declare an iterator object.

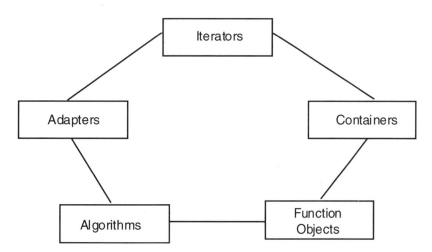

Figure 14.6 Cooperating STL Components

Sample Iterator Application

We used a number of forward iterators in the general display function to dump the list elements (see p. 233):

```
template<class T>
void dumpList(T& t) {
  T::iterator iter;

  try {
    if ((iter = t.begin()) == t.end())
      throw ListException();

    for (iter = t.begin(); iter != t.end(); iter++)
      cout << " " << (*iter) << " ";
  }

  catch (ListException) {
    cout << " Empty list found in dumpList()" << endl;
  }
}
```

The `begin()` and `end()` functions return the position of the start of the list and just past the end of the list, respectively. These functions are used by the iterator object `iter` to advance forward through the list. Note that we can dereference the iterator (`*iter`) just like an ordinary pointer to gain access to an element in that particular position. We also use the increment operator++() to advance the iterator to the next element.

There is also a set of reverse iterators that have the same format as the forward iterators. Here is an example of how we can implement the display function using reverse iterators:

```
template<class T>
void dumpList(T& t) { //using reverse iterators
  T::reverse_iterator iter;

  try {
    if ((iter = t.rbegin()) == t.rend())
      throw ListException();

    for (iter = t.rbegin(); iter != t.rend(); iter++)
      cout << " " << (*iter) << " ";
  }

  catch (ListException) {
    cout << " Empty list found in dumpList()" << endl;
  }
}
```

```
Output:
```

```
Merged lists dList1 & dList2:
2.3  24  7.1  0  -2.9  3.14  6.4  3.88

Sorted dList1:
24  7.1  6.4  3.88  3.14  2.3  0  -2.9

Checking dList2:
Empty list found in dumpList()
```

The iterator object `iter` is now a reverse iterator making use of the `rbegin()` and `rend()` functions. We see that the lists are now traversed in the opposite direction to what was illustrated in Section 14.8.

14.16 Algorithms

C++ developers are not confined to the set of iterators listed in the iterator header to manipulate container objects. A number of efficient algorithms are also available for manipulation of elements in the various generic classes. These algorithms can be accessed from the `algo.h`, `algobase.h`, `algoif.h`, and `algbaoif.h` header files. The last two are stripped versions of `algo.h` and `algobase.h`, respectively. Here is a list of some of these algorithms:

```
adjacent_find          prev_permutation
binary_search          push_heap
copy                   random_shuffle
copy_backward          remove
count                  replace
find                   replace_if
lower_bound            reverse
max                    rotate
merge                  sort
nth_element            swap
partition              transform
pop_heap               upper_bound
```

Here are the specifications of some of the algorithms:

```
// File: algobaif.h (stripped version of algobase.h)

#include <pair.h>
#include <iterator.h>

template <class ForwardIterator1, class ForwardIterator2,
          class T>
inline void __iter_swap(ForwardIterator1 a,
                        ForwardIterator2 b, T*);
```

```
template <class ForwardIterator1, class ForwardIterator2>
inline void iter_swap(ForwardIterator1 a, ForwardIterator2 b);

template <class T>
inline void swap(T& a, T& b);

template <class T>
inline const T& min(const T& a, const T& b);

template <class T, class Compare>
inline const T& min(const T& a, const T& b, Compare comp);

template <class T>
inline const T& max(const T& a, const T& b);

template <class T, class Compare>
inline const T& max(const T& a, const T& b, Compare comp);

template <class InputIterator, class Distance>
void __distance(InputIterator first,
                InputIterator last, Distance& n,
                input_iterator_tag);

template <class ForwardIterator, class Distance>
void __distance(ForwardIterator first,
                ForwardIterator last, Distance& n,
                forward_iterator_tag);

template <class BidirectionalIterator, class Distance>
void __distance(BidirectionalIterator first,
                BidirectionalIterator last,
                Distance& n, bidirectional_iterator_tag);

template <class RandomAccessIterator, class Distance>
inline void __distance(RandomAccessIterator first,
                       RandomAccessIterator last,
                       Distance& n,
                       random_access_iterator_tag);

template <class InputIterator, class Distance>
inline void distance(InputIterator first,
                     InputIterator last, Distance& n);

template <class InputIterator, class Distance>
void __advance(InputIterator& i, Distance n, input_iterator_tag);

template <class ForwardIterator, class Distance>
void __advance(ForwardIterator& i, Distance n,
forward_iterator_tag);

template <class BidirectionalIterator, class Distance>
void __advance(BidirectionalIterator& i, Distance n,
               bidirectional_iterator_tag);
```

Some of the algorithms we have already used include sort(), merge(), and count(). There are literally dozens of algorithms that can be used in connection with container objects, including min(), max(), swap(), and the creation of random numbers. Proficiency with these functions is quickly gained as we use them in actual applications.

14.17 Function Objects

Many of the STL functions used to manipulate containers can be specified as objects. There are three general categories of function objects:

- Predicates—return the values *true* or *false*, just as for any C/C++ predicate, and are used to initiate an action based on the result.

- Comparators—also return the values *true* or *false*, and are used to order elements, e.g., the *less* or *greater* we have witnessed previously.

- General Functions—return some numeric value and perform operations based on the parameters passed.

Sample Function Object Application

We will use the `greater` comparator as a sample function object for a vector container of doubles. The function object is specified as `greater<double>()` and is passed as a parameter in the sort() function to have the vector elements sorted in a descending order:

```
// File: funcobj.cpp

#pragma warning (disable : 4290) // new, exception
#include <iostream.h>
#include <algo.h> // include before vector.h
#include <vector.h>

class ContainerException {};

template<class T>
void dumpContainer(T& t);

int main () {
  vector<double> dVec;

  dVec.push_back(67.4);
  dVec.push_back(11.9);
  dVec.push_back(201.79);

  sort(dVec.begin(), dVec.end(), greater<double>());
```

```
    cout << " Vector sorted in descending order:" << endl;
    dumpContainer(dVec);
  return 0;
  }

template<class T>
void dumpContainer(T& t) { //using forward iterators
  T::iterator iter;

  try {
    if ((iter = t.begin()) == t.end())
      throw ContainerException();

    for (iter = t.begin(); iter != t.end(); iter++)
      cout << " " << (*iter) << " ";
  }

  catch (ContainerException) {
    cout << " Empty container found in dumpContainer()" << endl;
  }
}
```

```
        Vector sorted in descending order:
        201.79   67.4   11.9
```

Some of the other algorithms that accept this type of comparator as a function object include:

binary_search()	push_heap()
lower_bound()	set_difference()
make_heap()	set_intersection()
merge()	set_union()
pop_heap()	sort_heap()

These functions can be found in the `algo.h` header file.

14.18 Exception Handling

The C++ ANSI standard specifies that error conditions detected within the STL should be reported via the C++ exception handling mechanism. The problem is that the STL standard does not specify which exceptions should be used. There is only a weak reference to "using a subset of the standard C++ exceptions."

Here is a likely hierarchy of exceptions that the STL functions will be using, where the indentation level indicates the inheritance hierarchy:

- exception—the C++ abstract root exception
  - bad_alloc—memory allocation error
  - logic_error—abstract base class for exceptions related to violations of preconditions
    - domain_error—attempt to access illegal domain
    - invalid_argument—attempt to declare a container with an illegal size, e.g., -1.
    - length_error—attempt to declare a string with an illegal length
    - out_of_range—attempt to reference a container item using an index that is out of range
  - runtime_error—abstract base class for exceptions related to various run-time errors.
    - range_error—value of a variable is outside the legal range.
    - overflow_error—result is larger than the number of bits available for the size of that type, e.g., attempt to divide by zero.
    - underflow_error—result is smaller than the smallest allowable value for this implementation

The abstract classes `logic_error` and `runtime_error` inherit from the root class `exception`. All the other exceptions inherit from either `logic_error` or `runtime_error`. A class diagram of the suggested exception classes is shown in Figure 14.7. We will provide an implementation of this structure in Section 14.19.

This hierarchy is reasonably straightforward and easily extendible in both dimensions. Virtual member functions can be used to take advantage of the polymorphic behavior. Even if there is run-time overhead associated with this mechanism, it is of little significance, since the primary purpose of an exception is to document the "where" and "what" of a particular exceptional condition. We will provide a C++ implementation of this structure in Section 14.19.

Using the STL Exceptions

Attempting to use the "standard" STL exceptions can be an extremely frustrating experience if we are moving between development platforms. The exceptions are supposed to be contained within the <stdexcept.h> header or a header with a similar name. Different vendors are implementing their own versions, however, and there is no "standard' in this area. Here is an example of what you can expect from the Borland 5.0x version:

```
// Excerpt from the Borland C++ 5.01 <stdexcep.h>:
//
#ifndef __RWSTD_EXCEPTION_SEEN
```

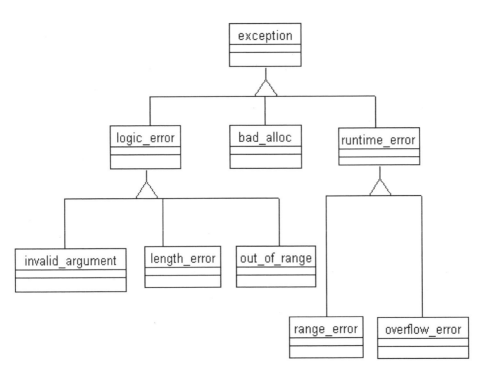

Figure 14.7 Exception Class Hierarchy

```
#ifndef RWSTD_NO_NAMESPACE
namespace std {
#endif
extern char RWSTDExport __rw_stdexcept_NoNamedException[];

class RWSTDExport exception {
public:
  exception () RWSTD_THROW_SPEC_NULL {;}
  exception (const exception& rhs) RWSTD_THROW_SPEC_NULL
                       { str = rhs.str; }
  exception& operator= (const exception& rhs)
                               RWSTD_THROW_SPEC_NULL
```

Borland is licensing the Rogue Wave STL implementation, which is littered with "RW" macros and unique "features." It becomes extremely annoying to move to a new C++ development version and find that your code will no longer compile.

The Microsoft version is a little cleaner, but it also includes macros. Here is an excerpt from Visual C++ version 4.2:

```
// Excerpt from <stdexcept> in Visual C++ version 4.2 and 5.0:
// ...
class logic_error : public exception {
public:
  explicit logic_error(const string& _S)
            : exception(""), _Str(_S) {}
  virtual ~logic_error() {}
  virtual const char *what() const {
    return (_Str.c_str());
  }
protected:
  virtual void _Doraise() const {_RAISE(*this);}
private:
  string _Str;
};

// CLASS domain_error
class domain_error : public logic_error {
public:
  explicit domain_error(const string& _S)
        : logic_error(_S) {}
  virtual ~domain_error() {}
protected:
  virtual void _Doraise() const {_RAISE(*this);}
};

// CLASS invalid_argument
class invalid_argument : public logic_error {
public:
  explicit invalid_argument(const string& _S)
          : logic_error(_S) {}
  virtual ~invalid_argument() {}
protected:
  virtual void _Doraise() const {_RAISE(*this);}
};

// CLASS length_error
class length_error : public logic_error {
public:
  explicit length_error(const string& _S)
          : logic_error(_S) {}
  virtual ~length_error() {}
protected:
  virtual void _Doraise() const {_RAISE(*this);}
};
// ...
```

We notice the macro _RAISE rather than the C++ `throw`. Here again, this code is not portable between C++ platforms due to vendor-unique implementations of "standard" C++ features.

The biggest problem we run into in attempting to adjust our code to a vendor's STL implementation is the extreme recursive nature of the header files. As we attempt to include the new header files, literally hundreds of compiler errors occur due to a different library structure. A solution to this problem is to create an independent set of exception classes, similar to the structure shown in Figure 14.6. This is outlined in the next section.

14.19 A Hierarchy of Exception Classes

An independent, portable hierarchy of exception classes can greatly reduce the time and frustration that is usually expended on moving between different development platforms.

Integrating this type of a hierarchy with the rest of the STL classes may require some modifications to an existing STL version. An example of such a modification includes the replacement of a call to an `exit()` function in an allocator by raising a bad_alloc exception. This is a small price to pay compared to the havoc that may result when a vendor decides to include some or all of the STL functionality into their other C++ libraries. A suggested version of a hierarchy of exception classes is shown in Figure 14.8.

```
// File: stlxcept.cpp

#include <iostream.h>
#include "kstring.h"

class exception {
public:
  exception() : msg(0) {}
  exception(const exception& rhs) : msg(rhs.msg) {}
  exception& operator=(const exception& rhs) {
    if (this == &rhs)
      return *this;
    msg = rhs.msg;
    return *this;
  }

  virtual ~exception() {}
  virtual const char* what() {
    return ((msg.size() == 0) ? "UnKnownException" : msg.data());
  }
protected:
  exception(const string& name) : msg(name) {
    cout << " msg.data()=" << msg.data() << endl;
  }
private:
  string msg;
};

class bad_alloc : public exception {
```

```
public:
  bad_alloc(const string& name) : exception(name) {}
  const char* what() {
    cout << " bad_alloc::what() " << exception::what() << endl;
    return 0;
  }
};

class logic_error : public exception {
public:
  logic_error(const string& name) : exception(name) {}
  const char* what() { // ... }
};

class invalid_argument : public logic_error {
public:
  invalid_argument(const string& name) : logic_error(name) {}
  const char* what() { // ... }
};

class length_error : public logic_error {
public:
  length_error(const string& name) : logic_error(name) {}
  const char* what() { // ... }
};

class out_of_range : public logic_error {
public:
  out_of_range(const string& name) : logic_error(name) {}
  const char* what() { // ... }
};

class runtime_error : public exception {
public:
  runtime_error(const string& name) : exception(name) {}
  const char* what() { // ... }
};

class range_error : public runtime_error {
public:
  range_error(const string& name) : runtime_error(name) {}
  const char* what() { // ... }
};

class overflow_error : public runtime_error {
public:
  overflow_error(const string& name) : runtime_error(name) {}
  const char* what() { // ... }
};
```

Figure 14.8 Exception Classes

A problem associated with using STL with other C++ libraries is the likely existence of different "String" classes. All of the STL classes, iterators, and functions assume the existence of a "string" class, spelled with all lowercase characters. Some versions of the STL have a <bstring.h> file, others have a <cstring.h> file.

We are including a "kstring.h" file here to indicate a unique string class that can be used with the STL components. Sometimes we also have to include the regular C <string.h> to manipulate character strings, e.g. strcpy().

The use of `namespace` can prevent the problems associated with multiple classes having the same name. This is a relatively new language feature and is not yet supported by all C++ compilers. Several of the applications demonstrated in this chapter, using Visual C++ 4.2, have been modified with the `namespace` feature for Visual C++ 5.0, and are included on the floppy disk.

14.20 Summary

Obtaining a copy of the STL, either from an independent vendor or as part of a C++ development environment, is highly recommended. It will take some time to understand the structure of the library and learn how to use it in C++ applications. But this expense in money and time will be a worthwhile effort. Creating common data structures from scratch requires a significant development effort which the use of the STL will avoid. Since the STL is now accepted as a part of the C++ language specification, portability across platforms is "guaranteed."

The use of the STL has a number of advantages for C++ developers:

- A standard set of dynamic data structures already exist and don't have to be hand-crafted.
- Efficient sorting and searching algorithms are available.
- Data structures do not have to be redesigned half-way through the project. If the data structure we have chosen proves to be inadequate, we simply pick a different data structure that will satisfy our requirements.
- The use of generic classes replaces an equivalent inheritance hierarchy and should improve run-time efficiency.

Disadvantages of using the STL include a significant learning curve for understanding the full complement of the generic classes and their associated functions and iterators. Some C++ development systems do not yet support the STL template operations, and C++ developers using these systems will have to create and manipulate their own data structures.

Even though this is a large chapter that covers all the components of the STL and how to use them, we have only scratched the surface! Proficiency with this library can only be attained through continued use of the various features as they are implemented in actual C++ applications.

The significance and value of this library will continue to grow as more and more developers learn the incredible amount of data structures that are available here for immediate reuse in C++ applications.

References

1. Ellis, M.A., and Stroustrup, B., *The Annotated C++ Reference Manual*, Addison-Wesley, Reading, MA, 1990.

2. Stepanov, A. and Lee, Meng, *The Standard Template Library*, July 7, 1995. stepanov@mti.sgi.com, lee@hpl.hp.com

3. Working Paper for Draft Proposed International Standard for Information Systems - Programming Language C++, Doc No: X3J16/96-0225, WG21/N1043, 2 December 1996.

4. Stepanov, A. and Lee, Meng, *The Standard Template Library*, Doc No: X3J16/94-0140, WG21/N0527, July 29, 1994. stepanov@hpl.hp.com

5. Modena Software, STL++, modena@netcom.com, (408)354-0846

6. ObjectSpace, STL<toolkit>, http://www.objectspace.com, 1-800-OBJECT1

7. Rogue Wave Software, Standard C++ Library, http://www.roguewave.com

15

Creating Robust Code with `const`

One of the most important contributions of C++ over C is the potential for creating more robust code. This can be accomplished with the use of the C++ `const` feature. C++ overloads the use of the `const` construct, and in this chapter we will investigate five separate categories for the use of `const`:

- Constant Variables
- Constant Parameters in a Function Parameter List
- Constant Class Members
- Constant Pointers
- Constant Return Type References

15.1 Constant Variables

There is a single const programming construct in C, but its semantics is different from C++. The declaration of a constant variable in C defaults to external linkage, i.e., it cannot be used in a header file. The following declaration can be used in both C and C++:

```
const int MaxBuf = 512;
```

Since this defaults to external (global) linkage in C, it has limited usefulness. In C++, however, the linkage is internal (local) and this declaration can be placed in a header file.

A common programming style in C is to use the #define statement for global constants. To take advantage of C++ type checking, the C-style #define statements should be replaced by a constant:

```
#define MaxBuf 1024  // don't use this anymore
const int MaxBuf = 1024;  // use this in C++
const char Message[] = "Hello World";
const char* Str = &Message;
```

Note that a global constant must be initialized in the declaration, since in subsequent code, MaxBuf cannot appear on the left hand side of an assignment statement. This has some interesting implications for constant data members, which we will discuss in Section 15.3.

The compiler will flag any attempts to change the value of a constant symbol. We are thus shifting error checking from run-time debugging to compile-time type checking. An infamous example of run-time problems facing C and C++ programmers is the following if-statement:

```
...
if (MaxBuf = 1024)  // we wanted '=='
...
```

Under non-const rules, the compiler would let us assign the value 1024 to MaxBuf. Since we have declared MaxBuf to be const, however, this will be flagged as a compilation error rather than appearing later as an annoying run-time mystery.

15.2 Constant Parameters in a Function Parameter List

If actual parameters are passed to a function by value, a local copy is made within that function. To avoid the copying, formal parameters are usually specified by reference. This is especially important for passing large objects, since the performance of a system could be seriously affected by multiple copying of several large objects.

A potential problem with passing objects by reference is that they can be modified inside the function they are passed to without the knowledge of the calling function. The use of const for the formal parameters prevents a function from modifying actual parameters passed by reference:

```
class String {
public:
  String();
  ~String();
  String& String(const String& copyStr);
  // ...
  Boolean operator==(const String& aStr);
...
private:
```

```
    // ...
  };
```

Whenever the copy constructor is invoked, the new string object will be initialized to the `copyStr` object that is passed in. If the copy constructor attempts to modify the `copyStr` object, the compiler will issue an error message to that effect. Similarly, if the equivalence operator attempts to modify the `aStr` object, the compiler will also issue an error message.

It is important to realize that the actual parameter passed does not have to be a constant type. The `const` shown in the formal parameter list for both the String copy constructor and the comparison operator represents a type qualifier. This qualifier protects the actual parameter passed in to the function from being modified inside the function.

The use of `const` to protect actual parameters passed to a function is recommended for any formal parameter specified as a reference or pointer that should be treated as read-only. This is not necessary when we are passing by value, since only a copy of the actual parameter is used inside the function.

15.3 Constant Class Members

The `const` keyword can be used with both data members and member functions. In this section, we will illustrate how we can specify constant data members and the effect that has on object construction. We will also show how we can specify constant member functions by extending the signature.

Constant Data Members

We have already seen (Section 15.1) how we can declare constant global variables using `const`. We can also declare constant data members using `const`. Here is a code snippet from the packing order header file in the Horizon application (see Section 11.2):

```
class PackingOrder {
public:
  PackingOrder(const Customer& cust, const Invoice& inv,
               const Date& deliv);
  // ...
private:
  // ...
  // Data Members
  String orderId;
  const Customer& theCustomer;
  Address shippingAddress;
  Date deliveryDate;
  multimap<List<String>, Item> listOfInvoices;
};
```

Since there will always be exactly one unique customer associated with a packing order, the embedded customer object (theCustomer) is made a const reference.

The use of a const data member may seem straightforward, but there is a hitch that applies to all const data members, regardless of whether they are declared by value or by reference. Data members can only be initialized by constructors. Constant values cannot be changed after their initialization. The only way to initialize constant data members is to use the member initialization syntax from a constructor:

```
PackingOrder::PackingOrder(const Customer& cust,
                           const Invoice& inv, const Date& deliv)
     : theCustomer(cust) {
   deliveryDate = deliv;
                 // can also use init syntax for this data member
   // add the invoice etc
}
```

Since an alias must contain a reference to an actual object when the alias is created, the only way to initialize the data member theCustomer is to use the member initialization syntax. This is also true for any constant data member that is an embedded object, regardless of whether it is of a built-in or user-defined type.

Constant Member Functions

One of the categories described for the four types of member functions was *access* functions. The purpose of the functions in this category is to provide users with the current values of data members in protected and private access sections.

The only purpose of an access function is to return the value of a hidden object. Such a function should never modify any of the data member values they are returning. This type of non-mutability by a function can be implemented in C++ by extending the signature with a const qualifier, as shown in the following code snippet of the PackingOrder class interface:

```
class PackingOrder {
public:
  // ...

  // Access Functions
  void Display() const;
  void Print() const;
  String& GetCustomerId() const;
  String& GetOrderId() const;
private:
  // ...
};
```

We see here how the functions Display(), Print(), GetCustomerId(), and GetOrderId() have the const qualifier in the prototype as an extension of the signature. This qualifier guarantees that the function will only access data members in read-only mode. Any attempt to change the value of any of the data members will be flagged by the compiler as an error.

When the `const` qualifier is used to extend the signature of a member function, it adds a restriction regarding how this member function can be invoked on behalf of an object: Only const member functions can be invoked by a `const` class instance. A `const` member function can also be invoked on behalf of a non-const object. Here is an example to illustrate this restriction:

```
// File: string.cpp

#include <iostream.h>

class exception {};

class String {
public:
  String(const char* str) : theString((char*)str) {}
  char& operator[](int index) {
    cout << " non-const operator[] invoked" << endl;
    if(index <= 0)
      throw exception();
    return theString[index];
  }
  const char& operator[](int index) const {
    cout << " const operator[] invoked" << endl;
    if(index <= 0)
      throw exception();
    return theString[index];
  }
private:
  char* theString;
};

int main() {
  const String cStr1 = "San Diego";
  String str2 = "Chicago";

  cout << " Using operator[] in main(). Fifth char of cStr1 = "
       << cStr1[4] << endl;
  cout << " Using operator[] in main(). Fifth char of str2 = "
       << str2[4] << endl;

  return 0;
}
        Output:

        const operator[] invoked
        Using operator[] in main(). Fifth char of cStr1 = D
        non-const operator[] invoked
        Using operator[] in main(). Fifth char of str2 = a
```

We see here how the proper index operator gets invoked based on whether the object type is const String or non-const String, respectively.

If we had not provided the operator[ ]() const, we would get the following error message:

```
error C2678: binary '[' : no operator defined which takes a left-
hand operand of type 'const class String *' (or there is no ac-
ceptable conversion)
```

Since the object cStr1 is constant, the compiler is looking for a corresponding const operator[ ].

Note that the example with the two operators illustrates an extended form of overloading: The two parameter lists of operator[ ] are identical, but the signature of the second operator has been extended with the const qualifier.

The ability to declare const member functions adds to the robustness of a class design, and should be implemented for all member functions that only need read-only access to data members.

15.4 Constant Pointers

The use of constant pointers as data members has the same ramifications as for aliases regarding how they are initialized. All constant data members must be initialized with the member initialization syntax:

```cpp
// File: string.cpp

#include <iostream.h>

class exception {};

class String {
public:
  String(const char* str) : theString((char*)str),
                            nullString("null") {}
  char& operator[](int index) {
    cout << " non-const operator[] invoked" << endl;
    if(index <= 0)
      throw exception();
    return theString[index];
  }
  const char& operator[](int index) const {
    cout << " const operator[] invoked" << endl;
    if(index <= 0)
      throw exception();
    return theString[index];
  }
  const char* getNullString() {return nullString;} // non-const
private:
```

```
   char* theString;
   const char* nullString;
};


int main() {
   const String cStr1 = "San Diego";
   String str2 = "Chicago";

   cout << " Using operator[] in main(). Fifth char of cStr1 = "
        << cStr1[4] << endl;
   cout << " Using operator[] in main(). Fifth char of str2 = "
        << str2[4] << endl;
   cout << " Null String = " << cStr1.getNullString(); // error

   return 0;
}
```

If we try to access the nullString data member via the cStr1 object, as shown here, we get the following compiler error message:

```
error C2662: 'getNullString' : cannot convert 'this' pointer from
'const class String *' to 'class String *const
```

This indicates that there is no `const` getNullString() corresponding to the constant cStr1 object. This example works fine when we change the access function to a `const`:

```
// File: string.cpp

#include <iostream.h>

class exception {};

class String {
public:
   // same as above
   const char* getNullString() const {return nullString;} // const
private:
   char* theString;
   const char* nullString;
};


int main() {
   // same as above
return 0;
}
```

```
   Output:

        const operator[] invoked
        Using operator[] in main().  Fifth char of cStr1 = D
```

```
non-const operator[] invoked
Using operator[] in main().  Fifth char of str2 = a
Null String = null
```

Besides showing the use of the member initialization syntax for the constant pointer nullString, this example also underscores the fact that access to member functions via constant instances requires the existence of the overloaded corresponding const member functions (as discussed in Section 15.3).

15.5 Return Type References

A function can return a const or non-const reference to an object. The choice between these two must be made depending upon how the returned value is used.

We noted in the previous sections of this chapter that we sometimes have to provide both a const and a non-const version of the same member function. The const version is required for accessing a member function on behalf of a constant class instance. In a similar fashion, expressions using the values returned by function calls must match the type of what is returned.

The use of a reference return type is required for any expression that needs an lvalue returned. The requirement of a const reference is a bit more obscure. We will illustrate the two different reference types with an application using a String class.

Non-Const Reference Type

Our first attempt at providing a suitable interface for a String class is shown in the following header file:

```cpp
// File: stringkn.h

#ifndef STRINGKN_H
#define STRINGKN_H

#include <iostream.h>

enum Bool {False, True};
class bad_alloc {}; // exception
class out_of_range {}; // exception

class String {
   friend ostream& operator <<(ostream& os, String& sStr);
   friend istream& operator >>(istream& is, String& sStr);
public:
   String();
   String(const char* chStr);
   String(const String& sStr);
```

```
  ~String();

    char& operator[](int index);
    char& operator[](int index) const;
    String& operator=(const char* chStr);
    String& operator=(const String& sStr);
    String& operator+=(const String& sStr);
    String operator+(const String& sStr);
    Bool operator==(const String& sStr);
  private:
    int length;
    char* theStr;
  };

  #endif
```

In addition to the usual constructors and destructors, we have provided the `const` index operator[ ](). This uses a non-`const` reference as its return type, just like the non-`const` index operator.

The implementations of the two index operators are identical, and both return a non-`const` reference:

```
  // File: string.cpp

  #include <iostream.h>
  #include "stringkn.h"
  #include <string.h>

  const int MaxSize = 256;

  String::String() : length(0), theStr(NULL) {}

  String::String(const char* chStr) {
    length = strlen(chStr);
    theStr = new char[length + 1];
    strcpy(theStr, chStr);
  }

  String::String(const String& sStr) {
    length = sStr.length;
    if (sStr.theStr == NULL) {
      theStr = NULL;
      return;
    }
    theStr = new char[length + 1];
    strcpy(theStr, sStr.theStr);
  }

  String::~String() {delete theStr;}

  char& String::operator[](int index) {
    if (index < 0 || index >= length)
```

```
      throw out_of_range();
    return theStr[index];
  }

  char& String::operator[](int index) const {
    if (index < 0 || index >= length)
      throw out_of_range();
    return theStr[index];
  }
  // other operators
  //  ...
```

We can now use this class in an application and declare both constant and non-constant String objects:

```
// File: refmain.cpp
// Using references as return types.

#include <iostream.h>
#include "stringkn.h"

int main() {
  try {
    String str1("Park City");
    const String str2("Taos");

    cout << " Third letter of str1 = " << str1[2] << endl;
    cout << " Third letter of str2 = " << str2[2] << endl;

    str1[2] = str2[0];
    cout << " Third letter of str1 = " << str1[2] << endl;
  }
  catch(bad_alloc& /*except*/) {
    cout << " bad_alloc exception caught in main()" << endl;
  }
  catch(out_of_range& /*except*/) {
    cout << " out_of_range exception caught in main()" << endl;
  }
  return 0;
}
          Output:

            Third letter of str1 = r
            Third letter of str2 = o
            Third letter of str1 = T
```

The String object str1 is declared as a variable String, whereas str2 is declared a constant String. In the assignment statement str1[2] = str2[0], the non-const index operator is invoked on behalf of str1 and the const operator on behalf of str2.

Note that the const index operator does not have to return a reference, since the assignment operator can use an rvalue on the rhs. The non-`const` index operator, however, must return a reference, since the lhs must be an lvalue.

`const` Reference Type

Why would we ever need to return a constant reference as a return type? The only case for this is if we specifically want to prevent the invocation of a member function on behalf of an object that is on the lhs of an assignment statement.

As a design issue for the String class, this kind of return type could be used if we wanted to prevent the assignment of elements from one String object to another. We could then declare the non-`const` index operator with the following return type:

```
// File: stringkn.h

// same as above

class String {
   // same as above
public:
   // same as above
   const char& operator[](int index);
   char& operator[](int index) const;
   // same as above
};
```

If the design of a class required read-only access to class instances for certain member functions, we would declare those functions as `const` members that return `const` references as their return types. In the case of the index operators for the String class, we would only need one:

```
// File: stringkn.h

// same as above

class String {
   // same as above
public:
   // same as above
const char& operator[](int index) const;
   // same as above
};
```

This operator will get invoked on behalf of both constant and non-constant String objects. Elements of the non-constant objects can only be accessed in a read-only fashion.

15.6 Summary

We should always use const for better type checking, protection of actual parameters passed to a function, and controlling the legal use of member functions. The use of this design guideline will result in more robust code. The const keyword can be used in the following different contexts:

- Constant Objects—used whenever we need a global or local constant that should not be changed during the life of the application. This style replaces the use of #define in C.

- Constant Parameters in a Function Parameter List—used to guarantee that actual parameters passed to a function will not be modified within the function.

- Constant Class Members—includes const data members and member functions. The specification of const member functions is required for member functions invoked on behalf of a const class instance. Data members declared const must be initialized with the member initialization syntax. A const member function will be invoked on behalf of a non-const instance if no non-const member function has been specified.

- Constant Return Type References—used with const member functions to prevent a member function from being invoked on behalf of an object that is the rhs of an assignment statement, i.e., guarantees read-only access.

PART 4

Persistent Data

Data persistence refers to the lifetime of data elements that are part of a C++ program, or that exist as part of a database system. Data elements survive with different lifetimes, depending on how they are used within an application. A local object created with a C++ constructor will only last until it is destroyed by a corresponding destructor. A global object will persist as long as the application is running. A database element must persist during the execution of an application, as well as between application invocations.

The focus of this part is on a description of the various forms of persistent data required in C++ applications and how we program their corresponding lifetimes. A review discussion is provided of the more traditional Relational Database Management Systems (RDBMSs).

A common method of accessing an RDBMS is via the Structured Query Language (SQL) interface. A fairly recent interface mechanism for an RDBMS is the Object Database Connectivity (ODBC) specification created by Microsoft. We describe the general features of the ODBC interface and illustrate how we can access an RDBMS from a C++ application via ODBC without any SQL interface.

16

C++ Static Members

Data persistence is a requirement for every application that contains data elements whose states can change while the application is executing. This can be as simple as maintaing a count of how many times a particular function has been called, and as complex as a distributed database in a client/server environment across multiple computers. This suggests two primary categories: persistence in *time* between application invocations, and persistence in *space* to accommodate client/server systems. The type of persistence required depends entirely on the application we are developing.

Traditional programming languages do not include any programming constructs for dealing with database issues. They only address the lifetime of data elements that are designed as data structures required for an application. C++ is no exception in this regard, it only includes language features that deal with persistence of internal data structures associated with a C++ application.

In this chapter, we will describe data persistence in time that can be implemented with the C++ programming language:

- Class variables that can be shared among a set of objects belonging to the same class
- Own-variables that persist between function invocations
- Lifetime of objects created within the application
- Storage of data elements in flat files using the C++ I/O library features

Later chapters in this part include descriptions of how C++ programs can interface with separate database management systems.

16.1 Class Variables versus Instance Variables

When an instance of a class is constructed, memory is allocated for each data member that is declared within that class. These data members are referred to as Instance Variables and have the same lifetime as the object they belong to. When that object is destroyed by a destructor, the data members are also destroyed. C++ does not provide any direct language support for saving the data members of an object. Some of the `iostream` file handling functions can be used to save data members in a flat file.

Class Variables

If we want to save the state of a data member past the destruction of an object, we can create Class Variables using the `static` keyword. Class variables maintain their state and can be shared among any number of instances of the same class. Let's assume that we have a requirement to maintain the name of a class in an inheritance hierarchy during execution. This can be considered a minimalist requirement for RTTI data. Here is one way this can be accomplished:

```
// File: static1.h

class Object {
public:
  // ...
    virtual char* GetClassName() const {return "Object";}
};

class NewClass : public Object {
public:
  //...
    virtual char* GetClassName() const {
      return className;
    }
private:
  static char className[];
};

// File: NewClass.cpp
//...
char NewClass::className[] = "NewClass";
//...
```

Classes derived from the Object base class override the `GetClassName()` function which returns a static string. All objects instantiated from the same derived class share the single static string containing their class name. This is thus a primitive way to obtain RTTI data for the class name of an object. A more sophisticated mechanism of dealing with RTTI data will be described when we discuss MFC features in Chapter 22.

A different use of a class variable is where we want to keep a running total of an amount associated with objects that are created and destroyed. Here is an example of how we can tally the total amount of sales from a number of invoices:

```
// File: static2.h

class Date {};

class Invoice {
public:
   Invoice();
   ~Invoice();
   static void UpdateSales(double add) {Totals += add;}
   //...
private:
   char* InvoiceId;
   Date InvoiceDate;
   //...
   static double Totals;
};

//File: Invoice.cpp
//...
double Invoice::Totals = 0.0;
//...
```

Each instance of an `Invoice` object can now update the tally of the total sales from the time a collection of invoices is created.

We can summarize the common characteristics of static data members as follows:

- A static data member is shared among all instances of its class
- A static data member can be accessed via the class and scope operator
- A static data member can only be initialized after the class declaration, prefer-ably in a separate .cpp file
- A static data member can be made non-public, different from an ordinary global variable
- A static data member is not entered into the application's global name space. This can prevent accidental name conflicts.

Instance Counter

A common use for a static data member, is an instance counter, i.e., a counter that records the number of current instances of a particular class. Here is an example of a counter used to maintain the count of Array objects:

```
// File: tarray.h
```

```
#ifndef TARRAY_H
#define TARRAY_H

typedef unsigned int UINT;
const UINT size1 = 5;
const UINT size2 = 7;
const UINT size3 = 10;

class out_of_range {};   // exception

template<class T>
class Array {
public:
  Array(UINT aSize) {
    theSize = (aSize > 0) ? aSize : 1;
    dataPtr = new T[theSize];
    numInstances++;
  }
  ~Array() {
    delete [] dataPtr;
    numInstances-;
  }

  UINT getSize() const {return theSize;}

  T& operator[](int index) {
    if (index < 0)
      throw out_of_range();
    return dataPtr[index];
  }

  static UINT getNumInstances() {
    return numInstances;
  }
protected:
  static UINT numInstances;
  UINT theSize;
  T* dataPtr;
};

template<class T>
UINT Array<T>::numInstances = 0;
#endif
```

The instance counter `numInstances` gets incremented in the constructors and decremented in the destructor, and maintains the current count of how many instances of the Array<T> class exist in the application. Here is a small application using this array class:

```
// File: tarrmain1.cpp
#include <iostream.h>
#include "tarray.h"
```

```
int main() {
  int i;
  int n = 1;
  double d = 10.0;
  cout << endl;
  Array<int> intArr(size1);

  cout << " intArr[i]: ";
  for (i = 0; i < size1; i++) {
    intArr[i] = i + n;
    cout << intArr[i] << " ";
  }

  cout << " \n There are currently "
       << intArr.getNumInstances()
       << " active instance(s) of class Array<int>" << endl;

  cout << " dArr[i]: ";
  Array<double> dArr(size2);
  for (i = 0; i < size2; i++) {
    dArr[i] = i + d;
    cout << dArr[i] << " ";
  }

  cout << " \n There are currently "
       << dArr.getNumInstances()
       << " active instance(s) of class Array<double>" << endl;

  return 0;
}
```

Output:

```
intArr[i]: 1  2  3  4  5
There are currently 1 active instance(s) of class Array<int>
dArr[i]: 10  11  12  13  14  15  16
There are currently 2 active instance(s) of class Array<double>
```

The static instance counter is automatically incremented in the constructor each time a new object is created. The current value is returned via the access function Array<T>:: getNumInstances(), where the class is instantiated for the particular type of array.

The access function can also be invoked on behalf of any array object, e.g., dArr.getNumInstances(). It makes more sense to use the class notation and scope operator, however, since we are dealing with a static *class* variable.

16.2 Lifetime of Data Elements

Data members that are part of an object will only survive as long as their respective objects survive. Once an instance of a class is destroyed by a destructor, all the associated data members are also destroyed.

Static class variables have different lifetimes than the non-static variables. The lifetime of a class variable is tied to the existence of objects of the class, and will survive as long as there is at least one object of that class in the application. We can demonstrate this lifetime using the Array class from the previous section as shown in Figure 16.1.

```cpp
// File: tarrmain.cpp

#include <iostream.h>
#include "tarray.h"

int main() {
// same as above

   cout << " \n There are currently "
        << Array<double>::getNumInstances()
        << " active instance(s) of class Array<double>" << endl;

   dArr1.~Array(); // explicit
   dArr2.~Array(); //    destruction

   cout << " \n There are currently "
        << Array<double>::getNumInstances()
        << " active instance(s) of class Array<double>" << endl;

   return 0;
}
```

Output using Microsoft Visual C++ 4.2 and 5.0:

```
intArr[i]:  1  2  3  4  5
There are currently 1 active instance(s) of class Array<int>
dArr1[i]:   10  11  12  13  14  15  16
dArr2[i]:   20  21  22  23  24  25  26  27  28  29
There are currently 2 active instance(s) of class Array<double>

There are currently 0 active instance(s) of class Array<double>
```

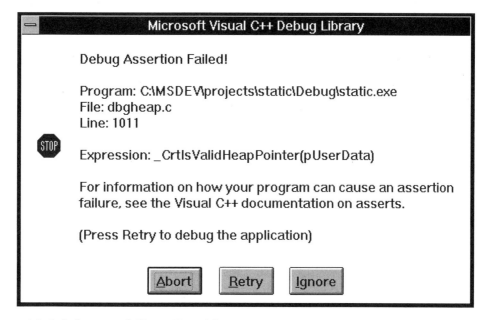

Figure 16.1 Lifetime of Class Variables

After we explicitly call the destructor for the two `Array<double>` objects, it appears that we get the correct number of remaining objects, i.e., zero. We actually get a run-time error from trying to access the class variable which no longer exists.

Attempting to access a class variable after all instances of that class have been destroyed appears to be implementation dependent. Here is the behavior for Borland's C++ version, after modifying the required syntax for accessing the destructor:

```
#include "tarray.h"

int main() {
  // same as above
  cout << " \n There are currently "
       << Array<double>::getNumInstances()
       << " active instance(s) of class Array<double>" << endl;

  dArr1.Array<double>::~Array(); // syntax required
  dArr2.Array<double>::~Array(); // by Borland C++

  cout << " \n There are currently "
       << Array<double>::getNumInstances()
       << " active instance(s) of class Array<double>" << endl;

  return 0;
}
```

`Output Using Borland C++ 5.01:`

```
intArr[i]:  1  2  3  4  5
There are currently 1 active instance(s) of class Array<int>
dArr1[i]:  10  11  12  13  14  15  16
dArr2[i]:  20  21  22  23  24  25  26  27  28  29
There are currently 2 active instance(s) of class Array<double>

There are currently 0 active instance(s) of class Array<double>
```

This completed with a normal return from main(), without any problems regarding accessing memory for the class variable which no longer exists.

16.3 Object Creation and Destruction

The type of persistence described in the previous sections applies to an application while it is executing. The lifetimes of both static and non-static objects are tied to the lifetime of the application, and the data associated with those objects is not saved when the application exits.

If data must be saved between invocations of an application, a database scheme of some type must be used. This can be as simple as using a "flat file" with the functions available in the iostream library. These features must be considered primitive and should only be used for simple applications. Some randomized indexing can be performed, but the general scheme is to store the data in files without any query capabilities.

Large, data oriented applications usually require database features that include query capabilities and security features to control data access. The most common database type used today are RDBMSs, with various ODBMSs slowly gaining acceptance for general use.

The table-driven design of an RDBMS is not particularly well suited for an interface to the object-oriented nature of a C++ application. Microsoft's specification of the Open Database Connectivity [1] has opened the opportunity for merging a C++ application with an RDBMS. The remaining chapters in this part will describe the general features of an RDBMS and how we can interface our C++ applications to these databases.

16.4 Summary

C++ has only limited features for storing and retrieving persistent data. The static keyword can be used to maintain class variables during execution of an application as instances are created and destroyed.

The common characteristics of static data members can be summarized as follows:

- A static data member is shared among all instances of its class.
- A static data member can be accessed via the class and scope operator, or via any instance of the same class.
- A static data member can only be initialized after the class declaration, preferably in a separate .cpp file.
- A static data member can be made non-public, different from an ordinary global variable.
- A static data member is not entered into the application's global name space. This can prevent accidental name conflicts.

Storing and retrieving persistent data between application invocations can be accomplished with the file handling functions in the `iostream` library.

Any significant data storage schemes should be designed using the various database interfaces available to C++ programs. This is the topic of the next two chapters.

References

1. Microsoft ODBC 3.0 Programmer's Reference and SDK Guide, Microsoft Press, Redmond, WA 1997.

17

Relational Database Management Systems

A traditional method for maintaining persistent data between application invocations has been the use of database management systems (DBMSs). A database can be defined as a collection of related data elements that model some aspects of real world abstractions, e.g., for banking, financial, or air traffic control applications. A DBMS includes a database and the necessary interfaces to create, access, control, and maintain the database. In general, a DBMS allows several related applications shared access to the same database.

The most prominent approach to the use and creation of databases in the last couple of decades has been the Relational Database Management System (RDBMS). Loosely defined, an RDBMS is a DBMS whose database consists of a number of relations (tables) that are connected via certain relationships. Each table is composed of a number of columns (data fields or attributes) and rows (records or tuples). Each row can be accessed via a primary key value. Access to a related table is accomplished via a foreign key in the target table which is a primary key in the related table.

The primary objective of this chapter is to describe the main features and construction of a traditional RDBMS. In the next chapter, we will describe the main features and construction of the ODBC interface, and the administrative tasks of interfacing to an RDBMS from a C++ application.

17.1 Background

A DBMS is the primary tool used to create and maintain persistent data that can be shared by a group of related applications. There are a number of features expected from every DBMS, regardless of type:

- Ability to change real-world data—The values of data elements can be changed without affecting the applications using the data
- Support for data structures that model the real world—A conceptual model to describe real-world entities, data items, and relationships
- Protection against corruption of data elements by authorized users
- Protection against data access by unauthorized users—Includes control of read, write, and delete permissions
- Support for simultaneous access by multiple users—Concurrency control by locking tables, rows or individual columns and providing atomic operations (no partial read or write of a data element)
- Recovery from software and hardware failures—Includes transaction processing where an update will only be `committed` if the entire transaction is completed. A `rollback` to the original state will be issued if a failure is detected.
- Ease of information transfer—Use of query languages, e.g., SQL, GUIs, and report writers
- Reasonable run-time performance—Performance can be measured in terms of response time to a particular request, or the number of transactions completed per unit time (second or minute). This should not be adversely affected in a multi-user environment.

Every access to a DBMS by an application can be described in terms of the three-level architecture shown in Figure 17.1.

The external view is represented as the view of an individual user. The conceptual schema includes all the data in the database, all identified constraints on the data elements, and the logical design of the database. The internal schema includes the details of how the data is stored, and how the data is accessed, e.g., via indexes.

Note that modern DBMSs do not allow direct access to the internal data view by an application. This would violate the encapsulation and modularity of having a separate DBMS from the application. Every application that is allowed direct access to the internal schema or below, will have to be recoded and recompiled when the internal data formats change.

17.2 RDBMS Structure

The relational database model is based on a set of relations (tables), each of which contain all the data elements associated with a particular real-world entity. The tables are connected via certain relationships. Each table consists of a number of columns (attributes or data fields) and a set of rows (records or tuples) that represent the current data for that table. One or more fields constitute a unique primary key. Other fields may contain foreign keys that correspond to primary keys in other tables. The relationships between tables are established via the primary and foreign keys.

17.3 Database and Tables

The creation of an RDBMS can be illustrated with an application that consists of Student, Enrollment, Section, Course, and Instructor relations (taken from the Datasheet View in Microsoft Access of the Stdreg32 database). An example of a table is the Student table shown in Figure 17.2. Each student (row) has a unique student Id with associated name and graduation year (columns).

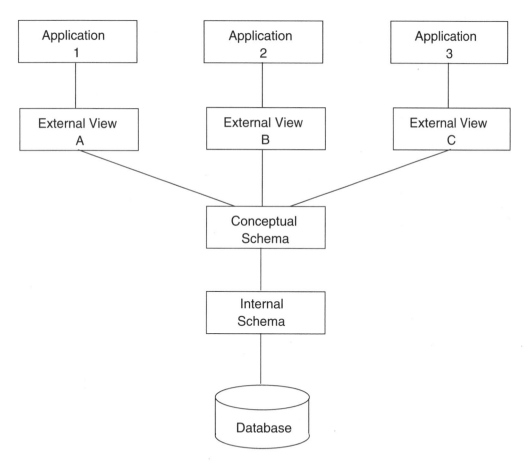

Figure 17.1 Three-Level Information Architecture

Student : Table

StudentID	Name	GradYear
1004	Shannon, Eric	98
1005	Foster, Susan	97
1006	Jefferson, Nancy	99
1007	Tuner, Bob	97
1008	Holm, David	98
1009	Reynolds, Don	97
1010	Taylor, Robert	98
1011	Karr, Dave	97
1012	Tannant, Tim	97
1013	Marcus, Susan	98
1014	Butterfield, Rita	98
1015	Amon, Craig	98
1016	Anderson, Sandra	97
1017	Cooper, Linda	99

Record: 4 of 17

Figure 17.2 Student Table

This table consists of three columns and 17 rows. Any number of rows can be added or deleted. Changing column names or modifying the number of columns, however, will represent a change to the structure of the table and the relationships to the other tables.

According to the relational model, each table must comply with the following *structural rules*:

- There are no duplicate rows
- There is no order to the rows (i.e., top to bottom)
- There is no order to the columns (i.e., left to right). By convention, however, the columns making up the primary key are placed first (on the left).
- The column values are atomic, i.e., there is one and only one value in each table cell

The remaining tables in the Student Registration data source and their relationships are shown in the sections that follow.

17.4 Primary and Foreign Keys

The StudentID in the Student table provides a unique identifier, i.e., *a primary key*, for each student (row). Primary keys are sometimes composed of multiple columns to provide a unique identification. In the Enrollment table shown in Figure 17.3, for example, both the StudentID, CourseID, and SectionNo fields make up the primary key.

Each of the StudentID, CourseID, and SectionNo fields refers to a row in the tables Student, Course, and Section, respectively. These fields are called *foreign keys*. A foreign key is a column value in a table that is not that table's primary key and which makes a reference to a primary key in another table.

In the Section table shown in Figure 17.4, the CourseID and SectionNo fields make up the primary key. The CourseID, SectionNo, and InstructorID fields are all foreign keys that make references to other tables.

The two remaining tables in the Student Registration database are shown in Figures 17.5 and 17.6. The CourseID is the primary key of the Course table, and InstructorID is the primary key of the Instructor table.

In addition to the table rules listed in Section 17.3, tables must also comply with certain integrity rules:

- Entity integrity—No part of a primary key can be null.

- Referential integrity—The value of a foreign key must either be null, or be one of the proper values of the primary key in the related table.

StudentID	CourseID	SectionNo	Grade
1001	MATH101	1	A
1002	MATH101	1	B
1003	MATH101	1	C
1004	MATH101	1	A
1005	MATH201	2	B
1006	MATH201	2	A
1007	MATH201	2	C
1008	MATH202	1	C
1009	MATH202	1	B
1010	MATH202	1	A
1011	MATH202	2	B
1012	MATH202	2	B

Record: 1 of 16

Figure 17.3 Enrollment Table

CourseID	SectionNo	InstructorID	RoomNo	Schedule	Capacity
MATH101	1	KLAUSENJ	KEN-12	MWF10-11	40
MATH101	2	ROGERSN	WIL-1088	TTH3:30-5	15
MATH201	1	ROGERSN	WIL-1034	MWF2-3	20
MATH201	2	SMITHJ	WIL-1054	MWF3-4	25
MATH202	1	KLAUSENJ	WIL-1054	MWF9-10	20
MATH202	2	ROGERSN	KEN-12	TTH9:30-11	15
MATH202	3	KLAUSENJ	WIL-2033	TTH3-4:30	15

Record: 1 of 7

Figure 17.4 Section Table

CourseID	CourseTitle	Hours
MATH101	Algebra	4
MATH201	Calculus I	4
MATH202	Calculus II	4

Record: 1 of 3

Figure 17.5 Course Table

InstructorID	Name	RoomNo
KLAUSENJ	Klausen, Jim	HAN-171
ROGERSN	Rogers, Nancy	HAN-163
SMITHJ	Smith, Jane	HAN-155

Record: 1 of 3

Figure 17.6 Instructor Table

The deletion of rows in related tables is governed by the Referential Integrity rule. No row is deleted if a null foreign key is allowed. The row of a non-null foreign key is deleted in the related table whenever the corresponding row is deleted in the table referencing the relationship.

With a basic understanding of the RDBMS table structure and the use of primary and foreign keys, we will next describe how table relationships and cardinalities are represented.

17.5 Relationships and Cardinalities

One of the primary disadvantages of an RDBMS is the limited ability to deal with relationships between major data entities. There is no concept of the object-oriented aggregation relationship, for example. The relationships can only be represented as two dimensional tables using primary and foreign keys to link the tables. There is no encapsulation of data and operations, and data manipulations are usually accomplished via various forms of SQL queries.

The relationships between the tables in the student registration database are shown in Figure 17.7. The connecting lines between the tables represent the relationships and the cardinalities. For example, the StudentID in the Enrollment table refers to exactly one student in the Student table; each student can be associated with multiple course enrollments in the Enrollment table.

The use of the infinity sign for a cardinality corresponds to our use of zero or more in the object-oriented model.

17.6 Normalization Rules

Relational tables are usually constructed using certain *normalization* rules, where normalization is the process of analyzing and grouping data according to inherent characteristics. In particular, the use of normalization simplifies the updating and deletion of data elements in target rows and related rows. Some of the design principles involving normalization include:

- Logically related data items are grouped to form an entity (e.g., the Student table shown in Figures 17.2 and 17.7)

- The data in a group can be distinguished by a unique identifier (i.e., the primary key)

- The data in a group describes only a single entity (e.g., separate tables for Section and Enrollment)

Each table is designed according to a set of normal forms that provides a level of encapsulation and promotes robustness:

- A table is in first normal form (1NF) if there are no repeating groups. We could, for example, have added a number of courses to the Student table as repeating groups. This would greatly complicate the Student table, however, and would violate the single-entity design stipulated above.

- A table is in second normal form (2NF) if the non-key columns are dependent on the fields that make up the primary key.

- A table is in third normal form (3NF) if all of the non-key columns are dependent on the primary key, on the whole key, and nothing but this key.

Most RDBMSs are designed to comply with the 3NF. All the tables shown in Figure 17.7 are in the 3NF. In the Section table, for example, the non-key columns RoomNo, Schedule, and Capacity are all dependent on the primary key, which is made up of CourseID and SectionNo.

17.7 Referential Integrity

Referential Integrity pertains to rules that apply to relationships between tables. These rules must be defined via business rules for every relationship. This includes when a foreign key can be null, and how rows should be deleted in a related table.

For the tables listed in the Student Registration database, the only foreign key that could be allowed to be null is the InstructorID in the Section table. This is based on the business rule that a section may be allowed to be printed in a course catalog before an instructor is assigned.

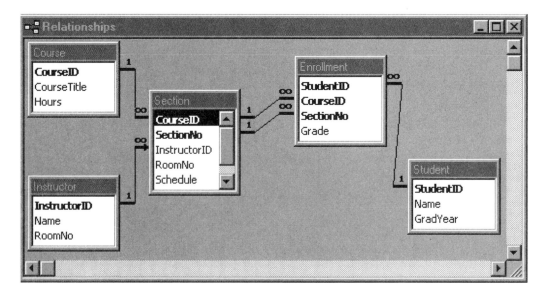

Figure 17.7 Student Registration Table Relationships

Deletion of rows is tied directly to the referential integrity rules. There are three primary options for deleting rows:

- Cascading—When the target row is deleted, delete all rows in related tables
- Restricted—Deletions are restricted to rows where there are no related tables
- Nullifying—When the target row is deleted, set the foreign key to null in all related rows

The deletion rules are not uniform across RDBMSs. Microsoft Access, for example, only implements the cascading delete.

17.8 SQL

The data contained in the various tables that make up each database is accessed via SQL statements to create the necessary forms and reports. Information hiding can be created with the SQL interface, if this is the only access mechanism to the data tables. Most programming languages, however, provide opportunities for direct access to the data tables and a potential violation of data integrity. Many applications have been implemented by hard-wiring access directly to the data tables without any form of encapsulation and information hiding.

We do not intend to cover the SQL syntax or use here. A suggested SQL reference is [1].

17.9 C++ and RDBMS

The primary disadvantage of using an RDBMS with a C++ application is the limited set of data types that can be used for data elements in the relational model. This limitation is directly orthogonal to the unlimited set of user-defined types available with C++.

The predominant method of accessing an RDBMS from a C++ application is via the ODBC mechanism explained in Chapter 18. This mechanism permits a C++ application to open a data source (e.g., Oracle, Sybase, or Access) that is registered with the operating system and for which there is a driver that can translate the internal data formats.

C++ applications can also potentially access an RDBMS via a special SQL interface and a native driver. This solution provides for limited portability and is really a way of hard-wiring an application to a particular database. This should only be an option if there are no ODBC drivers available for the database of choice.

17.10 Summary

RDBMSs have been the capstan of database technology and use for the last few decades. The primary problem with using an RDBMS in a C++ application is the limited set of data types that can be used for data elements in the relational model. This limitation is directly orthogonal to the unlimited set of user-defined types available with C++.

RDBMSs are designed according to a set of integrity and normalization rules that promote encapsulation and robustness.

An RDBMS database consists of a set of two-dimensional tables. Each table represents a real-world entity and is composed of a number of columns as data fields and rows as instances of a set of column values. Tables are related via primary and foreign keys.

RDBMSs are slowly, but surely, being replaced by ODBMSs. The latter solves the impedance mismatch of limited RDBMS data types and C++ classes as user-defined types.

C++ applications can access RDBMSs via the ODBC connection, provided a data source is registered and the appropriate drivers are available. Some drivers also allow connections to ODBMSs (e.g., POET) from traditional RDBMS applications

Good sources about relational theory and RDBMS design and implementation can be found in [2] and [3].

References

1. Bowman, J. et al., *The Practical SQL Handbook*, Addison-Wesley, Reading, MA, 1993.

2. Codd, E. F., "A Relational Model of Data for Large Shared Data Banks," *Comm. ACM* 13(7), pp. 377-87.

3. McFadden, F. and Hoffer, J., Modern Database Management, Fourth Edition, Benjamin/Cummings, Redwood City, CA 1994.

18

Open Database Connectivity

The Open Database Connectivity (ODBC) specification was written to allow various applications access to databases with different formats and schemas. The requirements for this type of access are that a suitable ODBC driver exists for the specific formats, e.g., Oracle, DB2 or Sybase, and that the user must register the database and tables using an administrative tool.

Since this book is about the creation of C++ applications, this chapter describes how a C++ application can access an existing RDBMS via the ODBC interface. This can provide an interim solution in lieu of a pure object database solution

The primary objective of this chapter is to describe the main features and construction of the ODBC interface, and how to do the administrative tasks of preparing to use a DBMS by an application.

18.1 Background

The Open Database Connectivity (ODBC) was originally authored by Microsoft [1], and is now supported by a number of different software development vendors. The objective of the ODBC specification and its associated software API is to provide a bridge between different DBMSs and between the DBMS and ODBMS world.

18.2 ODBC Interface

The use of ODBC can allow applications access to data in different DBMSs by registering a data source (database and individual tables) and specifying an ODBC software driver capable of converting from one database format to another. A Btrieve database, for example, can be translated to be used in a Microsoft Access application. Similarly, an Access RDBMS database can be translated to be used with a Microsoft Windows C++ application. Another view of an ODBC interface is that one application can access data from a number of different databases.

The ODBC specification defines the following structures and standards for accessing and manipulating databases:

- An API consisting of a library of ODBC functions that permit applications to access databases, execute SQL statements, and retrieve results from the queries
- A standard set of error codes
- A set of standard representations for common data types
- A standard interface for connecting to and logging on to a DBMS
- SQL syntax rules which are based on the X/Open and SQL Access Group (SAG) SQL CAE.

The execution of SQL statements is performed by passing the statements as parameters in the API function calls.

18.3 The ODBC Architecture

The interface between a C++ application and a DBMS is shown in Figure 18.1, and illustrates the various components involved in the ODBC architecture.

This is a layered, multi-tier architecture that is similar in structure to the three-level architecture of an RDBMS.

A Data Source includes the database, the associated OS functions, and network (if any) required to access the DBMS. A data source is a specific instance of a database and the run-time system required to access the data. Examples include:

- An Oracle RDBMS running under Windows NT on a server and accessed by a client C++ application
- A local POET ODBMS running under Windows 95 and used by a client Microsoft Access application running on the same platform

Note that these two examples represent both the translation from an RDBMS to a C++ application and from an ODBMS to an application (Access) that uses an RDBMS.

The Application performs various internal processing tasks and calls the ODBC API functions to submit SQL requests and retrieve results. The results are reported via a suitable user interface, and potential error messages are logged and reported. Specific application tasks associated with the use of the ODBC include:

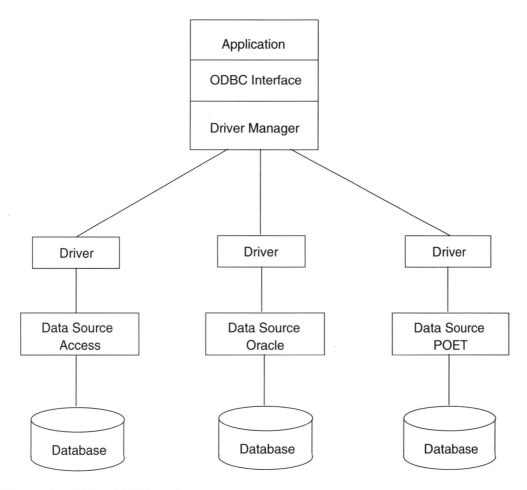

Figure 18.1 The ODBC Architecture

- Requesting a connection (session) with a data source
- Creating and maintaining data structures and data formats for the results of SQL requests
- Sending SQL requests to the data source
- Requesting results to be returned to the application
- Performing error processing
- Passing results back to users
- Requesting *commit* or *rollback* operations for transaction processing

The Driver Manager includes a dynamic link library (a DLL which is transparent to the application) and its primary function is to load unique database drivers specified by the application, e.g., a driver for Oracle, DB2, or Sybase. This manager makes use of the ODBC Cursor Library (a DLL) to handle scrolling through the data.

Each Driver contains a DLL which implements the ODBC function calls and provides an interface to the data source. Specific functions performed by a driver include:

- Creating a connection to a data source
- Submitting requests to the data source
- Translating data formats
- Returning query results to the application
- Formatting error messages from the data source into standard ODBC error codes

From our view as C++ developers, the most interesting aspect of this architecture is how we gain access to the data elements in the data source. This is highly dependent on the development platform we are using. In Chapter 25, we will see that the MFC has ODBC classes that permit access without using SQL statements.

18.4 ODBC Administration

An ODBC Administrator is used to configure a DBMS and make it available to an application. A data source must be registered and configured before it can be accessed by an application. Drivers must be matched to a particular application.

The ODBC Administrator tool is used to add and remove data sources. Depending on a particular ODBC driver, a new data source can also be created. Data sources can be accessed locally or across a network. Drivers are usually installed with a development environment, e.g., Borland C++ or Microsoft Visual C++ during the setup procedure. A driver is matched to the data source required by a particular application. The 32-bit ODBC Administrator is located on the Control Panel for Windows NT, as shown in Figure 18.2. How to use the administration tool is illustrated later in this chapter.

18.5 Matching Applications and ODBC Drivers

The completion of an application includes testing the ODBC interface with a particular data source. A major advantage of ODBC is that the same application can be used with other data sources without recompiling the source code and retesting the modules.

When the application is written, it is not targeted to a specific data source. Additional data sources can be accessed at a later time, provided, of course, that the appropriate drivers are available.

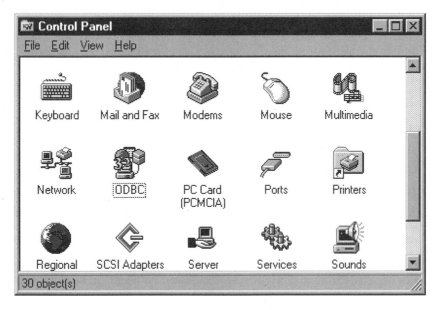

Figure 18.2 ODBC Administrator in Windows NT

This may, at first, sound like nirvana, but the reality is that different drivers are written to a specific *conformance level*. This complicates the portability issue and requires a careful consideration of the available drivers. The specification of a driver will include a description of the conformance levels that it supports. An application can obtain information about a driver's conformance levels by calling `SQLGetInfo()`, `SQLGetFunction()`, and `SQLGetTypeInfo()`.

Here is a list of the drivers provided with Microsoft Visual C++ 4.x:

- SQL Server
- Microsoft Access
- Microsoft FoxPro
- Microsoft Excel
- Borland dBase
- Borland Paradox
- Text Files (.csv, .txt, and .asc)

Numerous other drivers are now available from various software vendors such as Intersolv and Btrieve Technologies. We will make additional comments about the selection of drivers after we have discussed conformance levels in the next section.

18.6 ODBC Conformance Levels

The ODBC specification defines conformance levels for the ODBC API and the ODBC SQL.

ODBC API Conformance

The ODBC API conformance levels include:

- Core API—The set of basic functionality that all drivers are expected to support
- Level 1 API—Includes all the Core API functions. Additional capabilities include the use of dialog boxes for making connections, sending only a portion of a parameter value, and retrieving only a part of a requested result.
- Level 2 API—Includes all the Core API Level 1 functions. Additional capabilities include browsing for available data sources and connection information, sending arrays of parameter values, using scrollable cursors, and retrieving catalog information about access privileges, keys and procedures.

ODBC SQL Conformance

The ODBC SQL conformance levels include:

- Minimum SQL Grammar—The basic functionality includes a Data Definition Language (DDL) to create and drop a table; a Data Manipulation Language (DML) to select, insert, and update a table; simple expressions (e.g., A > B + C); and primitive data types (CHAR, VARCHAR, AND LONG VARCHAR).
- Core SQL Grammar—Includes the Minimum SQL Grammar and data types. Additional capabilities include further manipulations of a table; a DML with full SQL SELECT; expression subqueries with functions such as sum() and min(); and additional data types (DECIMAL, NUMERIC, SMALLINT, INTEGER, REAL, FLOAT, DOUBLE PRECISION).
- Extended SQL Grammar—Includes the Minimum and Core SQL Grammar and data types. Additional capabilities include more DML functions, such as outer joins and unions; expressions that allow invocations of functions for substrings, absolute values, date, time, and timestamps; additional data types (e.g., BIT, BINARY, VARBINARY, DATE, TIME, and TIMESTAMP); batch SQL statements; and procedure calls.

Since each driver is designed to a certain combination of conformance levels for the API and SQL, it is essential that we understand the specifications for that driver before we attempt to use it in an application. Any one driver may satisfy all of our requirements for the API, but only some of the SQL requirements. If an ideal driver is not available, we may have to analyze trade-offs in capabilities before a particular driver is chosen.

18.7 Selecting the Required Functionality

The ODBC API functions and SQL statements supported by a specific driver are usually determined by the features of the associated data source. Some drivers may exceed those features and have additional functionality built in.

The functionality required by an application depends on a number of different factors. Here are some of the considerations to be made in selecting the functionality:

- The minimum functionality required by the application
- The required run-time performance for accessing the data source
- How many different data sources the application must access and the level of interoperability required for moving between these data sources
- The functionality included in the drivers that are applicable and available to the application

It is clearly the application developer's responsibility to carefully evaluate the functionality required for the application and the features available with existing drivers.

The functionality of available drivers may sometimes be augmented by export/import features associated with a specific data source. Peachtree Accounting for Windows (PAW), for example, has an export feature allowing tables in Btrieve format to be exported in text format (.csv files). These tables can then be imported, e.g., into Microsoft Access, and converted to that application's RDBMS format. With the data in an RDBMS format, we can then use the Access ODBC driver to use the data in a C++ application. Note that in the ODBC notion, the data source is now associated with Access, not with PAW.

18.8 Multiple ODBC Connections

An application can register more than one data source and request multiple connections to these data sources. Each connection is considered to execute in a separate transaction space. An active connection can maintain one or more processing streams to different applications.

It is the driver that maintains a transaction for each active connection. The application can request an automatic commit action to be performed by the driver upon a successful completion. If the application simply submits a transaction request without a commit specification, the driver waits for an explicit commit request from the application. After a commit or rollback function is performed, the driver resets all statements associated with that transaction.

The Driver Manager (see Figure 18.1) maintains the environment that permits the application to switch between connections while a transaction is in progress on the current connection.

18.9 Example of Using ODBC

With the introduction of ODBC features and capabilities presented above, we will now illustrate how we register data sources and select drivers under Windows NT.

Selecting a Driver

We add a data source by first selecting a driver and then specifying the associated data source. We start by double clicking on the "32 ODBC" icon appearing in the Control Panel in Figure 18.2. The Data Sources dialog comes up, as shown in Figure 18.3, with a display of currently registered data sources.

Data sources currently registered include Perhello associated with the POET driver and StudentRegistration, associated with the Access driver. We will now add a data source, which was imported from PAW, by clicking the Add... button in the Data Sources dialog. The Add Data Source dialog shown in Figure 18.4, appears for user input. We are really picking the driver here, not the data source yet.

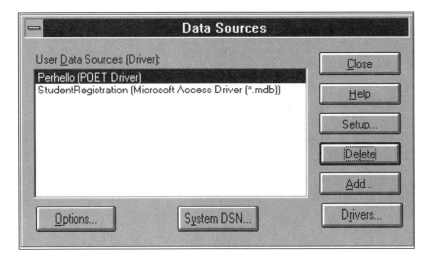

Figure 18.3 Currently Registered Data Sources

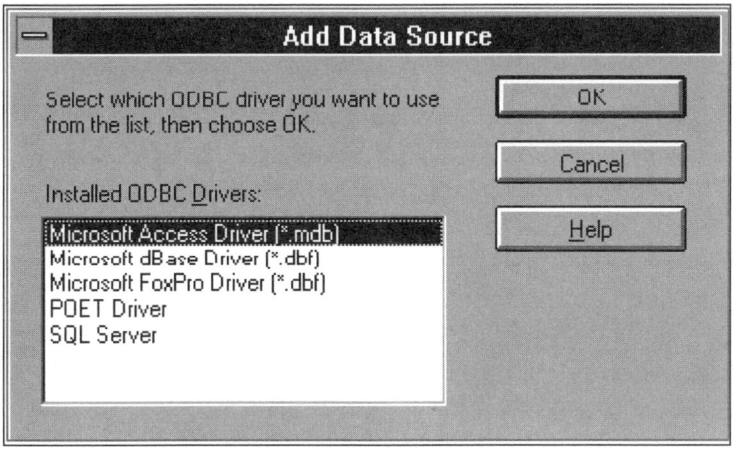

Figure 18.4 Selecting a Driver for a Data Source

Adding a Data Source

After selecting the Access driver, the ODBC data source setup dialog appears for that driver, as shown in Figure 18.5.

We use the Select... button to locate the physical data source, PAW401.mdb. The logical name InvoicePAW is entered for the Data Source Name. This becomes the data source we specify in an application, e.g., an MFC C++ application that requires access to a table in InvoicePAW.

The Advanced... button can be used to set access privileges and assign a password.

After clicking on the OK button in the setup window, the new addition to registered data sources appears in the Data Source dialog, as shown in Figure 18.6.

18.10 C++ and ODBC

We now have three registered data sources in the system that can be accessed from any application that supports connections to that data source. Two of the data sources are associated with the Access ODBC driver. The third is associated with the POET driver. We will demonstrate how to build MFC C++ applications that use the Access data sources in Chapter 25.

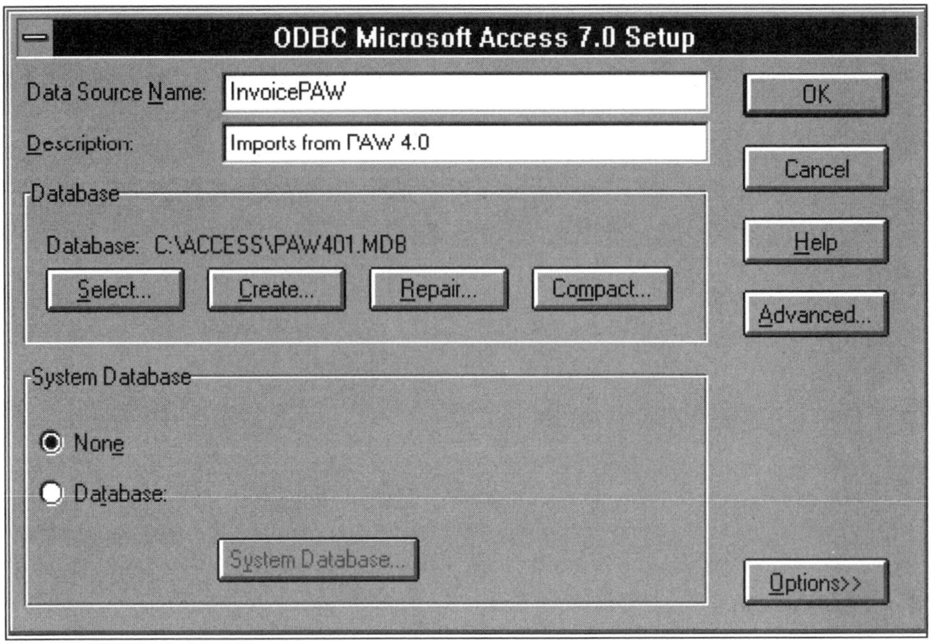

Figure 18.5 Selecting a Data Source

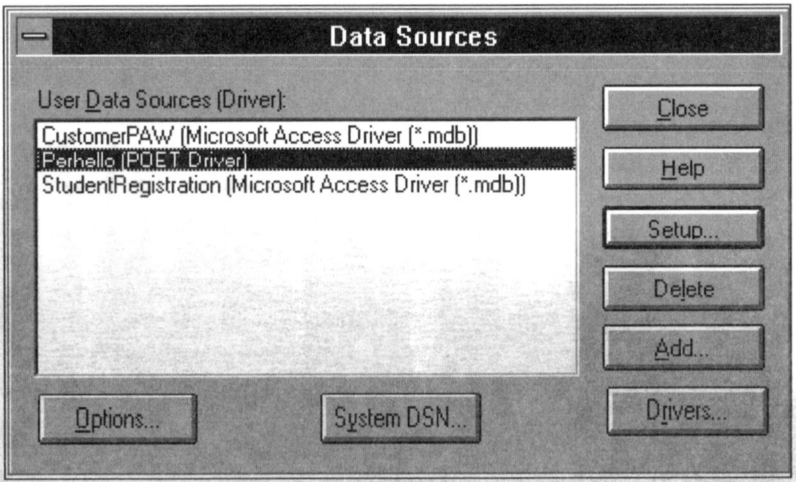

Figure 18.6 Registered ODBC Data Sources

18.11 Summary

The ODBC mechanism is a powerful tool for allowing applications access to a wide variety of DBMSs without recoding the application for each DBMS.

A data source includes the database and DBMS access mechanism for that database. Before an application can use a DBMS, the associated data source must be registered by using the ODBC Administration program. There must also be an ODBC driver available for the particular data source.

ODBC drivers are designed for specific API and SQL conformance levels. Every application developer must scrutinize the capabilities of a potential driver to make sure it has the required functionality.

References

1. Microsoft ODBC 3.0 Programmer's Reference and SDK Guide, Microsoft Press, Redmond, WA 1997.

PART 5

C++ Frameworks

Frameworks have become a mainstay for object-oriented software development. Their primary strengths are manifested in code reuse and consistency in class design. There are a number of frameworks available, both as part of visual development environments, as well as individual products developed by third-party vendors.

An object-oriented framework is developed for a specific programming language. The two primary object-oriented programming languages in use today are C++ and Smalltalk. We will focus exclusively on C++ frameworks here.

The use of a C++ framework can provide a significant reduction of the total development time for a large application. This is particularly true for GUI intensive programming, where user interface elements such as windows, buttons, dialogs, and menus are part of a particular framework.

Some of the C++ frameworks that are commercially available include Microsoft's MFC, Borland's OWL, Inmark's zApp, Zinc Software's Zinc, Hewlett-Packard's UIM/X, and XTV Software's XTV. These frameworks differ significantly with respect to architecture and capabilities. The features of each framework are constantly changing and a comparison of their capabilities is outside the scope of this book. Articles discussing the comparison of C++ frameworks can be found in [1, 2] at the end of chapter 19.

We will first briefly describe the components and creation of an independent C++ framework. The major emphasis of this part of the book is how the Microsoft Foundation Class (MFC) library is structured and how we can use the MFC framework within the Microsoft Visual C++ development environment.

19

Creating a Framework

A C++ framework is more than a library of classes. It also includes mechanisms that can manipulate the elements of the framework. In this chapter, we will first describe the structure and components that make up a framework. Then we will explore the different mechanisms that automatically glue the various components together. Finally, we will describe the different architectural schemes used in typical C++ frameworks.

19.1 Components of a Framework

Every framework consists of at least a C++ library with simple and generic classes. Some frameworks may also include C structs, especially when a framework has evolved over time. Remember, the only difference between C++ classes and structs is that the default access for a class is private and public for a struct.

The classes in a framework will usually support a number of functional categories that are required for a large C++ application:

- Memory management
- Domain-specific, e.g., banking, graphics applications, and air traffic control
- Domain-neutral, e.g., Windows, X/Motif, math libraries, and multi-tasking
- Database support
- Synchronization support for multithreaded applications
- Exception handling
- Common data structures

- Cross-platform support

In addition to the usual set of functional categories, some frameworks include aides to lessen a sometimes steep learning curve:

- On-line help, preferably context-sensitive
- Tutorials
- Sample files and applications
- Debugging aids

Some of the early C++ frameworks were implemented merely as thin wrappers to existing C APIs, e.g., the Microsoft Windows Software Development Kit (SDK). This is not the architecture we expect from a modern framework. A typical, robust C++ framework includes a hierarchy of C++ classes with an extensible architecture that provides efficient run-time execution. The classes in the framework encapsulate the capabilities required for a particular domain, e.g., the support for windows, menus, and dialog boxes in a GUI application.

Robustness is expected from a modern C++ framework, and can be supported with a uniform design strategy of exception handling within each of the C++ classes.

The capability to extend an existing framework is important, since there will usually be some required functionality that is not supported by the framework we chose.

The level of desired extensibility ranges from simply deriving a new C++ class from a base class in the framework to the integration of a third-party tool or library such as Rogue Wave's *tools.h++* or the STL.

Run-time efficiency can be affected with a balance between a limited use of inheritance and generic classes. The current trend in framework design is to rely heavily on generic class structures, and minimize the use of inheritance hierarchies. This minimizes the run-time overhead associated with polymorphism.

The primary feature that distinguishes a framework from a mere C++ library is the implementation of built-in mechanisms. These are discussed in the next section.

19.2 Framework Mechanisms

Booch [3] defines a mechanism as "A structure whereby objects collaborate to provide some behavior that satisfy some requirement of the problem." We can think of a mechanism as the hidden "glue" that automates an extended functionality beyond the particular function we call in a library. Examples of mechanisms that may play a role in a framework include the following:

- Use of polymorphism—Automated run-time mechanism for picking the invocation of a member function

- Use of aggregation—Embedded objects are created and destroyed automatically using the built-in C++ constructor/destructor mechanism
- Use of templates—Instantiation of a generic class, and making use of built-in iterators
- Built-in exception handling—The use of exceptions instead of, for example, the use of assert() to detect and handle exceptional conditions
- Storage Management (beyond the new() and delete() associated with C++ constructors and destructors)—For example, a memory pool for dynamic allocations that includes automatic garbage collection
- Built-in help—The use of special function keys, e.g., F1 to invoke context-sensitive help screens
- Synchronization to allow concurrent access to data structures—The use of built-in features to provide mutex, semaphores, critical sections, etc.
- Locking of files or records for protection of shared data structures—Automated features built into a database system to provide data integrity for multi-user access.

A major part of the learning curve for a new framework is to understand the various mechanisms employed and how they will affect the execution of our application.

19.3 C++ Framework Structure

Modern C++ frameworks are structured with an architecture that combines an inheritance hierarchy and generic classes using the C++ template feature. Early frameworks were constructed with a heavy reliance on inheritance since the template feature is a relatively new implementation by compiler vendors.

Single-Tree Model

The two primary architectures employing inheritance hierarchies are the single-tree model and the forest model. The single-tree model is anchored by a root base class, sometimes called *Object*. Every class in the hierarchy is derived from the single root class. An example of this structure is the first widely-known C++ library, which was created at the National Institute of Health and referred to as the NIHCL [4]. A partial hierarchy of the NIHCL is shown in Figure 19.1.

This structure was based on the Smalltalk model and every class in the hierarchy is derived from the *Object* root class. One oddity produced with this type of structure is noted by the *Date* class which doesn't seem to belong with the rest of the container classes.

Other oddities included at the same level as the *Date* class are *Time*, *Random*, *Semaphore*, and *Scheduler*. None of these classes relate well to container classes, and a better representation could be provided by creating other sets of related classes, separate from the containers.

Forest Model

The hierarchical structure of most modern frameworks is based on the forest model (or class families). The rationale for using class families, rather than a single-tree hierarchy, can be summarized as follows:

- Selecting a component from the library is associated with less complexity and overhead
- Support for the structure of related groups (families) of classes is included
- Extending the framework by including other libraries is simplified

An example of class families is shown in Figure 19.2 and illustrates a reorganization of a small set of the NIHCL classes.

The hierarchy shown in Figure 19.2 represents a class family that provides support for the creation of different types of containers. The hierarchy illustrated in Figure 19.3 represents a different class family, which provides concurrency support for the management of multiple processes.

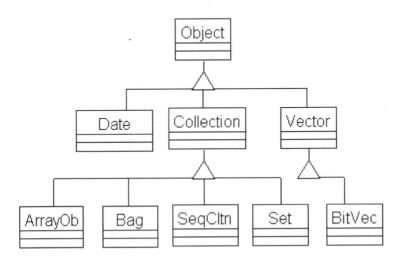

Figure 19.1 NIHCL Hierarchical Structure

Hybrid

A variation of the strict single-tree or forest model is a hybrid between these two models. Class families can be represented as individual branches originating from the same root, i.e., a single-tree model. Collections of other related classes can be specified independent of the primary tree structure. These collections may originate from a different base class, or from no base class at all.

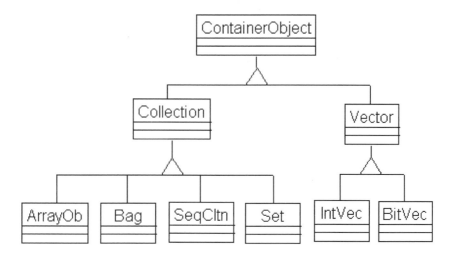

Figure 19.2 A Container Family Hierarchy

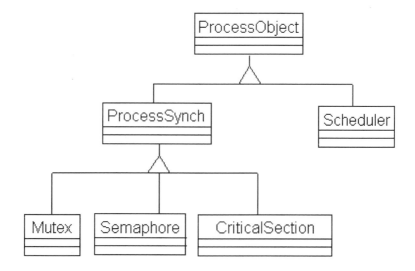

Figure 19.3 A Process Management Family Hierarchy

The MFC structure falls into this category. A sample of two families originating from the same base root class is shown in Figure 19.4. One class family includes classes for the construction of dialog boxes, the other includes classes for graphical drawing objects. (The vertical representation is used to make all the derived classes fit on the same page.)

Two different collections of related classes are shown in Figure 19.5. The first collection includes classes that support run-time features to archive objects, dump the context of an object, and provide RTTI of an object. The second collection includes array, list, and map containers for pointers.

Neither of these two groups of classes derive from the root CObject. They are still part of the same library (MFC), but cannot be classified as either single-tree or forest models.

Choosing a Hierarchy

An important issue to consider before choosing a C++ framework is the depth of the inheritance hierarchy. A deep hierarchy may result in significant run-time overhead associated with polymorphism, i.e., run-time binding. This is a feature that is inherent in the run-time mechanism and cannot be turned off.

A significant change in the philosophy of framework design is to replace the older, deep inheritance hierarchies with an extended use of generic classes via the C++ template feature. This will increase compilation-time, but is likely to reduce run-time overhead significantly. Most modern C++ frameworks employ a balanced design between inheritance hierarchies and generic classes for maximum run-time efficiency.

Very few C++ applications are developed today without the use of a framework. In the remaining chapters of this part, we will explore the concepts discussed here using the MFC as a typical representation of a modern C++ framework.

19.4 Root Classes

The development of a class library includes an important design decision regarding what types of features should be included in the root base class for each class family. Each root class is usually implemented as an abstract base class representing the common interface for all the derived classes. We will use the MFC root class CObject to illustrate an example of a common interface.

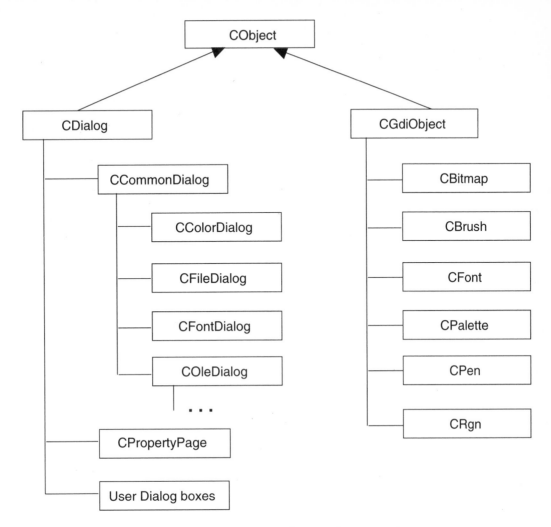

Figure 19.4 MFC Hierarchical Structure of Two Class Families

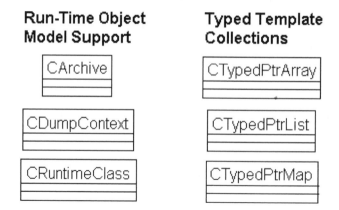

Figure 19.5 MFC Collections of Two Class Families

MFC CObject

A simplified version of the root class CObject used in the MFC is shown in Figure 19.6. This code snippet is taken from the header file <afx.h>.

```
class CObject {
public:
virtual ~CObject();   // virtual destructors are necessary

    // Diagnostic allocations
    void* operator new(size_t, void* p);
    void* operator new(size_t nSize);
    void operator delete(void* p);

    // Access functions
    virtual CRuntimeClass* GetRuntimeClass() const;

#ifdef _DEBUG
    // for file name/line number tracking using DEBUG_NEW
    void* operator new(size_t nSize, LPCSTR lpszFileName, int
                    nLine);
#endif

    // Disable the copy constructor and assignment by default so
    // you will get compiler errors instead of unexpected behavior
    // if you pass objects by value or attempt to assign objects.

protected:
  CObject();

private:
  CObject(const CObject& objectSrc);
```

```
      void operator=(const CObject& objectSrc);

  public:
    BOOL IsSerializable() const;
    BOOL IsKindOf(const CRuntimeClass* pClass) const;

  // Overridables
    virtual void Serialize(CArchive& ar);

    // Diagnostic Support
    virtual void AssertValid() const;
    virtual void Dump(CDumpContext& dc) const;

  public:
    static CRuntimeClass AFXAPI_DATA classCObject;
  };
```

Figure 19.6 CObject, MFC Root Class

Even though the CObject class represents a common interface, it is not implemented as an abstract base class. Instances of this type can only be declared via derived classes, however, as witnessed by the default constructor in the protected section.

Note how the design is emphasizing efficiency by disallowing any calls by value, since the copy constructor is in the private section. Passing parameters by reference will be the calling mechanism of choice. This prevents copying of large objects to be used as locals inside a function.

Assignment of one CObject to another is also disallowed by placing the assignment operator in the private section.

One of the general services provided is the determination of whether or not an object is serializable, i.e., if it can be written or read using the Serialize() archiving function. The IsKindOf() function returns a boolean value regarding whether or not the pointer passed in is referencing a derived CObject instance.

Diagnostic support is provided with the AssertValid() and Dump() functions. Special versions of new and delete are used to manage storage associated with the diagnostic support.

The GetRuntimeClass() function returns a pointer to a structure (the static classObject) corresponding to the calling object's class. Elements of the structure include such data as the class name and the size of the object in bytes.

The way Microsoft has implemented the CObject class for the MFC library indicates the types of features that can be placed in the common interface of a root class. Most of these common features can be used for most domain libraries other than a GUI implementation, and can thus provide a starting point for the design of a root class interface.

19.5 Summary

Most large-scale C++ development projects can increase productivity by using a framework that matches the particular problem domain. Significant code reuse can be accomplished using existing C++ classes via standard interfaces.

We discussed the C++ Standard Template Library (STL) in Chapter 14. The STL certainly qualifies as a major framework. The use of templatized functions and classes is inherent in the library structure. The primary built-in mechanism in the STL is the comprehensive set of iterators that can be used in creating and manipulating the ten different categories of containers. No coding extensions are required to use this library. All the features required for using the algorithms, containers, and iterators are already available for use in C++ applications. Another automated mechanism is the built-in memory allocation as elements are added to the various containers.

Other frameworks include Microsoft's MFC and Borland's OWL for developing Windows programs on PCs. We will investigate the structure, features, and built-in mechanisms of the MFC throughout the remainder of this book.

The primary disadvantage of using a framework is the learning curve required to understand the overall architecture and the built-in mechanisms that automate the run-time behavior. The time invested in learning how to use the STL, MFC, OWL, etc., are well worth the effort, however. Once we get past the, sometimes steep!, learning curves of these frameworks, our productivity increases dramatically compared with having to create applications from scratch.

References

1. O'Brien, L., Comparing Application Frameworks, *Software Development*, p. 23, June 1995.

2. O'Brien, L., C++ Application Frameworks, *Software Development*, p. 84, October 1995.

3. Booch, G., *Object-Oriented Analysis and Design with Applications*, Second Edition, Benjamin/Cummings, Redwood City, CA 1994.

4. Gorlen, K.E., et al., *Data Abstraction and Object-Oriented Programming in C++*, John Wiley, New York, NY 1990.

20

Microsoft Foundation Class (MFC) Library

The MFC is a comprehensive C++ library designed specifically for the development of applications running on the Windows 3.x, Windows 95, and Windows NT platforms. Development tools have been added to allow the MFC to also be used for applications running on Macintosh, DEC Alpha, IBM RISC, and MIPS machines.

The MFC is used in conjunction with Microsoft Visual C++, which has become a major development tool for Windows applications. In this chapter, the emphasis is on the architecture of the MFC:

- MFC class hierarchies
- Some of the primary data structures used to support the MFC architecture
- Some of the built-in mechanisms that operate behind the scenes

We will describe the overall structure of the MFC and the major components and mechanisms that play a role in creating Windows C++ applications.

20.1 Visual C++ Components

The Microsoft Visual C++ development environment consists of a number of tools that can be used to create Windows or DOS C++ applications. The Microsoft Developer Studio is the overall development platform that integrates the C++ compiler, linker, loader, text editor, wizards, debuggers, and on-line help functions.

Individual C++ development tools include the AppWizard for automating the creation of a number of different applications, as shown in Figure 20.1. Each application is created within a Project Workspace, which integrates all the header and source files included in an application.

The focus of the chapters in this part is on using the MFC to create a Windows C++ application. The visual development platform also allows the creation of other types of Windows applications as shown in Figure 20.1, e.g., by direct access to the API ("Application"), and DOS programs ("Console Application").

Other tools included in the development platform encompass a ClassWizard for the specification of new classes, a ResourceEditor for creating dialog boxes, menus, tool bars, etc., text editor, and source code debugger The text editor used for creating and modifying header and source files has built-in drag-and-drop features, similar to Word for Windows 6.0 and higher, and color-coded highlighting for special code such as keywords and comments.

A special feature of the C++ tool kit is the Component Gallery, which contains different categories of classes that can be included in an application. The Component Gallery dialog is shown in Figure 20.2 and illustrates two categories of C++ classes that can be added to an application: (1) various Microsoft classes, and (2) OLE Controls (OCXs). The other two categories refer to classes that have been generated for the application (enroll) and the data source to be accessed (e.g., PAW401, see Chapter 18).

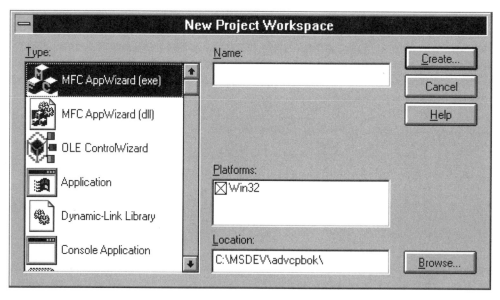

Figure 20.1 AppWizard and Project Workspace

20.2 Creating Windows Applications

Creating a Windows application from scratch is no simple matter, regardless of whether we are using C and the Windows Software Development Kit (SDK) or C++ and MFC. The learning curve for either approach is steep.

The API of the SDK contains more than 1,000 functions that may be required in a C Windows program. C programmers who want to use the MFC have to first learn C++ before they can tackle the creation of an MFC application. The task of C++ programmers is a bit simpler since they "only" need to understand the structure and use of the MFC.

The primary advantage of the C++/MFC approach is the tremendous amount of automated code generation supported by the AppWizard, the ease of adding class members via the ClassWizard, the code reuse from the MFC C++ classes, and the built-in run-time mechanisms that support the application. For example, the creation and deletion of window objects is performed automatically via C++ class constructors, and the message loop is hidden and encapsulated within the framework mechanism.

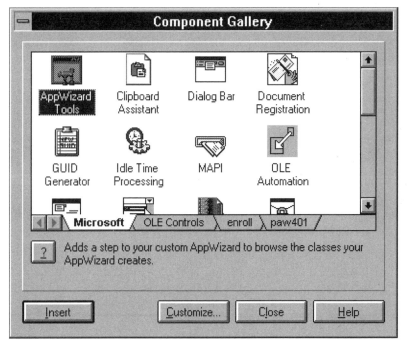

Figure 20.2 The Component Gallery

20.3 The Structure of the MFC Framework

The MFC consists of a set of C++ classes and structs that support certain functionalities of a Windows application. The C++ classes are organized into a hierarchical library that takes advantage of the C++ inheritance features. The concept of a framework was described in Chapter 19 as a superset of a C++ library. The additional features of a framework (besides the library) are the built-in mechanisms that automate the run-time execution of an application. Examples of mechanisms within an MFC Windows application include:

- Creation and destruction of windows objects
- Automatic inclusion and execution of WinMain()
- Automatic processing of the message loop
- Automatic mapping of events, and macros to handle the events
- When a user opens a window for a document, a view is created automatically and attached to the document (document/view architecture)
- Raising of exceptions within a try block, and the propagation of exceptions to the scope of a handler
- Built-in diagnostic support
- Built-in RTTI support
- Serialization of persistent data as archived data elements to a file

The primary emphasis of the rest of this chapter is on the C++ class hierarchies and some of the supporting structs. Some of the primary framework mechanisms are also discussed.

20.4 C++ Class Hierarchies

The MFC class hierarchies have evolved from the original version 1.0 to the current version 5.0. This version includes unique features for Windows 95 and NT, e.g., 32-bit processing and multi-threading. We will primarily be referring to the latest version here. Occasionally, we may point out differences regarding threaded and non-threaded features of the various MFC versions.

From earlier chapters, we have seen that the two primary architectures used in creating C++ libraries are inheritance and templatized classes. The MFC is primarily built on inheritance structures, and fits into the hybrid model described in Chapter 19. Several families of related classes form individual branches of inheritance hierarchies that derive from a common root class.

One way to look at the set of MFC classes could be strictly from an inheritance point of view. This view would have to consider all the classes in a particular derivation hierarchy, and is not very sensible, given the large number of different classes. Also, there are a number of classes that are not related via inheritance.

A simpler way to analyze the MFC classes is to group them into a number of functional hierarchies that relate to the features and mechanisms that are present in Windows applications. Some of the MFC classes supplied with Visual C++ 5.0 that are derived from the CObject class are illustrated in Figure 20.3.

The classes in the categories shown in Figure 20.3 are all derived from the CObject base class, and can take advantage of the inheritance and polymorphism mechanism inherent in a C++ hierarchy. They also benefit from the various built-in MFC mechanisms. There is another set of MFC C++ classes that are not derived from the CObject base class:

- Internet Server API
- Run-time Object Model Support
- Simple Value Types
- Structures
- Support Classes
- Typed Template Collections
- OLE Typed Wrappers
- OLE Automation Types
- Synchronization

Each of these categories includes a collection of related classes (and/or structs) that encapsulate certain Windows features, e.g., the classes CMultiLock and CSingleLock used in controlling access to resources in a multi-threaded program.

In this chapter, we will focus on the Application Architecture and Window Support classes shown in Figure 20.3, since they represent most of the classes we would use in a complex Windows application. We will ignore most of the classes that are not derived from CObject, except for some of the structures.

The MFC is using a special naming convention, where all the class names are prefixed by an uppercase "C," followed by an uppercase letter for each word-component contained in the class name, e.g., CMemoryException. Underscores are not used for class names, such as C_Memory_Exception. This naming convention permeates all of the Visual C++ tools, and should be followed for the sake of convenience. A lot of extra work would be required to undo the class names created by the built-in AppWizard, for example.

All the classes in the categories listed above, except the last three, are derived from the same root class: CObject. After a brief discussion of the purpose and structure of the CObject class, we will describe the classes in each of the categories.

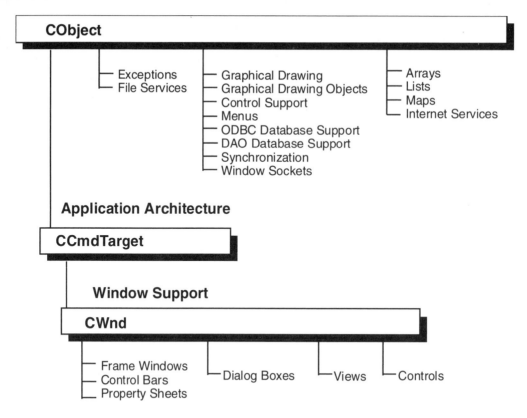

Figure 20.3 MFC Class Categories

The CObject Class

This class was introduced in Chapter 19 as an example of a root class anchoring a large C++ library. The purpose of this base class is to present a common interface for all of the subsequent derived classes. Here is a snapshot of the class declaration in the `<afx.h>` header file:

```
// class CObject is the root of all compliant objects

class CObject {
public:
  // Diagnostic Support
  virtual void Dump(CDumpContext& dc) const;
  virtual void AssertValid() const;

  // RTTI support
  virtual CRuntimeClass* GetRuntimeClass() const;
  BOOL IsKindOf(const CRuntimeClass* pClass) const;
```

```
    // Serialization
    virtual void Serialize(CArchive& ar);
    BOOL IsSerializable() const;

    virtual ~CObject();

protected:
    CObject();

private:
    CObject(const CObject& objectSrc); // no implementation
    void operator=(const CObject& objectSrc); // no implementation
    ...
};
```

The common interface includes features for diagnostic support, RTTI support, and serialization, with increasing levels of sophistication. The simplest level of support is the diagnostic support used in the debugger to track down miscellaneous run-time error conditions. The general purpose, free-standing CDumpContext class provides a context between data to be dumped and a monitor screen or a file. The AssertValid() function is used to validate the data members of an object. Both of these two functions should be overridden in the derived class to provide the required functionality.

The next level of support is run-time class information. Objects of classes derived from CObject can be queried for class name and memory size at run-time. This can be useful when we are passing void* pointers or in a polymorphic structure where the class identity of objects is hidden (or at best ambiguous). Whereas the diagnostic support is automatic, run-time class information can only be obtained if we add the appropriate macros:

```
    // In header file:
    DECLARE_DYNAMIC(CDerivedClass)

    // In the corresponding implementation file:
    IMPLEMENT_DYNAMIC(CDerivedClass, CObject)
```

Every class derived from CObject is assigned an object of type CRuntimeClass, which contains run-time data about the derived instances.

The highest level of support offered by CObject is *serialization*. This is a process to archive the values of an object's data members to provide data persistence as permanent storage. No indexing is available, and object data must be restored in exactly the same order as it was written to a file. This process encapsulates the complex file handling normally required for data storage, and provides a simple archiving mechanism. This mechanism allows data members to be written to a file in a serial order and read back later in the same serial order.

The default constructor is protected to allow the construction of objects in the derived classes. Note the private copy constructor and assignment operator. This prevents copying and assignment of CObject instances outside the scope of this class. In particular, this prevents the copy mechanism in a function if we attempt to pass large objects by value. Large objects should be passed by reference.

20.5 Application Architecture

An *application* represents an executable program that a user can invoke by double-clicking on an application icon or a *.exe* file. A Windows application is created automatically by the AppWizard in the Microsoft Developer Studio, using the application name that we specify. Every application, e.g., CEnrollApp, created by this tool is of type CWinApp:

```
// File: CEnrollApp
// See enroll.cpp for the implementation of this class
//

class CEnrollApp : public CWinApp {
public:
  CEnrollApp();
// ...
};
```

There is exactly one application object (derived from CWinApp) for each Windows application program:

```
// File: enroll.cpp
// ...
// CEnrollApp construction
CEnrollApp::CEnrollApp() {
  // TODO: add construction code here,
  // Place all significant initialization in InitInstance()
}
// ...
// The one and only CEnrollApp object
CEnrollApp theApp;  // global declaration

// CEnrollApp initialization

BOOL CEnrollApp::InitInstance() {
// ...
}
```

The application instance `theApp` is automatically declared as a global object in the application source file (.cpp). This (hidden) instance encapsulates the message loop relating to the events and message passing mechanism.

The structure of the CWinApp class (from which every Windows application class is derived) is shown in Figure 20.4. This class is a descendant of the CObject class and can, thus, support run-time diagnostics, RTTI data, and serialization. We are ignoring the two intermediate classes, CCmdTarget and CWinThread, for now; they are not important in the context of how an application is created.

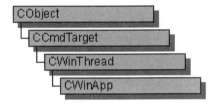

Figure 20.4 Structure of the CWinApp Class

The declaration of the CWinApp class is in the <afxwin.h> header file and has a number of member functions, some of which we may have to override:

```
// File: afxwin.h
// ...
class CWinApp : public CWinThread {
  DECLARE_DYNAMIC(CWinApp) // RTTI support
public:

// Constructor
  CWinApp(LPCTSTR lpszAppName = NULL);
                     // app name defaults to EXE name

// Overrides for implementation
  virtual BOOL InitInstance(); // override in CMyApp
  virtual int Run();
  virtual BOOL OnIdle(LONG lCount); // return TRUE if more idle
                                    //   processing
  virtual int ExitInstance(); // return app exit code
  virtual LRESULT ProcessWndProcException(CException* e,
                                          const MSG* pMsg);
public:
  virtual ~CWinApp();
// ...
};
```

The two primary member functions we may have to override in our application are InitInstance() and Run(). The first determines how an instance of the application object is created. This is overridden to specialize the application's main window object. The Run() function automates the execution of the standard message loop (event loop), and can be overridden to tailor the message loop handling. Note that we can override the handling of a Windows exception in ProcessWndProcException().

Each application that uses the MFC can only have one object derived from CWinApp. This object is declared globally, outside the class scope, and is constructed when other C++ global objects are constructed. The application is already available when Windows calls the WinMain() function, which is supplied by the MFC library.

The creation and execution of a C++ Windows application that uses the MFC is shown in Figure 20.5. The WinMain() function is supplied by the MFC framework.

```
int WinMain() {
  CMyApp::InitInstance();
          // Initializes an instance of CMyApp
  CWinApp::Run();
          // Maintains the message loop
          // Calls OnIdle() to check idle processing
          // Calls ExitInstance()
          // Provides clean-up
          // Returns resources
  return 0;
}
```

Figure 20.5 CWinApp Processing

Figure 20.5 does not represent the exact C++ code of `WinMain()`, and is only intended to show the order of processing. An instance of the application object is created as a global object and is initialized by calling the (almost always) overridden `InitInstance()`. We will examine the contents of this function later, when we discuss the creation of windows and frames.

Application Processing

After the necessary window objects are created and displayed, `WinMain()` then calls `Run()` to maintain the default message loop. If we want to customize the message loop, we must override this function to get the required functionality.

`Run()` calls `OnIdle()` to check on idle processing. This function can be overridden to provide customized idle processing. When an application has completed its processing, `Run()` calls `ExitInstance()` for clean-up processing and return of allocated resources. `ExitInstance()` can also be overridden for customized exit processing.

20.6 Frame Windows

Window objects are constructed from various frame elements. The type of frame used depends on the type of Windows application we are creating. A snapshot of the class hierarchy of frame window classes is shown in Figure 20.6.

These classes are all derived from the CWnd class and are used to build and maintain the window objects needed for Single Document Interface (SDI), Multiple Document Interface (MDI), and OLE applications. The SDI and MDI frame classes will be discussed in detail in Chapter 22.

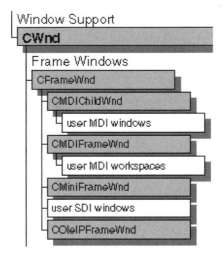

Figure 20.6 Hierarchy of Frame Window Classes

20.7 Documents and Views

Documents are among the most important elements of the application structure, since they are one of the required parts of the document/view architecture. In general, a document holds the data associated with an application, and the data can be displayed in one or more views.

Documents

The CDocument class resides high in the hierarchy, as illustrated in Figure 20.7.

Every application created with the *AppWizard* has source code generated for the built-in document/view architecture. A set of a header and a corresponding source file is created automatically for both the document and its associated view(s).

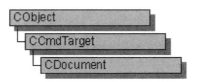

Figure 20.7 The CDocument Hierarchy

A user document class is derived from CDocument and holds the data that will be displayed to the users in one or more of the views. The document represents the data (e.g., the text and formats that make up a Word for Windows file) that the user typically opens with a File/Open command and saves with a File/Save or File/Save As... command.

Here is an example of a user-defined document that will hold the Student data table from the Stdreg32 data source in an ODBC application:

```
// File: enrollDoc.h

class CEnrollDoc : public CDocument {
protected:
  CEnrollDoc();
  DECLARE_DYNCREATE(CEnrollDoc)

// Attributes
public:
  CStudentSet m_StudentSet; // data in Student table

// Implementation
public:
  virtual ~CEnrollDoc();
// ...
};
```

The CEnrollDoc class is the user-defined document class containing the data in the Student table. This data will be displayed in a user window as part of a CEnrollView object.

The relationships between documents and views is probably the most important design aspect of an MFC application that is built with the *AppWizard* and will be discussed in great length in Chapter 22.

Views

The data held by a document object is displayed to users via one or more view objects associated with the document. A view represents an image of the document data in a frame window. The view object interprets user input as operations on the document via menu clicks and keyboard input. There is thus a dual functionality associated with a view: (1) provide an interface for user input; and (2) display data in a particular format, as requested by a user. The hierarchy of the CView class is shown in Figure 20.8.

The CView class is considered a window element and is derived from CWnd. We have included the CScrollView class here, since it is simply a CView class with scrolling capabilities. Note that a document is considered a part of the application architecture, whereas a view is represented as a window object. Here is a user-defined view class for the Enroll application:

```
// File: enrollView.h

class CEnrollView : public CScrollView {
protected:
  CEnrollView();
  DECLARE_DYNCREATE(CEnrollView)

// Attributes
public:
  CStudentSet* m_pSet; // ptr to data held by the doc

// Operations
public:
  CEnrollDoc* GetDocument(); // linking a view to a doc
// ...
// Implementation
public:
  virtual ~CEnrollView();

// ...
};
```

The user-defined view is derived as a scroll view. The pointer m_pSet is of the same type as the actual data object declared in the CEnrollDoc class. A view can be linked to its associated document object by calling the GetDocument() function.

A document can have multiple views associated with it. When a user opens a window of a document, the MFC framework creates a view and attaches it to the document. A document template specifies the type of view and frame window that should be used to display each type of document. Document templates are discussed in Chapter 22.

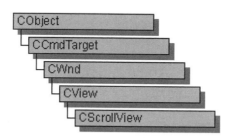

Figure 20.8 The CView Class Hierarchy

20.8 Dialog Boxes

The CDialog class is the base class used for creating and displaying dialog boxes on the screen. Dialog boxes come in two categories: modal and modeless. A modal dialog box must be closed by the user before the application continues. A modeless dialog box allows the user to display the dialog box and return to another task without canceling or removing the dialog box.

The CDialog class hierarchy is shown in Figure 20.9. A dialog is considered a kind of window and provides an interface for user commands.

Figure 20.10 shows a simple example of a modal dialog for the Help/About menu item of the Enroll application.

A CDialog object is a combination of a dialog template and a user-defined class derived from the CDialog class. The ResourceEditor is first used to create the dialog template and save it as a resource. ClassWizard is then used to create a class derived from CDialog. Each control and button on the dialog is mapped to a member function (message handler) in the derived class.

20.9 Exceptions

MFC version 4.0 and later integrates C++ exceptions with the rest of the framework. The Structured Exception Handling (SEH) that was used with macros in previous versions is no longer used. The hierarchy of exception classes is shown in Figure 20.11.

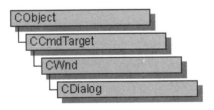

Figure 20.9 CDialog Class Hierarchy

Figure 20.10 Modal Dialog for Help/About

The exceptions listed in Figure 20.11 are integrated into the design of the MFC framework, and any one of them may be raised whenever an exceptional condition is detected by the run-time system. A strategy for handling exceptions was discussed in Chapter 13 and should be included with any C++ application using the MFC.

20.10 ODBC Database Support

We saw in Chapter 18 how we can interface a C++ application to an RDBMS via the Open Database Connectivity (ODBC) mechanism. The MFC classes shown in Figure 20.12 are used to support ODBC for Windows applications. These classes are derived directly from CObject. They are included in the <afxdb.h> header file.

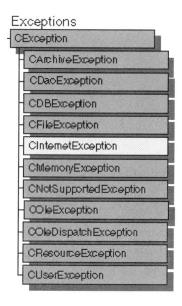

Figure 20.11 Hierarchy of MFC Exception Classes

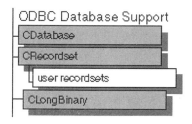

Figure 20.12 MFC ODBC Database Support

A CDatabase object is used to create a connection to a data source. This object will allow us to operate on the data source. We can have one or more CDatabase objects active at a time in an application. Managing the switching between data sources is performed by the Driver Manager, as explained in Chapter 18.

A CRecordset object is usually declared as an aggregation of a document object. A recordset object contains a set of records (rows) selected from a particular data source. These objects are typically used in two forms: dynasets and snapshots. A dynaset stays synchronized with data updates made by other users in a multi-user environment, whereas a snapshot is a static view of that data.

Here is an example of creating a user recordset of the Student table for the Stdreg32 data source where the new object is a part of a document object:

```
// File: enrollDoc.h

class CEnrollDoc : public CDocument {
protected:
  CEnrollDoc();
  DECLARE_DYNCREATE(CEnrollDoc)

// Attributes
public:
  CStudentSet m_StudentSet; // CRecordSet object

// Overrides
  // ...
// Implementation
public:
  virtual ~CEnrollDoc();
  // ...
};
```

The CStudentSet class was created in ClassWizard and linked there to the Stdreg32 data source. This topic will be explored in detail in Chapter 25.

The CLongBinary class was used in earlier versions of MFC for very large binary data objects (BLOBs) in a database, e.g., a record field in an SQL table might contain a bitmap representing a picture. A CLongBinary object can store such an object and keep track of its size.

The CLongBinary class has been superseded by the CByteArray class in conjunction with the DFX_Binary function which is used to transfer data between a recordset and a data source. Using CByteArray provides more functionality under Win32, since there is no longer the size limitation associated with 16-bit CByteArray objects. The CByteArray is a collection class that we will discuss in Chapter 21.

20.11 File Services

The MFC includes a set of classes that are used to interface with disk files, in-memory files, OLE streams, and Windows sockets. The base class for this set of classes is CFile, which is derived directly from the root class CObject. The structure of the file services classes is shown in Figure 20.13.

All the classes derived from CFile can be used in conjunction with the CArchive class to perform serialization. Here is a brief description of some of the file services classes:

- CFile—provides an interface to binary disk files
- CMemFile—provides an interface to files kept in memory
- CSharedFile—provides an interface to shared files kept in memory
- COleStreamFile—provides an interface to OLE compound files
- CSocketFile—provides an interface to a Windows Socket
- CStdioFile—provides an interface to buffered stream disk files
- CFileException—file-oriented exception raised within some of the file services functions

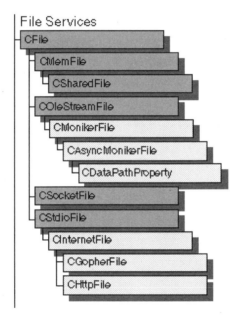

Figure 20.13 MFC File Services

The common interface for these classes includes functions to open, close, read, write, etc. Here is a snapshot of the CFile class found in the `<afx.h>` file:

```
// File: afx.h
// ...
class CFile : public CObject {
  DECLARE_DYNAMIC(CFile)
public:
// Flag values
  enum OpenFlags {
    modeRead =          0x0000,
    modeWrite =         0x0001,
    modeReadWrite =     0x0002,
   // ...
  };

  enum Attribute {
    normal =     0x00,
    readOnly =   0x01,
    hidden =     0x02,
    system =     0x04,
    volume =     0x08,
    directory = 0x10,
    archive =    0x20
  };

  enum SeekPosition { begin = 0x0, current = 0x1, end = 0x2 };

  enum { hFileNull = -1 };

// Constructors/destructor
  CFile();
  CFile(int hFile);
  CFile(LPCTSTR lpszFileName, UINT nOpenFlags);
  virtual ~CFile();


// Operations
  virtual BOOL Open(LPCTSTR lpszFileName, UINT nOpenFlags,
                    CFileException* pError = NULL);
  virtual UINT Read(void* lpBuf, UINT nCount);
  virtual void Write(const void* lpBuf, UINT nCount);
  virtual void Close();

  DWORD SeekToEnd();
  void SeekToBegin();
  virtual LONG Seek(LONG lOff, UINT nFrom);

  virtual CFile* Duplicate() const;
  virtual void SetLength(DWORD dwNewLen);
  virtual DWORD GetLength() const;

// ...
```

```
// Attributes
  UINT m_hFile;

protected:
  BOOL m_bCloseOnDelete;
  CString m_strFileName;
};
```

Most of the member functions seen here are also available in the various iostream header files. The question then becomes: Which library to use, MFC or the standard C++ I/O library?

If we are primarily developing Microsoft Windows applications without any concern for portability, the simplest solution will be to use the MFC file services. Since all the file services classes are derived from the CObject root class, we have a uniform set of utilities which is not limited to the file services. The exception handling, serialization, RTTI, and debug features are built-in mechanisms available with all classes derived from CObject.

If our applications will be ported to other platforms, however, we should use the standard C++ I/O library.

20.12 Graphics Support

The Windows API provides a variety of drawing tools that can be used in various device contexts. Graphical objects include pens to draw lines, brushes to fill interiors, and fonts to draw text. MFC provides a number of graphic-object classes that encapsulate the drawing tools in Windows.

Graphical objects are not drawn directly on a window, but via a device context. This provides for a general drawing mechanism that is independent of the physical characteristics of a particular hardware device.

The MFC includes two sets of classes for accomplishing drawing in Windows applications: (1) graphical device context classes that support an interface between the application and the devices; and (2) the graphical object classes that provide the actual objects such as pens, brushes, circles, etc.

Graphical Device Contexts

A device context is a data structure that contains data elements used to describe the drawing attributes of a particular device, e.g., a laser printer or a monitor display. These device contexts allow device-independent drawing in Windows applications. The same graphical objects can be sent to a printer or a display by simply choosing the appropriate device context. The set of MFC device context classes is shown in Figure 20.14.

The CDC (device context) base class is derived from the root class CObject. Here is a brief description of the device context classes:

- CDC—Concrete base class for all the device context classes
- CClientDC—Manages a display context associated with a window's client area
- CMetaFileDC—Associates a device context with a metafile (i.e., a sequence of programming instructions)
- CPaintDC—Encapsulates calls to BeginPaint() and EndPaint(), the traditional API functions used to paint a window
- CWindowDC—Manages a display context associated with an entire window, including the client area, frame window, and controls

The CDC base class defines the common interface for all the device-context classes. This includes a set of member functions for working with a device context, such as a display or printer, as well as members for working with a display context associated with the client area of a window. A metafile is used as a reusable set of programming instructions.

In general, drawing is performed via the member functions associated with a CDC instance. This class provides member functions for device-context operations and drawing tools. Other features include working with color palettes, drawing text, working with fonts, scrolling, and playing back metafiles.

Graphical Objects

The graphical objects are used as drawing tools for a particular device context. The hierarchy of these classes is shown in Figure 20.15.

Drawing in a Device Context

Now that we have seen the two different sets of classes required for drawing, let's do an example showing a typical use of a context and how we can draw in that context.

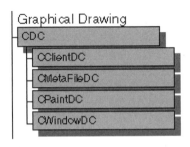

Figure 20.14 MFC Device Context Classes

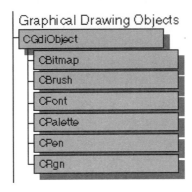

Figure 20.15 MFC Graphical Object Classes

The primary mechanism used for drawing objects is to include the necessary code in the virtual `OnDraw()` function that is created automatically by the AppWizard. Here are some code snippets for drawing a colored circle in the client area:

```
// drawView.h : interface of the CDrawView class

class CDrawView : public CView {
public:
  CDrawDoc* GetDocument();
  virtual void OnDraw(CDC* pDC);   // overridden to draw this view
protected:
  CDrawView();
private:
  CRect m_rectEllipse;
  int   m_nColor;
// ...
};


// drawView.cpp : implementation of the CDrawView class

CDrawView::CDrawView() : m_rectEllipse(50, 50, 300, 300),
                         m_nColor(LTGRAY_BRUSH) {
}

void CDrawView::OnDraw(CDC* pDC) {
  pDC->SelectStockObject(m_nColor);
  pDC->Ellipse(m_rectEllipse);
}
```

Drawing is performed within the View component of the architecture created by the AppWizard (see Chapter 22 for a discussion of the Document/View design pattern). We've added the two data members, m_rectEllipse, to describe the bounds of an ellipse, and m_nColor, an integer value used to designate the color fill of the ellipse. (See Figure 20.16.)

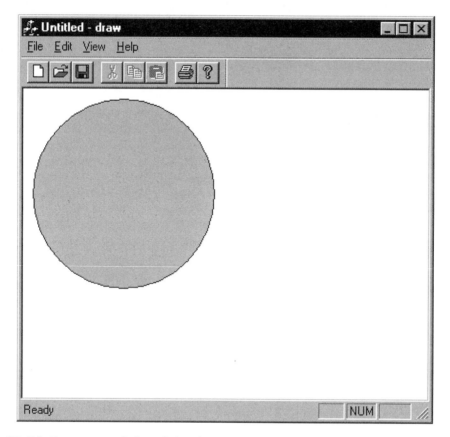

Figure 20.16 Drawing a Colored Circle in a Device Context

In Figure 20.16, one of the drawing objects is a light gray brush used as fill color in the circle. The `Ellipse()` function in the API is used to actually draw the circle, but note that we are calling this function via the pointer to the context CDC.

Even though this is a very simple example for drawing an object, all drawing is performed in the same manner: We first select the device context for which we will be using the polymorphic `OnDraw()` function. We then select the particular brush, pen etc. to be used for the drawing object, including the dimensions and origin of the object. Finally, we include the required function calls inside the `OnDraw()` functions.

The drawing encapsulation mechanism inherent in the MFC greatly simplifies the coding effort compared to interfacing directly with the API. The primary advantage of drawing to a device context is that the gory details of the hardware interfaces have been hidden, i.e., we are performing device independent drawing.

A device context is treated as a Windows resource, of which there is a limited supply. Whenever we are finished using a context, we must remember to release it back to the system.

20.13 Data Structures

Some of the Windows API structures are encapsulated in the MFC with simple C++ classes that derive directly from their equivalent API structs. A POINT API data structure defines the x- and y-coordinates of a point and has the following form:

```
typedef struct tagPoint {
    int x; // x-coordinate of point
    int y; // y-coordinate of point
} POINT;
```

The equivalent MFC class, CPoint, is derived from the Windows POINT structure and includes member functions to manipulate CPoint and POINT structures:

```
class CPoint : public tagPOINT { // in <afxwin.h>
public:
// Constructors
    CPoint();
    CPoint(int initX, int initY);
    CPoint(POINT initPt);
    CPoint(SIZE initSize);
    CPoint(DWORD dwPoint);

// Operations
    void Offset(int xOffset, int yOffset);
    void Offset(POINT point);
    void Offset(SIZE size);
    BOOL operator==(POINT point) const;
    BOOL operator!=(POINT point) const;
    void operator+=(SIZE size);
    void operator-=(SIZE size);

// Operators returning CPoint values
    CPoint operator+(SIZE size) const;
    CPoint operator-(SIZE size) const;
    CPoint operator-() const;

// Operators returning CSize values
    CSize operator-(POINT point) const;
};
```

It may at first seem surprising that we can derive a C++ class from a struct. The thing to remember is that the only semantic difference between structs and classes is that the default access rule for struct data members is `public`, as opposed to `private` for class data members.

Other MFC encapsulations that have a similar structure to the CPoint class are CSize and CRect for rectangular window structures. A CPoint object can be used wherever a POINT structure is used. The member functions of this class that interact with a "size" accept either CSize objects or SIZE structures, since the two are interchangeable. Also note the operators that take a SIZE parameter and return a CPoint object, as well as the operator that takes a POINT parameter and returns a CSize object.

This has been a short description of some of the various families of classes represented in the MFC structure. Complete references to the MFC can be found in [1–3] and the on-line help included with the Visual C++ CD.

We have omitted one set of classes here: the Collection classes. They will be described in the next chapter and compared to the features of the STL.

In the next section, we will discuss some of the mechanisms inherent in the MFC framework. The set of built-in mechanisms constitutes the part that distinguishes a framework from a mere C++ library.

20.14 MFC Mechanisms

In Chapter 19, we described a C++ framework as an architecture of a set of related classes and the mechanisms that are automatically invoked when we create instances of these classes in an application. In this chapter, we have described several of the class families that make up the MFC framework. The focus of this section is on some of the built-in mechanisms in the MFC.

Automatic Inclusion of `WinMain()`

Every Windows application has a WinMain() function as the entry point for starting a Windows application. If we are interfacing directly with the API, we have to create our own WinMain() function. Here is a prototype for this function [4]:

```
int PASCAL
WinMain (HINSTANCE hInstance,       // Who am I?
         HINSTANCE hPrevInstance,   // Any older siblings?
         LPSTR     lpszCmdLine,     // Ptr to command line.
         int       cmdShow);        // How to open my window?
```

In addition to providing the entry point for a Windows application, the WinMain() function must also include code to register one or more call-back functions for handling messages; register a window as a particular "class;" create the window; show the window; and load resources, such as accelerator keys, the icon to be used in a minimized state, and the particular shape of the cursor. All this (drudgery) code is hidden by the MFC and is created automatically behind the scenes.

Encapsulated Message Loop

After a Windows application is started, the program executes a message loop (sometimes referred to as the "message pump") to handle events originating from the user interfacing via keyboard strokes and mouse clicks. In a typical C program (or C++ code that doesn't use the MFC), the message loop looks like this [4]:

```
int PASCAL
WinMain (HINSTANCE hInstance,       // Who am I?
         HINSTANCE hPrevInstance,   // Any older siblings?
         LPSTR     lpszCmdLine,     // Ptr to command line.
         int       cmdShow)         // How to open my window?
{
  // ...
  while (GetMessage(&msg, 0, 0, 0)) {
    if (!TranslateAccelerator (hwnd, hAccel, &msg)) {
    TranslateMessage(&msg); // Convert KEYDOWNs to CHARs
    DispatchMessage(&msg);  // Transmit message to WndProc
    }
  }
  return 0;
}
```

This message loop is hidden by the MFC and is incorporated within the automated message handling (see Chapter 23 for details of how messages and call-backs are handled).

Automatic Mapping of Events

Windows applications are event-driven, with messages passed as a result of hitting keys on the keyboard and clicking on menus and other controls. Without using the MFC, this mechanism has to be coded explicitly. Here is a call-back function to handle File menu requests [4]:

```
LRESULT CALLBACK
AccelWndProc (HWND    hwnd,    // For whom is message sent?
              UINT    mMsg,    // What is exact message?
              WPARAM  wParam,  // ...message details.
              LPARAM  lParam)  // ...message details.
{
  switch (mMsg) {
    case WM_COMMAND: {
      char buffer[80];
      char *npch;

      switch (wParam) {
        case IDM_FILE_NEW:
          npch = "File.New";
          break;
        case IDM_FILE_OPEN:
          npch = "File.Open...";
          break;
        case IDM_FILE_SAVE:
```

```
                npch = "File.Save";
                break;
            case IDM_FILE_SAVEAS:
                npch = "File.Save As...";
                break;
            case IDM_FILE_PRINT:
                npch = "File.Print";
                break;
            case IDM_FILE_EXIT:
                npch = "File.Exit";
                break;
// ... etc. for Edit menu requests
        }

// Display message box with name of selected menu item.
        wsprintf (buffer, "%s command selected.", (LPSTR)npch);
        MessageBox (hwnd, buffer, achAppName, MB_OK);

// If user selected File.Exit, simulate {-}.
// Close menu selection
        if (wParam == 6) {
            SendMessage (hwnd, WM_SYSCOMMAND, SC_CLOSE, 0L);
        }
    }
    break;

    case WM_DESTROY:
        PostQuitMessage(0);   // Handle application shutdown.
        break;

        default:
            return(DefWindowProc(hwnd,mMsg,wParam,lParam));
            break;
    }
    return 0L;
}
```

The call-back mechanism to handle these messages is automated within the MFC. As a minimum, the cascading menus File, Edit, and Help are included as window features (see Figure 20.16), and the code for all the call-backs associated with the menu items is included as defaults (see Chapter 23 for details).

Document/View Architecture

When a user opens a window for a document (which holds the data), a view is created automatically and attached to the document. This is the basic Document/View design pattern, which is inherent in all MFC programs created using the AppWizard. This constitutes the primary mechanism for how data is attached to a document, and how that data is displayed in various forms in a window. The details of this architecture are described in Chapter 22.

Diagnostic Support

Automated diagnostic support can be associated with any of the classes that derive from the root class CObject. Here is a code snippet from the CObject class:

```
// File: afx.h

class CObject {
public:

  // Diagnostic allocations
  void* PASCAL operator new(size_t nSize);
  void* PASCAL operator new(size_t, void* p);
  void PASCAL operator delete(void* p);

#if defined(_DEBUG) && !defined(_AFX_NO_DEBUG_CRT)
  // for file name/line number tracking using DEBUG_NEW
  void* PASCAL operator new(size_t nSize,
                            LPCSTR lpszFileName, int nLine);
#endif

  // Diagnostic Support
  virtual void AssertValid() const;
  virtual void Dump(CDumpContext& dc) const;
};
```

Diagnostic features are available by setting the system variable _DEBUG, which determines the version of the overloaded new() to use.

The virtual member function AssertValid() provides run-time checks of an object's internal state. This includes, typically, assertions on all the object's member variables to see if they contain valid values. For example, AssertValid() can check that all pointer data members are not NULL. If an object is determined to be invalid, AssertValid() halts the program.

The virtual member function Dump() is used to dump the contents of the data members associated with the object on whose behalf the function is invoked. The output is dumped to the specific device context referenced as the parameter. Here is an example of how we can override the Dump() member function [1]:

```
// File: person.h

class CPerson : public CObject {
public:
#ifdef _DEBUG
  virtual void Dump( CDumpContext& dc ) const;
#endif

  CString m_firstName;
  CString m_lastName;
  int     m_nAge;
  // etc. ...
};
```

```
// File: person.cpp

#ifdef _DEBUG
void CPerson::Dump( CDumpContext& dc ) const {
  // call base class function first
  CObject::Dump( dc );

  // now do the stuff for our specific class
  dc << "last name:  " << m_lastName  << "\n"
     << "first name: " << m_firstName << "\n"
     << "age:        " << m_nAge      << "\n";
}
#endif
```

When the `Dump()` function is overridden in a derived class, it calls the base class `Dump()` first, and then performs the specialized dumping action. Note how we can use the "`<<`" operator in association with the referenced device context.

RTTI Support

Run-time type information (RTTI) is now a part of the C++ standard specification, but is not yet widely available on C++ compilation systems. The MFC structure has built-in RTTI support for all classes derived from CObject. This is different from the standard C++ RTTI features. Here are the code sections of CObject that apply to the RTTI data:

```
// File: afx.h

class CObject {
public:
  // ...
  virtual CRuntimeClass* GetRuntimeClass() const;
  BOOL IsKindOf(const CRuntimeClass* pClass) const;
  // ...
public:
  static const AFX_DATA CRuntimeClass classCObject;
};
```

Each class has a static object of type `CRuntimeClass` that contains data associated with its class, such as class name, size of an object, and a pointer to the `CRuntimeClass` of the base class.

The virtual `GetRuntimeClass()` member function returns a pointer to the object's `CRuntimeClass` structure, which contains the run-time information.

The member function `IsKindOf()` returns `True` if the object referenced belongs to the specified class or to a class derived from the specified class.

The MFC has thus implemented its own RTTI mechanism independent of the C++ features specified in the standard.

Persistent Data

Many applications need to save persistent data to a permanent storage device, e.g., a disk or a tape. The MFC has included a "Serialization" feature to accomplish this task. The term serialization refers to data that is stored in a "flat file" where the data is read in the same order as it was written. The serialization feature is available for all classes derived from the CObject class. Here are the pertinent member functions:

```
// File: afx.h

class CObject {
public:
  // ...
  BOOL IsSerializable() const;

// Overridables
  virtual void Serialize(CArchive& ar);

  // ...
};
```

The non-virtual predicate function `IsSerializable()` returns `True` if the "this" object can be serialized; otherwise False. This function tests whether the object is eligible for serialization. The eligibility is determined by checking if the class declaration contains the DECLARE_SERIAL macro, and if the corresponding implementation contains the IMPLEMENT_SERIAL macro.

The virtual Serialize() function is used to perform both read and write actions. Here is a simple serialization example [1] using the same CPerson class we saw in the Diagnostic Support section above:

```
void CPerson::Serialize(CArchive& ar) {
  if (ar.IsStoring()) {
    ar << m_firstName;
    ar << m_lastName;
    ar << m_nAge;
  }
  else {
    ar >> m_firstName;
    ar >> m_lastName;
    ar >> m_nAge;
  }
}
```

The reference to the CArchive object is associated with a file object that has the attribute CArchive::Store for a write operation or CArchive::Load for a read operation. The predicate IsStoring() returns True for the Store attribute, and False otherwise. This is how we can use the same Serialize() function for both reading and writing.

The overloaded insertion and extraction operators are defined in the CArchive class. Note how the data members are read in the exact same order as they were written.

The use of the MFC serialization mechanism is simpler than using the standard C++ I/O features, but is, of course, non-portable.

Users of the earlier versions of the MFC should note that the serialization mechanism now has an alternative, more efficient way of handling persistent data: the use of Data Access Objects (DAO). The details of the DAO mechanism are described in [1].

Exception Handling

Exception handling is a C++ feature, and in itself doesn't qualify as a mechanism. When it is integrated into the architecture of a C++ library, however, it can be considered a mechanism built into the framework.

The raising of exceptions within try blocks, and the propagation of those exceptions to the appropriate scope of a handler, is a mechanism the Windows program can take advantage of by creating the required handlers and supplying the desired fault tolerant features.

The details of the exception handling mechanism built into the MFC are discussed in Chapter 24.

20.15 Summary

The MFC is a framework tailored for the domain of Windows programming. The library structure is a hybrid between a single-tree and a forest model. Several class families branch from the same root class CObject. Other related collections of classes are independent classes that do not originate from the CObject class.

The root class CObject provides a common interface for a number of features, including

- Diagnostic support
- RTTI
- Serialization

The CObject copy constructor is made private to make the passing of objects by value illegal. The assignment operator is also made private to prevent assignment of CObject instances.

Class families are provided to support the creation of windows, frames, documents, views, dialog boxes, menus, controls, drawing of graphics, writing of text, etc. A set of collection classes supports various types of containers. Other classes include support for

- Internet Server API

- Run-time Object Model Support
- Simple Value Types
- Structures
- Support Classes
- Typed Template Collections
- OLE Typed Wrappers
- OLE Automation Types
- Synchronization

Each Windows application is constructed as either a Single Document Interface (SDI) or Multiple Document Interface (MDI). The architecture of these applications is based on the Document/View design pattern. A document holds the data associated with an application, and that data can be displayed in multiple forms as one or more views. SDI applications have a single document and one view associated with the document. MDI applications can have multiple documents and multiple views associated with each document.

The MFC includes a number of built-in mechanisms that are invoked automatically, including:

- Automatic Inclusion of `WinMain()`
- Encapsulated Message Loop
- Automatic Mapping of Events
- Document/View Architecture
- Diagnostic Support
- RTTI Support
- Serialization
- Exception Handling

References

1. Microsoft Visual C++ Version 4.0, Programming with MFC, Volume 2, Microsoft Press, Redmond, WA 1995.

2. Microsoft Visual C++ Version 4.0, MFC Class Library Reference, Volume 3, Microsoft Press, Redmond, WA 1995.

3. Microsoft Visual C++ Version 4.0, User's Guide, Volume 1, Microsoft Press 1995.

4. Yao, Paul, *Peter Norton's Windows 3.1 Power Programming Techniques*, 2nd Edition, Bantam Books, New York, NY 1992.

21

MFC Collection Classes

We have seen the importance of collection classes in connection with the implementation of the aggregation relationship between classes. C++ does not have a language construct to implement this relationship, and we use the concept of collections (or containers) to embed a set of objects as an attribute of an application class.

The Standard Template Library (STL), which is now a part of the C++ ISO/ANSI standard specification, was described in Chapter 14. We noted there that the STL consists of ten different containers distributed among three primary groups:

- Sequence containers:
  - vector<T>
  - deque<T>
  - list<T>

- Associative containers:
  - set< key, compare>
  - multiset<key, compare >
  - map< key, T, compare >
  - multimap< key, T, compare >

- Adapter containers:
  - stack<Container<T> >
  - queue< Container<T> >
  - priority_queue< Container<T>, compare>

The focus of this chapter is on the various collection classes that Microsoft has implemented with the MFC C++ class library. The various design features utilized in the classes are of particular interest; especially the use of templates. We will also provide a comparison between the MFC collection classes and the STL containers.

21.1 MFC Collection Class Hierarchies

The MFC containers are referred to as "collection classes." These classes support the creation of arrays, lists, and maps. These three types are also referred to as different "shapes." The arrays are just like ordinary C++ arrays, except that memory allocation is handled automatically. The list structures are doubly linked lists. The map structures associate a value with a key. Maps are sometimes referred to as "dictionaries."

There are two primary groups of MFC collection classes [1, p. 117]:

- Template-Based Collection Classes—These classes came into existence when templates were supported by the Visual C++ compiler

- Non-Template Collection Classes—These classes were released with the original MFC version

The collection classes are organized into two separate structures. One set represents all the collection classes derived directly from the root class CObject. The other set is a group of independent, typed template collections, which are derived from a BASE_CLASS specified as a template parameter.

We will show the class hierarchies for the arrays, lists, and maps first. The class hierarchy for the array collections derived from CObject is shown in Figure 21.1.

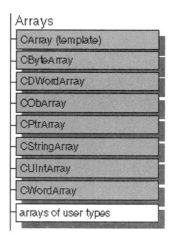

Figure 21.1 Array Collection Classes

These classes include the templatized CArray, and the "hard-coded" array classes for specific types, e.g., instances of type CObject, WORD, and CString. The CArray class is similar to the STL vector<T> class. Memory allocations in a CArray object are made automatically based on how many elements are added to the array.

The list collection classes derived from CObject are shown in Figure 21.2.

We recognize the same combination of collections as for the array classes: the templatized class CList, and the specific lists for pointers (void*), CObject, and CString objects. The CList class is similar to the STL list<T> container class. They are both doubly linked structures.

The map collections derived from CObject are shown in Figure 21.3.

We notice the templatized CMap class and non-template classes for specific associations between a key and a value, e.g., CMapStringToString for mapping a CString key to a CString object. The CMap class is similar to the STL map<key, T, compare> class, except that there is no specification for a comparison function object. (The complete set of mapping types for the non-template classes are listed in the summary in Table 21.3.)

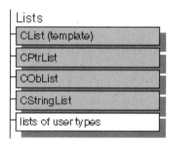

Figure 21.2 List Collection Classes

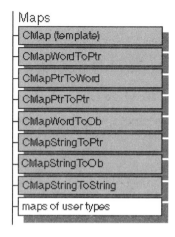

Figure 21.3 Map Collection Classes

Type-Safe Collections

The second group of collection classes, i.e., the set of collections that are not derived from CObject is shown in Figure 21.4. These classes are derived from a specific BASE_CLASS, and there is one class for each of the three basic shapes.

These collections are templatized and are considered type-safe. Type safety is defined as the assurance that a function will not be passed any actual parameters of a type it cannot handle. This can happen when we are passing a pointer to an object of a derived class. The compiler can't detect an erroneous run-time call. The best assurance of type safety is the use of template classes, where all type checking is performed at compile time.

These collection classes are considered type-safe because their member functions only operate on the specified collection of the derived class or the base class.

We will now take a closer look at the design features of the three different shape collections which are summarized in Tables 21.1 through 21.3.

21.2 Array Collections

The type information associated with MFC array collections is summarized in Table 21.1.

Table 21.1 provides a list of all the various array collection classes. The two template classes are listed first. CArray is derived directly from CObject. CTypedPtrArray is a type-safe class derived from a designated BASE_CLASS. The column designated Type 1 shows the kind of objects that are stored with a particular collection. The Type 2 column is only used with the typed collection to designate the type of object in the collection. Note that CObArray is a collection of pointers to CObject instances.

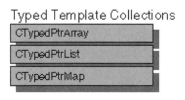

Figure 21.4 Typed Template Collections

Table 21.1 MFC Array Classes

Class	Shape	Type1	Type 2	Type-Safe
CArray	array	T		no
CTypedPtrArray	array	BASE_CLASS	T	yes
CByteArray	array	BYTE		yes(1)
CDWordArray	array	DWORD		yes(1)
CObArray	array	CObject*		no
CPtrArray	array	void*		no
CStringArray	array	CString		yes(1)
CUIntArray	array	unsigned int		yes(1)
CWordArray	array	WORD		yes(1)

(1) The class is type-safe if used as intended, e.g., using CStringArray to store CString objects is type-safe, but not for char*.

Members of Array Collections

The templatized collections are found in `afxtempl.h`, the non-template collections in afxcoll.h. Here is a summary of the members in the CArray collection:

```
// File: afxtempl.h
// ...
template<class TYPE, class ARG_TYPE>
class CArray : public CObject {
public:
// Construction
  CArray();

// Attributes
  int GetSize() const;
  int GetUpperBound() const;
  void SetSize(int nNewSize, int nGrowBy = -1);

// Operations
  // Clean up
  void FreeExtra();
  void RemoveAll();

  // Accessing elements
  TYPE GetAt(int nIndex) const;
  void SetAt(int nIndex, ARG_TYPE newElement);
```

```
    TYPE& ElementAt(int nIndex);

    // Direct Access to the element data (may return NULL)
    const TYPE* GetData() const;
    TYPE* GetData();

    // Potentially growing the array
    void SetAtGrow(int nIndex, ARG_TYPE newElement);
    int Add(ARG_TYPE newElement);
    int Append(const CArray& src);
    void Copy(const CArray& src);

    // overloaded operator helpers
    TYPE operator[](int nIndex) const;
    TYPE& operator[](int nIndex);

    // Operations that move elements around
    void InsertAt(int nIndex, ARG_TYPE newElement, int nCount = 1);
    void RemoveAt(int nIndex, int nCount = 1);
    void InsertAt(int nStartIndex, CArray* pNewArray);

// Implementation
protected:
    TYPE* m_pData;      // the actual array of data
    int   m_nSize;      // # of elements (upperBound - 1)
    int   m_nMaxSize;   // max allocated
    int   m_nGrowBy;    // grow amount

public:
    ~CArray();
    void Serialize(CArchive&);
#ifdef _DEBUG
    void Dump(CDumpContext&) const;
    void AssertValid() const;
#endif
};
```

Numerous member functions are included for creating, inserting, removing, and obtaining information about array collections of any type. We note the absence of the general iterators that are part of the STL. Access to individual array elements can be obtained by looping through the collection and using the operator[]().

The data members of CArray are straightforward with a pointer to the actual collection, and various integer variables designating the size of the collection and how it should grow.

Members of Non-Template Array Collections

We can now compare the member functions of the generic array collection CArray to one of the hard-coded collection classes, using the CStringArray as an example. Here is a summary from the `afxcoll.h` file:

```
// File: afxcoll.h
// ...
class CStringArray : public CObject {

  DECLARE_SERIAL(CStringArray)
public:

// Construction
  CStringArray();

// Attributes
  int GetSize() const;
  int GetUpperBound() const;
  void SetSize(int nNewSize, int nGrowBy = -1);

// Operations
  // Clean up
  void FreeExtra();
  void RemoveAll();

  // Accessing elements
  CString GetAt(int nIndex) const;
  void SetAt(int nIndex, LPCTSTR newElement);
  CString& ElementAt(int nIndex);

  // Direct Access to the element data (may return NULL)
  const CString* GetData() const;
  CString* GetData();

  // Potentially growing the array
  void SetAtGrow(int nIndex, LPCTSTR newElement);
  int Add(LPCTSTR newElement);
  int Append(const CStringArray& src);
  void Copy(const CStringArray& src);

  // overloaded operator helpers
  CString operator[](int nIndex) const;
  CString& operator[](int nIndex);

  // Operations that move elements around
  void InsertAt(int nIndex, LPCTSTR newElement, int nCount = 1);
  void RemoveAt(int nIndex, int nCount = 1);
  void InsertAt(int nStartIndex, CStringArray* pNewArray);

// Implementation
protected:
  CString* m_pData;     // the actual array of data
  int      m_nSize;     // # of elements (upperBound - 1)
  int      m_nMaxSize;  // max allocated
  int      m_nGrowBy;   // grow amount
```

```
public:
  ~CStringArray();

  void Serialize(CArchive&);
#ifdef _DEBUG
  void Dump(CDumpContext&) const;
  void AssertValid() const;
#endif

protected:
  // local typedefs for class templates
  typedef CString BASE_TYPE;
  typedef LPCTSTR BASE_ARG_TYPE;
};
```

This set of member functions and data members is exactly the same as for the templatized CArray collection class. The only difference is that the ARG_TYPE in CArray has been hard-coded with the CString type in the CStringArray class. The same holds true for the other non-template array collections.

The last code section of CStringArray includes the two typedefs BASE_TYPE and BASE_ARG_TYPE. These can be used to derive type-safe template collection classes similar to CTypedPtrArray.

The other non-template array collection classes also have the same set of members as the CStringArray class.

21.3 List Collections

The MFC list collection classes are shown in Table 21.2.

The two list template classes are listed first, followed by the non-template classes. Note that the type used with the CObList is a pointer to CObject rather than the object itself.

Table 21.2 MFC List Collection Classes

Class	Shape	Type1	Type 2	Type-Safe
CList	list	T		no
CTypedPtrList	list	BASE_CLASS	T	yes
CPtrList	list	void*		no
CObList	list	CObject*		no
CStringList	array	CString		yes

The general structure of a list is a collection of nodes with each node consisting of pointers to the next and previous nodes, and the data element itself. Data members include pointers to the head and tail of the set of nodes, as well as a counter for how many nodes are currently stored in the collection. These members are illustrated in the next section.

Members of List Collections

Here is a summary of the members found in the `afxtempl.h` header for the CList collection class:

```
// File: afxtempl.h

// ...

template<class TYPE, class ARG_TYPE>
class CList : public CObject {
protected:
   struct CNode {
      CNode* pNext;
      CNode* pPrev;
      TYPE data;
   };
public:
// Construction
   CList(int nBlockSize = 10);

// Attributes (head and tail)
   // count of elements
   int GetCount() const;
   BOOL IsEmpty() const;

   // peek at head or tail
   TYPE& GetHead();
   TYPE GetHead() const;
   TYPE& GetTail();
   TYPE GetTail() const;

// Operations
   // get head or tail (and remove it) - don't call on empty list
!
   TYPE RemoveHead();
   TYPE RemoveTail();

   // add before head or after tail
   POSITION AddHead(ARG_TYPE newElement);
   POSITION AddTail(ARG_TYPE newElement);

   // add another list of elements before head or after tail
```

```
      void AddHead(CList* pNewList);
      void AddTail(CList* pNewList);

      // remove all elements
      void RemoveAll();

      // iteration
      POSITION GetHeadPosition() const;
      POSITION GetTailPosition() const;
      TYPE& GetNext(POSITION& rPosition); // return *Position++
      TYPE GetNext(POSITION& rPosition) const; // return *Position++
      TYPE& GetPrev(POSITION& rPosition); // return *Position-
      TYPE GetPrev(POSITION& rPosition) const; // return *Position-

      // getting/modifying an element at a given position
      TYPE& GetAt(POSITION position);
      TYPE GetAt(POSITION position) const;
      void SetAt(POSITION pos, ARG_TYPE newElement);
      void RemoveAt(POSITION position);

      // inserting before or after a given position
      POSITION InsertBefore(POSITION position, ARG_TYPE newElement);
      POSITION InsertAfter(POSITION position, ARG_TYPE newElement);

      // helper functions (note: O(n) speed)
      POSITION Find(ARG_TYPE searchValue,
                    POSITION startAfter = NULL) const;
        // defaults to starting at the HEAD, return NULL if not found
      POSITION FindIndex(int nIndex) const;
        // get the 'nIndex'th element (may return NULL)

  // Implementation
  protected:
    CNode* m_pNodeHead;
    CNode* m_pNodeTail;
    int     m_nCount;
    CNode* m_pNodeFree;
    struct CPlex* m_pBlocks;
    int m_nBlockSize;

    CNode* NewNode(CNode*, CNode*);
    void FreeNode(CNode*);

  public:
    ~CList();
    void Serialize(CArchive&);
#ifdef _DEBUG
    void Dump(CDumpContext&) const;
    void AssertValid() const;
#endif
};
```

The CList class can be used to create doubly-linked lists of any type. The list is constructed as a set of nodes, where each node has the usual next and previous pointers, and a data element.

Member functions include features for adding and removing elements at both the head and the tail of the list. There are also functions to insert in the middle of the list: InsertBefore() and InsertAfter(). Note the comments for the iterators GetNext() and GetPrev() regarding how the respective positions are incremented and decremented. Also, note the slow speed of the Find() function.

The data members include pointers to the head and the tail of the list, as well as structures for memory management.

The last section of the class declaration includes the virtual functions from CObject for serialization and diagnostic features.

Members of Non-Template List Collections

The non-template list classes have the same set of members as the templatized CList class. The only difference is the hard-coded types for the particular list, e.g., a pointer to a CObject instance in the CObList class:

```
// File: afxcoll.h

// ...

class CObList : public CObject {
protected:
  struct CNode {
    CNode*    pNext;
    CNode*    pPrev;
    CObject* data;
  };
  // ...
  POSITION InsertAfter(POSITION position, CObject* newElement);
  // ...
  // local typedefs for class templates
  typedef CObject* BASE_TYPE;
  typedef CObject* BASE_ARG_TYPE;
};
```

This is exactly the same design as we noted above when we compared the non-template array classes to the CArray class. The parameter types and the node type are now hard-coded with the CObject* type. The typedefs are used by derived template classes, e.g., CTypedPtrList.

21.4 Map Collections

The MFC map collection classes are summarized in Table 21.3.

Table 21.3 MFC Map Collection Classes

Class	Shape	Type1	Type 2	Type-Safe
CMap	map	key	T	no
CTypedPtrMap	map	BASE_CLASS	key, T	yes
CMapWordToPtr	map	WORD	void*	no
CMapPtrToWord	map	void*	WORD	no
CMapPtrToPtr	map	void*	void*	no
CMapWordToOb	map	WORD	CObject*	no
CMapStringToPtr	map	CString	void*	no
CMapStringToOb	map	CString	CObject*	no
CMapStringToString	map	CString	CString	yes

The types listed in the Type 1 column represent the key that will be used to look up the associated value of the types listed in the Type 2 column.

The BASE_CLASS shown for `CTypedPtrMap` in the Type 1 column is the base class from which this collection class is derived. The types for the key and its associated value are both listed in the Type 2 column for this collection class.

The general structure of a map includes an association construct which consists of a pointer to the next association, a hashing value, the key, and the associated value. The data members include an array of pointers to the associations, the size of the hash table, the number of associations currently stored in the collection, and miscellaneous memory management constructs. These members are illustrated in the next section.

Members of Map Collections

Here is a summary of the members found in the `afxtempl.h` header for the CList collection class:

```
// File: afxtempl.h

// ...

template<class KEY, class ARG_KEY, class VALUE, class ARG_VALUE>
class CMap : public CObject {
protected:
  // Association
  struct CAssoc {
    CAssoc* pNext;
```

```
      UINT     nHashValue;  // needed for efficient iteration
      KEY      key;
      VALUE    value;
   };
public:
   // Construction
   CMap(int nBlockSize = 10);

   // Attributes
   // number of elements
   int GetCount() const;
   BOOL IsEmpty() const;

   // Lookup
   BOOL Lookup(ARG_KEY key, VALUE& rValue) const;

   // Operations
   // Lookup and add if not there
   VALUE& operator[](ARG_KEY key);

   // add a new (key, value) pair
   void SetAt(ARG_KEY key, ARG_VALUE newValue);

   // removing existing (key, ?) pair
   BOOL RemoveKey(ARG_KEY key);
   void RemoveAll();

   // iterating all (key, value) pairs
   POSITION GetStartPosition() const;
   void GetNextAssoc(POSITION& rNextPosition,
                     KEY& rKey, VALUE& rValue) const;

   // advanced features for derived classes
   UINT GetHashTableSize() const;
   void InitHashTable(UINT hashSize, BOOL bAllocNow = TRUE);

// Implementation
protected:
   CAssoc** m_pHashTable;
   UINT     m_nHashTableSize;
   int      m_nCount;
   CAssoc*  m_pFreeList;
   struct CPlex* m_pBlocks;
   int m_nBlockSize;

   CAssoc* NewAssoc();
   void FreeAssoc(CAssoc*);
   CAssoc* GetAssocAt(ARG_KEY, UINT&) const;

public:
   ~CMap();
   void Serialize(CArchive&);
#ifdef _DEBUG
```

```
    void Dump(CDumpContext&) const;
    void AssertValid() const;
 #endif
 };
```

Whereas the "node" is the key feature for a list, the "association" is the key construct for a map. The CAssoc struct includes a link to the next association, a hash value used for fast lookup, the key, by which a value is stored, and the associated value.

The member functions include features to get the number of associations in the collection, look up an association by a key value, add and remove associations, iterators for start position and iterating through the entire collection, and memory management features.

The data members include an array of pointers to the list of associations, the size of the hash table, the number of associations in the collection, and various memory management structures.

The last class section has the serialization and diagnostic features, just as for the CArray and CList classes.

Members of Non-Template Map Collections

The non-template map classes have the same set of members as the templatized CMap class. The only difference is the hard-coded types for the particular list, e.g., a pointer to a CObject instance in the CMapStringToOb class:

```
// File: afxcoll.h

// ...

class CMapStringToOb : public CObject {
protected:
  // ...
  struct CAssoc {
    CAssoc*  pNext;
    UINT     nHashValue;   // needed for efficient iteration
    CString  key;
    CObject* value;
  };

public:
  // ...
  // iterating all (key, value) pairs
  void GetNextAssoc(POSITION& rNextPosition,
                CString& rKey, CObject*& rValue) const;
  // ...
protected:
  // local typedefs for CTypedPtrMap class template
  typedef CString BASE_KEY;
```

```
        typedef LPCTSTR BASE_ARG_KEY;
        typedef CObject* BASE_VALUE;
        typedef CObject* BASE_ARG_VALUE;
    };
```

This is exactly the same design as we noted above when we compared the non-template array classes to the CArray class, and the list classes to the CList class. The association is now hard-coded with CString as the type of the key and CObject* as the type of the value.

In the GetNextAssoc() iterator, the key parameter is a reference to a CString object, and the value parameter is a reference to a CObject* instance.

The typedefs are used by template classes, e.g., CTypedPtrMap.

21.5 Using Template-Based Collection Classes

We have seen that the template-based collections are subdivided into two sets of classes:

- Collection classes derived from the root CObject
- Typed collection classes that are not derived from CObject, but that are type-safe

The templatized collection classes derived from CObject that are not type-safe include:

- CArray—A vector of any data type; ordered, and can be indexed by an int type. Duplicate elements are allowed.
- CList—A doubly-linked list structure for any data type which is ordered but cannot be indexed. Duplicate elements are allowed.
- CMap—A map structure that associates an object of any data type with a key. This container is not ordered, but is indexed with a key of any data type. The key must be unique, but multiple values are allowed to be associated with each key (i.e., a multimap).

The class declarations for these three shapes are listed in the `<afxtempl.h>` file, and are summarized above in Sections 21.2–21.4, respectively. We will now look at how we can use some of these classes.

Using CArray

The MFC CArray class is similar to the STL vector class. One thing that is different from the STL implementation is the second parameter ARG_TYPE, which is used to templatize some of the member functions. Here is an example using CArray and a Person class:

```cpp
// File: arramain.cpp

#include <string.h>

class Person {
public:
  Person(char* aName, int aAge) : name(aName), age(aAge) {}
  Person(const Person& rhs) {
    name = new char[(sizeof(rhs.name))];
    strcpy(name, rhs.name);
  }
  const char* getName() const {return name;}
  int getAge() const {return age;}
private:
  char* name;
  int age;
};


#include <iostream.h>

int main() {
  // ...
  Person aPerson("Peter", 25); // create an instance
  CArray<Person, Person&> theArray; // create the collection
  theArray.Add(aPerson); // add an instance
  // ...
  cout << "Name: " << theArray[0].getName()
       << "Age: "  << theArray[0].getAge() << endl;
  return 0;
}
```

The second argument in the instantiation of the CArray class is the type of the parameter passed to the Add() member function, i.e., the newElement formal parameter will reference a Person object.

In building the CArray class (as well as the CList and CMap classes), Microsoft is using the template features to create generic member functions.

Using the CArray, CList, and CMap is similar to the STL vector, list, and map, respectively. There are no adapter containers, however, so stacks, queues, and prioritized queues will have to be implemented separately. There are also no algorithms in the MFC structure. Iterators are implemented as member functions for each collection, rather than as a reusable set of components.

We will now shift our attention to the other set of templatized collections: the typed collection classes.

21.6 Using the Type-Safe Collections

The set of templatized containers that are not derived from CObject include

- CTypedPtrArray—A collection of pointers to instances of an array data type. This container is derived from either CObArray or CPtrArray.
- CTypedPtrList—A collection of pointers to nodes of a list type. This container is derived from either CObList or CPtrList.
- CTypedPtrMap—This container is derived from CMapPtrToWord, CMapPtrToPtr, CMapStringToPtr, CMapWordToPtr, or CMapStringToOb.

Each of these three classes is derived from a specified base class. The member functions of the instantiated template class use encapsulated calls to the member functions of the base class to enforce type safety. We illustrate this encapsulation in the following section.

CTypedPtrArray

Here is a snippet of the `afxtempl.h` header file for the class declaration of CTypedPtrArray, which can be derived from the non-template array collection classes:

```
// File: afxtempl.h

// ...

template<class BASE_CLASS, class TYPE>
class CTypedPtrArray : public BASE_CLASS {
public:
  // Accessing elements
  TYPE GetAt(int nIndex) const
    { return (TYPE)BASE_CLASS::GetAt(nIndex); }

  TYPE& ElementAt(int nIndex)
    { return (TYPE&)BASE_CLASS::ElementAt(nIndex); }

  void SetAt(int nIndex, TYPE ptr)
    { BASE_CLASS::SetAt(nIndex, ptr); }

// Potentially growing the array
  void SetAtGrow(int nIndex, TYPE newElement)
    { BASE_CLASS::SetAtGrow(nIndex, newElement); }

  int Add(TYPE newElement)
    { return BASE_CLASS::Add(newElement); }

  int Append(const CTypedPtrArray<BASE_CLASS, TYPE>& src)
```

```
                    { return BASE_CLASS::Append(src); }

        void Copy(const CTypedPtrArray<BASE_CLASS, TYPE>& src)
           { BASE_CLASS::Copy(src); }

        // Operations that move elements around
        void InsertAt(int nIndex, TYPE newElement, int nCount = 1)
          { BASE_CLASS::InsertAt(nIndex, newElement, nCount); }

        void InsertAt(int nStartIndex,
                      CTypedPtrArray<BASE_CLASS, TYPE>* pNewArray)
          { BASE_CLASS::InsertAt(nStartIndex, pNewArray); }

        // overloaded operator helpers
        TYPE operator[](int nIndex) const
          { return (TYPE)BASE_CLASS::operator[](nIndex); }

        TYPE& operator[](int nIndex)
          { return (TYPE&)BASE_CLASS::operator[](nIndex); }
     };
```

We recognize the same member functions that are used in the CArray class. Note, however, that all of these functions make "encapsulated" calls to the corresponding member functions in the base class. This guarantees type safety, since all actual parameters passed can be handled by the member functions of the base class.

The other two class declarations for CTypedPtrList and CTypedPtrMap are structured in exactly the same way. They also make the same type of encapsulated calls to their base class member functions.

Using Typed Arrays and Lists

The typed template classes CTypedPtrArray and CTypedPtrList both take two parameters: BASE_CLASS and TYPE. These classes can store data of any type, but they can only be derived from a non-template collection base class that stores pointers to objects. For typed arrays, this means deriving from CPtrArray (stores void*) or CObArray (stores CObject*). For typed lists, the base classes include CPtrList (stores void*) and CObList (stores CObject*).

The declaration of a typed array or list collection object includes the instantiation based on the two required class parameters:

```
        CTypedPtrArray<CObArray, Person*> persCollection;
        CTypedPtrList<CPtrList, Alerts*> alertCollection;
```

The first declaration creates an array collection instance for pointers to Person objects. The class Person must be derived from CObject, since the typed collection class is derived from the base class CObArray, which stores CObject pointers.

The second declaration creates a list collection instance for pointers to Alerts objects. The Alerts class is not derived from CObject, and this form can be used for storing pointers to any collection of objects that are not derived from CObject. This is still type-safe, since the base class CPtrList is a collection of (void*) pointers.

If the value parameter is specified as just a class (or struct) without a pointer or reference, a copy constructor for that type must exist. This is required to allow the creation of a local copy of a parameter passed by value to any of the member functions. Having such a copy constructor may affect the run-time efficiency for large collections. One of the design features built into the CObject class is to prevent such copying by placing the copy constructor in the private section,

Using Typed Maps

The use of the type-safe CTypedPtrMap requires an instantiation with the three parameters base class, key, and value:

```
CTypedPtrMap<CMapPtrToPtr, CString, Alerts*> alertPtrMap;
CTypedPtrMap<CMapStringToOb, CString, Person*> alertPtrMap;
```

The first declaration creates a map collection that associates pointers to Alerts objects with a CString key object. This provides type safety even though Alerts is not derived from CObject, since the base class stores (void*) pointers.

The second declaration creates a map that associates pointers to Person objects with a CString key. The type safety is assured by the correspondence between the CObject* value in CMapStringToOb and the Person* value in the typed collection, where Person is derived from CObject.

Of the two kinds of template collection classes, the simple collections of CArray, CList, and CMap are certainly easier to use. They are not type-safe, however, and the typed template collections would be safer.

21.7 Comparing MFC and STL Containers

The MFC containers consist of the three basic "shapes" array, list, and map. The equivalent STL containers are vector, list, and map. The STL has several additional containers: deque, set, multiset, multimap, stack, queue, and priority_queue. The last three are implemented as adapters for the other containers. The MFC collections have no comparable features, e.g., we have to create our own priority queue using the available shapes.

The STL has iterators and algorithms implemented as separate components of the architecture. The MFC has specialized iterators for each shape class, but no algorithms.

Using the MFC collection classes CArray, CList, and CMap is similar to using the STL vector, list, and map, respectively.

All the STL containers are type-safe and template-based. The MFC collection classes consist of three different structures:

- Simple template collections that are not type-safe
- Non-template collections with hard-coded types for each collection. These classes are derived from the root class CObject
- Type-safe template collections derived from the non-template collections

The MFC simple template collections and the non-template collections are as easy to use as the STL containers. Using the MFC typed collections requires significant preparations regarding which collection will be appropriate.

Choosing between the STL containers and the MFC collection classes is not easy, since it is difficult to second-guess what Microsoft is planning for future MFC versions. Using the MFC collections will create non-standard, non-portable C++ applications. The advantage is that the serialization, diagnostics, and RTTI features from CObject are available with collections derived from CObject. The lack of adapter containers is a serious drawback to using the MFC collections.

One approach could be to mix the STL and MFC to take advantage of the advanced STL features. This might induce significant run-time overhead, however, and will also be non-portable. The preferred approach would be to use only the STL, but this is nearly impossible because the automated code generation features of AppWizard include the use of the MFC collections.

The reality of working within the MFC framework, and accepting the automated mechanisms, is to use the available MFC classes, including the collection classes, with the resulting non-portable and non-standard C++ programs.

21.8 Summary

There are three separate sets of MFC collection classes:

1. Simple template collections that are not type-safe.
2. Non-template collections with hard-coded types for each collection. These classes are derived from the root class CObject.
3. Type-safe template collections derived from the non-template collections.

The simple, templatized collection classes derived from CObject that are not type-safe include:

- CArray—A vector of any data type; ordered, and can be indexed by an int type. Duplicate elements are allowed.

- CList—A doubly-linked list structure for any data type which is ordered but cannot be indexed. Duplicate elements are allowed.

- CMap—A map structure that associates an object of any data type with a key. This container is not ordered, but is indexed with a key of any data type. The key must be unique, but multiple values are allowed to be associated with each key (i.e., a multimap).

The class declarations for these three shapes are listed in the `<afxtempl.h>` file. The non-template collections have hard-coded types and are derived from CObject. They include:

- Array shapes—CByteArray, CDWordArray, CObArray, CPtrArray, CStringArray, CUIntArray, CWordArray (see Table 21.1)

- List shapes—CPtrList, CObList, CStringList (see Table 21.2)

- Map shapes—CMapWordToPtr, CMapPtrToWord, CMapPtrToPtr, CMapWordToOb, CMapStringToPtr, CMapStringToOb, CMapStringToString (see Table 21.3)

The class declarations for these three shapes are listed in the `<afxcoll.h>` file. The set of templatized containers that are not derived from CObject include

- CTypedPtrArray—A collection of pointers to instances of an array data type. This container is derived from either CObArray or CPtrArray.

- CTypedPtrList—A collection of pointers to nodes of a list type. This container is derived from either CObList or CPtrList.

- CTypedPtrMap—This container is derived from CMapPtrToWord, CMapPtrToPtr, CMapStringToPtr, CMapWordToPtr, or CMapStringToOb.

The class declarations for these three shapes are listed in the `<afxtempl.h>` file.

None of the collection classes listed can function as adapters, i.e., there are no facilities comparable to the STL stack, queue, and priority_queue.

Iterators are implemented as member functions of the various collection classes. There are no algorithms available, in contrast to the STL containers.

Serialization, diagnostics, and RTTI features from the root class CObject are available to the collections derived from CObject.

The set of member functions and data members for the non-template collections is almost exactly the same as for the corresponding simple, templatized collection class. The only difference is that the ARG_TYPEs in the template collections have been hard-coded with the corresponding type, e.g., BYTE, WORD, CString, etc.

It appears that Microsoft could move the two typedefs that now reside in the non-template collection classes to the CObject class. The three simple collections CArray, CList, and CMap could then be restructured to become type-safe, and none of the other collection classes would be needed. This would greatly simplify the current structure and retain the same features. This would, of course, mean that a lot of MFC code would have to be recompiled, since the root class interface would change.

On the surface, the STL containers would be a clear choice over the equivalent, non-standard MFC classes regarding portability and the use of standard C++ features. This will be difficult to implement, however, if we also want to take advantage of the MFC framework mechanisms, especially the automated code generation built into the AppWizard.

It will be interesting to see how the future versions of MFC containers will be structured. Hopefully, Microsoft will join the C++ standardization effort and use the STL rather than their current containers that include the relics of the first MFC version.

References

1. Microsoft Visual C++ Version 4.0, Programming with MFC, Volume 2, Microsoft Press, Redmond, WA 1995.

22

Windows Encapsulations in MFC

Windows applications created with C code have traditionally been using various versions of the Microsoft Windows Software Development Kit (SDK) as the primary API. The use of SDK and C code has been replaced by C++ programming and the MFC as the primary API.

Early versions of the MFC were simply thin wrappers in the form of header files that provided function calls to the SDK. More recent MFC versions contain actual encapsulations of Windows entities in the form of C++ libraries and associated framework mechanisms. The discussions provided in this chapter are based on MFC version 4.2.

In this chapter, we will describe how the Windows programming structures and mechanisms normally created with C code have been encapsulated with the MFC C++ class library and framework. Many of the MFC features and mechanisms noted in Chapter 20 will be discussed in further detail here, including:

- Creating a frame structure as the basis for window displays
- Using the document/view architecture in SDI and MDI applications
- Creating dynamic document templates for documents and views
- Using RTTI functions and macros
- Creating and initiating window objects

After a brief overview of the major components of a Windows application created with the MFC framework, we will discuss in detail the architecture and management of these components.

22.1 The Application

Every Windows application consists of a number of components that make up the visual user interface. Some of these components can handle user commands in the form of menu selections and mouse clicks. Other components are dedicated to storing an application's data, drawing graphical objects, and displaying graphical and textual data inside windows.

We usually associate an application with an executable file that can be activated by double-clicking on its icon on the desktop or by sending a "run" command to the operating system.

In this chapter, we will look at an application as an instance of the CWinApp class which is created by the MFC framework, as a component of a Windows program. We will also discuss how this component interacts with the other primary components of a Windows program.

22.2 Window Frames

All Microsoft Windows applications use "windows" as the primary user interface. These windows have at least one frame that contains the necessary menus, tool bars, command buttons, and status windows for a particular application. The window display contained within a frame is referred to as a client area. This area represents the primary user display of the application for handling mouse clicks, drag-and-drop features, etc.

A main frame for a Windows NT Notepad application is shown in Figure 22.1. The title bar contains the name of the application (Notepad) and the name of the file displayed in the client area (nvertinh.cpp). The button on the far left represents the system menu. The buttons on the right can be used to minimize, maximize or close the window. The vertical scroll bar and frame boundaries surround the client area.

This style of Windows application is referred to as a single document interface (SDI) application, since only one document (or file) can be open at any one time. If we attempt to open another file, the present file will automatically close first.

Window frames are encapsulated in the MFC with the C++ Frame Windows class family hierarchy as shown in Figure 22.2.

A frame is considered a type of window, and is thus derived from the CWnd class. Since a frame usually has menus, it is a direct descendant from the CCmdTarget class, the topmost class that can handle menu commands.

The CMDIChildWnd class provides the functionality of a Windows multiple document interface (MDI) child window, along with members for managing the window. An MDI child window looks much like a typical frame window, except that the MDI child window appears nested inside an MDI frame window, rather than on the desktop.

An MDI child window does not have a menu bar of its own, but instead shares the menu of the MDI frame window. The framework automatically changes the MDI frame menu to represent the currently active MDI child window.

```
// File: nvertinh.cpp

#include <iostream.h>
#include "nvertinh.h"

HWDevice::HWDevice() {
   cout << " Constructor for hardware device " << endl;
}

HWDevice::~HWDevice() {
   cout << " Virtual destructor for hardware device  " <<
}

void HWDevice::print() {
   cout << " Virtual print() in the base class " << endl;
}
```

Figure 22.1 Frame Structure for Notepad Application

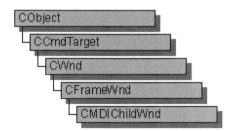

Figure 22.2 Hierarchy of Frame Classes

Each frame contains a window that represents a user view. The frame is responsible for coordinating the tasks required to translate user commands into the corresponding actions and display. If a user clicks on the File/Open... menu, for example, the frame is responsible for displaying the Open dialog box from which the user can select a particular file to open.

Different frame structures are required for SDI and MDI applications. The `CFrameWnd` class is used as a base class for SDI applications. User SDI windows are derived directly from the `CFrameWnd` class. Here is an example of a frame for a sample SDI application:

```
// File: MainFrm.h (interface to the CMainFrame class)
//
class CMainFrame : public CFrameWnd {
protected:
  CMainFrame();
  DECLARE_DYNCREATE(CMainFrame)
public:
  virtual ~CMainFrame();
  virtual BOOL PreCreateWindow(CREATESTRUCT& cs);
protected:   // control bar embedded members
  CStatusBar  m_wndStatusBar;
  CToolBar    m_wndToolBar;
// ...
};
```

An SDI application of this type has a main frame derived from the CFrameWnd class, and includes a status bar and tool bar.

MDI applications can have multiple documents (and their associated windows) open at any one time. An example of the MS Word 97 application used to create one of the chapters for this book is shown in Figure 22.3.

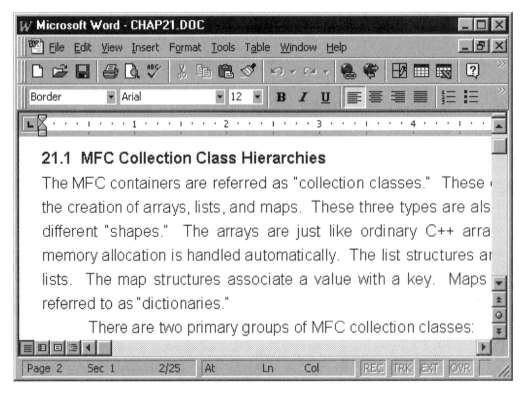

Figure 22.3 MDI Application with Open Documents

Aside from the toolbars, which can be customized for each document, note the elaborate menus that are structured for an open document. The <u>W</u>indows menu is always present for an MDI application and has a list of documents currently open. A representation of an MDI application with no open documents is shown in Figure 22.4.

Note the shorter list of menu items and the lack of a file name in the title bar when no documents are open.

Each MDI application has one main frame (CMDIFrameWnd, derived from CFrameWnd) that contains a special client area. The client area includes a child frame (CMDIChildWnd, derived from CFrameWnd) for each window that is open. Each child frame manages a child client area that is used for displaying the data of an open document. Here is an example of a main frame and a child frame for a sample MDI application:

```
// File: MainFrm.h (interface to the CMainFrame class)

class CMainFrame : public CMDIFrameWnd {
  DECLARE_DYNAMIC(CMainFrame)
public:
  CMainFrame();
public:
  virtual ~CMainFrame();
  virtual BOOL PreCreateWindow(CREATESTRUCT& cs);
```

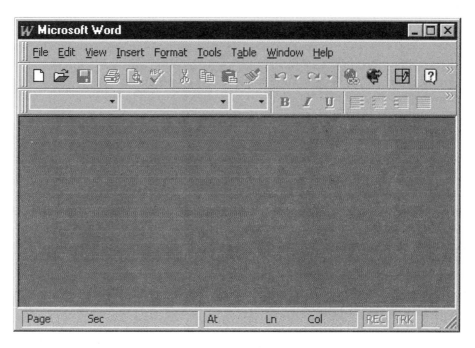

Figure 22.4 MDI Application with No Open Documents

```
protected:   // control bar embedded members
   CStatusBar   m_wndStatusBar;
   CToolBar     m_wndToolBar;
// ...
};

// File: ChildFrm.h (interface to the CChildFrame class)

class CChildFrame : public CMDIChildWnd {
   DECLARE_DYNCREATE(CChildFrame)
public:
   CChildFrame();
   virtual ~CChildFrame();
   virtual BOOL PreCreateWindow(CREATESTRUCT& cs);
// ...
};
```

Each MDI application will have an instance of a CMainFrame class and one CChildFrame for each view of an open document.

22.3 The Document/View Pattern

As designers and implementers of GUI-based applications, we are responsible for determining a number of important design decisions, including:

- Which component holds and owns the application's data?
- Which component is responsible for updating the application's data when data elements are changed?
- Which component should respond to user commands.?
- How the data should be displayed.
- How persistent data should be stored and retrieved.

A Windows application created with the MFC framework simplifies many of these design decisions by automating the application arch ecture and the facilities for handling user interfaces.

Windows applications created using the MFC framework are based on the document/view design pattern. Document classes own and hold the application's data, and the associated view classes are responsible for user input commands and the display of the data in various formats in the child windows. A frame structure is also included to handle menu requests.

The document/view paradigm is the default structure for all Windows applications created with the AppWizard. This provides default support for saving and retrieving files, printing and print preview, and includes a set of standard menus and dialogs.

There are two separate features of the MFC framework that contribute to the resulting Windows application: the automatic code generation performed by the AppWizard and the document/view architecture created by the MFC framework.

The primary advantage of the document/view architecture is the support for a clear separation of an application's data and how the data should be displayed to the user. The document represents the data source, and the view represents the place to present the data to the user.

When a Windows application is created, instances of four different components must be constructed: the application, window frames, documents, and view objects. The last three components are managed by the document template structure. We will now take a closer look at the various components that make up a Windows application.

22.4 Documents

The foundation for the document/view architecture is the document, which represents a data source. Examples of documents include a simple text file, a rich text file, a bit map, a Word document, and a Rational Rose/C++ file.

Each document contains data in a unique format that can be managed by a particular application, e.g., a Word document can be a combination of text, formatting information, and embedded bit maps.

When an application is created by the MFC framework, a document class for that application is derived from the MFC CDocument class. The hierarchy for the CDocument class is shown in Figure 22.5.

The CDocument class provides the base class with member functions for operations such as creating a document, retrieving it from various storage media, and saving it. The MFC framework manages documents by using the interface provided by CDocument.

As a direct descendant of the CCmdTarget class, the CDocument class can receive and respond to command messages from toolbars and menus. Here is a code snippet of the CDocument class from the header afxwin.h:

```
// File: afxwin.h
// ...
class CDocument : public CCmdTarget {
public:
  CDocument();
```

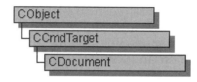

Figure 22.5 CDocument Class Hierarchy

```cpp
// Attributes
public:
    const CString& GetTitle() const;
    virtual void SetTitle(LPCTSTR lpszTitle);
    const CString& GetPathName() const;
    virtual void SetPathName(LPCTSTR lpszPathName,
                             BOOL bAddToMRU = TRUE);
    CDocTemplate* GetDocTemplate() const;

// Operations
    void AddView(CView* pView);
    void RemoveView(CView* pView);
    virtual POSITION GetFirstViewPosition() const;
    virtual CView* GetNextView(POSITION& rPosition) const;

    // Update Views (simple update - DAG only)
    void UpdateAllViews(CView* pSender, LPARAM lHint = 0L,
                        CObject* pHint = NULL);

// Overridables
    virtual BOOL OnNewDocument();
    virtual BOOL OnOpenDocument(LPCTSTR lpszPathName);
    virtual BOOL OnSaveDocument(LPCTSTR lpszPathName);
    virtual void OnCloseDocument();
public:
    virtual ~CDocument();

// overridables for implementation
    virtual HMENU GetDefaultMenu(); // get menu depending on state
    virtual HACCEL GetDefaultAccelerator();

    virtual BOOL OnCmdMsg(UINT nID, int nCode, void* pExtra,
                          AFX_CMDHANDLERINFO* pHandlerInfo);
    friend class CDocTemplate;

protected:
    // file menu commands
    //{{AFX_MSG(CDocument)
    afx_msg void OnFileClose();
    afx_msg void OnFileSave();
    afx_msg void OnFileSaveAs();
    //}}AFX_MSG
};
```

We see various member functions that deal with document titles and their directory paths. Another group of functions supports the management of views. Several member functions are included for opening, saving, and closing files. One set of functions provides support for menu and keyboard input, as well as general command messages.

Also note that friend privilege is given to the CDocTemplate class. This is the class that manages documents, views, and frames, which we will get back to in a later section.

We will now present an example of a document class created by the MFC framework for an application we have called AdvCpp:

```
// AdvCppDoc.h : interface of the CAdvCppDoc class

class CAdvCppDoc : public CDocument {
protected: // create from serialization only
  CAdvCppDoc();
  DECLARE_DYNCREATE(CAdvCppDoc)

// Attributes
public:

// Operations
public:

// Overrides
  // ClassWizard generated virtual function overrides
  //{{AFX_VIRTUAL(CAdvCppDoc)
  public:
  virtual BOOL OnNewDocument();
  virtual void Serialize(CArchive& ar);
  //}}AFX_VIRTUAL

// Implementation
public:
  virtual ~CAdvCppDoc();
#ifdef _DEBUG
  virtual void AssertValid() const;
  virtual void Dump(CDumpContext& dc) const;
#endif

protected:

// Generated message map functions
protected:
  //{{AFX_MSG(CAdvCppDoc)
    // NOTE - the ClassWizard will add and remove member
    //        functions here.
    //    DO NOT EDIT what you see in these blocks of
    //    generated code !
  //}}AFX_MSG
  DECLARE_MESSAGE_MAP()
};
```

We notice the virtual member function OnNewDocument(), which we can tailor for creating new documents. The other features of the CDocument class can be invoked either by calling the member functions directly, or via polymorphism for the virtual functions.

The serialization and diagnostic features in the CAdvCppDoc class are inherited from the CObject class. We defer an explanation of how the message maps are implemented to the next chapter.

22.5 Views

Each document has one or more associated views. Views are used to display the data owned by a document in various formats, and to provide a user interface.

The general functionality of views is represented by the MFC CView class. The class hierarchy for this class is shown in Figure 22.6.

A view is considered to be a kind of window, and can handle messages resulting from a user moving objects or resizing windows. It also inherits from CCmdTarget and can thus receive command messages from menus and controls.

A view can be considered a child of a frame window which can be shared by more than one view. An example of this type of sharing is a splitter window with two views and a single frame. When a user creates a new window, or splits an existing one, the framework constructs a new view and attaches it to the associated document.

A view can only be associated with a single document, but a document can have multiple views attached to it simultaneously. As an example, a word processing program can provide both a complete text view of a document and an outline view that shows only the section headings. The two different types of views can be placed in separate frame windows or in separate panes of a single frame window managing a splitter window.

A view receives user commands forwarded to it by its frame window. If the view does not wish to handle certain commands, it simply forwards them to its associated document. We saw previously that a view can function as a command target, since it is derived from the CCmdTarget class. Command messages are handled by the view via a message map or virtual functions. (This will be explained in detail in Chapter 23.)

The functionality encapsulated in a view can be gleaned from the CView member functions. Here is a code snippet of CView from the `afxwin.h` header:

```
// File: afxwin.h
// ...
class CView : public CWnd {
protected:
  CView();
```

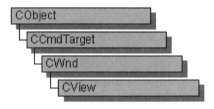

Figure 22.6 CView Class Hierarchy

```
public:
  CDocument* GetDocument() const;

  virtual BOOL OnScroll(UINT nScrollCode,
                        UINT nPos, BOOL bDoScroll = TRUE);
  virtual BOOL OnScrollBy(CSize sizeScroll,
                          BOOL bDoScroll = TRUE);
protected:
  virtual void OnActivateView(BOOL bActivate,
                              CView* pActivateView,
                              CView* pDeactiveView);
  virtual void OnActivateFrame(UINT nState,
                               CFrameWnd* pFrameWnd);

  // General drawing/updating
  virtual void OnUpdate(CView* pSender, LPARAM lHint,
                        CObject* pHint);
  virtual void OnDraw(CDC* pDC) = 0; // pure virtual

public:
  virtual ~CView();

  virtual void CalcWindowRect(LPRECT lpClientRect,
                              UINT nAdjustType = adjustBorder);
protected:
  CDocument* m_pDocument;

  virtual BOOL OnCmdMsg(UINT nID, int nCode, void* pExtra,
                        AFX_CMDHANDLERINFO* pHandlerInfo);
  // friend classes that call protected CView overridables
  friend class CDocument;
  friend class CDocTemplate;
  friend class CPreviewView;
  friend class CFrameWnd;
  friend class CMDIFrameWnd;
  friend class CMDIChildWnd;
  friend class CSplitterWnd;

  //{{AFX_MSG(CView)
  afx_msg int OnCreate(LPCREATESTRUCT lpcs);
  afx_msg void OnDestroy();
  afx_msg void OnPaint();
  afx_msg int OnMouseActivate(CWnd* pDesktopWnd,
                              UINT nHitTest, UINT message);
};
```

This class is an abstract base class with the default constructor in the protected section. Several member functions are available for dealing with user scrolling and activation of views and frames. The OnUpdate() function is used to update the data in a view when the user has made changes.

Note the pure virtual member function OnDraw(). This function must be overridden in the application view class to perform the required drawing (painting) of a particular view. This function will be called when the application view receives a `WM_PAINT` message.

The primary data member is the `m_pDocument` pointer which associates a particular view object with its document.

The command handling capability is evidenced by the general command handler OnCmdMsg() for `WM_COMMAND` messages, and the specialized message handlers, e.g., OnPaint() for `WM_PAINT` messages.

A suspicious design trend for this class is the granting of friend privileges to several classes. Data encapsulation is thus severely compromised, making us wonder what happened to the object orientation for this class.

The MFC framework creates a view class for each application. Here is the class created for our AdvCpp application:

```
// File: AdvCppView.h

class CAdvCppView : public CView {
protected: // create from serialization only
  CAdvCppView();

// Attributes
public:
  CAdvCppDoc* GetDocument();

// Operations
public:

// Overrides
  // ClassWizard generated virtual function overrides
  //{{AFX_VIRTUAL(CAdvCppView)
public:
  virtual void OnDraw(CDC* pDC); // overridden
  virtual BOOL PreCreateWindow(CREATESTRUCT& cs);
protected:
  virtual BOOL OnPreparePrinting(CPrintInfo* pInfo);
  virtual void OnBeginPrinting(CDC* pDC, CPrintInfo* pInfo);
  virtual void OnEndPrinting(CDC* pDC, CPrintInfo* pInfo);
  //}}AFX_VIRTUAL

// Implementation
public:
  virtual ~CAdvCppView();
#ifdef _DEBUG
  virtual void AssertValid() const;
  virtual void Dump(CDumpContext& dc) const;
#endif

// Generated message map functions
protected:
  // ...
};
```

```
#ifndef _DEBUG  // debug version in AdvCppView.cpp
inline CAdvCppDoc* CAdvCppView::GetDocument()
   { return (CAdvCppDoc*)m_pDocument; }
#endif
```

The section for the overrides includes OnDraw(), PreCreateWindow(), and a number of print functions. We must provide an implementation of OnDraw() to be able to paint in the view. Overriding PreCreateWindow() is only necessary if we want to change the window style furnished by the framework. Print functions are normally handled by the frame objects and usually don't have to be overridden.

The diagnostic features of the CObject class can be overridden with the AssertValid() and Dump() access functions.

The release version of the GetDocument() function is implemented by returning the inherited pointer to the associated document with a cast to the "this" application document.

22.6 Document/View Frames

We have seen how the document/view architecture separates the design concerns of how the data is handled by a document and how that data is displayed to the user in the view. There is a third component involved with this architecture: the frame. The frame acts as a bounding box of a view and surrounds it with borders, scroll bars, toolbars, and menus.

A view can handle user commands in the form of mouse clicks, drag-and-drop, drawing, and text editing. The surrounding frame will handle menu commands, scroll bar manipulations, and window resizing.

An SDI application has only one type of document, and only one document can be open at a time. The view associated with an SDI document is bounded by a main frame, which is shared by all documents for that application. An example of an SDI main frame is shown in Figure 22.1 for the Notepad application. The SDI main frame is derived from CFramewnd, as discussed in Section 22.2.

Frames containing views for an MDI application are considerably more complex than SDI frames. An MDI application can have multiple documents open at the same time, and these documents can be of different types. A spreadsheet application, for example, can include formatted documents to hold the data, as well as bit maps to render various drawings of that data. Each MDI document can have different views that are used to represent the data.

There are two basic frames associated with MDI applications: (1) the main frame used for opening files or creating new files when no document is open, as shown in Figure 22.4 for the Word application; and (2) the child frames associated with the views of a document, as shown in Figure 22.3.

The MDI main frame is derived from the CMDIFrameWnd, and each child frame is derived from the CMDIChildWnd, as discussed in Section 22.2. We will now take a closer look at the SDI and MDI document/view architecture, using class diagrams to illustrate the class relationships and cardinalities.

22.7 SDI Document/View Architecture

The SDI application SampleSDI with an open document demo1.sdl is shown in Figure 22.7.

The main frame of SampleSDI includes the title bar, menu list, toolbar, status bar, and a border bounding the client area used to display a view. In this case the document is empty, and there is no display of a view.

The class model for the SampleSDI application is shown in Figure 22.8. The classes CSampleSDIApp, CMainFrame, CSampleSDIDoc, and CSampleSDIView are all created by the AppWizard as the application is built.

The CSampleSDIApp application is derived from CWinApp and is composed of exactly one main frame instance of type CMainFrame, zero or one document instance of type CSampleSDIDoc, and zero or one view of type CSampleSDIView.

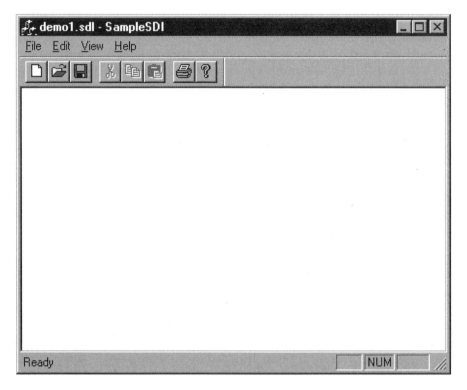

Figure 22.7 SDI Application

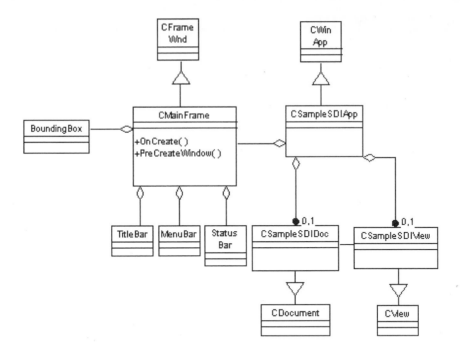

Figure 22.8 SDI Application Class Diagram

The CMainFrame is derived from the CFrameWnd and is composed of a title bar, a menu bar, a status bar, and a bounding box. The latter contains the frame for the view and may include scroll bars.

The CSampleSDIDoc class is derived from the CDocument class, and CSampleSDIView from the Cview class. We also note the association relationship between the document and view classes.

22.8 MDI Document/View Architecture

The primary differences between SDI and MDI applications are that MDI applications can have multiple documents open at the same time, and that each document can be associated with multiple views. The MDI application SampleMDI, with two open documents demo1.mdx and demo2.mdx, and two views of each document, is shown in Figure 22.9. This time we included vertical scroll bars to bound the views.

The main frame surrounds the entire set of views. Each view is bounded by a child frame. The main frame still has a toolbar and status bar. It now has two sets of menus: (1) the limited main frame menus that are used when no document is open; and (2) the menus that are unique for a given document type.

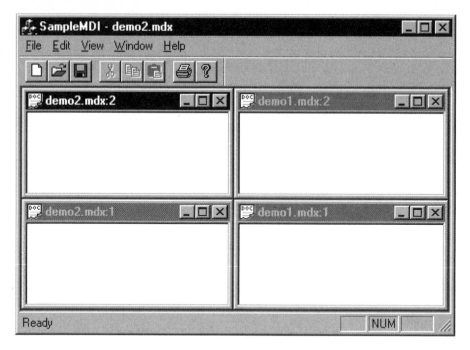

Figure 22.9 MDI Application

The class model of our SampleMDI application is shown in Figure 22.10. The application class CSampleMDIApp is composed of a main frame derived from the CMDIFrameWnd class, a CChildFrame class derived from CMDIChildWnd. We have left out the main frame aggregates to keep the diagram simple, and to focus on the primary components. The CSampleMDI application is composed of one main frame, and zero or more CChildFrame objects, CSampleMDIDoc documents, and CSampleMDIView objects.

In addition to the differences of having multiple documents open at one time, we notice that some of the MDI classes created by the framework are derived from different base classes. The CMainFrame class is derived from CMDIFrameWnd, and CChildFrame from CMDIChildWnd. The fact that the CSampleMDIView class is derived from CScrollView, is the result of a choice we made in AppWizard. This choice is also available for SDI applications.

Now that we have seen the class diagrams for the SDI and MDI applications, we should expect this architecture to be implemented in the respective header and source files, with embedded objects for the frames, documents, and views. This is not quite the case, however, because the MFC framework includes a mechanism for managing frames, documents, and views. This mechanism is based on the Document Template paradigm, and is an implementation of the Abstract Factory design pattern [1, p. 87].

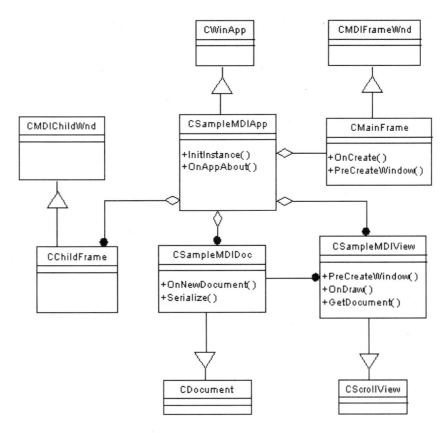

Figure 22.10 MDI Application Class Diagram

22.9 SDI Document Templates

A document template can be considered a factory, with classes and objects created and managed dynamically. An MDI application can declare a set of document templates, and thus manage a set of child frames, documents, and views. A document template for an SDI application manages an associated set of a main frame, document, and view.

The modified class model for the SampleSDI application is shown in Figure 22.11. The intervening class CSingleDocTemplate manages the frame, document, and view objects. This template is derived from the MFC CDocTemplate class, and is instantiated with the CMainFrame, CSampleSDIDoc, and CSampleSDIView classes.

The application object maintains a list of other objects that can create documents and views dynamically. These objects are implemented as document templates. When a user sends a command to open a new file, the application searches its list of document templates until it finds the corresponding document. The given template is used to create the required document/view object combination dynamically, before the application continues its execution.

Here is a document template for a sample SDI application, where the declarations are made within the main application source file (SampleSDI.cpp):

```
// File: SampleSDI.cpp
//...
BOOL CSampleSDIApp::InitInstance() {
```

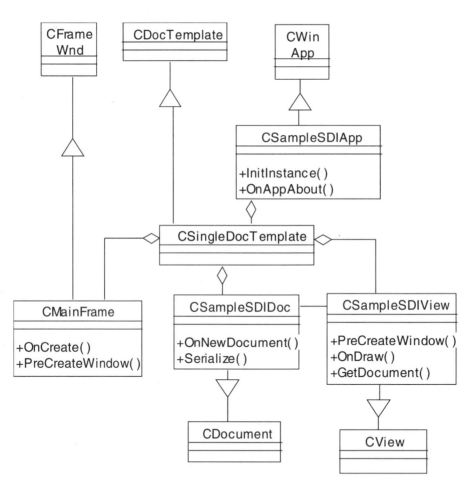

Figure 22.11 SDI Class Model with CSingleDocTemplate

```
    // Register the application's document templates.
    // Document templates serve as the connection between
    //   documents, frame windows and views.

    CSingleDocTemplate* pDocTemplate;
     pDocTemplate = new CSingleDocTemplate(
       IDR_MAINFRAME,
       RUNTIME_CLASS(CSampleSDIDoc),
       RUNTIME_CLASS(CMainFrame),         // main SDI frame window
       RUNTIME_CLASS(CSampleSDIView));
     AddDocTemplate(pDocTemplate);

 // ...

    return TRUE;
  }
  //...
```

The IDR_MAINFRAME is a resource identifier used to associate a menu and various other resources with the object created via the template.

The RUNTIME_CLASS() macro returns a pointer to a data structure that contains RTTI data for the corresponding class. This data structure (CRuntimeClass) is described below.

The first of the three run-time class structures is a description of the CSampleSDIDoc class, which is derived from CDocument. Objects of this class represent documents of this SDI type, e.g., text files for the Notepad application.

The CMainFrame class structure specifies the type of frame (derived from CFrameWnd) that will contain the SDI view.

The CSampleSDIView class structure includes run-time information about the CSampleSDIView class derived from CView.

The function AddDocTemplate() (member function of CWinApp) is used to register the document template with the framework. This will be the only document template for the SDI application. An MDI application will have one document template for each type of document associated with that application.

Hierarchy of SDI Document Template

The hierarchy of the SDI document template class is shown in Figure 22.12. Since the root class of this hierarchy is CObject, the MFC RTTI features are supported for the CSingleDocTemplate class. We also recognize the Serialize() function in the CSampleSDIDoc class. The persistent data owned by the document can thus be saved and restored using the serialization feature.

The implementation of CDocTemplate architecture is an example of the Factory Method design pattern [1, p. 107].

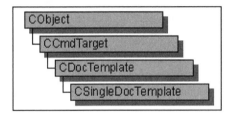

Figure 22.12 Hierarchy of SDI Document Template Class

22.10 MDI Document Templates

An MDI application has one document template for each document type that it supports. The application uses these templates when the user creates new documents. The document types are displayed to the user in a list box under the File/New or File/Open menus. When the user has selected a document type, the application creates a document object, a frame object, and a view object and links them via the document template. The modified class diagram for the SampleMDI application is shown in Figure 22.13.

The CMultiDocTemplate is used to manage child frames, documents, and the associated views. The main frame is a separate component that includes the tool bar, status bar, and the limited menu when no document is open.

Here is an example of the use of a document template for the SampleMDI application taken from the application source file:

```
// File: samplemdi.cpp
// ...
BOOL CSampleMDIApp::InitInstance() {
   // Register the application's document templates.
   // Document templates serve as the connection between
   // documents, frame windows and views.

   CMultiDocTemplate* pDocTemplate;
   pDocTemplate = new CMultiDocTemplate(
      IDR_SAMPLETYPE,
      RUNTIME_CLASS(CSampleMDIDoc),
      RUNTIME_CLASS(CChildFrame), // custom MDI child frame
      RUNTIME_CLASS(CSampleMDIView));
   AddDocTemplate(pDocTemplate);

   // create main MDI Frame window
   CMainFrame* pMainFrame = new CMainFrame;
   if (!pMainFrame->LoadFrame(IDR_MAINFRAME))
      return FALSE;
   m_pMainWnd = pMainFrame;
```

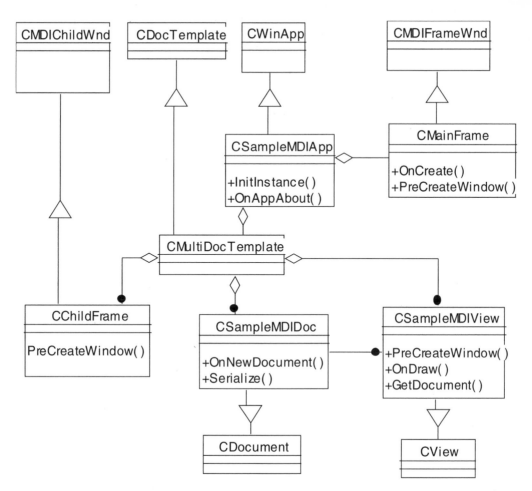

Figure 22.13 MDI Class Model with CMultiDocTemplate

```
// ...
  // The main window has been initialized, so show and
  //   update it.
  pMainFrame->ShowWindow(m_nCmdShow);
  pMainFrame->UpdateWindow();

  return TRUE;
}
// ...
```

Note that the IDR_SAMPLETYPE identifier is unique for an MDI application to accommodate two levels of menu bars: one for the main frame (with the identifier
IDR_MAINFRAME) and one for each document type.

The RUNTIME_CLASS() macro returns a pointer to a data structure that contains RTTI data for the corresponding class. This data structure (CRuntimeClass) is described in Section 22.11.

The structure of the document template creation is similar to that for the SDI application. One major difference is the creation of a custom MDI child frame for each document, rather than the single main frame for an SDI application.

The function AddDocTemplate() (member function of CWinApp) is used to register the document template with the framework. This adds the current document template to the application's list of available document templates.

We see from the InitInstance() function how the main frame is created as a separate component, and that the main frame object is used to display the main window.

Hierarchy of MDI Document Template

The hierarchy of the MDI document template class is shown in Figure 22.14. This class is also derived from the CObject class, and RTTI data are thus available.

Each document template has enough information stored about its corresponding classes to create instances of those classes at run-time from requests by the application object. To support the dynamic creation of instances, MFC has implemented its own version of Run-Time Type Information (RTTI), which we will discuss in the next section.

22.11 MFC and Run-Time Type Information

The C++ language specification includes support for run-time type information (RTTI), but few vendors have yet to implement this with their C++ development systems. The MFC structure includes a special version of RTTI that is a combination of C++ constructs and macros. Table 22.1 includes a list of the MFC constructs and the C++ equivalents.

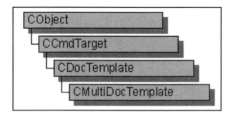

Figure 22.14 Hierarchy of MDI Document Template Class

Table 22.1 MFC RTTI Constructs

MFC Construct	C++ Equivalent
CObject::IsKindOf()	dynamic_cast< >
CObject::GetRuntimeClass()	typeid()
CRuntimeClass (struct)	type_info (class)

The `CObject::IsKindOf()` function is used to determine if an object corresponds to a given class. It has the equivalent functionality of the C++ `dynamic_cast<>`, but is not a true casting operator like the latter. The `CObject::GetRuntimeClass()` function is used to return a pointer to an object's `CRuntimeClass` information. It has the equivalent functionality of the C++ `typeid()`. Every class derived from CObject has a `CRuntimeClass` structure associated with it. This structure is used to obtain RTTI data about an object or its base class during run-time. Here is the declaration for the `CRuntimeClass` struct:

```
// File: afx.h
// ...
struct CRuntimeClass{
// Attributes
  LPCSTR m_lpszClassName;
  int    m_nObjectSize;
  UINT   m_wSchema; // schema number of the loaded class
  CObject* (PASCAL* m_pfnCreateObject)();

#ifdef _AFXDLL
  CRuntimeClass* (PASCAL* m_pfnGetBaseClass)();
#else
  CRuntimeClass* m_pBaseClass;
#endif

// Operations
  CObject* CreateObject();
  BOOL IsDerivedFrom(const CRuntimeClass* pBaseClass)
                                              const;

// Implementation
  void Store(CArchive& ar) const;
  static CRuntimeClass* PASCAL Load
                (CArchive& ar, UINT* pwSchemaNum);

// CRuntimeClass objects linked together in simple list
  CRuntimeClass* m_pNextClass;
                  // linked list of registered classes
};
```

The run-time information for each class derived from `CObject` is stored in this static structure and used by the various MFC RTTI functions and macros. We have already seen how the `RUNTIME_CLASS()` macro was used to return pointers to data structures that contains RTTI data for the document, frame, and view classes linked by the document templates.

Here is the prototype for `CObject::IsKindOf()`:

```
BOOL IsKindOf(const CRuntimeClass* pClass);
```

The `pClass` pointer is used to identify the data structure associated with a particular class derived from `CObject`. `IsKindOf()` uses the `m_pBaseClass` data member of the `CRuntimeClass` struct to navigate the class hierarchy to determine if the object is an instance of the given class or a class derived from the given class.

Here is an example of how we can use `IsKindOf()` with an RTTI capability:

```
class CInvoice : public CObject { ... };
//...
CInvoice invoice(011234);
//...
ASSERT(invoice.IsKindOf(RUNTIME_CLASS(CInvoice)));
ASSERT(invoice.IsKindOf(RUNTIME_CLASS(CObject)));
```

The object `invoice` is checked to see if it is an instance of the `CInvoice` and `CObject` classes. The appropriate pointers to the `CRuntimeClass` structs are returned by the `RUNTIME_CLASS()` macros for `CInvoice` and `CObject`, respectively.

The `CRuntimeClass` is a struct that contains RTTI data about classes derived from the `CObject` class. Two restrictions are imposed on RTTI support for MFC classes: (1) they must be derived from `CObject`, and (2) the RTTI functions only work for classes declared with the `DECLARE_DYNAMIC()` and `DECLARE_SERIAL()` macros. These macros are discussed further in the next section.

22.12 MFC RTTI Macros

Support for RTTI data of a class has been added by the MFC in the form of a number of macros. Some of these macros have to be used in pairs with one "declare" macro in a header file and one "implement" macro in the corresponding source file, as shown in Table 22.2. The set of macros to be used for a given application must be chosen, based on the run-time support required. Each pair of macros in the table adds an incremental run-time capability over the previous pair(s) listed in the table.

The `DECLARE_DYNAMIC()` macro is used to declare support for basic RTTI data, i.e., we only expect to interrogate objects for information about their respective classes. Here is the macro expansion for DECLARE_DYNAMIC():

```
#define DECLARE_DYNAMIC(class_name) \
public: \
    static AFX_DATA CRuntimeClass class##class_name; \
```

```
virtual CRuntimeClass* GetRuntimeClass() const; \

#define IMPLEMENT_DYNAMIC(class_name, base_class_name) \
  _IMPLEMENT_RUNTIMECLASS(class_name, base_class_name,
                          0xFFFF, NULL)
```

If we need to create classes and objects dynamically, we include the
DECLARE_DYNCREATE() macro for a class. The dynamic creation capability is in addition to the basic RTTI support obtained via the DECLARE_DYNAMIC() macro. Here
is an example of the use of this macro in the sample SDI application:

```
// File: SampleSDIView.h
class CSampleSDIView : public CView {
protected: // create from serialization only
  CSampleSDIView();
  DECLARE_DYNCREATE(CSampleSDIView)
...
};
```

Here is the macro expansion for DECLARE_DYNCREATE():

```
#define DECLARE_DYNCREATE(class_name) \
  DECLARE_DYNAMIC(class_name) \
  static CObject* PASCAL CreateObject();
```

Note how the DECLARE_DYNAMIC() macro is nested as a recursive unit inside the macro
expansion. This supports the notion that the "dyncreate" capability is an incremental feature added to the "dynamic" capability. Here is the "implement" part of the paired
declaration:

```
// File: SampleSDIView.cpp
...
  IMPLEMENT_DYNCREATE(CSampleSDIView, CView)
...
```

Table 22.2 MFC RTTI Macros

MFC Macro	RTTI Support
DECLARE_DYNAMIC()	declares RTTI information about an object's class
IMPLEMENT_DYNAMIC()	IsKindOf(), GetRuntimeClass()
DECLARE_DYNCREATE()	declares RTTI information and dynamic creation
IMPLEMENT_DYNCREATE()	ConstructObject(), CreateObject()
DECLARE_SERIAL()	declares RTTI information, dynamic creation, and serialization
IMPLEMENT_SERIAL()	CreateObject(), ReadObject()
RUNTIME_CLASS()	returns a pointer to a CRuntimeClass struct

Here is the macro expansion:

```
#define IMPLEMENT_DYNCREATE(class_name, base_class_name) \
CObject* PASCAL class_name::CreateObject() \
   { return new class_name; } \
   _IMPLEMENT_RUNTIMECLASS(class_name, base_class_name, 0xFFFF, \
   class_name::CreateObject)
```

The DECLARE_SERIAL() macro is used when we want to add a serialization capability to the other run-time support. This means that we can store and retrieve objects and their associated data members at run-time. Here is the macro expansion:

```
#define DECLARE_SERIAL(class_name) \
   DECLARE_DYNCREATE(class_name) \
   friend CArchive& AFXAPI operator>>(CArchive& ar, \
                                      class_name* &pOb);


#define IMPLEMENT_SERIAL(class_name, base_class_name, \
                         wSchema) \
   CObject* PASCAL class_name::CreateObject() \
     { return new class_name; } \
   _IMPLEMENT_RUNTIMECLASS(class_name, base_class_name, \
                wSchema, class_name::CreateObject) \
   CArchive& AFXAPI operator>>(CArchive& ar, class_name* \
                               &pOb) \
   { pOb = (class_name*) ar.ReadObject \
                   (RUNTIME_CLASS(class_name)); \
      return ar; } \
```

Since the MFC RTTI macros are not part of the C++ specification, there are some restrictions that must be noted.

Every class that requires RTTI support must be derived from the root class CObject.

The only use of multiple inheritance with the MFC is a combination of an MFC class derived from CObject and one or more mix-in classes, or two or more non-CObject classes. This prevents the use of MFC RTTI with any MFC multiple inheritance class structure.

The only type of dynamic casts that are available with MFC RTTI are pointer casts; reference casts are not supported.

22.13 Creating Windows Objects

We have seen how an application created using the automated features of AppWizard is based on the MFC document/view architecture. The major components of an MFC application include an application object, a main frame, child frames for MDI applications, document objects, and views. We also saw how the document template structure is used to manage frames, documents, and views.

We will now discuss how the various components of an MFC application get created and how the application is initiated.

In general, the application object manages the document templates, and each template object handles the corresponding document, frame window, and view. These objects are created dynamically, in response to user requests for opening a specific document or for creating a new file. The dynamic creation is facilitated via the DECLARE_DYNAMIC() macro for each of the three types of objects:

```
// MainFrm.h : interface of the CMainFrame class
//
class CMainFrame : public CFrameWnd {
protected:
  CMainFrame();
  DECLARE_DYNCREATE(CMainFrame)
// ...


// SampleSDIDoc.h : interface of the CSampleSDIDoc class
//
class CSampleSDIDoc : public CDocument {
protected:
  CSampleSDIDoc();
  DECLARE_DYNCREATE(CSampleSDIDoc)
// ...


// SampleSDIView.h : interface of the CSampleSDIView class
//
class CSampleSDIView : public CScrollView {
protected: // create from serialization only
  CSampleSDIView();
  DECLARE_DYNCREATE(CSampleSDIView)
// ...
```

The document template (only one for an SDI application) is managed by the application object and is created in the InitInstance() member function:

```
// SampleSDI.cpp:
//
// ...
BOOL CSampleSDIApp::InitInstance() {
// ...
// Register document templates

  CSingleDocTemplate* pDocTemplate;
  pDocTemplate = new CSingleDocTemplate(
    IDR_MAINFRAME,
    RUNTIME_CLASS(CSampleSDIDoc),
    RUNTIME_CLASS(CMainFrame),  // main SDI frame window
    RUNTIME_CLASS(CSampleSDIView));
  AddDocTemplate(pDocTemplate);
// ...
```

The document template is registered using the `CWinApp::AddDocTemplate()` member function.

After the application has initialized the necessary template(s), new window frame and document objects, and their associated views, can be created on demand by the users. Application documents are created in response to menu requests of `File/New`, `File/Open`, or if users double click on a file associated with a particular application.

The initial user requests are handled by the member functions `OnFileNew()` or `OnFileOpen()` of the MFC `CWinApp` class. These member functions are implemented as message handlers for the corresponding menu and mouse clicks. If we're using the AppWizard, the code for the message maps is added automatically:

```
// SampleSDI.cpp: implementation for an application object
// ...
BEGIN_MESSAGE_MAP(CSampleSDIApp, CWinApp)
  //{{AFX_MSG_MAP(CSampleSDIApp)
  ON_COMMAND(ID_APP_ABOUT, OnAppAbout)
  //}}AFX_MSG_MAP
  // Standard file based document commands
  ON_COMMAND(ID_FILE_NEW, CWinApp::OnFileNew)
  ON_COMMAND(ID_FILE_OPEN, CWinApp::OnFileOpen)
  // Standard print setup command
  ON_COMMAND(ID_FILE_PRINT_SETUP, CWinApp::OnFilePrintSetup)
END_MESSAGE_MAP()
// ...
```

The WM_COMMAND messages resulting from a user request to create a new file or to open an existing file, are passed on to the respective handlers in CWinApp. The process for creating the objects managed by the document template is shown in Figure 22.15.

A document is opened in `OpenDocumentFile()` if the name passed as a parameter matches a saved file. If the file name is a null string, a new file is created.

There are two member functions of the CDocTemplate class used to create the necessary objects. The function `CreateNewDocument()` is called to create a new document of the type associated with the document template, and `CreateNewFrame()` is called to produce the frame. The frame constructor invokes the necessary functions to create the view(s) associated with the document. Here are the specifications for these two functions:

```
// File: afxwin.h
// ...
  virtual CDocument* CreateNewDocument( );

  virtual CFrameWnd* CreateNewFrame( CDocument* pDoc,
                                     CFrameWnd* pOther );
```

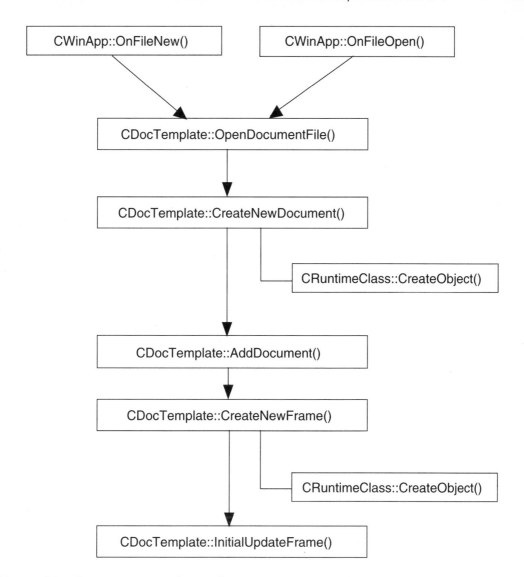

Figure 22.15 Creating Windows Objects

The two "create" functions use the run-time class information associated with the particular class and call the `CreateObject()` function of the `CRuntimeClass` struct to have the instances created.

As soon as the document templates have been initialized with the required document, frame, and view run-time class information, the frame work does the rest. The `IntitialUpdateFrame()` function is called to cause the views in that frame window to receive their `OnInitialUpdate()` calls. This function is called automatically as a result of a user activating the File/New or File/Open menus.

This discussion may lead us to believe that the entire mechanism for handling document templates is performed within the application object. This is not entirely true, as Microsoft moved some of this functionality into the class `CDocManager` when they created MFC 4.0. This class is undocumented (i.e., we can't find it in the Help files) for versions 4.x and 5.0. Here is a snapshot of the class declaration from `afxwin.h`:

```
// File: afxwin.h
// ...
// CDocManager

class CDocManager : public CObject {
  DECLARE_DYNAMIC(CDocManager)
public:
  CDocManager();

  //Document functions
  virtual void AddDocTemplate(CDocTemplate* pTemplate);
  virtual POSITION GetFirstDocTemplatePosition() const;
  virtual CDocTemplate* GetNextDocTemplate(POSITION& pos) const;
  virtual void RegisterShellFileTypes(BOOL bCompat);
  virtual CDocument* OpenDocumentFile(LPCTSTR lpszFileName);
  virtual BOOL SaveAllModified(); // save before exit
  virtual void CloseAllDocuments(BOOL bEndSession);
  virtual int GetOpenDocumentCount();

  virtual void OnFileNew();
  virtual void OnFileOpen();

// Implementation
protected:
  CPtrList m_templateList;
// ...
```

The CWinApp functions that were associated with the document templates in MFC versions prior to 4.0 are now simply calling the corresponding CDocManager member functions. The latter functions select a document template and call the appropriate CDocTemplate:: member functions shown in Figure 22.15. The primary data structure for managing document templates is the protected data member `m_templateList`. Here is a small snapshot of the implementation of `CDocManager::OpenDocumentFile()` from the MFC `docmgr.cpp` file:

```
CDocument* CDocManager::OpenDocumentFile(LPCTSTR lpszFileName) {
  // find the highest confidence
  POSITION pos = m_templateList.GetHeadPosition();
  CDocTemplate* pBestTemplate = NULL;
// ...
  return pBestTemplate->OpenDocumentFile(szPath);
}
```

Even though this code snippet is highly elided, we recognize the `CDocManager` data structure `m_templateList` and the call to `CDocTemplate::OpenDocumentFile()` via the pointer `pBestTemplate`.

This little diversion has shown how Microsoft successfully moved a major encapsulated capability from the application object to the new document manager without changing the structure of MFC. This also demonstrates how we can extend the MFC by deriving a new class from CObject, and treating existing MFC member functions as wrappers for the member functions of the new class.

22.14 Summary

There are two types of Windows applications:

- SDI applications—Each application has one type of document, and only one document can be open at a time
- MDI applications—Each application can have different document types, and more than one document can be open at once

A Windows application created by the MFC automated features includes a number of components:

- An application object—Responsible for the creation and management of the other components
- A main frame—Includes a toolbar, status bar, main frame menu, and a bounding box for one or more windows
- Child frames—Used in MDI applications to bound a child window
- Document—Owns and manages data
- Views—Representations of how data is displayed in a window

The document/view architecture is an inherent feature of an MFC application, and separates the data from its representation. The document holds the data, and the associated view displays the data in a window.

Frames, documents, and views are managed by document templates. CSingleDocTemplate is the class used for instantiating SDI components. CMultiDocTemplate is used for instantiating MDI components. The implementations of CSingleDocTemplate and CMultiDocTemplate are examples of the Factory Method design pattern [1, p.107].

MFC implements RTTI via a set of macros, rather than using the standard C++ constructs. The primary data structure used for RTTI support is the CRuntimeClass struct. This structure has information about a class, including its name, size of a class instance, a function pointer for creating an object of the class, and a function pointer for getting the base class.

The document/view architecture is an excellent implementation of a GUI design. Components and design features embody a clear separation of capabilities for handling user commands. Since the various components can all handle multiple types of user commands, the designer of an MFC application must carefully consider which component should handle a specific command. This is discussed further in the next chapter, where we look at the message mapping mechanism used in MFC.

References

1. Gamma, E. et al., *Design Patterns*, Addison-Wesley, Reading, MA 1995.

23

Message Mapping in MFC

All Windows applications are event driven. Whenever a user activates a menu, toolbar icon, or a button on a dialog box, an event is registered by the Windows system. Each event is transformed into a message that is handled either by the application or the Windows system. Each Windows application, regardless of whether it is a C application created with the SDK/API or a C++/MFC application, has a message loop service that processes events that have been translated into messages. The MFC has a built-in mechanism that handles the message loop; a C++/MFC application does not have to add any code for this functionality.

In this chapter, we describe how the MFC maps messages to message handlers using macros. The MFC mechanism is contrasted with the normal C++ mechanism of polymorphism using virtual functions. Both of these two mechanisms are used in a complementary fashion in C++/MFC applications. The emphasis of this chapter is placed on:

- How the Windows programming structures normally created with C code have been encapsulated with C++ classes and macros using message maps
- Data structures used by the message maps
- How messages are forwarded to a particular handler
- Design decisions related to which component should handle a particular message or set of messages

23.1 Windows Messages

The basic mechanism for handling GUI requests in a Windows application is that each request is considered an event for which there is a corresponding message. The application component includes a message loop ("message pump") that forwards each message to an appropriate handler.

There are two types of Windows messages that must be accepted and forwarded by the message loop:

- Command messages—Messages resulting from a user activating a menu item or a control (e.g., hitting a button in a dialog box). These messages are described with the common name of WM_COMMAND.

- General Windows messages—Messages resulting from a user manipulating the elements of a window. These messages have specific names such as WM_SIZE if a user has changed the size of a window, or WM_PAINT if the user has made a change to the contents of a window that will require redrawing that window.

In a C/API application, these messages are handled by coding monstrous switch statements that include a case for every conceivable message that should be handled by that handler. Since there is a total of more than 150 general Windows messages and numerous combinations of command messages, this is one of the most tedious aspects of writing Windows applications using C/API. Here is an example of a message handler in a C/API application [1]:

```
LRESULT CALLBACK
AccelWndProc (HWND    hwnd,      // For whom is message sent?
              UINT    mMsg,      // What is exact message?
              WPARAM  wParam,    // ...message details.
              LPARAM  lParam)    // ...message details.
{
   switch (mMsg) {
     case WM_COMMAND: {
        char buffer[80];
        char *npch;

        switch (wParam) {
          case IDM_FILE_NEW:
            npch = "File.New";
            break;
          case IDM_FILE_OPEN:
            npch = "File.Open...";
            break;
          case IDM_FILE_SAVE:
            npch = "File.Save";
            break;
          case IDM_FILE_SAVEAS:
            npch = "File.Save As...";
```

```
        break;
      case IDM_FILE_PRINT:
        npch = "File.Print";
        break;
      case IDM_FILE_EXIT:
        npch = "File.Exit";
        break;
// ... etc. for Edit menu requests
   }

// Display message box with name of selected menu item.
   wsprintf (buffer, "%s command selected.", (LPSTR)npch);
   MessageBox (hwnd, buffer, achAppName, MB_OK);

// If user selected File.Exit, simulate {-}.
// Close menu selection
   if (wParam == 6) {
      SendMessage (hwnd, WM_SYSCOMMAND, SC_CLOSE, 0L);
   }
 }
 break;

case WM_DESTROY:
   PostQuitMessage(0);   // Handle application shutdown.
   break;

   default:
     return(DefWindowProc(hwnd,mMsg,wParam,lParam));
     break;
 }
 return 0L;
}
```

The MFC framework hides most of the drudgery of message handling code behind message mapping macros. These macros encapsulate the message type and the corresponding C++ handler, where the handler is written as a member function of one of the major Windows components.

The MFC framework also handles the forwarding of messages to the appropriate handler. This mechanism is rather elaborate, however, and is the most mysterious part of the entire message handling package. One reason why it is mysterious, is that each Windows component is given a choice of whether or not to handle a message. If a component does not handle a particular message, it gets passed to the next component for a similar choice. Another reason is the fact that command messages and Windows messages are handled differently and take different routes to their respective handlers.

23.2 Design Approach

A naive C++ approach to message handling could be to create virtual member functions in base classes associated with frame and window objects for handling mouse events and keyboard commands. Derived classes for window and view objects could then declare overridden functions to handle specific events. The C++ run-time environment would determine the appropriate function to be called for a specific event via polymorphism.

The overhead associated with the use of polymorphism was discussed in Chapter 10. We would need approximately 150 virtual functions spread over about 25 different classes to handle all the specified messages. Since each derived class needs a vtable with an entry for each virtual function, this would represent a significant storage and run-time overhead. Another problem associated with this approach is that it would be almost impossible to anticipate suitable virtual base functions for all the different buttons and menus that would be required for future applications.

The general message handling mechanism chosen for MFC is the use of macros to map Windows messages to C++ functions. Does this mean that virtual functions are not used at all for handling messages? The answer is a qualified "no." Virtual functions are used to perform certain operations and may be called from a message handler. Strictly speaking, they are not part of the message map mechanism. We'll say more about this in a later section.

An important design issue regarding the use of message handlers is the determination of which C++ classes and window components they should be associated with. We will indicate these design decisions in the ensuing sections.

23.3 Message Map Data Structures

There are two primary data structures used for the MFC message handling mechanism:

- Message Entry—Holds the details of a map between a message and its handler. Includes items such as message Id and a function pointer for the corresponding C++ handler.

- Message Map—Includes a pointer to the base class's message map structure and an array of message entries.

Here is a code snippet from afxwin.h that includes these two data structures:

```
// File: afxwin.h
// ...
struct AFX_MSGMAP_ENTRY {
  UINT nMessage;     // windows message id
  UINT nCode;        // control code or WM_NOTIFY code
  UINT nID;          // control ID (or 0 for windows messages)
```

```
   UINT nLastID;      // used for entries specifying a range of
                      // control id's
   UINT nSig;         // signature type (action) or pointer to
                      //   message #
   AFX_PMSG pfn;      // routine to call (or special value)
};


struct AFX_MSGMAP {
  const AFX_MSGMAP* pBaseMap;
  const AFX_MSGMAP_ENTRY* lpEntries;
};
```

The message map entry includes a message number; a control code for `WM_COMMAND` messages, or for `WM_NOTIFY`; a control Id for `WM_COMMAND` messages (0 for Windows messages); a signature type used to describe the return type and parameters of the message handler function; and a pointer function for the message handler.

The message map structure includes a pointer to the base class. This is used to forward the message upward in the hierarchy, in lieu of using polymorphism. We can thus traverse an inheritance structure using a linked list. This is significantly more efficient than the built-in vtables that are part of the C++ polymorphic structure. The framework traverses the message map up into the hierarchy until it finds a handler function for the message. The top-most class that can handle a message is the CCmdTarget class.

The second part of this structure is an array of message map entries for a particular class. Classes having member functions that can act as message handlers will include this data structure as a static object.

23.4 Message Handling with MFC Macros

MFC provides an alternative to the switch statement used in traditional Windows programs to handle messages sent to a window. A mapping from messages to member functions may be defined so that when a message is to be handled by a window, the appropriate member function is called automatically. This message-map facility is designed to be similar to virtual functions, but has additional benefits not possible with C++ virtual functions.

The message handlers are declared as member functions in classes derived from the CCmdTarget class. Each message handler needs an entry in the message map, a function prototype, and the function body.

There are three macros associated with the message map mechanism. These macros are the `DECLARE_MESSAGE_MAP`, `BEGIN_MESSAGE_MAP`, and `END_MESSAGE_MAP`. The first of these is included at the end of the header file of a class that includes data members as message handlers. The last two create a "sandwich" for the message mapping information in the .cpp file.

Declaring a Message Map

The message map macros are installed by AppWizard when a project is first created. Here is a snapshot of code from the SampleMDI application (see Chapter 22):

```
// File:  SampleMDI.h

class CSampleMDIApp : public CWinApp {
public:
  CSampleMDIApp();

// Overrides
  // ClassWizard generated virtual function overrides
  //{{AFX_VIRTUAL(CSampleMDIApp)
public:
  virtual BOOL InitInstance();
  //}}AFX_VIRTUAL

// Implementation

  //{{AFX_MSG(CSampleMDIApp)
  afx_msg void OnAppAbout();
  // NOTE - the ClassWizard will add and remove member
  //        functions here.
  //  DO NOT EDIT what you see in these blocks of generated code
!
  //}}AFX_MSG
  DECLARE_MESSAGE_MAP()
};
```

This is the header file created by the AppWizard for the SampleMDI application, and contains the message handler OnAppAbout(). The event associated with this handler is the invocation of the Help About... menu item that is usually the last item (rightmost) of any Windows compliant application. The `afx_msg` is just an MFC tag; it is not part of the return type specification.

In the introductory remarks to this chapter, we mentioned that MFC actually incorporates both the message map mechanism and the use of virtual functions. We notice the `AFX_VIRTUAL` MFC tags as evidence of a section dealing with virtual member functions; only InitInstance() in this case. We will get back to the merits of the two competing mechanisms in a later section.

There were really no design decisions to be made here. AppWizard created the message handler OnAppAbout() and placed it in the application class for us. Note that this is the only logical place for this message handler since the Help/About... menu item is always associated with the application and not with any particular frame, document, or view.

The `DECLARE_MESSAGE_MAP()` Macro

The `DECLARE_MESSAGE_MAP()` macro declares the following three members for a class:

- A private array of `AFX_MSGMAP_ENTRY` entries called _messageEntries
- A protected `AFX_MSGMAP` structure called `messageMap`, that points to the _messageEntries array
- A protected virtual function called `GetMessageMap()` that returns the address of `messageMap`

The two data structures were described in Section 23.3. Here is the macro expansion from `afxwin.h`:

```
#define DECLARE_MESSAGE_MAP() \
private: \
  static const AFX_MSGMAP_ENTRY _messageEntries[]; \
protected: \
  static AFX_DATA const AFX_MSGMAP messageMap; \
  virtual const AFX_MSGMAP* GetMessageMap() const; \
```

This macro is placed in the declaration of any class using message maps. By convention, it is placed at the end of the class declaration.

Implementing Message Handlers

The implementation of the message handler is placed in the corresponding source file:

```
// File: SampleMDI.cpp
//  Defines the class behaviors for the application.
// ...

BEGIN_MESSAGE_MAP(CSampleMDIApp, CWinApp)
  //{{AFX_MSG_MAP(CSampleMDIApp)
  ON_COMMAND(ID_APP_ABOUT, OnAppAbout)
  // NOTE - the ClassWizard will add and remove mapping
  //        macros here.
  // DO NOT EDIT what you see in these blocks of
  //   generated code!
  //}}AFX_MSG_MAP
  // Standard file based document commands
  ON_COMMAND(ID_FILE_NEW, CWinApp::OnFileNew)
  ON_COMMAND(ID_FILE_OPEN, CWinApp::OnFileOpen)
  // Standard print setup command
  ON_COMMAND(ID_FILE_PRINT_SETUP, CWinApp::OnFilePrintSetup)
END_MESSAGE_MAP()

//...
```

The message handler `OnAppAbout()` is placed in the code block sandwiched between the macros `BEGIN_MESSAGE_MAP(CSampleMDIApp, CWinApp)` and `END_MESSAGE_MAP()`. When a user invokes the Help/About... event, a `WM_COMMAND` message is created with the `ID_APP_ABOUT` menu identifier. This message will be handled by the OnAppAbout() function, which creates the modal dialog box, as illustrated in Figure 23.1.

Note the additional message handlers associated with File/New, File/Open..., and File/Print Setup.... These are common to all applications (if we select them in AppWizard), and their declarations are placed in the `CWinApp` class:

```
class CWinApp : public CWinThread {
   DECLARE_DYNAMIC(CWinApp)
public:
// ...
// Constructor
   CWinApp(LPCTSTR lpszAppName = NULL);
                    // app name defaults to EXE name
// ...
// Command Handlers
protected:
   // map to the following for file new/open
   afx_msg void OnFileNew();
   afx_msg void OnFileOpen();

   // map to the following to enable print setup
   afx_msg void OnFilePrintSetup();
// ...
};
```

These three events are directly associated with every application that uses the standard File menu. And, again, we didn't have to make any design decisions regarding their placement.

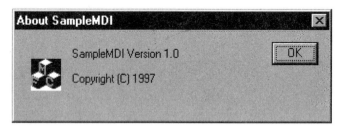

Figure 23.1 Modal Dialog Box

The Implementation Macros

The BEGIN_MESSAGE_MAP() macro declares the following members for a class:

```
#define BEGIN_MESSAGE_MAP(theClass, baseClass) \
  const AFX_MSGMAP* theClass::GetMessageMap() const \
    { return &theClass::messageMap; } \
  AFX_DATADEF const AFX_MSGMAP theClass::messageMap = \
  { &baseClass::messageMap, &theClass::_messageEntries[0] }; \
  const AFX_MSGMAP_ENTRY theClass::_messageEntries[] = \
  { \
```

The END_MESSAGE_MAP() macro provides the logical end to the message map block:

```
#define END_MESSAGE_MAP() \
  {0, 0, 0, 0, AfxSig_end, (AFX_PMSG)0 } \
}; \
```

The expanded code for these macros in the SampleMDI application will look like the following:

```
// File: SampleMDI.cpp
//  Defines the class behaviors for the application.
// ...

const AFX_MSGMAP* CSampleMDIApp::GetMessageMap() const
    { return &CSampleMDIApp::messageMap; }

AFX_DATADEF const AFX_MSGMAP CSampleMDIApp::messageMap =
  { &CWinApp::messageMap, &CSampleMDIApp::_messageEntries[0] };

const AFX_MSGMAP_ENTRY CSampleMDIApp::_messageEntries[] =
{
  ON_COMMAND(ID_APP_ABOUT, OnAppAbout)
  ON_COMMAND(ID_FILE_NEW, CWinApp::OnFileNew)
  ON_COMMAND(ID_FILE_OPEN, CWinApp::OnFileOpen)
  ON_COMMAND(ID_FILE_PRINT_SETUP, CWinApp::OnFilePrintSetup)
  {0, 0, 0, 0, AfxSig_end, (AFX_PMSG)0 }
};
```

The first part of this expansion includes the GetMessageMap() function which is used by the framework, and returns a pointer to the message map.

The second part is the message map data structure which includes a pointer to the message map of the base class CWinApp. This is part of the linked list used by the framework to traverse up the hierarchy as it looks for a message handler function. The second element of this data structure is a pointer to the first element of the message map entry.

The third part constitutes the other data structure, the actual message map entries, and is initialized with the maps for the WM_COMMAND messages. Each mapping includes an Id for the menu entry and the corresponding message handler function.

Note how the OnAppAbout() function of this class is used to handle the <u>H</u>elp/<u>A</u>bout menu item, whereas the <u>F</u>ile/<u>N</u>ew, <u>F</u>ile/<u>O</u>pen, and <u>F</u>ile/<u>Pr</u>int Setup menu items are handled by the base class CWinApp.

The last entry of `_messageEntries[]` terminates the list of entries, and shows the actual values that make up the six data elements of a map entry. The data elements of the mappings are filled in by the macro `ON_COMMAND()`. Here is one version of this macro, as listed in `afxmsg.h`:

```
// File: afxmsg.h
// ...
#define ON_COMMAND(id, memberFxn) \
  { WM_COMMAND, CN_COMMAND, (WORD)id, (WORD)id, AfxSig_vv,
(AFX_PMSG)&memberFxn },
```

The signature `AfxSig_vv` identifies a void return type and empty (void) parameter list. There are a number of other variations of this macro listed in `afxmsg.h`, as well as the macros for all the Windows messages.

23.5 Message Routing

Messages take different routes to their destination handler, depending on their type. Command messages are handled differently than Windows messages.

In general, all messages are first dispatched to the `AxfWndProc()` function with the handle of the window from which the message originated. This function translates the window handle into a pointer to a window, and then calls the corresponding `CWnd::WindowProc()`. Since `WindowProc()` is a virtual function, this means the message is first sent to the active window (derived from `CWnd`) where that message was created by the user.

If the message is a Windows message, and there is a message map entry for the message, the message gets passed on to the message map handler for processing, as shown in Figure 23.2. If no entry is found, the message is passed on for default processing.

When an entry is found in the message map, the handler performs the necessary processing. This may include calling an appropriate virtual member function. For example, the `WM_PAINT` message invokes the OnPaint() message handler which, in turn, calls the virtual OnDraw() function to perform the actual painting in the window.

If the message passed to `Wnd::WindowProc()` is a command message or a notify message, the message is passed on to `CWnd::OnCommand()` for further processing, as shown in Figure 23.3.

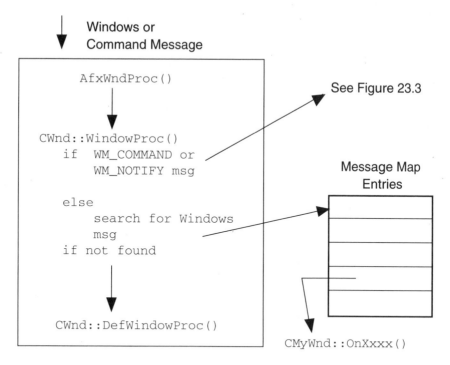

Figure 23.2 Routing of Windows Messages

The framework calls the virtual OnCommand() member function whenever a user selects an item from a menu, when a child control sends a notification message to its parent, or when an accelerator keystroke is translated. If a notification message is received, OnCommand() calls the appropriate OnChildNotify() function to handle the message. Command messages are passed on to the virtual `CCmdTarget::OnCmdMsg()`

`CCmdTarget::OnCmdMsg()` is called by the framework to route and dispatch command messages and to handle the update of command user-interface objects. This is the main implementation routine of the framework command architecture.

Whenever a command message is passed to it, OnCmdMsg() dispatches a command to other objects or handles the command itself after performing the message map lookup.

The MFC message routing mechanism is the most complex and intricate of all the MFC built-in framework mechanisms. We have only provided a brief overview of the MFC message-routing implementation here. For additional details about this mechanism and the associated functions, see the excellent article in [2].

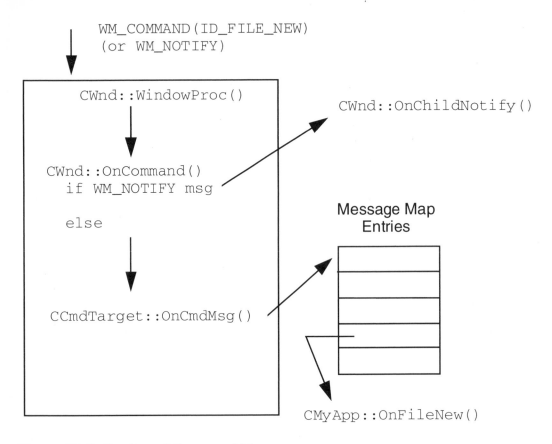

Figure 23.3 Routing of Command Messages

23.6 Chain of Responsibility Design Pattern

The mechanism for handling command messages is an implementation of the Chain of Responsibility Design Pattern [3, p.223]. This design pattern is used to decouple the sender of a message from a set of receivers. Each receiver has the option of either handling a message or passing it on to the another receiver. The receivers are chained together via a specific ordering scheme, e.g., the first receiver is the active window where the command was initiated.

The MFC senders are menus, toolbar buttons, and accelerator keys. Receivers are mainframe windows, documents, and views.

The Chain of Responsibility design pattern has a number of advantages that can be utilized in various C++ applications:

* Whenever more than one object can handle a request, the appropriate handler

can be determined at run-time

- A request can be made to one of several receivers without having to specify the receiver explicitly

23.7 Using Virtual Member Functions

The use of the special MFC message handler macros and the use of C++ virtual functions are two complementary approaches for event driven Windows applications. We illustrated the use of message macros above, and have only briefly indicated how virtual functions are used. Here is an example of using a virtual function within a view class for painting a window:

```
// File: enrollView.h

class CEnrollView : public CScrollView {
protected:
  CEnrollView();
  DECLARE_DYNCREATE(CEnrollView)

// Attributes
public:
  CStudentSet* m_pSet; // CRecordSet ptr

// Operations
public:
  CEnrollDoc* GetDocument();

// Overrides
  // ClassWizard generated virtual function overrides
  //{{AFX_VIRTUAL(CEnrollView)
public:
  virtual void OnDraw(CDC* pDC);
  virtual BOOL PreCreateWindow(CREATESTRUCT& cs);
protected:
  virtual void OnInitialUpdate();
  virtual BOOL OnPreparePrinting(CPrintInfo* pInfo);
  virtual void OnBeginPrinting(CDC* pDC, CPrintInfo* pInfo);
  virtual void OnEndPrinting(CDC* pDC, CPrintInfo* pInfo);
  //}}AFX_VIRTUAL
// ...
};
```

The OnDraw() function will be called indirectly as a result of a WM_PAINT message. This message maps to either an OnPaint() or OnPrint() function. Both of these functions call OnDraw() for painting on either a window or a printer, depending on the device context pDC.

This is a general strategy employed throughout the MFC. All of the classes involved with the creation of Windows elements have virtual functions that we can override in a derived class. These overridden member functions can be called from the message handlers to perform specific tasks.

23.8 Placement of Message Handlers

A Windows application consists of four major components: an application object, one or more frames encapsulating windows, one or more documents holding data values, and views displaying the data owned by a document. Each of these components can potentially handle a user interface action, including the opening and closing of files.

In addition to the components that we create for each unique application, the MFC hierarchy includes high-level classes with virtual functions for handling user commands. As designers and implementers, we need to carefully place the various message handling functions in the appropriate component, or leave a message for default processing by the MFC high-level classes. Here is a summary of suggested design decisions for placement of message handlers:

- In CWinApp—Default processing for Print menu handlers. These are common to all applications
- In the application object—General help regarding the application, e.g., OnAppAbout() for the Help/About. This menu item is always associated with the application and not with any particular frame, document, or view.
- In the main frame—Handlers for menu items and accelerators that deal with opening, closing, and deleting documents
- In the document object—Handlers for updating and saving data associated with a document, and for attributes common to multiple views.
- In the view object—Handlers for drawing, text editing, window resizing, etc.

23.9 Summary

There are two types of messages represented by the MFC framework: command messages and Windows messages. Command messages are used for interfaces with menu items, accelerator keyboard actions, and controls, and have the common name WM_COMMAND. Windows messages are used for interfaces inside views, and have unique names such as WM_SIZE and WM_PAINT.

Messages in the MFC framework are represented with: (1) message maps, and (2) the virtual functions of the CCmdTarget C++ class and various derived classes. An MFC message map uses two primary data structures:

- Message Entry—Holds the details of a map between a message and its handler. Includes items such as message id and a function pointer for the corresponding C++ handler.

- Message Map—Includes a pointer to the base class's message map structure and an array of message entries.

The message mapping mechanism is implemented with three message macros: (1) `DECLARE_MESSAGE_MAP()`, which is placed at the end of the class declaration in the header file; (2) `BEGIN_MESSAGE_MAP`(derived class, base class), which is placed in the .cpp file at the beginning of the message map section; and (3) `END_MESSAGE_MAP()`, which is placed at the end of the message map section.

Routing of Windows messages is relatively simple. Routing of command messages is complex and circuitous. Windows messages are handled via a direct route to the message handler and corresponding virtual function. Command messages are handled using the Chain of Responsibility design pattern. The architecture of the command message handling starts with the CCmdTarget class. Every class that descends from this class can receive command messages. The routing starts with the active window where the command was initiated. This component decides whether it wants to handle the message or not. If not, it passes the message to the next component in the chain, etc., thus we have the Chain of Responsibility.

Message maps and virtual functions are used in a complementary fashion. The general strategy is to first locate a message handler using the message map structures. When a message handler is found, it calls virtual functions to perform the actual interface function. This permits a Windows object to pass off the interface operation to another object higher in the hierarchy, or to activate default processing.

The placement of message handlers is an important design decision and should be selected with care.

References

1. Yao, Paul, *Peter Norton's Windows 3.1 Power Programming Techniques*, 2nd Edition, Bantam Books, New York, NY 1992.

2. DiLascia, Paul, Meandering Through the Maze of MFC Message and Command Routing, *Microsoft Systems Journal*, July 1995.

3. Gamma, E. et al., *Design Patterns*, Addison-Wesley, Reading, MA 1995.

24

MFC and Exception Handling

The older versions of the MFC used a "home grown" non-C++ style of exception handling referred to as Structured Exception Handling (SEH). This included the use of macros to simulate the C++ try, catch, and throw constructs. Starting with version 4.0, the MFC framework incorporates the standard C++ exception handling mechanism, and retains backwards compatibility to the SEH mechanism. Some Windows applications developed with the older MFC versions may have a mixture of SEH and C++ exception code.

The basis for the MFC exception handling is the CException class derived from CObject. In this chapter, we will describe the C++ MFC exception class hierarchy, how the MFC has implemented its exception handling strategy as part of the framework, and how we, as applications programmers, can use the MFC exception handling features.

24.1 CException Class Hierarchy

The MFC includes a hierarchy of exception classes, as shown in Figure 24.1. The class CException is the base class for the various exceptions that may be raised within the MFC member functions.

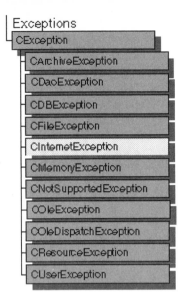

Figure 24.1 MFC Exception Hierarchy

CException is derived from the CObject class and is the base class of the exception hierarchy. It has the inherited features from CObject, including RTTI, diagnostics, and serialization. Here is a short description of the derived classes:

- CArchiveException—Archive-specific exception (#include afx.h)
- CDaoException—Data access object (DAO) exception (#include afxdao.h)
- CDBException—Exception raised in classes based on ODBC (#include afxdb.h)
- CFileException—File-specific exception (#include afx.h)
- CInternetException—Exception raised in classes used to implement Internet operations. (#include afxinet.h)
- CMemoryException—Out-of-memory exception (#include afx.h)
- CNotSupportedException—Request for an operation that is not supported (#include afx.h)
- COleException—Exception raised for OLE operations (#include afxole.h)
- COleDispatchException—OLE dispatch (automation) exception (#include afxdisp.h)
- CResourceException—Requested Windows resource not found or cannot be created (#include afxwin.h)
- CUserException—Used for an application-specific exception (#include afxwin.h)

Even though the hierarchy shown in Figure 24.1 is part of the official Microsoft documentation, this isn't quite the story we find if we look in the `afx.h` file that contains the declarations for some of the exception classes. One of the classes not shown in Figure 24.1 is the CSimpleException class. The correct, but undocumented, hierarchy for the exception classes declared in `afx.h` is shown in Figure 24.2.

The undocumented class CSimpleException is used as a base class for resource-critical MFC exceptions. The member functions of this class handle ownership and initialization of error messages. The two derived classes are used to raise exceptions when an application is erroneously requesting the use of an unsupported feature, or memory or resources are exhausted. A specific resource Id can be passed back to the application via exceptions from these classes.

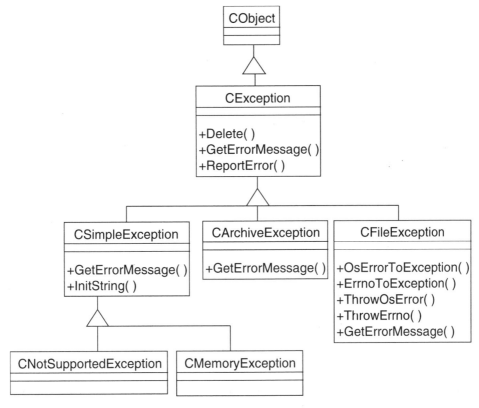

Figure 24.2 The MFC Exception Class Hierarchy (afx.h)

Class CException

The base class CException doesn't have a what() function like we saw in Chapter 13 for the Standard C++ exception hierarchy. It does have similar functions, however, as shown in the following code section from `afx.h`:

```
// File: afx.h

class CException : public CObject {
  // abstract class for dynamic type checking
  DECLARE_DYNAMIC(CException)

public:
// Constructors
  CException();    // sets m_bAutoDelete = TRUE
  CException(BOOL bAutoDelete);
              // sets m_bAutoDelete = bAutoDelete

// Operations
  void Delete();  // use to delete exception in 'catch' block

  virtual BOOL GetErrorMessage(LPTSTR lpszError,
                      UINT    nMaxError,
                      PUINT   pnHelpContext = NULL);
  virtual int ReportError(UINT nType = MB_OK,
                      UINT nMessageID = 0);

// Implementation (setting m_bAutoDelete to FALSE is advanced)
public:
  virtual ~CException();
  BOOL m_bAutoDelete;
#ifdef _DEBUG
  void PASCAL operator delete(void* p);
protected:
  BOOL m_bReadyForDelete;
#endif
};
```

The function ReportError() uses GetErrorMessage() to return a string describing the error type, and then calls AfxMessageBox() to put up a dialog box which displays the error message. This is similar to using the C-style assert() macro which displays a line number and file where an error condition occurred.

A unique feature of the CException class is the Delete() function. This function is used to delete an instance of type CException, independent of the C++ operator new. Here is the implementation of this function:

```
// File: except.cpp
// ...

void CException::Delete() {
```

```
    // delete exception if it is auto-deleting
    if (m_bAutoDelete > 0) {
#ifdef _DEBUG
    m_bReadyForDelete = TRUE;
#endif
      delete this;
    }
}
```

We notice the rather drastic operation of deleting the very object on whose behalf this function is called! We'll revisit this operation to illustrate how it can be used in Section 24.4.

Class CArchiveException

Instances of this class can be used to report error conditions associated with a serialization operation. Here is the class declaration:

```
// File: afx.h
// ...

class CArchiveException : public CException {
  DECLARE_DYNAMIC(CArchiveException)
public:
  enum {
    none,
    generic,
    readOnly,
    endOfFile,
    writeOnly,
    badIndex,
    badClass,
    badSchema
  };

// Constructor
  CArchiveException(int cause = CArchiveException::none,
                    LPCTSTR lpszArchiveName = NULL);

// Attributes
  int     m_cause;
  CString m_strFileName;

// Implementation
public:
  virtual ~CArchiveException();
#ifdef _DEBUG
  virtual void Dump(CDumpContext& dc) const;
#endif
```

```
virtual BOOL GetErrorMessage(LPTSTR lpszError,
                             UINT   nMaxError,
                             PUINT  pnHelpContext = NULL);
};
```

The anonymous (type tag omitted) enum declaration includes a number of conditions that can be reported as a cause of an archiving exception. The name of the archiving medium can also be created as a part of the exception object.

Class CFileException

Specific file exceptions can be created and reported whenever errors occur in file I/O operations. Here is the class declaration:

```
// File: afx.h
// ...

class CFileException : public CException {
  DECLARE_DYNAMIC(CFileException)

public:
  enum {
    none,
    generic,
    fileNotFound,
    badPath,
    tooManyOpenFiles,
    accessDenied,
    invalidFile,
    removeCurrentDir,
    directoryFull,
    badSeek,
    hardIO,
    sharingViolation,
    lockViolation,
    diskFull,
    endOfFile
  };

// Constructor
  CFileException(int     cause = CFileException::none,
                 LONG    lOsError = -1,
                 LPCTSTR lpszArchiveName = NULL);

// Attributes
  int     m_cause;
  LONG    m_lOsError;
  CString m_strFileName;
```

```
  // Operations
    // convert a OS dependent error code to a Cause
    static int PASCAL OsErrorToException(LONG lOsError);
    static int PASCAL ErrnoToException(int nErrno);

    // helper functions to throw exception after converting
    // to a Cause
    static void PASCAL ThrowOsError(LONG    lOsError,
                                    LPCTSTR lpszFileName = NULL);
    static void PASCAL ThrowErrno(int      nErrno,
                                  LPCTSTR lpszFileName = NULL);

  // Implementation
  public:
    virtual ~CFileException();
#ifdef _DEBUG
    virtual void Dump(CDumpContext&) const;
#endif
    virtual BOOL GetErrorMessage(LPTSTR lpszError,
                                 UINT   nMaxError,
                                 PUINT  pnHelpContext = NULL);
  };
```

We recognize an anonymous enum type similar to the one specified in
CArchiveException for reporting the exact cause of a file error.

Additional member functions are included for converting an error number into a
"cause" before the exception is created.

Standard Exception Throws

To design a C++ exception handling mechanism into our applications requires a carefully laid out schema of naming exceptions and placing the corresponding handlers.
There may be times when we would like to just raise an exception and have it propagate to a window without going through our own handlers. The MFC includes a set of
functions for just this purpose:

```
  // File: afx.h

  // Standard exception throws

void AFXAPI AfxThrowMemoryException();
void AFXAPI AfxThrowNotSupportedException();
void AFXAPI AfxThrowArchiveException(int cause,
                                     LPCTSTR lpszArchiveName =
                                     NULL);
void AFXAPI AfxThrowFileException(int cause,
                                  LONG lOsError = -1,
                                  LPCTSTR lpszFileName = NULL);
```

If we are doing our own memory management, e.g., by calling malloc(), and the memory allocation fails, we can call AfxThrowMemoryException(). This will automatically generate a memory exception, independent of our own exception handling strategy. We do not use this for the operator new because it raises the CMemoryException which we will have to handle.

We can call the AfxThrowNotSupportedException() function in a similar fashion whenever we receive a failure notification regarding an operation that is not supported.

The other two standard throw functions can be used to display specific information about serialization or file handling, respectively. We can pass these functions the cause of a failure and the name of the particular archive or file where the error occurred.

24.2 Catching and Deleting Exceptions

The syntax and semantics of the C++ exception handling mechanism of declaring, raising, handling, and propagating exceptions was described in detail in Chapter 13. The emphasis here is on what Windows applications programmers using the MFC have to be concerned with.

We are used to the automatic destruction of local objects that are part of the stack frame. The matching of the new() and delete() operations for dynamic heap objects is also a familiar programming paradigm. What is different in using the MFC exceptions is the requirement to delete an exception after it has been handled.

We noticed above that the MFC includes a unique Delete() function that is specified as a member function of the CException class. Here is how we can use this function:

```
void FuncX() {
  Invoice* theInvoice = new Invoice;
  try {
    theInvoice->FuncY(); // may throw an exception
  }
  catch (CException* except) {
    TRACE ("Exception raised in FuncX()\n");
    ...
    // now delete the exception
      except->Delete(); // MFC Delete()
  }
  // Delete the local object
  delete theInvoice; // C++ delete
}
```

The MFC CException::Delete() is used to free memory associated with the except exception shown in this code section. The C++ delete operation should not be used to release memory for a CException instance, because it may not have been allocated from the heap. The delete operation is used normally, however, to free non-CException objects, such as the Invoice instance referenced to by the `theInvoice` pointer.

24.3 Positioning of CException Handlers

We discussed in Chapter 13 how the run-time system goes looking for a matching handler as soon as an exception is raised. Whenever we are using a class hierarchy for creating instances of exceptions, we need to carefully place the handlers for these exceptions. Here is an example of how we can place handlers for some of the exceptions shown in the hierarchies in Figures 24.1 and 24.2:

```
void myFunc() {
  try {
    // statements that may raise exceptions
    ...
  }
  catch (CMemoryException* exc) {
    // out-of-memory handler here
  }
  catch (CFileException* exc) {
    // file exception handler here
  }
  catch (CDBException* exc) {
    // ODBC exception handler here
  }
  catch (COleException* exc) {
    // OLE exception handler here
  }
  catch (CException* exc) {
    // handle other MFC exceptions here
  }
  catch(...) {
    // handle all unknown (non-CExceptions) exceptions here
  }
}
```

The specific handlers must be placed first, in any order. The rest of the CExceptions will be caught by the last handler. If we place the general CException handler first, all of these exceptions will be caught by this handler, and we would have to use the RTTI features or other member functions to decipher which particular CException is raised.

The very last handler is used to catch any non-CException exceptions that may be raised. Since we do not know what type of exception this could be, we use the no-name handler.

24.4 Freeing Exception Objects

Since the normal program flow of an application is altered when exceptions are thrown, objects must be disposed of in an orderly fashion in conjunction with the normal C++ destructor mechanism. If this is not done properly, it could result in serious memory leaks.

To illustrate the potential problems that may occur when exceptions are thrown, here is an example of problematic code that may result in a memory leak:

```
void FuncX() {
  Invoice* theInvoice = new Invoice;
  theInvoice->FuncY(); // may throw an exception
  // ...
  // Delete the local object
  delete theInvoice; // C++ delete
}
```

If an exception is thrown within `FuncY()` (or in its calling hierarchy), the object pointed to by `theInvoice` will not be recovered. Since there is no handler placed in this function, the exception will be propagated to the next enclosing block, thus resulting in a memory leak. The regular C++ mechanism will delete the pointer `theInvoice` as the stack is unwound, but not the object it is pointing to.

We will now discuss the two basic mechanisms we can use to solve the potential problems with memory leaks.

Handling an Exception Locally

The first mechanism for avoiding memory leaks is to handle exceptions locally with try/catch blocks; and then destroy all objects:

```
void FuncX() {
  Invoice* theInvoice = new Invoice;
  try {
    theInvoice->FuncY(); // may throw an exception
  }
  catch (CException* except) {
    // handle the exception here
    ...
    // now delete the exception
      except->Delete(); // MFC Delete()
  }
  // Delete the local object
  delete theInvoice; // C++ delete
}
```

Since normal program flow will follow the exception handling, we must ensure that the exception is destroyed within the handler.

Destroying Objects, then Re-Raising the Exception

The second mechanism for avoiding memory leaks is to first destroy objects in a catch block; and then to re-raise the exception which will be propagated outside the block:

```
void FuncX() {
  Invoice* theInvoice = new Invoice;
  try {
    theInvoice->FuncY(); // may throw an exception
  }
  catch (CException* except) {
    delete theInvoice; // C++ delete
    throw; // re-raising exception
  }
  // Normal program flow
  delete theInvoice; // C++ delete
}
```

Note that the exception must not be deleted, as it was in the first mechanism. The execution of the throw statement implies the existence of a "current exception" (see [1, p. 358]). It also imples that the `except` exception must be deallocated after we exit the handler.

24.5 General Exception Handling Strategy

The newer versions of MFC (starting with version 4.0) use only the standard C++ exception handling mechanism; the SEH macros are no longer used.

Application programmers can derive any number of additional exceptions from the MFC CException base class. An independent hierarchy of exception classes is not recommended, since this would introduce a second method for destroying exceptions.

To catch an exception of unknown type, we use the CException class and the `CObject::IsKindOf()` member function to determine the type. User-defined exceptions derived from CException must be declared with the `IMPLEMENT_DYNAMIC` macro to be able to use this RTTI feature.

In general, do not mix the SEH and C++ exception handling mechanisms. In particular, never use SEH macros and C++ keywords inside the same code block. The way exception objects are deleted is different between the SEH mechanism and the C++ destructors. Mixing the two mechanisms is almost guaranteed to create memory management problems.

Windows application-unique exceptions should be derived from the MFC CException base class. This hierarchy already includes a mechanism for deleting exceptions that are raised, i.e., the Delete() function declared in the CException base class.

24.6 Summary

An exception handling mechanism, based on the C++ exception feature, is integrated with the MFC framework. This mechanism does not use the previous MFC Structured Exception Handling (SEH).

The base class of the exception hierarchy is CException. This class is derived from CObject and thus inherits the RTTI, diagnostic, and serialization features of CObject. The hierarchy includes general exceptions for memory handling, file I/O, and archiving errors, as well as more specialized exceptions for dealing with DAO objects and the OLE mechanism.

A set of standard exception throws can be used to raise exceptions directly, independent of the normal declaring, raising, and handling mechanism.

A unique feature of the CException class is the inclusion of the Delete() function. This member function should be used to free the memory associated with an instance of CException, and not the C++ operator delete.

Any number of specialized exceptions can be derived from the CException hierarchy for an application. Several virtual functions are included in the hierarchy for overriding in a derived class.

References

1. Ellis, M.A., and Stroustrup, B., *The Annotated C++ Reference Manual*, Addison-Wesley, Reading, MA, 1990.

25

MFC and ODBC

We described the basic features of the ODBC interface in Chapter 18, and mentioned how we can access a DBMS from a C++ application by registering the DBMS database as a data source and specifying the corresponding driver.

In this chapter, we will describe the MFC ODBC classes that encapsulate the ODBC functionality in the API, and how we can create an MFC C++ Windows application using the Visual C++ AppWizard and ClassWizard. The data source we interface with in the C++ application is an RDBMS structure created with the application Access.

The primary reference material for this chapter can be found in [1, 2].

25.1 The MFC ODBC Classes

The MFC includes a set of ODBC classes that encapsulate the functionality required to access a DBMS from a C++ application. These classes can be used directly by the developer, or they can be integrated automatically by using the Visual C++ AppWizard. In either case, they greatly simplify the interface to the ODBC API.

The MFC ODBC classes have evolved considerably since the early versions of Visual C++. We will only be concerned with the 32-bit versions included in Visual C++ 4.2 here. The ODBC class hierarchy derived from CObject is shown in Figure 25.1.

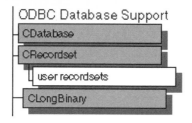

Figure 25.1 MFC ODBC Classes

The MFC classes shown in Figure 25.1 are the only "pure" ODBC classes. There are other MFC classes involved in a C++ application using the ODBC features , however. Here is a brief description of the ODBC classes and related classes:

- CDatabase—Encapsulates a connection to a database. This connection enables us to operate on a data source.

- CRecordset—Encapsulates a set of table rows (records) selected from a data source. This class enables scrolling between the rows, and includes a set of member functions for manipulating the records.

- CLongBinary—Used to encapsulate large objects such as bitmaps, photographs, etc. These type of objects are usually referred to as BLOBs (binary large objects). One restriction on objects of this type is that they cannot be used as parameters in function calls.

- CRecordView—Provides a form view that is directly connected to a recordset object. The dialog data exchange (DDX) mechanism provides automated data exchange between the recordset and the form view.

- CDBException—Used for exceptions that may be raised in an attempt to access a database.

- CFieldExchange—Provides support for record field exchange (RFX) routines used by the database classes. RFX exchanges data between the field data members of a recordset object and the corresponding columns of the current record on the data source. RFX manages the exchange in both directions, from the data source and to the data source.

C++ applications that use the MFC ODBC classes will have at least a CDatabase for the database connectivity and a CRecordset object for each table. Appropriate exception handlers will have to be provided by the developers to catch potential exceptions that may be raised in accessing a database.

We will now provide a description of the primary MFC ODBC classes that are likely to be used in a C++ application. These descriptions include class members in the following categories:

- Data Members
- Construction (Managers)
- Attribute Functions (Access Functions)
- Operations (Implementers)
- Overridables (Virtual Functions)

These categories are a little different from the member function classifications we have been using in earlier chapters. We are using this set here because it matches the Microsoft documentation [2]. Note that some of the functions in the Attribute Functions category include "set" operations and, thus, do not strictly match our earlier notion of Access Functions, which should only return a value.

25.2 CDatabase

A CDatabase object is used to create a connection to a data source. This class is derived directly from the CObject class, as shown in Figure 25.2, and its declaration is in the <afxdb.h> header file.

Here is a portion of the CDatabase code from afxdb.h:

```
// File: afxdb.h
// ...
class CDatabase : public CObject {
  DECLARE_DYNAMIC(CDatabase)

// Constructors
public:
  CDatabase();

    enum DbOpenOptions
    {
        openExclusive =        0x0001, // Not implemented
        openReadOnly =         0x0002, // Open database read
                                       // only
        useCursorLib =         0x0004, // Use ODBC cursor lib
        noOdbcDialog =         0x0008, // Don't display ODBC

                                       //     Connect dialog
        forceOdbcDialog =      0x0010, // Always display ODBC
                                       //     connect dialog
    };
```

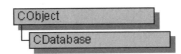

Figure 25.2 CDatabase Hierarchy

```cpp
    virtual BOOL Open(LPCTSTR lpszDSN, BOOL bExclusive = FALSE,
                      BOOL bReadonly = FALSE,
                      LPCTSTR lpszConnect = _T("ODBC;"),
                      BOOL bUseCursorLib = TRUE);
    virtual void Close();

// Attributes
public:
    HDBC m_hdbc;

    BOOL IsOpen() const;
    BOOL CanUpdate() const;
    BOOL CanTransact() const;

    CString GetDatabaseName() const;
    const CString& GetConnect() const;

// Operations
public:
    void SetLoginTimeout(DWORD dwSeconds);
    void SetQueryTimeout(DWORD dwSeconds);

    // transaction control
    BOOL BeginTrans();
    BOOL CommitTrans();
    BOOL Rollback();

    void ExecuteSQL(LPCTSTR lpszSQL);

    // Cancel asynchronous operation
    void Cancel();

// Overridables
public:
    // set special options
    virtual void OnSetOptions(HSTMT hstmt);

// Implementation
public:
    virtual ~CDatabase();

#ifdef _DEBUG
    virtual void AssertValid() const;
    virtual void Dump(CDumpContext& dc) const;

    BOOL m_bTransactionPending;
#endif //_DEBUG

protected:

    // friend classes that call protected CDatabase overridables
    friend class CRecordset;
    friend class CFieldExchange;
```

```
    friend class CDBException;
};
```

Data Members

The following data member is included in the CDatabase class:

m_hdbc—ODBC connection handle to a data source. Type: HDBC.

Normally, there is no need to access this connection handle directly. The framework assigns a handle when the Open() function is called for the data source. If, however, there is a need to make a direct call to the ODBC API, here is an example of how to use the connection handle [2, p. 407]:

```
// Using m_hdbc for a direct ODBC API call
// m_db is the CDatabase object; m_hdbc is its HDBC
// member variable
...
nRetcode = ::SQLGetInfo(
                m_db.m_hdbc,
                SQL_ODBC_SQL_CONFORMANCE,
                &nValue, sizeof(nValue), &cbValue);
```

The handle of a data source is passed to the API to obtain information about the driver and data source associated with the handle [3].

Construction

Here are some of the functions used to manage database objects:

- CDatabase()—Constructs a CDatabase object. The object must be initialized by calling Open().
- virtual BOOL Open(....)
  throw (CDBException, CMemoryException)—Establishes a connection to a data source via the appropriate ODBC driver. Note that this function may raise the exceptions CDBException and CMemoryException.
- virtual void Close()—Closes the connection to the data source.

Note that the Open() and Close() virtual functions are included here in the Construction category and not in the Database Overridables section.

Database Attributes

Here are some of the functions used in set/get operations:

- `const CString& GetConnect() const`—Returns the ODBC connect string used in connecting the CDatabase object to the data source.
- `BOOL IsOpen() const`—Returns true (nonzero) if the CDatabase object is currently connected to a data source.
- `CString GetDatabaseName() const`—Returns the name of the database currently in use.
- `BOOL CanUpdate() const`—Returns true (nonzero) if the CDatabase object is updatable (not read-only).
- `BOOL CanTransact() const`—Returns true (nonzero) if the data source supports transactions.
- `void SetLoginTimeout( DWORD dwSeconds )`—Sets the number of seconds after which a data source connection attempt will time out.
- `void SetQueryTimeout( DWORD dwSeconds )`—Sets the number of seconds for a time-out of database query operations. All subsequent Open(), AddNew(), Edit(), and Delete() calls are affected by this operation.

Database Operations

Here are some of the functions used in database operations:

- `BOOL BeginTrans()`—Starts a "transaction" (a series of reversible calls to the AddNew(), Edit(), Delete(), and Update() member functions of class CRecordset) on the connected data source. The data source must support transactions for BeginTrans() to have any effect.
- `BOOL CommitTrans()`—Completes a successful transaction begun by BeginTrans(). All the commands in the transaction (that alter the data source) have been completed before this function is called.
- `BOOL Rollback()`—Reverses changes made during the current transaction. The data source returns unaltered to its previous state, as defined at the BeginTrans() call.
- `void Cancel()`—Cancels an asynchronous operation.
- `void ExecuteSQL(LPCSTR lpszSQL) throw(CDBException)`—Executes an SQL statement. No data records are returned, but an exception may be raised if anomalies are detected.

Database Overridables

Here is a virtual function used to set certain connection options:

- `virtual void OnSetOptions(HSTMT hstmt)`—Called by the framework to set standard connection options. The default implementation sets the query time-out value and the processing mode (asynchronous or synchronous). These options can be established a priori by calling SetQueryTimeout() and SetSynchronousMode().

25.3 CRecordset

A CRecordset object contains a set of rows (records) selected from a data source. These objects are referred to as "recordsets," and are available in two forms: *dynasets* and *snapshots*.

A dynaset is a dynamic recordset that stays synchronized with updates by multiple users. A snapshot is a static recordset that reflects the state of the database at the time the snapshot was taken. Each object form represents a set of rows fixed at the time the recordset is opened. Scrolling to a record in a dynaset, however, reflects changes subsequently made to the record, either by other users or by other recordsets in the application.

The CRecordset class is derived directly from the CObject base class, as shown in Figure 25.3. The class declaration is in the `<afxdb.h>` header file.

Here is a portion of the CRecordset code from afxdb.h:

```
// File: afxdb.h
// ...

class CRecordset : public CObject {
   DECLARE_DYNAMIC(CRecordset)

// Constructor
public:
   CRecordset(CDatabase* pDatabase = NULL);

public:
   virtual ~CRecordset();
```

Figure 25.3 CRecordset Hierarchy

```
        virtual BOOL Open(UINT nOpenType = AFX_DB_USE_DEFAULT_TYPE,
                          LPCTSTR lpszSQL = NULL,
                          DWORD dwOptions = none);
        virtual void Close();

    // Attributes
    public:
        HSTMT m_hstmt;             // Source statement for this resultset
        CDatabase* m_pDatabase;    // Source database for this resultset

        CString m_strFilter;       // Where clause
        CString m_strSort;         // Order By Clause

        BOOL CanAppend() const;    // Can AddNew be called?
        BOOL CanRestart() const;   // Can Requery be called to restart
                                   //    a query?
        BOOL CanScroll() const;     // Can MovePrev and MoveFirst be
                                    //    called?
        BOOL CanTransact() const;   // Are Transactions supported?
        BOOL CanUpdate() const;     // Can Edit/AddNew/Delete be
                                    // called?

        const CString& GetSQL() const; // SQL executed for this
                                       // recordset
        const CString& GetTableName() const;        // Table name

        BOOL IsOpen() const;       // Recordset successfully opened?
        BOOL IsBOF() const;        // Beginning Of File
        BOOL IsEOF() const;        // End Of File
        BOOL IsDeleted() const;     // On a deleted record

        long GetRecordCount() const;    // Records seen so far or -1
                                        // if unknown
        void GetStatus(CRecordsetStatus& rStatus) const;

    // Operations
    public:
        // cursor operations
        void MoveNext();
        void MovePrev();
        void MoveFirst();
        void MoveLast();
        virtual void Move(long nRows,
                          WORD wFetchType = SQL_FETCH_RELATIVE);

        // edit buffer operations
        virtual void AddNew();     // add new record at the end
        virtual void Edit();       // start editing
        virtual BOOL Update();     // update it
        virtual void Delete();      // delete the current record

    // Overridables
```

```
public:
    // Get default connect string
    virtual CString GetDefaultConnect();

    // Get SQL to execute
    virtual CString GetDefaultSQL();

    // set special options
    virtual void OnSetOptions(HSTMT hstmt);

    // for recordset field exchange
    virtual void DoFieldExchange(CFieldExchange* pFX);

// Implementation
public:
#ifdef _DEBUG
    virtual void AssertValid() const;
    virtual void Dump(CDumpContext& dc) const;
#endif //_DEBUG

    friend class CFieldExchange;
    friend class CRecordView;
};
```

Data Members

Here are the CRecordset data members:

- `m_hstmt`—Contains the ODBC statement handle for the recordset. Type: `HSTMT`.
- `m_pDatabase`—Contains a pointer to the CDatabase object through which the recordset is connected to a data source.
- `m_strFilter`—Contains a CString object that specifies an SQL `WHERE` clause. This is used as a filter to select only those records that meet certain criteria.
- `m_strSort`—Contains a CString object that specifies an SQL `ORDER BY` clause. This is used to control how the records should be sorted.

Construction

Here are the functions used to manage CRecordset objects:

- `CRecordset()`—Constructor for a CRecordset object. A derived class must provide a constructor that calls this one.
- `virtual BOOL Open(....)throw(CDBException, CMemoryException, CFileException)`—Opens the recordset by retrieving the table or performing the

query that the recordset represents. Note the exceptions that may be raised.

- `virtual void Close()`—Closes the recordset and the ODBC HSTMT (handle) associated with it.

Recordset Attributes

Here are some of the access functions used to return information about CRecordset objects:

- `BOOL CanAppend() const`—Returns nonzero if new records can be added to the recordset via the `AddNew()` member function.
- `BOOL CanRestart() const`—Returns nonzero if `Requery()` can be called to run the recordset's query again.
- `BOOL CanScroll() const`—Returns nonzero if we can scroll through the records.
- `BOOL CanTransact() const`—Returns nonzero if the data source supports transactions.
- `BOOL CanUpdate() const`—Returns nonzero if the recordset can be updated (i.e., add, update, or delete records).
- `long GetRecordCount() const`—Returns the number of records in the recordset.
- `void GetStatus(CRecordsetStatus& rStatus) const`—Gets the status of the recordset: the index of the current record and whether a final count of the records has been obtained. `CRecordsetStatus` is the following struct:

```
struct CRecordsetStatus {
    long m_lCurrentRecord;
    BOOL m_bRecordCountFinal;
};
```

This struct is used to determine if a valid record can be established.

- `const CString& GetTableName() const`—Returns the name of the table associated with the recordset.
- `const CString& GetSQL() const`—Returns the SQL string used to select records for the recordset.
- `BOOL IsOpen() const`—Returns nonzero if Open() has previously been called.
- `BOOL IsBOF() const`—Returns nonzero if the recordset has been positioned before the first record, i.e., the recordset is empty. There is no current record, and MoveFirst() must subsequently be called to position us at the first record.
- `BOOL IsEOF() const`—Returns nonzero if the recordset has been positioned after the last record. There is no current record.

- BOOL IsDeleted() const—Returns nonzero if the recordset is positioned on a deleted record.

Recordset Update Operations

Here are functions used to update CRecordset objects:

- virtual void AddNew() throw(CDBException, CFileException)—Prepares for the addition of a new record. Update() must be called to complete the addition.
- virtual void Delete() throw(CDBException)—Deletes the current record from the recordset. An explicit scroll to another record must be executed after the deletion.
- virtual void Edit() throw (CDBException, CFileException, CMemoryException)—Prepares for changes to the current record. Update() must be called to complete the edit.
- virtual void Update() throw(CDBException)—Completes an AddNew() or Edit() operation by saving the new or edited data on the data source.

Recordset Navigation Operations

Here are functions used to navigate within a recordset:

- virtual void Move(long lRow, WORD wFetchType) throw (CDBException, CFileException, CMemoryException)—Positions the recordset to a specified number of records from the current record in either direction.
- void MoveFirst() throw (CDBException, CFileException, CMemoryException)—Positions the current record on the first record in the recordset. We must test for IsBOF() first, as in this example:

```
void CEnrollView::OnDraw(CDC* pDC) {
  int y = -500;
  CString fStr; // used with Format & TextOut

  if (m_pSet->IsBOF()) // empty?
    return;

  pDC->TextOut(50, -50, "Student ID  Student Name     Grad
Year");
  m_pSet->MoveFirst(); // 1st record

  while (!m_pSet->IsEOF()) { // get all records
```

```
        fStr.Format("%ld",m_pSet->m_StudentID); // long
        pDC->TextOut(50, y, fStr);

        pDC->TextOut(1600, y, m_pSet->m_Name);

        fStr.Format("%d",m_pSet->m_GradYear); // int
        pDC->TextOut(5000, y, fStr);

        m_pSet->MoveNext(); // next record
        y -= 300; // next line 0.3 in
    }
}
```

- `void MoveLast() throw (CDBException, CFileException, CMemoryException)`—Positions the current record on the last record in the recordset. Must test for IsEOF() first.
- `void MoveNext() throw (CDBException, CFileException, CMemoryException)`—Positions the current record on the next record in the recordset. Must test for IsEOF() first.
- `void MovePrev() throw (CDBException, CFileException, CMemoryException)`—Positions the current record on the previous record in the recordset. Must test for IsBOF() first.

Note that most of these member functions may raise exceptions that will first get propagated back to the caller. We need to prepare handlers for these exceptions and encapsulate the calls in various *try* blocks.

Recordset Overridables

Here are various virtual functions:

- `virtual void DoFieldExchange(CFieldExchange* pFX) = 0; throw(CDBException)`—Called to exchange data (in both directions) between the field data members of the recordset and the corresponding record on the data source. Implements record field exchange (RFX). Note that this is a pure virtual function that can raise an exception.
- `virtual CString GetDefaultConnect()`—Returns a pointer to the default connect string.
- `virtual CString GetDefaultSQL() = 0`—Returns a pointer to a string that holds the default SQL statement to be executed.
- `virtual void OnSetOptions(HSTMT hstmt)`—Called to set options for the specified ODBC statement.

25.4 CRecordView

A CRecordView object provides a form view that is directly connected to a recordset object. This is an example of the document/view architecture. The document holds the recordset, and the view displays the data to the user.

The dialog data exchange (DDX) mechanism exchanges data between the recordset and the controls of the record view. Like all form views, a record view is based on a dialog template resource. Record views also support moving from record to record in the recordset, updating records, and closing the associated recordset when the record view closes.

The CRecordView class is not derived directly from the CObject class like CDatabase and CRecordset, and the structure is more complex, as shown in Figure 25.4. The class declaration for CRecordView is also in the `<afxdb.h>` header file.

The CRecordView class is not strictly an ODBC class. Since it is derived from the CScrollView and CFormView classes, it has built-in features for scrolling and forms display.

Data Members

There are no specialized data members for the CRecordView class.

Construction

Here are the constructors:

- `CRecordView( LPCSTR lpszTemplateName )`—Constructor
- `CRecordView( UINT nIDTemplate )`—Constructor

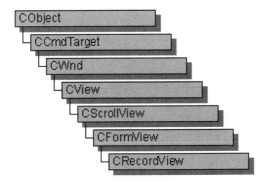

Figure 25.4 CRecordView Hierarchy

These two constructors are in a protected section, and we use a derived class to have CRecordView objects created. Here is an example of how we can create a CFormView object from a derived record view class:

```
CMyRecordView::CMyRecordView()
  : CRecordView( IDD_MYFORM ) {
  //{{AFX_DATA_INIT( CMyRecordView )
  // NOTE: the ClassWizard will add member initialization here
  //}}AFX_DATA_INIT
  // Other construction code, such as data initialization
}
```

The identifier of our form view, IDD_MYFORM, is passed up to the CRecordView constructor for the object creation.

Attribute Functions

Here are access functions:

- virtual CRecordset OnGetRecordset() = 0—Returns a pointer to a successful object creation of a class derived from CRecordset. ClassWizard will override this function and create the recordset if necessary.
- BOOL IsOnFirstRecord()—Returns nonzero if the current record is the first record in the associated recordset.
- BOOL IsOnLastRecord()—Returns nonzero if the current record is the last record in the associated recordset

Operations

Here is a move function:

- virtual BOOL OnMove(UINT nIDMoveCommand)—Used to move to a different record in the recordset and display the fields in the controls of the record view. If the current record has changed, that record is first updated on the data source, before the move to the specified record (next, previous, first, or last) is executed.

Overridables

There are no overridables of higher-level virtual functions in the CRecordView class.

Now that we have presented the major ODBC classes and their class members, we will illustrate how to create an ODBC C++ application using the MFC and associated framework.

25.5 Creating a C++ ODBC Windows Application

To demonstrate how we can use an Access RDBMS in a C++ Windows application, we first look at the data source we intend to use.

The Access Data Source

The data source we registered in Chapter 18 as Stdreg32.mdb is shown as an Access database in Figure 25.5.

The relationships between the various tables are shown in Figure 25.6. This includes the cardinalities between the table entities.

This RDBMS database consists of a number of tables (relations), one of which is the Student table shown in Figure 25.7. This is the table we will access within a C++ Windows application.

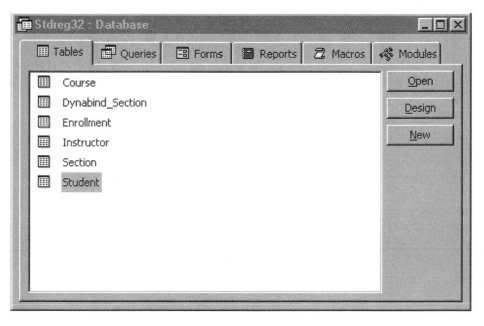

Figure 25.5 Microsoft Access Data Source

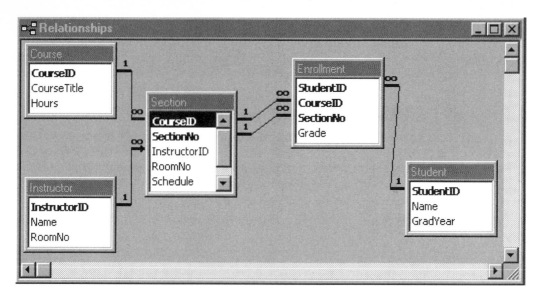

Figure 25.6 Student Registration Table Relationships

StudentID	Name	GradYear
1001	Smith, Randy	98
1002	Maples, Alex	99
1003	Jones, Thomas	98
1004	Shannon, Eric	98
1005	Foster, Susan	97
1006	Jefferson, Nancy	99
1007	Tuner, Bob	97
1008	Holm, David	98
1009	Reynolds, Don	97
1010	Taylor, Robert	98
1011	Karr, Dave	97
1012	Tannant, Tim	97
1013	Marcus, Susan	98
1014	Butterfield, Rita	98
1015	Amon, Craig	98
1016	Anderson, Sandra	97
1017	Cooper, Linda	99

Record: 1 of 17

Figure 25.7 Student Table in Stdreg32 Data Source

Building the MFC Application

The C++ application is built using the AppWizard and specifying the ODBC options, as shown in Figure 25.8.
We have selected the "Dynaset" option to utilize the dynamic update feature for the recordset.

Next, we need to select the specific table(s) in the data source that we want to interface with, as shown in Figure 25.9. In this case, we selected the Student table.

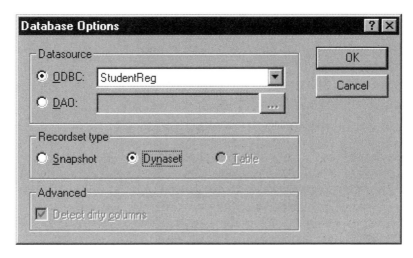

Figure 25.8 Selecting the Data Source

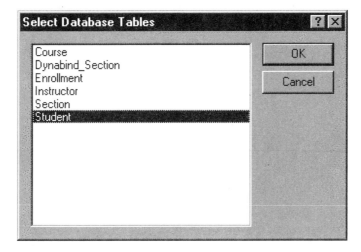

Figure 25.9 Selecting the Student Table

Using ClassWizard

We can use the ClassWizard to link column names in the table with the corresponding C++ data members, as shown in Figure 25.10.

We have now linked the database table columns GradYear, Name, and StudentID with the corresponding C++ data members m_GradYear, m_Name, and m_StudentID. Here is the header file for the new class:

```
// StudentSet.h : header file

class CStudentSet : public CRecordset {
public:
  CStudentSet(CDatabase* pDatabase = NULL);
  DECLARE_DYNAMIC(CStudentSet)

// Field/Param Data
  //{{AFX_FIELD(CStudentSet, CRecordset)
  long    m_StudentID;
  CString m_Name;
  int     m_GradYear;
  //}}AFX_FIELD

// Overrides
  // ClassWizard generated virtual function overrides
  //{{AFX_VIRTUAL(CStudentSet)
  public:
  virtual CString GetDefaultConnect();
  virtual CString GetDefaultSQL();
  virtual void DoFieldExchange(CFieldExchange* pFX); // RFX sup-
port
  //}}AFX_VIRTUAL

// Implementation
#ifdef _DEBUG
  virtual void AssertValid() const;
  virtual void Dump(CDumpContext& dc) const;
#endif
};
```

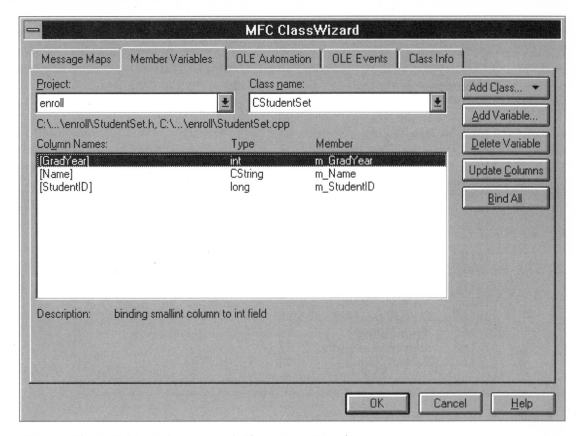

Figure 25.10 Table Columns and Class Data Members

Of the member functions that deal with the database, GetDefaultConnect() connects to the default Student Registration data source, GetDefaultSQL() associates the recordset object with the default table Student, and DoFieldExchange() provides record field exchange (RFX) for moving data beteen the database table and the recordset object.

The three data members m_StudentID, m_Name, m_GradYear correspond to the columns in the database table.

The MFC application resulting from accepting the AppWizard options of SDI and database support with header files only is shown in Figure 25.11.

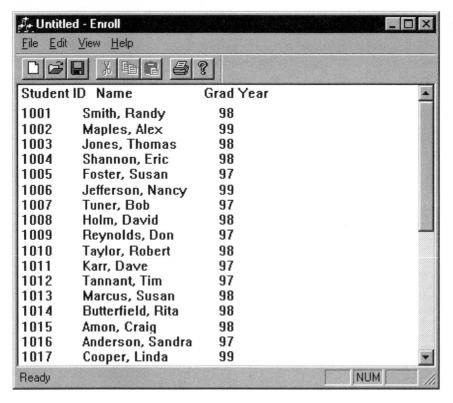

Figure 25.11 Accessing the Data Source

To display the data in the Student table, we have simply added a header line to distinguish between the column names. The data in the rows is identical to the data shown in the Access RDBMS format in Figure 25.7.

After having described how we can create a C++ interface to an RDBMS via the ODBC mechanism, we'll now take a closer look a the architecture of this application.

25.6 Architecture

The Enroll ODBC application was created with the MFC AppWizard which included the default document/view architecture (see Chapter 22). Since we selected an SDI model, the application includes a main frame, a document, and a view object. The static class model for the Enroll ODBC application is shown in Figure 25-12.

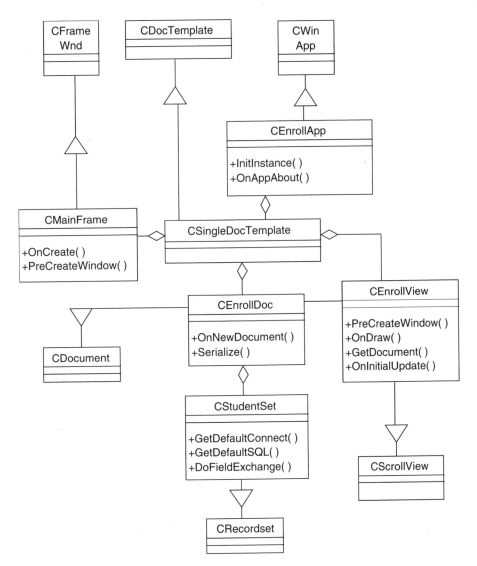

Figure 25.12 Enroll Application Class Diagram

We notice the same document/view structure that was discussed in Chapter 22. The CSingleDoc template is modelled as a class factory and controls the related classes CMainFrame, CEnrollDoc, and CEnrollView.

In this case, the document component is different from the usual document or file we have seen in previous chapters. Here is the header for the document class:

```
// EnrollDoc.h : interface of the CEnrollDoc class

class CEnrollDoc : public CDocument {
protected: // create from serialization only
   CEnrollDoc();
   DECLARE_DYNCREATE(CEnrollDoc)

// Attributes
public:
   CStudentSet m_studentSet; // CRecordset proxy

// Operations
public:
// Overrides
   // ClassWizard generated virtual function overrides
   //{{AFX_VIRTUAL(CEnrollDoc)
   virtual BOOL OnNewDocument();
   virtual void Serialize(CArchive& ar);
   //}}AFX_VIRTUAL

// Implementation
   virtual ~CEnrollDoc();
#ifdef _DEBUG
   virtual void AssertValid() const;
   virtual void Dump(CDumpContext& dc) const;
#endif

// Generated message map functions
protected:
   //{{AFX_MSG(CEnrollDoc)
      // NOTE - the ClassWizard will add and remove member
      //functions here.
      //       DO NOT EDIT what you see in these blocks of
      //       generated code !
   //}}AFX_MSG
   DECLARE_MESSAGE_MAP()
};
```

We notice the public data member *m_studentSet* which is of type *CStudentSet*. It is made public here for the sake of expediency. We do not want to have to supply a special access function, with the possibility of having to add a special constructor to return a copy within the access function.

The class *CStudentSet* is derived from CRecordset, as we illustrated in Section 25.4 (see Figure 25.10) and this data member will thus represent an instance of the actual Student Table of the data source Student Registration. The function of the Enroll document component models the design pattern Proxy [4, p. 207].

The Proxy Design Pattern

The document component in the Enroll application doesn't own the data as we have seen in previous document/view applications. In this case, the document has the role of a "proxy" for the database object. A proxy provides a surrogate or placeholder for another object, i.e., the recordset, and controls access to this object [4, p. 207].

When the document component part of the application is created, the constructor for the embedded data member m_studentSet gets invoked and creates the database table object. The recordset object gets connected to the RDBMS table in the CStudentSet class:

```
// StudentSet.cpp : implementation file

#include "stdafx.h"
#include "Enroll.h"
#include "StudentSet.h"

IMPLEMENT_DYNAMIC(CStudentSet, CRecordset)

CStudentSet::CStudentSet(CDatabase* pdb)
            : CRecordset(pdb) {
  //{{AFX_FIELD_INIT(CStudentSet)
  m_StudentID = 0;
  m_Name      = _T("");
  m_GradYear  = 0;
  m_nFields   = 3;
  //}}AFX_FIELD_INIT
  m_nDefaultType = dynaset;
}


CString CStudentSet::GetDefaultConnect() {
  return _T("ODBC;DSN=StudentRegistration");
}

CString CStudentSet::GetDefaultSQL() {
  return _T("[Student]");
}

void CStudentSet::DoFieldExchange(CFieldExchange* pFX) {
  //{{AFX_FIELD_MAP(CStudentSet)
  pFX->SetFieldType(CFieldExchange::outputColumn);
  RFX_Long(pFX, _T("[StudentID]"), m_StudentID);
  RFX_Text(pFX, _T("[Name]"), m_Name);
  RFX_Int(pFX, _T("[GradYear]"), m_GradYear);
  //}}AFX_FIELD_MAP
}

  // ...
```

We see here how the connections are made to the default data source Student Registration and the specified table Student. We also notice how the RFX mechanism is implemented for moving data between the database table and the data members (see the CStudenSet header file) that correspond to the column fields.

The entire ODBC mechanism for accessing a database from a C++ application is built into the MFC framework. The only two requirements are that we must register the database, and that there is an appropriate ODBC driver for that database.

The View

The view component serves the same function as we have seen in previous document/view applications: to display the data contained in the document. This is illustrated in Figure 25.11, which shows the view of the Student table.

The view class is derived from the CScrollView class. A pointer to a CStudentSet object (actually derived from the CRecordset class) is declared in enrollview.h:

```
// File: enrollview.h
//

class CEnrollView : public CScrollView {
protected:
  CEnrollView();
  DECLARE_DYNCREATE(CEnrollView)

// Attributes
public:
  CStudentSet* m_pSet; // CRecordset ptr

// Operations
public:
  CEnrollDoc* GetDocument();

// Overrides
  // ClassWizard generated virtual function overrides
  //{{AFX_VIRTUAL(CEnrollView)
public:
  virtual void OnDraw(CDC* pDC); // overridden to draw this view
  virtual BOOL PreCreateWindow(CREATESTRUCT& cs);
protected:
  virtual void OnInitialUpdate(); // called first time after
                                  // construction
  virtual BOOL OnPreparePrinting(CPrintInfo* pInfo);
  virtual void OnBeginPrinting(CDC* pDC, CPrintInfo* pInfo);
  virtual void OnEndPrinting(CDC* pDC, CPrintInfo* pInfo);
  //}}AFX_VIRTUAL

// Implementation
public:
```

```
    virtual ~CEnrollView();
    //...
protected:

// Generated message map functions
protected:
    //...
DECLARE_MESSAGE_MAP()
};
```

The m_pSet pointer is used to associate this view with the document component (which is the proxy for the database table). We recognize the familiar GetDocument() function which returns a pointer to this view's document, and is how the view component associates itself with the document component. Here is a portion of the view source code which illustrates how the view is associated with the database table:

```
// File: EnrollView.cpp
//

#include "stdafx.h"
#include "Enroll.h"

#include "StudentSet.h"
#include "EnrollDoc.h"
#include "EnrollView.h"

IMPLEMENT_DYNCREATE(CEnrollView, CScrollView)

void CEnrollView::OnDraw(CDC* pDC) {
int y = -500;
  CString fStr; // used with Format & TextOut

  if (m_pSet->IsBOF()) // empty?
    return;

  pDC->TextOut(50, -50,
      "Student ID  Student Name              Grad Year");
  m_pSet->MoveFirst(); // 1st record

  while (!m_pSet->IsEOF()) { // get all records
    fStr.Format("%ld",m_pSet->m_StudentID); // long
    pDC->TextOut(50, y, fStr);

    pDC->TextOut(1600, y, m_pSet->m_Name); // CString

    fStr.Format("%d",m_pSet->m_GradYear); // int
    pDC->TextOut(5000, y, fStr);

    m_pSet->MoveNext(); // next record
    y -= 300; // next line 0.3 in down
  }
}
```

```
void CEnrollView::OnInitialUpdate() {
  CScrollView::OnInitialUpdate();
  CSize sizeTotal(8000, 10500);

  SetScrollSizes(MM_HIENGLISH, sizeTotal);
  m_pSet = &GetDocument()->m_studentSet; // assoc to doc object
  // remember that documents/views are reused in SDI
  // applications!
  if (m_pSet->IsOpen()) {
      m_pSet->Close();
  }
  m_pSet->Open();
}
```

The association between the view and the document is established via the GetDocument() function called within OnInitialUpdate(). This function first returns a pointer to the document object. We then use the pointer member selection to access the (public!) data member m_studentSet. Finally, we use the address-of operator to assign the address of the document object (proxy for the database table) to the data member m_pSet. This pointer is then used to open the database table. (This is certainly an interesting exercise in remembering the rules for operator precedence and association!)

After the association is established, the m_pSet pointer is used to open the recordset. Since this is an SDI application, the open recordset (if any) is closed before the new recordset is opened.

The m_pSet CRecordset pointer is used by OnDraw() to paint the view of the table. The non-virtual navigation function MoveFirst() is called to make sure the recordset is not empty. Each column value is written with TextOut() by moving the fields horizontally across the screen. This could also have been accomplished by creating the entire string first before it was written only once.

Each record is accessed by moving through the set using the MoveNext() function. The output of the records in the Student table is shown in Figure 25-11.

25.7 Summary

The MFC ODBC mechanism supports access to DBMSs from a C++ application. The main MFC classes that encapsulate the ODBC features include:

- CDatabase—Encapsulates a connection to a database. This connection enables us to operate on a data source.

- CRecordset—Encapsulates a set of table rows (records) selected from a data source. This class enables scrolling between the rows, and includes a set of member functions for manipulating the records.

- CLongBinary—Used to encapsulate large objects such as bitmaps, photographs, etc. These type of objects are usually referred to as BLOBs (binary large objects). One restriction on objects of this type is that they cannot be used as parameters in function calls.

- CRecordView—Provides a form view that is directly connected to a recordset object. The dialog data exchange (DDX) mechanism provides automated data exchange between the recordset and the form view.

- CDBException—Used for exceptions that may be raised in an attempt to access a database.

- CFieldExchange—Provides supports for record field exchange (RFX) routines used by the database classes. RFX exchanges data between the field data members of a recordset object and the corresponding columns of the current record on the data source. RFX manages the exchange in both directions, from the data source and to the data source.

Only the first three of these classes are pure MFC ODBC classes. The other MFC classes are utilized by a C++ application to create the proper interface to a DBMS.

Interfacing to a DBMS requires a named data source and an ODBC driver for the database structure of that data source. The data source must be registered with the operating system before we can link to it.

The ClassWizard simplifies the linking of table columns from the data source with the corresponding data members in the C++ class that encapsulates the data object.

The MFC ODBC mechanism is implemented using a proxy design pattern for the actual recordset. The document/view architecture is employed, with the document as the proxy for the database table. This table is linked to an embedded object that is a data member of the document object.

The ODBC mechanism provides a straightforward method for accessing a database from a C++ application without the use of embedded SQL statements or an SQL interface.

References

1. Microsoft Visual C++ Version 4.0, Programming with MFC, Volume 2, p. 109, 527, Microsoft Press, Redmond, WA 1995.

2. Microsoft Visual C++ Version 4.0, MFC Class Library Reference, Volumes 3 & 4, Microsoft Press, Redmond, WA 1995.

3. Microsoft ODBC 3.0 Programmer's Reference and SDK Guide, Microsoft Press, Redmond, WA 1997.

4. Gamma, E. et al., *Design Patterns*, Addison-Wesley, Reading, MA 1995.

A

Summary of C++ Design and Programming Guidelines

This appendix contains a summary of the various C++ design and programming guidelines mentioned and used throughout the book. The design patterns used are also included. The section number where an item is used or referenced is listed in parenthesis, whenever appropriate.

A.1 Design Guidelines

Information Hiding (5.3)

- Initially, make all attributes private
- If a class is designed as a base class, make those attributes that are allowed to be manipulated by a derived class protected
- If instances of a base class should only be created by a derived class, make the base class constructor(s) protected
- Don't grant friend privileges unless absolutely necessary and harmless, e.g., for output functions that do not modify the data they display or print

Loose Coupling between Modules (5.3)

- Put all class declarations in header files (.h)
- Put all class definitions in separate source files (.cpp)
- Defer #include statements to the module where they are needed, e.g., put them in the .cpp file where needed, rather than nested within another header file

Designing Class Interfaces (8.1)

Class interfaces can be designed in terms of four categories of member functions:

- Managers—Object creation, initialization, destruction, memory management, etc.
- Implementers—Primary client interface reflected in the requirements
- Access—Will return values of (hidden) attributes
- Helpers—Internal operations used by the operations in categories 1-3

Access to Class Members (8.5)

- Managers (object creation, initialization, destruction, memory management, etc.) should be public
- Implementers (primary client interface reflected in the requirements) should be public
- Access Functions (return values of hidden attributes) should be public
- Helper Functions (internal operations used by the operations in the other categories) should be private or protected

Return Types (8.5)

Never return an address to an object that exits the function scope when the function completes! This can create the infamous dangling references when the local pointer goes out of scope.

Shortcut for Creating a Non-Static Shared Data Member (8.5)

Create an enumerated type within the architecture of the class declaration:

```
class NewClass {
public:
```

```
    //...
  private:
    //...
    enum {MaxBuff = 1024}; // ok
    char str[MaxBuff]; // ok
};
```

`MaxBuff` is now just like the static class variable that can be shared among all objects declared of the `NewClass` type.

Data Member/Base Constructor Initialization Syntax (8.7)

We can use the special initialization syntax mechanism in two different contexts: (1) to initialize data members without executable statements in the constructor body, and (2) to pass data values up to a base constructor for initialization of inherited data members.
    Required use of member initialization syntax includes the following:

- `const` non-static data members
- Reference type data members
- Passing initialization data to base constructors

Using Preprocessor Statements (8.8)

Use typed constants rather than #define:

```
#define maxBuff  1024 // avoid
const int maxBuff = 1024; // preferred
```

Bracket header files to prevent multiple inclusions of the same classes:

```
// File: stringx.h

#ifndef STRINGX_H
#define STRINGX_H

class String {
public:
  String();
  // ...
protected:
  // ...
};

#endif
```

Restricting Access (9.4)

We provide a dummy copy constructor and assignment operator in the protected or private part to prohibit copying and assignment. This is used for singleton objects, and secure applications, e.g., login name and password.

A protected or private copy constructor is also used to prevent passing parameters by value. Passing large objects by reference is more efficient.

Virtual Destructors (9.5, 10.6)

Whenever we have virtual functions declared in a base class, we should also declare a virtual destructor. The destructor mechanism will then automatically call the destructors for all derived objects in the reverse order of how they were created. This will prevent the kind of memory leaks that could occur if only a base object was reclaimed.

Characteristics of Various Class Operations (9.5)

Table A.1 Class Operation Characteristics

Operation	Inherited	Can Be Virtual	Can Have Return Type	Member or Friend	Generated by Default
constructor	no	no	no	member	yes
destructor	no	yes	no	member	yes
conversion	yes	yes	no	member	no
=	no	yes	yes	member	yes
()	yes	yes	yes	member	no
[]	yes	yes	yes	member	no
->	yes	yes	yes	member	no
op=	yes	yes	yes	either	no
new	yes	no	void*	static member	no
delete	yes	no	void	static member	no
other operator	yes	yes	yes	either	no
other member	yes	yes	yes	member	no
friend	no	no	yes	friend	no

Well-Designed Classes (9.6)

There is no minimal set of operations that should be specified for every class. Well-behaved classes can be used as a starting point for the class interface design:

- Default constructor
- Copy constructor
- Destructor
- Assignment operator
- Equality operator
- Inequality operator (can be based on the equality operator)

Multiple Inheritance (10.3)

If we are using multiple inheritance in a C++ library consisting of several branches, which are all anchored by the same base class, two major problems occur:

- Ambiguous calls to virtual functions
- Inclusion of multiple objects of repeated base classes

These problems are avoided if the base classes used in the multiple inheritance relationship derive from their (common) base class using *virtual* inheritance.

Creating Mixin Classes (10.3)

If we discover two or more classes we would like to use in a multiple inheritance relationship, we can clone all but one of the classes from the inheritance hierarchy as stand-alone, independent classes with different class names. Multiple inheritance will now only involve a single branch down the inheritance hierarchy, and the problems with ambiguous calls and multiple base objects are avoided.

Using *structs* versus Classes (11.10)

We have used the struct IPCMsg to represent the data structure for the message. In this case, we are modeling a message with just two int components. In a real system, this could be a nested struct including a header, the length of the message, etc. The main point here, is that we chose a struct rather than a class, because we are only dealing with data; there are no behaviors to encapsulate with a message object.

Using fstream Objects (11.10)

The conversion mechanism using *memcpy()* can also be used to write an object to a file as a byte stream. After the conversion from the object to the stream, the stream is written to a file as an ofstream object. The same stream can then be read back in as an ifstream object and converted back to the original object.

Using Template Functions (12.1)

Here is a brief summary of C++ generic functions and why they are so important for creating reusable algorithms:

- Generic functions represent a higher level of abstraction than old-style procedures and functions
- Functions that employ the same algorithm on data structures that only differ by type are ideal candidates for generic functions
- Template functions are instantiated with actual parameters at compile time. Storage is not allocated to a function template, only to a function instantiated with actual parameters.
- The instantiation is automatic, i.e., the compiler creates the functions without the use of any special syntax

Using Template Classes (12.4)

Here is a summary of the advantages of using C++ class templates:

- Complete type safety. Type checking is performed at compile time to assure proper matching of formal and actual parameters.
- We don't have to derive new classes from base classes. This saves on development time, since there is no need for testing of new classes and associated member functions.
- Several C++ template libraries are now available, including the STL, which is part of the C++ standard.

Parameterization (Using Templates) versus Inheritance (12.4)

Inheritance still has an important place in large C++ developments. Templates are ideal when we have algorithms operating on data structures that only differ by C++ types. We must also be able to specify a reasonable number of formal parameters for each template specification. For these types of classes and functions, the choice should be templates rather than inheritance. There are numerous instances, however, where a natural hierarchy of base classes and derived classes will occur. In this case, the choice is inheritance.

One way to summarize the difference between the reuse aspects of inheritance and templatized functions and classes is to consider inheritance the extensibility and re-use of types (classes), and the use of templates as reuse of source code.

A Taxonomy of Exceptions (13.1)

Here is a suggested taxonomy of exceptions that will support fault tolerance:

- Anticipated exceptional conditions
- Protection of server software.
- Detection and reporting of hardware failures
- Detection and reporting of unanticipated errors (bugs)

Declaring Exceptions (13.2)

C++ exceptions are treated as types and can be declared in several different ways:

- Nested classes
- Independent classes
- Enumeration types
- Inheritance hierarchy
- Throw list

Basic STL Components (14.2)

The basic components of the STL fall into the following five main categories:

- Container classes
- Iterators to provide traversal through containers
- Algorithms
- Function objects that encapsulate functions in objects for use by other components

- Adapters that adapt components to provide a different and suitable interface for other components

---

STL Container Classes (14.4)

There are ten basic categories of containers:

- vector<T>—sequential array
- deque<T>—sequential, double-entry queue, e.g., FIFO
- list<T>—doubly linked list
- set<key, compare>—set of items, elements are accessed with the key in an associative look-up
- multiset<key, compare>—same as set<T> with duplicate elements
- map<key, T, compare>—collection of 1:1 mappings between key and object
- multimap<key, T, compare>—collection of 1:N mappings
- stack<Container<T> >—adapter to use a container as a stack; LIFO only
- queue< Container<T> >—FIFO only
- priority_queue< Container<T>, compare>—sorted FIFO queue

Standard Exception Hierarchy (14.18)

The suggested C++ standard exception hierarchy is shown in Figure A.1.

Use of `const` (15.6)

We should always use `const` for better type checking, protection of actual parameters passed to a function, and controlling the legal use of member functions. The use of this design guideline will result in more robust code. The `const` keyword can be used in the following different contexts:

- Constant Objects—Used whenever we need a global or local constant that should not be changed during the life of the application. This style replaces the use of #define in C.
- Constant Parameters in a Function Parameter List—Used to guarantee that actual parameters passed to a function will not be modified within the function.

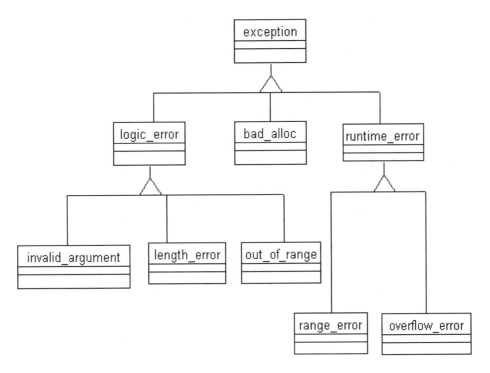

Figure A.1 C++ Standard Exception Hierarchy

- Constant Class Members—Includes const data members and member functions. The specification of const member functions is required for member functions invoked on behalf of a const class instance. Data members declared const must be initialized with the member initialization syntax. A const member function will be invoked on behalf of a non-const instance if no non-const member function has been specified.

- Constant Return Type References—Used with const member functions to prevent a member function from being invoked on behalf of an object that is the rhs of an assignment statement, i.e., guarantees read-only access.

Static Data Members (16.1)

We can summarize the common characteristics of static data members as follows:

- A static data member is shared among all instances of its class
- A static data member can be accessed via the class and scope operator, or via any instance of the same class

- A static data member can only be initialized after the class declaration, prefer-ably in a separate .cpp file
- A static data member can be made non-public, different from an ordinary global variable
- A static data member is not entered into the application's global name space. This can prevent accidental name conflicts

A.2 Design Patterns

In this section, we make references to the design patterns that have been illustrated throughout the book. We are using the same pattern names as those listed in [1].

Using the Singleton Design Pattern (9.4)

If we want to limit the creation of instances to a single object, the Singleton design pattern can be used, as suggested in [1, pp. 127-136]. The purpose of this design pattern is to ensure that a class has only one instance and to provide a global entry point for this instance.

The State Design Pattern (11.8)

An alternative to the C-based table-driven FSM is the object-oriented FSM approach based on the State design pattern [1, p. 305]. This model is also suggested in [FAI93]. The State pattern is based on a hierarchy of state classes, and allows an object to alter its behavior and class when its internal state changes.

Summary of the Object Oriented FSM Approach (11.8)

Here is a summary of the features, merits, and liabilities of the object oriented FSM approach:

- The STD model is represented directly by a class diagram
- A base class serves as an abstract root class
- Each state is modeled as a derived class
- The public virtual member functions represent events and are overridden in the derived classes

- State transitions are represented by class instances, inside the class hierarchy
- State objects are created and destroyed with each state transition
- Events that don't cause state transitions are ignored at the base class level
- The hierarchical structure makes it very easy to add states
- The coding convention of placing all events in a public section, and the corresponding actions in a private section, makes it easy to verify that the entire STD has been implemented
- There are no look-up tables for finding handler functions based on the system state
- Once an event is classified in the function ProcessNextEvent(), a single polymorphic function call is bound at run-time to the object that represents the current state
- An unknown issue is the run-time efficiency of the create/destroy mechanism for each state transition

Factory Method Design Pattern (11.9 and 22.9-22.10)

The Factory Method design pattern [1, p. 107] was created to solve the problem of run-time creation of instances of a particular class. This pattern is also known as the Virtual Constructor paradigm [3, p. 140]. This pattern can be used when a class cannot anticipate the class of objects it is required to create, or a base class wants its derived classes to specify the objects to be created.

Chain of Responsibility Design Pattern (23.5)

This pattern [1, p. 223] is used to decouple a sender object from a series of receiver objects. The sender only needs to know the address of the first receiver in the receiving chain. Each receiver has the opportunity to accept or reject the command received from the sender. This is the pattern used for the MFC `CCmdTarget::OnCmdMsg()` handling of `WM_COMMAND` messages.

The Proxy Design Pattern (25.6)

The document component in the Enroll application doesn't own the data as we have seen in previous document/view applications. In this case, the document has the role of a "proxy" for the database object. A proxy provides a surrogate or placeholder for another object, i.e., the recordset, and controls access to this object [1, p. 207].

A.3 Programming Guidelines

Here are a number of suggested programming guidelines that can make C++ code easier to read and provide a consistent style throughout a large project.

Pointer and Reference Declarations

Keep the reference and pointer operators with the type mark. This separates the type operators from the address-of and dereference operators, respectively:

```
char* szClassName;
const double& Getx() const {return x;}
ClassX::ClassX(const ClassX& Y) { ... } // copy ctor
```

Class Member Visibility

Always explicitly declare the public, protected, and private sections of a class, in that order.

Friend statements should appear first, i.e., before the public section and immediately after the class header in a class declaration.

Naming Convention Restrictions

Do not declare any names starting with two adjacent underscores, since this is normally reserved for system or environment parameters.

Formal Parameters

Always explicitly declare a meaningful formal parameter name after the type declaration in function prototypes.

Return Types

If no value is returned from a function, declare it as type `void` to avoid unintentional defaulting to type int.

Clean Header Files

No code should appear in header files unless it's extremely unlikely that these implementations will be changed, and that the resulting automatic inlining is acceptable. This minimizes recompilation of client software when changes to the server software are required, because the server implementation (which is changing) is in a separate source file. Clean header files also support precompiled headers used by compilers employing incremental compilation techniques. Constant definitions should be placed in header files.

Class Specifications

Place unrelated class specifications in separate header files. This provides for uncoupling of domain classes. Class hierarchies, e.g., exception classes, can be placed in the same header file.

Access Member Functions

Access member functions (member functions which are read-only) must be declared as `const`, with `const` formal arguments, unless the return values are passed back via a reference or pointer to these arguments.

Types of Formal Parameters

Use `const` when declaring formal parameters to functions unless the design mandates that the value of a parameter can change inside the function.

Infinite Loops

There must always be a way to exit a loop. Special care must be exercised for an infinite loop such as

```
while(1)   or   for(;;)
```

Accessing Class Variables

Always use the class scope operator when referencing a class variable. This is more readable than accessing via an object since a class variable is never associated directly with any object.

Friendly Access

Do not use the friend statement to allow access to private or protected data members of a class unless a public member function cannot be used, or the creation of numerous access functions does not make sense. Likely candidates for friendly access include the ios/iostream classes.

Virtual Destructors

Always declare a virtual destructor for base classes that have virtual member functions. Do not declare a virtual destructor for a non-virtual base class.

Exception Handling

Prepare to handle C++ exceptions raised within a class library supplied with the development system or purchased as a separate product. (This is our "Protection of Software" category.) Design the rest of the system with the C++ exception handling strategy we discussed in Chapter 13. Decide which of the four categories applies to the part of the application that doesn't use class libraries.

Visibility of Data Members in Exception Classes

Normally, data members should be declared in the private or protected sections of a class declaration. Data members in exception classes, however, should be made public since we are trying to provide as much information as possible about a fault condition. It does not make sense to create special access functions for this purpose.

References

1. Gamma, E. et al., *Design Patterns*, Addison Wesley, Reading, MA 1995.
2. Faison, T., Object-Oriented State Machines, *Software Development*, September 1993, p. 37.
3. Copelien, J., *Advanced C++:Programming Styles and Idioms*, Addison-Wesley, Reading, MA 1992.

Index

About The Floppy Disk ...

The enclosed floppy disk includes two sets of files:

1. **Rational Rose Design Files**—These .mdl files were created with Rational Rose 3.0.7, and can be viewed in either Booch or OMT notation. If you have Rational Rose 4.0 or later, you can also view the diagrams in UML notation. If you don't have Rational Rose C++, you can download an evaluation copy from "www.rational.com." The Rose files are zipped with WinZip. You can download an evaluation version of WinZip from the WinZip home page "www.winzip.com" or the GO WINZIP area on CompuServe.

   All the Rose files are collected in the folder "rose." See the file rosetoc.txt for further instructions and a Table of Contents.

2. **C++ Source Code**—These .h and .cpp files are used in demonstrating the various C++ programming concepts discussed in the book. They have been compiled using Microsoft Visual C++ 4.2 under Windows NT 3.51 and Visual C++ 5.0 under Windows NT 4.0. Many of the examples in the text have been expanded on the floppy to demonstrate new C++ features available with Visual C++ 5.0. One of the problems with Visual C++ 4.x was the inconsistent use of header files for the STL (see Chapter 14). This problem has been solved in version 5.0.

   New STL examples have been added to the floppy to show how to use namespace with the new set of STL header files. Files that will only compile with version 5.0 have been placed in separate folders. If you are using Borland C++, gcc, or other C++ compilers, you will have to adjust the STL header names to the proper include files.

   The C++ files are not zipped and can simply be copied to your hard drive. See the file cpptoc.txt for further instructions and a Table of Contents.

Contacting the Author

If you have comments or questions about the contents in this book, the author may be contacted at

73131.2125@CompuServe.com